W9-BZI-387

HISTORY OF THE OLD TESTAMENT

I

VOL. I

HISTORY OF THE

CLAUS SCHEDL

OLD TESTAMENT

THE ANCIENT ORIENT AND ANCIENT BIBLICAL HISTORY

alba house

A DIVISION OF THE SOCIETY OF ST. PAUL
STATEN ISLAND, NEW YORK 10314

Library of Congress Cataloging in Publication Data

Schedl, Claus.
History of the Old Testament.

Translation of Geschichte des Alten Testaments.
Includes bibliographical references.
CONTENTS: v. 1. The ancient Orient and ancient Biblical history.—v. 2. God's people of the covenant.—v. 3. The golden age of David. [etc.]
1. Bible. O. T.—History of Biblical events.
I. Title.
BS1197.S3213 221.9 70-38990
ISBN 0-8189-0231-0 (set)
ISBN 0-8189-0207-8 (v. 1)

Nihil Obstat:
Donald A. Panella, M.A., S.T.L., S.S.L.
Censor Librorum

Imprimatur:
James P. Mahoney
Vicar General, Archdiocese of New York
February 25, 1972

The nihil obstat and imprimatur are official declarations that a book or pamphlet is free of doctrinal or moral error. No implication is contained therein that those who have granted the nihil obstat and imprimatur agree with the contents, opinions or statements expressed.

Designed, printed and bound by the Fathers and Brothers of the Society of St. Paul as part of their communications apostolate.

FOREWORD

THE THEOLOGIAN AND THE OLD TESTAMENT

BY theologian we understand not merely the professional theologian who studies the Bible in connection with his vocation in order to qualify himself for the exercise of his office, but every believer for whom the Bible is an interesting and venerable document of the history of the ancient Eastern mind and religion. The Bible is not the private literature of a specially elect band of devotees, but the life book of God's people. It is in this book that the Word of God, binding on all men, has become flesh.

Just as the person of Christ "who, though he was in the form of God, did not count equality with God a thing to be grasped, but emptied himself, taking the form of a servant, being born in the likeness of men" (*Phil.* 2, 6-7) is the key to all theology, it is also the only approach to the Bible. Just as the God-man Jesus spans a mighty dichotomy in his person, by uniting what appear to be strictly disparate elements in one divine-human unity, so the word of the Bible is filled with a dynamism which surpasses human measurement. Are we now about to do away with this involvement in the sphere of human affairs by advancing a theology of the word of the Bible that concentrates too heavily on the overpowering splendor of that Word which was in the beginning with God and which is incapable of being incorporated into "the shards of letters"? [1]

Not at all. Just as the man who repudiates Christ's bodily existence and ascribes only a phantom human existence to the Incarnate Word is guilty of seriously misinterpreting Christ, so the man who refuses to recognize the fact of the Incarnation entirely misses the mystery of Scripture. Just as Christ was a true man of his times, speaking the Galilean dialect and wearing the dress of his century, so every word in the Bible is spoken in a concrete, unique, and historical setting. This very fact determined its fate. The dust of centuries has grown heavy upon it. The Word has made its way into history, as every other, earlier or later, profane document of history.

If we mean to approach this word, we must face the difficult task of entering into all the stipulations of historical development and not rest comfortably in our secure position by pointing to the fact of inspiration. Whoever wishes to approach the Bible in a scientific manner necessarily takes on the total load of a profane exegesis. The Old Testament is a written document of the Ancient Near East, and it has undergone a development over the course of more than a thousand years before reaching its present form. For the most part it is written in the Hebrew language. A scientific examination of the Old Testament, therefore, becomes impossible without the study and knowledge of this language. The man who bases his approach only on translations is always something of a stranger to the concrete call of the revealed word; for every translation is, in some respects, a betrayal. Only the original text is inspired, and not the translations, no matter how venerable they might be.

The Old Testament is also a literary document. Thus we are also obliged (and it would be a serious error to omit this task) to approach the text in terms of the principles of philology and literary criticism in order to critically test every passage. But

---

1. Origen, *Commentary on John,* Migne, P.G. 13, 29B-32B (cf.: Urs von Balthasar: *Geist und Feuer,* 1938, 165).

a literary criticism always runs the danger of being too removed from life and reality, unless it constantly keeps in sight the *Sitz im Leben* – its position in actuality.

The written document thus appeals to the mute witnesses of ancient history, which are made articulate by archaeological excavation. Philology, literary criticism, archaeology, and the history of the Ancient Near East are the guideposts for this profane exegesis; without them we are irrevocably lost in the realm of unreality, and we miss the full "incarnation of the Word." The personal religious conviction of the investigator plays no role in this. In fact, we might go so far as to claim that if there were one ideal technique for carrying out this methodology of examination, then the results of a study by an atheistic philologist and a believing theologian would be completely in agreement. And, in practice, to a large extent, this is exactly what happens.

But if we mean to rest content with this *profane exegesis*, we fail to recognize the inexhaustible reality of the Bible word. Profane exegesis must be enlarged upon, not only as a mere supplement, but as an ultimate fulfillment, by "pneumatic" exegesis. The primary source of Scripture is at once both human and divine. If one of the pillars is missing here, the whole construction collapses in ruin.

This is not the place to fully treat the nature of inspiration,[2] although the study of Scripture wanders about blindly without a clear idea of it. Both church and synagogue have always attested to the fact that the Bible contains God's word. Disagreements were only on questions concerning how the authorship of Scripture was to be ascribed to God, and how it was possible to speak of human authorship. The Patristic age[3] was fond of parables: the Holy Spirit, it was claimed, used the human author like a musical instrument (organ, flute, lyre, etc.). Though it is an attractive metaphor, it runs the risk of considering human

2. On inspiration, cf. A. Merk (New edition by A. Bea), *De Inspiratione S. Scripturae,* Institutiones Biblicae, Rome 1951.

3. Cf. J. Schildenberger, *Vom Geheimnis des Gotteswortes,* 1950, p. 17: "Der göttlich-menschliche Ursprung der Hl. Schrift."

cooperation too exclusively in terms of a dead "instrument," without any proper activity of its own. When God overshadows a human author, he does not extinguish human existence; he elevates it into greater light, into a freedom untrammeled by sin. Inspiration is the elevation of the human faculties. If God calls upon man to compose a book, he directs this call to a concrete, historically qualified man, who, under the divine impulse, takes up the historical source material available and forms it into a unity that has been revealed to him. In this process, it is only too easy to recognize the awkward hand of the human author, who was obviously not always an accomplished literary artist. But it is from this very defect that God's power sounds its clearest note. Thus the word formed by man becomes the true "bounty of the divine Word."[4] We can then speak of personal literary style, power of poetic expression, artistic or faulty composition without thereby calling into question the divine reality of inspiration.

Once the divine origin of Scripture is properly grasped, there are some ponderable conclusions. The basic concept of this book is divine and grandiose. It lays bare the deepest abysses of sin and judgment; but it also discloses the glories of forgiveness and grace. There is nothing superficial or monotonous about this book. It sounds depths of such great dimensions that they shine like lightning "from the beginning to the end of days." This book was not composed without a plan; it storms along towards its goal. The "shards of the individual words" announce the irresistible and passionate arrival of the Eternal Word. The words are all oriented towards *the* Word. The Old Testament is the "educator towards Christ." Thus, if you tell me how you look at Christ, I will tell you how you read the Old Testament. The ultimate understanding of Scripture comes only from faith and Spirit. Once a man has tasted the "sweetness of the word" (*Ps.* 34, 8), he is awake to the "passion of the divine." Since the Spirit who has inspired this book is passion and love, the man who has once experienced this "divine taste" can never

4. Origen, *Commentary on Jeremiah,* Migne, P.G. 13, 544 C.

again turn away. Even the mighty waters of boredom, which every study necessarily involves, will not be able to destroy this love. The final object of theological instruction does not consist in the imparting of knowledge, but in the development of the "theological eros." If this succeeds, the small spark becomes a conflagration which can inflame the entire world.

Thus we raise our voice in a complaint which is perhaps also an accusation: Why is there so much weakness and fragility in Christianity? Obviously, because the word has been dulled. We are taken up with New Testament exegesis and frequently lose ourselves in spiritualistic conclusions. The bread of the Old Testament is not broken enough. And still the Catholic Church is, much more than we dare to realize *the* Church of the Bible. The liturgical missal is almost exclusively Old Testament in its sung texts. If we would remove the Old Testament from our liturgy the Church would be without song. Take away the powerful readings from Law and Prophets from the liturgical year, and Christianity is made incomplete. The Old Testament is neither old nor ancient; [5] it is a living reality in our midst. But how many of us recognize the power coming from this book? Today, more than ever, we must call upon the tidings of the Old Testament, in order to recognize the hand of Yahweh in a world on the verge of collapse. Yahweh is a God of history, and he directs the chaos of human history towards a goal and purpose he has set.

The concluding words of this introduction are taken from Origen, one of the greatest Scripture scholars and interpreters of the Greek Church, and for that matter, the whole Church: "If we have once admitted that these writings owe their origin to the creator of the world, we must be convinced that whatever is encountered by those who examine into the fundamental meaning of the world will also be met with in the study of Scripture. The further we progress in reading, the higher the mountain

---

5. Cf. the discussion in my essay: "*Sieben Thesen wider des Alten Testamentes Verächter,*" Herder-Verlag, 1948.

of mysteries towers above us. And just as a man who sets out upon the sea in a tiny ship is unafraid so long as he is close to the land but, when he gradually approaches the high seas and the waves begin to swell and he begins to be lifted high upon their crests or, when they gape open and he begins to be swarmed under into the abyss, it is then that his spirit is seized by a monstrous fear and anxiety for having entrusted such a tiny ship to such monstrous floods – this is the experience we seem to have when, from the smallness of our merit and the narrowness of our spirit we dare to approach so wide a sea of mysteries." [6]

---

6. Origen, *Homily on Genesis.*

CONTENTS

PART ONE

HISTORY OF THE ANCIENT NEAR EAST

SECTION ONE

EGYPT

SECTION TWO

THE PEOPLES OF THE NEAR EAST

SECTION THREE

CANAAN AND ITS INHABITANTS

PART TWO

EARLY HISTORY OF THE BIBLE

SECTION ONE

ORIGIN OF THE WORLD

SECTION TWO

ORIGIN OF MAN

SECTION THREE

ORIGIN OF PEOPLES

ABBREVIATIONS

AASOR	Annual of the American School of Oriental Research
ABEL	F. M. Abel, *Géographie de la Palestine* (Études Bibliques), Paris, vol. I, 1933, vol. II, 1938
AfO	E. Weidner, *Archiv für Orientforschung,* Graz
AJA	American Journal of Archaeology
ANEP	J. P. Pritchard, *The Ancient Near East in Pictures relating to the Old Testament,* Princeton Univ. Press, 1954
ANET	J. P. Pritchard, *Ancient Near Eastern Texts relating to the Old Testament,* Princeton Univ. Press, 1955
AnglTR	Anglican Theological Review
Ann. PEF	Annual of the Palestine Exploration Fund, London
AnOr	Anacleta Orientalia, Rome
Ant.	Flavius Josephus, *Antiquitates Judaicae, Jüdische Altertümer*
AO	Alter Orient
AOB	H. Gressmann, *Altorientalische Bilder zum Alten Testament,* Berlin/Leipzig, 1927
AOT	H. Gressmann, *Altorientalische Texte zum Alten Testament,* 1926
APAW	Abhandlungen der Preussischen Akademie der Wissenschaften, Berlin
ARM	Archives Royales de Mari, Paris
Arch	Archaeology
ArOr	Archiv Orientálni
AT	Altes Testament
ATD	Hentrich and Weiser, *Das Alte Testament Deutsch,* Göttingen
BA	The Biblical Archaeologist
BASOR	Bulletin of the American Schools of Oriental Research

BB	Bonner Bibelkommentar
Bibl	Biblica
BiblArch	The Biblical Archaeologist
BibLex	H. Haag, *Bibellexicon*
BibLit	Bibel und Liturgie
BHK	R. Kittel, *Biblica Hebraica,* adapted by Stuttgart, 1954
BJRL	K. Galling, The Bulletin of the John Rylands Library
BK	M. Noth, *Biblischer Kommentar, Altes Testament,* Neukirchen
BRL	Biblisches Reallexicon
BZ	Biblische Zeitschrift, Neue Folge, Paderborn
BZAW	Beihefte zur ZAW
CalwK	Calwer Kommentar: Die Botschaft des Alten Testaments, Stuttgart
CBQ	The Catholic Biblical Quarterly
ClamB	Pirot-Clamer, *La Sainte Bible,* Latin and French text with both exegetical and theological comment Paris
DB	Vigouroux, *Dictionaire de la Bible,* Paris, 1861-1912
DBS	Supplément au Dictionaire de la Bible, Paris, 1926
DOT	Winton-Thomas, *Documents to the Old Testament*
EB	Echter Bibel, Würzburg
EinlAT	O. Eissfeldt, Einleitung in das Alte Testament unter Einschluss der Apokryphen und pseudepigraphen sowie der apokryphen und pseudepigraphenartigen Qumrān-Schriften. Entstehungsgeschichte des Alten Testaments, Tubingen, 1956
EnchBibl	Enchiridion Biblicum. Documenta ecclesiastica Sacram Scripturam spectantia, Rome, 1956
EncMikr	Encyklopaedia Mikra'it. Encyclopaedia Biblica. Thesaurus rerum biblicarum, Hebrew University, Jerusalem, 1950
EphThLov (ETL)	Ephemerides Theologicae Lovanienses
ET	The Expository Times
EvT	Evangelische Theologie
FF	Forschungen und Fortschritte, Berlin
Fs	Festschrift
GAV	H. Schmökel, *Geschichte des Alten Vorderasien,* Leiden, 1957

GTT	J. Simons, *The Geographical and Topographical Texts of the Old Testament,* Leiden, 1959
GVA	A. Moortgat, *Geschichte Vorderasien bis zum Hellenismus,* Munchen, 1950
HAT	Handbuch zum Alten Testament
HistM (HM)	Fritz Kern, *Historia Mundi,* 1952
HUCA	Hebrew Union College Annual, Cincinnati
IEJ	Israel Exploration Journal, Jerusalem
IntBib	The Interpreters Bible. A Commentary in twelve volumes, New York
JAOS	The Journal of the American Oriental Society
JBL	The Journal of Biblical Literature
JEArch	Journal of Egyptian Archaeology
JerB	Jerusalem Bible
JNES	The Journal of Near Eastern Studies
JSS	The Journal of Semitic Studies
KAT	E. Sellin, *Kommentar zum Alten Testament,* Leipzig
KB	Keilschriftliche Bibliothek
LexVT	L. Koehler – W. Baumgartner, *Lexicon in Veteris Testamenti Libros,* Leiden, 1953
LXX	Septuaginta
Migne, PG	Migne, *Patres Greci*
Migne, PL	Migne, *Patres Latini*
MiscBibl	Mischellania Biblica
MT	R. Kittel, *Masoretischer Text nach der Biblica Hebraica,* 1954
NouvRevThéol	Nouvelle Revue Théologique
OLZ	Orientalische Literaturzeitung, Leipzig
Or	Orientalia, Rome
PEQ	Palestine Exploration Quarterly, London
PG	Migne, *Patres Greci*
PL	Migne, *Patres Latini*
RA	E. Eberling and Br. Meisnner, *Reallexicon der Assyriologie*
RB	Revue Biblique, École Biblique, Jerusalem
RCB	Rivista di Cultura Biblica
REHM	Die Bücher der Könige, Echter Bibel, Würzburg, 1949
RSR	Recherches de Science Religieuse

Rev HistRel	Revue de l'Histoire des Religions, Paris
SAT	Gunkel – Gressmann, *Die Schriften des Alten Testaments,* Göttingen
ST	Studia Theologica
TGI	K. Galling, *Textbuch zur Geschichte Israels,* Tubingen, 1950
ThLZ	Theologische Literaturzeitung, Leipzig
ThZ	Theologische Zeitschrift, Basel
TTZ	Trierer Theologische Zeitschrift
UM	C. H. Gordon, *Ugaritic Manual,* Rome, 1955
VD	Verbum Domini
VT	Vetus Testamentum
WTJ	Westminster Theological Journal
ZAW	Zeitschrift für Alttestamentliche Wissenschaft
ZDMG	Zeitschrift der Deutschen Morgenländischen Gesellschaft
ZDPV	Zeitschrift des Deutschen Palästinavereines
ZKT	Zeitschrift für Katholische Theologie, Innsbruck
ZTK	Zeitschrift für Theologie und Kirche

INTRODUCTION

The first edition of this volume (1956) was soon sold out. Despite the impatient inquiries of dealers and the more gentle pressure from the publisher, I could not bring myself to publish a new edition with only a few simple changes.[1] There have been too many new developments. The completion of the whole series *History of the Old Testament,* now grown to five volumes, provided the impetus for a complete revision of the first volume. The new edition involved one very obvious change: the two sections "Ancient Near East" and "Biblical Prehistory" were transposed. Now the history of the Ancient Near East comes first, in its more logical position. For first we must delineate the larger outlines of ancient history before the Biblical prehistory can be properly understood against its contemporary background. The Ancient Near Eastern history was largely reworked and enlarged. New discoveries and more recent scholarship, moreover, forced me to completely rework the presentation of the Biblical prehistory.

In the second German edition of 1964, which has provoked considerable criticism, I developed my interpretation on the

1. An Italian translation of the first two volumes has in the meantime appeared, based on the second, unrevised edition, *Storia del Vecchio Testamento: I: Dalle Origini all 'Epoca dei Giudici,* Edizione Paoline, Rome, 1964.

basis of the so-called "toledot hypothesis," a hypothesis which in the form advanced there, can no longer be supported. In the scientific search for knowledge we must reckon on detours and cul-de-sacs as well. But the underlying principle, namely that the structure of the text is determined by number symbolism, has, in my opinion, only been substantiated by further scholarship. In order to preclude any possibility of subjectivism, I was determined to leave "not a jot or tittle" unexplored in my efforts to comprehend the basic structure of the text. The key to this interpretation was furnished by the oldest complete Hebrew manuscript of the Old Testament, the Leningrad Manuscript. I am deeply indebted to the Leningrad Library for the microfilm copies of this essential piece of evidence.

For the American edition, the Biblical prehistory has, accordingly, been completely reworked and revised, with the result that it is actually a third edition. It is the author's earnest hope that the direction here suggested for Pentateuchal criticism will prove to be a stimulus for further and more detailed investigation and make a worthwhile contribution to the theological understanding of prehistory. I am especially indebted, once again, to the Tyrolia Verlag, without whose urging and constant encouragement this work would never have appeared. My efforts continue to be dedicated to my predecessor, Aemilian Schoepfer.

The Second Vatican Council has given us the privilege of using the vernacular in divine service. This permission has paved the way for a reawakening of interest in the Old Testament. But the proper understanding of the sacred text requires interpretation. The difficult task of scientific work is thus, in the last analysis, truly a service to the Word.

Graz, Dec. 6, 1972

Dr. Claus Schedl
Professor at the University of Graz,
Austria

PART ONE

HISTORY OF THE ANCIENT NEAR EAST

SECTION ONE

EGYPT

THE ancient history of the Bible takes us back to the time of the Ancient Near East, with its peoples, kingdoms, cultures and religions. The Near East is generally referred to as the "lands of the fertile crescent."[1] On a map, if we draw a line from Egypt, over Palestine and Syria, all the way to the Upper Euphrates, and from there to the Persian Gulf, the result is a semi-circle which is not unlike a crescent.

When we attempt to determine the location and theater of biblical history along this extended arc of land, a narrow patch of fertility between sea and desert, we immediately notice the fact that the land of the Bible lies at the point of intersection between Egypt and Mesopotamia, and forms a land bridge between them. The spiritual, economic, religious, and political currents all cross here; something new that is neither purely Egyptian nor purely Mesopotamian develops.

The whole history of the Old Testament is determined by this geographical position in the midst of the Ancient Near East. Only in times of the political descendancy of both kingdoms to the

---

1. G. E. Wright and F. V. Filson, *The Westminster Historical Atlas to the Bible,* London 1946, 23: Fertile Crescent.

south and to the north was it possible to establish and maintain "middle kingdoms" on the Syro-Palestinian land bridge; when Egypt, or one of the great empires to the north rose to ascendancy, the independence of these middle kingdoms was over. Then Palestine was either under Egyptian sovereignty or the Assyrians, Babylonians, or Persians sent their armies, officials, and colonists into the "middle land."

For a full understanding of Old Testament history, it is necessary to have a more precise knowledge of the course of history of the Ancient Near East. The following three sections will be devoted to the three most important divisions of the "fertile crescent," beginning with Egypt in the south, and proceeding to the other end of the arc in the land between the two rivers and its surrounding mountain lands, and finally coming to rest on the geographical and ethnic structure of Canaan, the land of the Bible.

BIBLIOGRAPHY

1. H. Junker, *Die Ägypter, Geschichte der führenden Völker,* Freiburg i. Br. III (1933), 1–174. – H. Kees, *Ägypten, Handbuch der Altertumswissenschaften, Kulturgeschichte des Alten Orients* I: Munich 1933. – J. A. Scharff, *Geschichte Ägyptens von der Vorzeit bis zur Gründung Alexandreias,* Weltgeschichte in Einzeldarstellungen, Munich 1950. – M. A. Murray, *The Splendor that was Egypt.* A general Survey of Egyptian Culture and Civilization, London 1950. – J. A. Wilson, *The Burden of Egypt.* An Interpretation of Ancient Egyptian Culture, Chicago 1950. – *Ägypten,* Propyläen-Weltgeschichte, Berlin-Frankfurt-Wien II, 1961, 323–521. – E. Drioton – J. Vandier, *L'Égypte, Clio: Les peuples de l'Orient méditerranéen* II, Paris 1952[3] (with an elaborate bibliography, arranged by subject matter) – R. Anthes, *"Ägypten," Historia Mundi II,* 1953, 130–223: Grundlagen und Entfaltung der ältesten Hochkulturen, Bern 1953. – L. Cotrell, *Das Volk der Pharaonen,* Stuttgart 1956. – W. Wolf, *Die Welt der Ägypter,* Grosse Kulturen der Frühzeit, Stuttgart 1955 (with rich illustrative material). Helck – Otto, *Kleines Wörterbuch der Ägyptologie,* Wiesbaden 1956. – S. Moscati, *Die Kulturen des Alten Orients,* Munich 1962, 95–146. – D. J. Wiseman *Zwischen Nil und Euphrat,* Archäologische Erläuterungen zur Bibel, Wuppertal-Vohwinkel 1962. – P. Montet, *Das alte Ägypten und die Bibel,* translated from the French by M. Thurneysen, Zurich, 1960. (The

Biblical accounts need a revision) – E. Otto, *Ägypten, der Weg des Pharaonenreiches,* Urbanbücherei, Vol. 4, 1958. – W. Helck, *Zur Verwaltung des Mittleren und Neuen Reiches,* Leiden-Cologne 1958. – W. Wolf, *Die Kunst Ägyptens, Gestalt und Geschichte,* Stuttgart 1964.

CHAPTER I

THE LAND ON THE NILE

HERODOTUS called Egypt the "gift of the Nile." Whereas the rest of North Africa is desert for the greater part, along the banks of the Nile a narrow strip of fertile land has been spared. It was not without reason that Egypt was called the "great oasis," and its culture an oasis culture. This peculiar characteristic of the country was greatly affected by its geological development.[2] After the sea receded at the end of the Tertiary Period, the mouth of the Nile kept extending northward. The recession of the water did not progress at a constant tempo. It is true that Egypt did not experience a glacial age, but it did suffer periods of rain (pluvial periods), which alternated with periods of drought. This geological rhythm produced the Nile terraces. Investigation has established eight of these.[3] Since the Quarternary Period, the Nile has been flowing in its present form. At the end of the Tertiary Period, the Nile emptied into the sea at Fayum; today it extends its mouth farther towards the north. Within times of historical memory, there were seven branches to the delta, all of which are, today, joined into two principal branches.[4]

---

2. Drioton-Vandier, *L'Égypte,* pp. 1ff.

3. Sandford and Arkell, *Palaeolithic Man and the Nile Valley in Upper and Middle Egypt,* Chicago 1934.

4. Precise geographical sketches for the individual sections of Egypt can be found in Marcelle Baud, *Les Guides bleus*: *l'Egypte,* Paris 1950.

Egypt, in the stricter sense of the word, comprises only the lower and smaller part of the Nile valley, from the first cataract at Aswan, ancient Syene, up to the delta on the Mediterranean Sea. Along both sides of the river, beginning already in the south, there are two parallel mountain chains. The Nile valley is thus considerably constricted, so that it is never more than 15 km. across, and sometimes even less than one kilometer, whereas the delta area extends for some 200 km. Not only has the Nile inundated the land of Egypt, but its capricious activity has determined the economic, political, and social mores of the people. The ancient Egyptian provincial division developed as a logical adaptation to the flood waters of the Nile. The individual was powerless against this force of nature. If the flood waters were to be made useful, canals had to be constructed, and the farm land needed to be defined and divided over and over again. Thus, "stretching lines and hoeing lines in the ground" are among the oldest activities described, even being mentioned on the royal monuments, activities which, in the most ancient times, the king himself exercised.[5]

This natural phenomenon also gave rise to village settlements, as working communities, with their surrounding fields. Several villages were grouped together in a province or district. In later historical times, Egypt was divided into 42 such districts (22 in Upper Egypt, and 20 in Lower Egypt). At the beginning of historical times, these districts were all united in a combined state which, in this structure, survived some two and a quarter millennia. The individual districts were not only economic, but also religious communities, with a definite district symbol, a totem animal or some other religious symbol, and their own proper district divinity.[6]

Corresponding to these characteristics of the land, the wealth

---

5. Scharff, *Ägypten*, 7. – H. Kees, *Das Alte Ägypten. Eine kleine Landeskunde*, Berlin 1955.

6. The most extensive account of the Egyptian political subdivisions is to be found in Fritz Hommel, *Ethnologie und Geographie des Alten Orients*, 1926, 751–981.

of ancient Egypt lay in its agriculture. Stock raising also played a large role. Anyone familiar with the picture of everyday life as depicted in the Egyptian tombs knows that cattle were the pride and predilection of the ancients; that is why, with a certain degree of exaggeration, they loved to immortalize the great extent of their possessions for posterity. The king would bring home numerous cattle as booty from his military campaigns. The principal grazing area for these cattle was in the delta. When pasture was lacking due to the fall of the Nile, the cattle were driven into the still green "papyrus marsh district" of the delta. The form of economy was thus, in its regular alternation, not dissimilar to the economy of the Alpine meadows. The "coming of the cattle to the papyrus marsh district of the delta" forms a favorite theme in the tomb paintings of the Old Kingdom.[7]

This land along the Nile is generally called *miṣrâîm* (in the Vulgate *mesraim*) in the Bible, and a few times the singular form *māṣōr* occurs as a poetic expression for Egypt.[8] The basic meaning of this word appears to be *fortress* or *border district.* Thus, the word permanently expressed the first impression that the Semitic Bedouins had of Egypt. The same word form is to be found in the cuneiform texts (*mu-ṣur, mi-ṣir, mi-iṣ-ri-i*).[9] The most ancient native name was *Kmt,* that is, the "black" (black fertile land) in opposition to the red yellow of the desert. Other names are also used, however, such as "the two lands" (*t'.wy*), which expresses the fact that, from the most ancient times, Egypt is a double kingdom, the combined kingdoms of Upper and

---

7. King Sahure (5th dynasty) lists his booty from Libya as 123,400 cattle, 223,400 mules, 2,323,413 goats, 243,688 sheep. The number might be exaggerated, but it is still a large one. Cf. Kees, *Ägypten. Kulturgeschichte des AO* I, (1933), 18ff.

8. 2 Kings 19, 27; Is 19, 6; 37, 25; Mic 7, 12.

9. *Muṣir* also sometimes refers to the Sinai Peninsula and a Bedouin tribe that lived there. Cf. Hommel, *Ethnologie und Geographie des AO,* 1926, 15ff. Similarly, *miṣrâyîm,* in the Bible, frequently means only Lower Egypt, while Upper Egypt is called *patros* – "southland" (In the Assyrian form: *paturisi*); Gen 10, 14 and Ez 30, 14. On the derivation of Patros cf. Erman, ZAW 1890, 118ff.

Lower Egypt. This fact is most clearly evidenced in the imperial insignia. The Pharaoh wears a double crown, one white in the form of a leather head dress, for Upper Egypt, and a red one with a spiral wire for Lower Egypt. Similarly, there are two heraldic animals, the hawk for Upper Egypt and the uraeus for Lower Egypt; two heraldic plants, the lotus plant for Upper Egypt and the papyrus bush for Lower Egypt. In fact, Lower Egypt is frequently called simply the "land of the papyrus plant." Finally, this fact of the double kingdom is also expressed in the name given to the capital city of Memphis. The city itself bears its name from the magnificent pyramid of the Pharaoh Pepi (*Mn-nfr-pipy*), that is, "the beauty of Pepi abides." The Assyrian form for this is Mempi, in Babylonian, Nembi, and in Greek, Memphis. Another name frequently used was "the balance of the two lands" (*mh̲'t . t'wy*) or "the city of the white walls" (*inbw ḥd*).

It was the Greeks who first called the land on the Nile *Aigyptos,* a name that the whole world has taken over. But what does it mean? The word *Aigyptos* is also derived from a secondary name for the city of Memphis. The principal God of Memphis was Ptah. It was customary to speak of "the house of the God Ptah" (*h.t-k'-ptḥ* pronounced somewhat like *ḥikuptaḥ*), from which our word for Egypt is eventually derived. It was the religious designation of the Nile country which won out.[10]

Side by side with the land of Egypt proper, the land of the first cataract has a significant role to play in the course of history. Since the time of the Middle Kingdom, it was known by the name Cush (as a designation for Nubia) and the word made its way into the other Ancient Oriental languages. Thutmose I (1524-1502) took advantage of a revolt in Nubia and penetrated up to the fourth cataract, by Napata near Mt. Barkal, deep into the Sudan. This established the southern boundary of Egypt for the approximately 500 years of the New Kingdom. The country

---

10. For the derivation of the Egyptian words, cf. Erman-Grapow, *Wörterbuch der ägyptischen Sprache,* 6 Vols., 1925 to 1950.

up to the fourth cataract became an Egyptian province. It received its own administrator, who bore the title "prince of Cush." It was from this southern boundary of the kingdom that strong political forces developed in the later period, in the so-called Ethiopian epoch (715-663).[11]

Biblical history sees particular significance in the area assigned to the family of Jacob upon their migration to Egypt, called Gessen in the Vulgate, *gôšen* in Hebrew.[12] Gessen refers to the land north of On (Heliopolis), between the Tanitic branch of the Nile in the west and the Wadi Tumilat in the east, a valley which has been repeatedly crisscrossed by important canals, in both ancient and modern times. From the Lake of Timsah northward there is an uninterrupted series of lakes and swamps, a natural boundary which is very difficult to negotiate. By reason of its eastward position, this 20th Egyptian province bore the Semitic name of *Kedem,* that is, eastland. The more the Egyptian power extended towards Syria and Palestine, the more the political stress of the pharaonic kingdom was felt in the delta region. Thus, Ramses II (1301-1234) established his new capital in the eastern delta and named it after himself, "City of Ramses,"[13] in order to cast his own activity into relief.

Egypt is strictly isolated by its geographical position and condemned to a life of its own. This natural disadvantage was, however, a fertile ground for a strong Egyptian culture. The possibilities of extending the country are very limited. There are only two directions in which the Egyptian ambition for empire

11. H. von Zeissl, *Äthiopier und Assyrer in Ägypten.* Äg. Forsch., Heft 14. Glückstadt 1944.

12. *Gôšen* also occurs as a place name in South Palestine. The element *guš* is of frequent occurrence as the first member of a number of place names in North Palestine; its original meaning seems to be "hill, mound (of earth)." Albright, *From Stone Age to Christianity,* 1949, 433.

13. The French excavations under P. Montet in the ruins of ancient Tanis have established the fact that the place names Avaris (Hyksos era), Ramses City, Tanis (capital of the 21st dynasty), and the Biblical Zoan all refer to the same cities. Cf. Montet, *Le drame d'Avaris,* Paris 1941. *Dagegen B. Couroyer* in RB (1946), 75ff.

could expand: the one way led up the Nile towards the land of Cush, aimed at the great wealth of game available in inner Africa; the other led across Gessen to the copper mines of Sinai and the cedars of Lebanon. It was thus her geographical position which predetermined the route along which Egypt was to make her way into the land of the Bible.

a) THE INUNDATIONS OF THE NILE. The origin of the Nile, and the reason for its annually recurrent inundations, was unknown to the ancients; they located the source of this blessing in heaven, and thus accorded the stream divine honors as servant of God and man.[14] It is only the explorers of modern times who have managed to make their way to the sources of the Nile.

The Nile owes its origin to two rivers, the White and the Blue (clear and muddy), which unite in a single great stream at Khartoum. The White Nile contains three times as much water as the Blue Nile; it is also incomparably longer. The Blue Nile rises in the mountain heights of Abyssinia. The length of the river from Khartoum to its mouth is 2170 km. from Khartoum upwards to the source of the White Nile, approximately 4200 km. Some 220 km. below Khartoum, the river is joined by its only tributary, the Athbara, and then over a course of almost 2,000 km. it does not receive any additional water. The heavy precipitation in the Abyssinian mountains and the annual melting of the considerable snowfall supply the Blue Nile not only with a tremendous mass of water, but also great quantities of clay mire, which is washed down from the mountains. Towards the beginning of June, the rising of the Nile is noticeable in Egypt; in August, the stream overflows its banks and deposits the rich and abundantly fertile clay mire as an excellent natural fertilizer. If the Nile rises too high, the resultant inundations cause great destruction; if it does not rise high enough, the resultant drought takes a heavy toll, and the country is ripe for famine. In describing the most severe judgment that could be passed on Egypt, the prophets threaten the failure of the Nile and the drying up of its canals.[15]

The annual inundations are not only the basis for the country's fertility and its intensive agriculture; they have also played a decisive role in determining the general cultural development of the people. Irrigation, geometry, the division of land, the observation of the heavenly bodies to determine the seasons of the inundation, in connection with the estab-

---

14. E. Drioton, *Le Nil, serviteur des dieux et des hommes, in L'Amour de l'Art*, Paris 1948, 181-186.

15. Is 18, 1ff.; Jer 42, 7ff.

lishment of the calendar, the introduction of records and accounts to determine the boundaries of the inundated farmland, etc. – all this was furthered by the annual rise and fall of the Nile.

b) The Nile Year. It was already well known in classical antiquity that the Egyptians had a solar year of 365 days, which corresponded reasonably well to the "Julian calendar" introduced in Rome under Caesar, so that, in the last analysis, we might consider our solar year as the invention of the Egyptians (who, in turn, were influenced in this development by the land between the rivers). This ancient Egyptian year consisted of 12 months of 30 days each, together with 5 additional days at the end of the year, which were celebrated as the birthdays of the five great gods in the *Osiris* circle (*Isis-Osiris, Seth-Nephtys, Horus*). The names of the seasons, *Akhet* – inundation, *Peret* – sowing, and *Shemon* – harvest, testify to the supreme significance of the inundations for the country; the whole principle of division of time is based on the natural phenomenon of the Nile's inundations.

The Egyptian New Year's Day coincided with the beginning of the inundation. This arrangement must have taken place very early in Egyptian history. But since the Egyptian solar year, by reason of the fact that it lacked a leap year, no longer precisely coincided with the astronomical year, the New Year's Day kept getting farther away from the beginning of the inundation. In terms of arithmetic, this gradual divergence can be expressed in the following equation: 1461 Egyptian civil years are equal to 1460 Julian solar years of 365 and one-quarter days; in other words, within this interval of time there is a difference of a whole year. The inadequacies of the Julian calendar were remedied only by the Gregorian calendar reform, which determined that every 100 years the leap year was to drop.

The beginning of the Nile's inundation also coincided with an astronomical observation which was of significance for the Egyptian chronology. The Egyptians observed that the "Nile year" coincided with the course of the dog star Sirius (in Egyptian, Sothis, feminine!). Sothis was thus venerated as "the bringer of the Nile." When the civil New Year's Day had drifted away from the beginning of the Nile's inundation, the "emergence of Sothis" came to be celebrated as a second New Year's Day. In the rhythm of time – according to the equation established above, every 1460 years – it would necessarily happen that the civil New Year once again fell on the same day as the Sothis New Year. Such an occurrence in the course of Egyptian history is attested to by two documents: the *Ebers Papyrus* for the 18th dynasty (1570-1345) and the *Illahun Papyrus* for the Middle Kingdom (2052-1778). In order to precisely determine these Egyptian Sothis dates, we take as our point of departure for computation the information recorded by the Roman writer Censorinus regarding the end of a Sothis period on July 20, 138 A.D. On the basis of this year, which can be definitely established in terms of astronomy, we need only reckon 1460 years backwards, in order to arrive at the other ends or beginnings of the Sothis periods. But the actual use of these Sothis dates is a much contested point.[16] This also explains the uncertainty regarding the numbering of years in ancient Egyptian history. For the time before 2,000 B.C., only approximate dates are possible; even the chronology between 2,000 - 663 B.C. is subject to variations. In our account, we follow the later chronology of A. Scharff, which has also been taken over by R. Anthes in the *Historia Mundi.*

---

16. The discussion on the value of the Egyptian Sothis dating is still not over. Eduard Meyer, *Ägyptischen Chronologie* (Abh. Preuss. Ak. d. W. Berlin 1904) has established, on the basis of Sothis dates, the day of July 19, 4241, as the most ancient date that can be certainly established in human history. O. Neugebauer, in *Acta Orientalia* XVII, 169ff. maintains "the meaninglessness of the Sothis periods for the most ancient Egyptian chronology." Excellent literature on the present position of the question in Scharff, *Ägypten, Die Bedeutung des Sirius-(Sothis)-sterns für die Chronologie und die Sothisdaten,* 32-37. S. Schott, *Altägyptische Festdaten, zusammenfassende Darstellung der Kalenderentwicklung,* (Abh. Mainz. Ak. 1950, 10) studies the influence of the sun on the formation of the year. — The predominant influence of the moon cycle is investigated by R. A. Parker, *The Calendar of Ancient Egypt,* 1950. He postulates an original lunar year, from which the civil year derives as an "averaged lunar year," Or 22 (1953), 118-122.

CHAPTER II

THE INHABITANTS OF EGYPT

THE most ancient traces of human life in Egypt go back to the Early Stone Age (Palaeolithic Age), an era for which no dates can be determined, not even in terms of millennia. But it is possible to clearly point out the places where it is to be found. The most ancient inhabitants of Egypt lived on the heights along the Nile valley, where, today, there is no more plant life. In those "rain ages" which correspond to the European glacial ages, the Sahara was a verdant country, and the Nile valley was a swampy country uninhabitable by man, while the delta was only gradually forming. Upper Egypt was thus settled earlier than Lower Egypt. As to the race to which the early inhabitants belonged it is impossible to make any accurate statements; there are no skeletal remains from the Early Stone Age. In the Recent Stone Age (c. 5,000-4,000 B.C.), Egypt, together with Spain and Palestine, belongs to the North African culture, which is clearly distinct from the European. Around 3,000 B.C. it makes its entrance into history. But since both Egypt and Mesopotamia learned to work in copper at a very early age, the exit from the Recent Stone Age is also called the Copper Stone Age (*Chalcolithic*, up to 3200 or 2850).

Without going into more precise details here, we might distinguish three strata of culture in the Egypt of the Recent Stone

Age, all of which made a significant contribution to the rise and development of the classical Egyptian culture. In the Recent Stone Age, the delta was already settled. The same climatic and geographical conditions prevailed then as in historical times. Thus it has been possible to discover remains of this stone age culture in the delta region.[17]

One such excavation in the western delta has given its name to a culture, called the *Merimde* culture. The men of this time had already advanced beyond the state of hunters, nomads, and shepherds, and had settled in closed villages to practice agriculture. They buried their dead, in a squatting posture, under their own house, although without funeral gifts, which were offered to the departed from time to time at the banquet.

For Upper Egypt, the Recent Stone Age is established by the find at Badari and Naqada (north of Luxor). A characteristic note of the Badari and Naqada-I culture is the arrangement of the cemetery. Gifts were laid in the graves for the departed. It is here that we find the first evidence of handmade pottery. The clay vessels were painted white or yellow on a red background. The men of this culture are shepherds and cattle breeders; they belong to a class of people which appears in rock paintings in many places in North Africa. The Badari and Naqada-I culture thus obviously points to a North-African Hamite population.

The first culture common to both Upper and Lower Egypt can be established on the basis of further finds in Naqada, which are generally referred to as the Naqada-II culture. The clay vessels are now painted red on white background. This culture, too, developed from the south towards the north; it is also Egyptian-Hamite. Still, this culture shows many points of similarity with the Jemdet-Nasr culture in Mesopotamia. There are clear resemblances to Palestine and Asia Minor. For example,

---

17. R. Anthes, *Ägypten, Die vorgeschichtliche Zeit,* HM II (1953), 134-139. W. Kaiser, *Stand und Probleme der ägyptischen Vorgeschichtsforschung,* ZAeS 81 (1956), 87-109. For Merimde there are two recent carbon dates. Eight others oscillate between 4180 plus 110 and 3480 plus 120, WZKM 58 (1962), 202.

the cylinder seal is taken over from Mesopotamia towards the end of this period. During this era, it is probable that a Semitic-speaking population migrated to Egypt and gave a final stamp to the Egyptian language.

On the basis of these archaeological finds it is possible to distinguish three ethnic elements in prehistoric Egypt, all of which have contributed to the rise and development of Egyptian culture. The Berber-Hamite or northwest Hamite culture corresponds to the Merimde culture; the East Hamite corresponds to the Naqada-I and Badari culture, and it is possible to discern a Semitic element in the Naqada-II level.[18]

The Egyptians, as bearers of an independent culture and history, step out of the shadows of prehistory as a mixed race. In the table of nations (Gen. 10, 6) the inhabitants of Egypt are characterized as sons, that is, the posterity, of Ham; but Ham is Shem's brother. Thus we might say that the ethnic relationship between Egypt and the Semites is corroborated on the basis of archaeology.

Just as the Egyptian people are a mixed race, it is also possible to distinguish three distinct elements in the Egyptian language. The written monuments which date from around the year 3000 B.C. already show this mixed character. Old Egyptian is a combination of Berber-West Hamite, East Hamite, and ancient West Semitic elements. The happy mixture of these three elements gave rise to the classical Egyptian culture.[19]

The Egyptian language has undergone several periods of development in the course of the millennia, developments with

---

18. The names which refer to the early Egyptian cultures are somewhat different in some of the English literature. Naqada I is named Amratian, after the Upper Egypt site of El-Amrah; Naqada II is called Gerzean, from the site of Gerzeh. A good introduction to the prehistorical and early cultures of Egypt is to be found in Scharff, *Ägypten,* 10 ff. — E. J. Baumgärtel, *The culture of Phehistoric Egypt,* Oxford 1947. — H. Stock, *Das Ostdelta Ägyptens in seiner entscheidenden Rolle für die politische und religiöse Entwicklung des Alten Reiches,* WOr 3 (1948), 135-145.

19. Scharff, *Ägypten,* 17ff.

which the script has, to some extent, also kept pace. We distinguish three script systems: hieroglyphic, hieratic, and demotic.

The Egyptian script is not the result of a gradual development, but rather an invention. Since the art of writing had already been invented somewhat earlier by the Sumerians, the smouldering spark of this discovery could easily have leaped from Sumer into Egypt.[20] The Egyptian script, in its initial stage, was a picture writing: the object to be designated was portrayed in terms of signs and pictures (ideograms). But the discovery was quickly made that these pictures also had independent phonetic value. This was the step from picture signs to phonetic signs (phonograms). Now there were phonograms which could express words with three, two, or sometimes only one consonant; the vowels were *not* written. It was on the basis of these one-consonant phonograms that the next step was taken, alphabetic script. But the Egyptians, in the individuality of their complicated language, held fast to a mixed script composed of ideograms, phonograms, and alphabetic elements.

The script type known as hieroglyphic was used primarily for inscriptions on stone and wood. Side by side with the hieroglyphic writing there soon developed a cursive writing, which was called the priestly writing (hieratic script), because during the Greek era it was used exclusively by the priests. To borrow an expression from the famous decipherer of the hieroglyphic, Champollion, it is nothing more than a hieroglyphic shorthand. In late Egyptian times (since the end of the eighth century) this script was simplified even more, into a demotic or popular script. In the third century after Christ the Christian converts

---

20. Wilson, *Ägypten* 346 – Schott, *Hieroglyphen. Untersuchungen zum Ursprung der Schrift.* – Anthes, *Ägypten* 147, however, maintains that the dependence of hieroglyphic writing on Mesopotamian sources cannot be considered as proved. The two systems do have certain common characteristics, but they are essentially different in their formation. The contemporaneity of their invention is no proof of dependence. Both cultures were ripe for the invention of writing, as well as the potter's wheel.

among the Egyptians (the Copts) took over the Greek alphabet and supplied the missing letters from the demotic script.[21]

Within these various script systems, we are presented with a tremendously extensive literature, embracing almost all the areas of human endeavor, beginning with simple stories, including descriptions of daily life, and culminating in the great royal inscriptions and divine hymns in the temples.[22] For the history of religion, it is primarily the pyramid texts (inscriptions of a generally religious nature) which have particular significance; from the time of the fifth dynasty they were written on the walls of the burial chambers. Then there are the coffin texts, which begin in the first interim period (between the Old and Middle Kingdom, Heracleopolitan era) and cease towards the end of the Middle Kingdom. By coffin texts we understand a collection of some 200 magic formulas destined for the use of the departed in the hereafter; they are written in cursive, hieratic script on the inner walls of the sarcophagus. The various collections all bear the title: "Book of justification in the other world for N." At the

---

21. A good introduction to the Egyptian language is presented in the following grammars: A. Erman, *Ägyptische Grammatik, mit Schrifttafeln, Paradigmen und Übungsstücken*, 4th ed. Berlin 1928. Kurzer AbriB der ägyptischen Grammatik, Graz 1955[4]. A. H. Gardiner, *Egyptian Grammar*, Oxford 1927. G. Lefèbvre, *Grammaire de l'Égyptien classique* (Bibl. d'Etudes, vol. XIII), Cairo 1940. Erman-Grapow, *Wörterbuch der ägyptischen Sprache*, 6 vols. Leipzig-Berlin 1925-50. G. Roeder, *Ägyptisch, Praktische Einführung in die Hieroglyphen und die ägyptische Sprache mit Lesestücken und Wörterbuch*, Munich 1926[2]. S. Schott, *Hieroglyphen, Untersuchungen zum Ursprung der Schrift*, Wiesbaden 1950. H. Brunner, *AbriB der Mitteläqyptischen Grammatik*, Graz 1961. E. Edel, *Altägyptische Grammatik*, Rome 1955.

22. The peculiarities of Egyptian literature are well treated in: Erman, *Die Literatur der Ägypter*, Leipzig 1923. Pieper, *Literatur der Ägypter, im Handbuch der Literaturwissenschaften*, Vol. XIV, Potsdam 1927. Spiegelberg, *Die demotische Literatur*, ZDMG, N.S. X, Leipzig 1931. Roeder, *Altägyptische Märchen*, Jena 1927. Gilbert, *La poésie égyptienne*, Brussels 1949. H. Kees, *Aegyptologie-Literatur* (Handbuch der Orientalistik), 1952. W. von Bissing, *Altägyptische Lebensweisheit*, Zürich 1955. A. Hermann, *Altägyptische Liebesdichtung*, Wiesbaden 1959.

beginning of the 18th dynasty, these texts were written on papyrus and laid in the sarcophagus beside the mummy. All these texts are referred to as a group by the name *Book of the Dead.*[23]

If we are impressed and captivated by the insight into the culture of ancient Egypt afforded by these texts, our sense of wonder can only increase when we behold the artistic monuments, unequaled in their magnificence, in the fields of architecture, sculpture, and painting – so that the Egyptians must be counted not only among the oldest, but also among the greatest cultural peoples. The enduring stone of their confession of faith in a life after death still lives today in the mighty pyramids, a witness to the creative power of this people.[24]

---

23. For an introduction to the Books of the Dead, cf.: E. Otto, Or 8, 136-141. G. Thausing, *Der Auferstehungsgedanke in ägyptischen religiösen Texten,* 1943. E. Drioton, *Le théâtre égyptien,* Cairo 1942. S. Schott, *Das schöne Fest vom Wüstental. Festbräuche einer Totenstadt,* Mainz 1953. A. de Buck, *The Egyptian Coffin Texts,* Chicago 1951.

24. A. Scharff, *Ägypten, Handbuch der Archäologie,* I, 433-642, Munich 1939. H. G. Evers, *Staat aus Stein, Denkmäler, Geschichte und Bedeutung der ägyptischen Plastik während des Mittleren Reiches* I, II, Munich 1929. J. Vandier, *Manuel d'archéologie Égyptienne,* Paris 1952ff. W. Wolf, *Die Kunst Ägyptens, Gestalt u. Geschichte,* Stuttgart 1964. H. Schäfer, *Propyläen-Kunstgeschichte,* Vol. 2, Berlin. Steindorff, *Die Kunst der Ägypter,* Leipzig 1928. G. Maspéro, *L'archéologie égyptienne,* Paris 1911. reichem Bildmaterial). G. Maspéro, *L'archéologie égyptienne,* Paris 1911. *Histoire générale de l'art,* Paris 1911. A Rusch, *Geschichte der Kunst in Ägypten,* 2nd ed., Stuttgart 1925. V. Bissing, *Hatte die Pyramide mystisch-symbolische Bedeutung?* FF 26 1950, 113.

CHAPTER III

HISTORY OF EGYPT

1) DEVELOPMENT OF EGYPTIAN HISTORY

FOR the construction of Egyptian historical science, the history of Manetho is the work which paved the way. Manetho was a priest in Sebennytos in the delta. He lived under the second Ptolemy, about 280 B.C., and wrote a history of his country: *Ayguptiaka Upomnemata* – "Egyptian monuments." His work has been preserved only in fragments, in the chronicle of Julius Africanus. The division of Egyptian history into 30 dynasties dates back to him. Ptolemy begins the first dynasty with Menes and he continues the series up to the reconquest of Egypt by the Persians under Artaxerxes III in the year 343 B.C. The last Persian kings and Alexander the Great are added as dynasty 31.

Manetho's work can be partially supplemented and corrected by the various royal lists. First among these we must mention the royal papyrus of Turin, which dates to the Ramesside era and was apparently written in Memphis. It contains a list of kings beginning with the first dynasty and concluding with Ramses II (1301-1234). The Sakkara tablet contains the names of 58 kings, from the first dynasty down to Ramses II. There are also lists of kings in the temple of Seti I in Abydos, and in the temple at Karnak. On the basis of these royal lists we can determine the sequence of the Egyptian Pharaohs, if not with absolute certainty, at least with an ever closer approximation.

For the history of the Old Kingdom, the so-called Palermo stone is of the greatest importance; it is a black basalt block, with inscriptions on front and back. It contains information about the rule of the kings from the first beginnings down to the fifth dynasty.

Manetho's history, the various lists of kings which have been discovered, the astronomical Sothis dates, and, more particularly, archaeological comparison with finds in Asia Minor have, today, yielded a reasonably accurate system of Egyptian chronology.[25] More recent historical science tends to divide Egyptian history in terms of kingdoms. Today we distinguish the Old Kingdom, the Middle Kingdom, the New Kingdom, and the Recent Era. — We shall now present a brief sketch of Egyptian history, and then take up, somewhat more thoroughly, the position of Egypt in the Ancient Near East, since it is this area which is of particular significance for our understanding of the history of the Old Testament.

2) THE PRINCIPAL DIVISIONS OF EGYPTIAN HISTORY

a) Old Kingdom (dynasties 1 to 8, c. 2850 to 2190): The ancient Egyptian state is the embodiment, externally, of the form of an absolute monarchy. All power is concentrated in the Pharaoh. He himself is the "great god," the incarnate falcon god Horus himself, the son of the sun god Re. The Pharaoh is a divine being for his subjects, god on earth. The idea of a divine Pharaoh pervades the whole of Egyptian history; but it left its clearest stamp in the Old Kingdom.[26] The Old Kingdom thus presents the picture of a strongly centralized, theocratic state, which was administered by the officials of the Pharaoh. The capital of the Old Kingdom is Memphis, "the city of the white walls," the "balance of the two lands." The traditional unifier

---

25. The more recent questions are taken up in Scharff, *Ägypten*, 1950, "die zeitliche Festlegung der ägyptischen Geschichte" (25-37). R. Anthes, "Ägypten" *HM* II (1952), 130-134. J. V. Beckerath, "Die ägyptischen Königslisten des Manetho," *OLZ* 54 (1959), 5-11.

26. Hugo Müller, *Die formale Entwicklung der Titulatur der ägyptischen Könige* (Glückstadt, 1938), Äg. Forsch, Part 7. (The Pharoah is the incarnation of Horus!). A. Scharff, *Gott und König in der ägyptischen Königsplastiken,* Rosselinifest schrift, (Pisa, 1949). Only from the time of the 18th dynasty is the title Pharoah used, literally "great house."

of the kingdom was Menes, approximately 2850. It was he who welded Upper and Lower Egypt together into a unified state which, however, in its structure, always retained the stamp of double monarchy. The great Pharaohs of this epoch are: Juser, the builder of the first pyramid at Sakkara, then the pyramid builders Cheops, Chefren, and Mykerinos. During the 94-year reign of Pepi, the Pharaoh's power collapsed, and revolutionary powers make their appearance, leading to the end of the Old Kingdom.

b) THE FIRST INTERIM PERIOD, or Heracleopolitan Era (dynasties 9 and 10, c. 2190-2052): This dark epoch of the decentralization of the kingdom is somewhat illuminated by important works of literature. Among these are the stirring "Laments of Ipuwer," with the monotonous repetition of the words: "Yes, it is true, completely gone is what we yesterday saw. . . ." There is also the "Instruction for King Merikare," "The Laments of the Talkative Farmer," "The Account of the Argument between a Man Weary of Life and his Soul," and finally the "Potter's Song," which dreams of times gone by: "The gods who once were now sleep in their pyramids. . . ."[27]

c) MIDDLE KINGDOM (dynasties 11 to 12, c. 2025 - c. 1778): The battle among the provincial princes results in a victory for the Theban party. The administrative state of the Old Kingdom has now become a feudal state with a system of hereditary provincial princes. In order to consolidate the empire, the Pharaohs are constantly concerned with breaking the power of these provincial princes. The great kings of this epoch are Sesostris and Amenemhet. Their great accomplishments consist in the unification of the kingdom, the conquest of Nubia, the annexation and colonization of Fayum. The seventh year of Sesostris III

27. Texts in the above cited "*Literaturen der Ägypter.*" Cf. also: Joachim Spiegel, *Soziale und weltanschauliche Reformbewegungen im alten Ägypten* (Heidelberg, 1950). H. Kees, "Aus den Notjahren der Thebais," *Or* 21 (1952), 86-97.

(1878-1841) is known as a Sothis date, which is the basis for an exact chronology.

d) Second Interim Era (dynasties 13 and 14, 1778-1610) and Hyksos Period (dynasties 15 and 16, c. 1670-1570): the Middle Kingdom dissolved in the internal strife created by the provincial princes who once again rose to power; under the attack of the Hyksos it falls under the yoke of foreign rule, from the Near East; the center of power lay in the delta region.

e) New Kingdom (dynasties 17-21, 1570-950): liberation of the country from the south. During the Hyksos period Thebes enjoys a certain autonomy. In an effort to keep the kingdom safe, the Hyksos were pushed back into the country from which they originated, and, following their trail, it is the Pharaohs that become world conquerors. It is particularly the Thutmosides and the Ramessides who are responsible for a world empire, uniting Egypt and the Near East. Between these two powerful dynasties falls the Amarna era, a time of political descendancy and complete religious reconstruction. The New Kingdom, dependent upon the army, was definitely a military state.[27a]

f) Recent Era (dynasties 22-30, 950-332) presents a very spent Egypt. Political control was taken over first by the Libyans under Sheshonk (dynasty 22), then the Nubians under Shabaka and Taharka (dynasty 25), and finally the Persians. It was as their heir that Alexander the Great entered Egypt in 332. Under his successors, the Ptolemies, a new era began for Egypt.

3) EGYPT AND THE NEAR EAST

Apart from the prehistoric relationship of Egypt and the Near East (Naqada-II and Jemdet-Nasr culture), the sixth dynasty General Wenis ("Una"), in his funerary inscription in Abydos, reports a military campaign along the Syro-Palestinian

---

27a. R. O. Faulkner: "Egyptian Military Organization." *JEArch.* 39 (1953), 32-47.

coast. "The Lord returned home in fortune, after he had destroyed and cut in pieces the land of the sand-dwellers." The Old Kingdom was really not so isolated as was for a long time believed. Trade caravans made their way to the south, as far as the fourth cataract, and the sea trade went as far as Punt, the land of incense. Not only that, but the Pharaohs also attempted to make their way into the wooded country of Lebanon. For the Bedouins, fertile Egypt was the land of longing. In order to consolidate their advances and secure their trade routes, the Pharaohs constantly needed to undertake security expeditions against the "sand-dwellers," expeditions which, during the Old Kingdom, did not develop into an actual subjugation of Palestine.

In the Middle Kingdom too (2052-1778) Egypt remained true to its tendency towards Syria-Palestine as determined by its geographical position. Sesostris III (1878-1841) on a pillar in Abydos, declares that, in his military campaigns, he penetrated all the way to the city of Shechem.[28] His figure assumed legendary proportions. He became a military hero who was believed to have campaigned as far as Scythia and Colchis. But even in the Middle Kingdom there is no mention of any occupation of Palestine. Campaigns were undertaken for the purpose of intimidation, primarily in order to secure the wood trade with Byblos. The general state of affairs in Palestine and southern Syria is rather clearly presented in the Sinuhe story, the principal literary product of the Middle Kingdom.[29]

In the Hyksos era (c. 1670-1570), the Near East makes its first definite entry into the history of Egypt. The name "Hyksos" is not the proper name of a people, but an expression used as a title for "foreign rulers," literally "rulers of foreign countries." The Hyksos do not thus present the invasion of a conquering people in Egypt which can be racially determined with any degree

---

28. The texts of the Una and Sesostris inscriptions are best treated in Gressman, *AOT*, 80-81. The Sesostris text reads: "His Majesty succeeded in reaching as far as the territory called Sekmen."

29. "The Life of Sinuhe and His Adventures in Palestine," *AOT*, 55-61, or Galling, *TGI*, 12-19.

of certainty. It was the invasion of a very mixed Near East ethnic group, which were, in their turn, driven from their homes by the invasion of the Hurri who came from the Armenian mountain ranges. The Hurri were led by an Indo-Germanic ruling class and in north Syria they established the kingdom of Mitanni, which was well known in the New Kingdom of Egypt. It certainly cannot be maintained that these Hurri had established a giant empire in the Ancient Near East, including Egypt, nor that they forced their way into Egypt, with respect to their Indo-Germanic leadership, as Hyksos. The invasion of the Hurri into north Syria actually brought the peoples of Syria and Palestine into motion and confusion, and parts of them, yielding to the pressure, made their way further towards the south, eventually into Egypt. The Hyksos rule in Egypt cannot have lasted longer than a hundred years.

The center of their power lay in Avaris in the delta, a fortress city encompassed by walls and moats. Such gigantic walls could certainly have been constructed only by the most pitiless expenditure of forced labor. The probability that what we are here dealing with was originally a fortified war chariot camp, suggests the further conclusion that this was a feudal warrior class, capable of military service, that settled here with its leaders. But such concepts have no common ground with Semitic-Canaanite traditions. The Hyksos attempted to secure their position by establishing a circle of fortifications in Palestine-Syria; in south Palestine the fortresses of Sharuhen and Hebron, which were built seven years before Avaris in Middle Palestine, the fortresses of Megiddo and Hasor, and finally in Syria, the fortress city of Kadesh on the Orontes. This was to secure their connection with a line of retreat into north Syria. It was at this same time that the Hurrian "Mariannu," that is, chariot fighters, were erecting their system of small city states in Palestine.

The most important cultural contribution of these foreign conquerers in Egypt was the horse, not for riding, but for hitching to the war chariot. It is possible that the foreign conquerors owed their success to precisely this "new weapon." The horse originally comes from Syria; it apparently passed from Europe into the Balkans, or from southern Russia over the Caucasus to the Hittites of Asia Minor, and from there to the Hurri in northern Mesopotamia.[30]

In the New Kingdom, Egypt rose up against her conquerors from the Near East. Thutmose I (1524-1502) embarked upon a successful campaign all the way to the Euphrates, the "backward waters," so named because it flows in the opposite direction of the Nile. Along the Euphrates he hunted elephants, whose tusks he presented to the god Amon in Thebes. Thutmose I is the first great conqueror among the Pharaohs. He subjugated Nubia as far as the fourth cataract and Syria as far as the Euphrates.

Thutmose III (1502-1448), during his lengthy reign, undertook 16 campaigns against Syria, striking against the coalition of the Syro-Palestinian princes, who made regular efforts to shake off the yoke of Egyptian supremacy. The most important military event of this time is the battle at Megiddo (1480). The description of this battle, with the crossing of Mount Carmel, is preserved, in all its details, on one of the annal inscriptions on the walls of the temple at Karnak.[31] Around the year 1461 occurred the subjugation and destruction of Kadesh in northern Syria.

---

30. In addition to the description of the Hyksos Era in the general histories, see the individual studies of: Stock, "Studien zur Geschichte und Archäologie der 13-17. Dynastie unter besonderer Berücksichtigung der Skarabäen dieser Zeit," *Archäologische Forschungen*, Part 12 (Glückstadt, 1942). That the Hyksos are, essentially, not a new people, but merely represent a new, Asiatic dynasty which took up residence in the Delta city of Avaris around 1720 and subjugated larger and larger pieces of Egyptian territory from that point, is the result of the investigations of I. Save-Saderbergh in *JEArch.* 37 (1931), 53-71. On the problem of Indo-Arian Mariannu, cf. O'Callaghan, "New Light on the Mariannu as Charriot Warrior," *JkaF* 1 (1950-51), 309-324. A. Alt: "Die Herkunft der Hyksos in neuer Sicht," *Or* 24 (1955), 319. J. Leibovitch: "Le problème des Hyksos," *IEJ* 3 (1953), 99-112.

31. Galling, *TGI*: "Die Belagerung von Megiddo," pp. 12-19. A. Alt, "Neue Berichte über Feldzüge von Pharaonen des neuen Reiches nach Palästina," *ZDPV* 70 (1954), 62. W. Helck, "Die ägyptische Verwaltung

The central seat of unrest, however, lay further north in the kingdom of the Mitanni, which is somehow connected with the Hyksos. The conclusion of these twenty years of military campaigns apparently produced an agreement whereby the Syro-Palestinian conquests were secured for Egypt. Thus, the Egyptian kingdom achieved a vertical extension of some 3,200 km., from the mouth of the Orontes in northern Syria to Napata in Nubia, in the south, held together by the mighty personality of Thutmose III.

Amenhotep II (1448-1422), the successor of Thutmose III, had to reconquer the Palestino-Syrian provinces after the death of his predecessor. One particularly terrible tale is told of him; he had the bodies of seven dead Syrian princes suspended from the bow of his royal barge as he sailed up the Nile towards Thebes.

In the Amarna era, the Syro-Palestinian provinces were almost completely lost to the Egyptian empire, since Pharaoh Amenhotep IV, or, as he called himself, Ikhnaton (1377-1358), was more concerned with religious reform than with the affairs of state. In order to make a break with tradition, he abandoned the old capital of Thebes, and built a new residence in the neighborhood of the modern Arabic village of Amarna. In the year 1847 a part of his official archives were discovered here. This find consists of some 360 clay tablets, almost entirely made up of letters. This correspondence between the Pharaoh and the kings and princes of the Near East, especially those of Babylon, Ashur, Mitanni, Hatti and the Syro-Phoenician vassals, was carried on in Babylonian-Assyrian cuneiform script, and, with few exceptions, in that language as well. For the state of affairs in Palestine proper, the letters of Putiḫepas of Jerusalem are very illuminating; he sends one plea for help after another to the

---

in den syrischen Besitzungen," *MDOG* 92 (1960), 1-13. The conquered districts were subject to the "Overseer of the northern foreign lands."

Pharaoh, but is answered only with promises, never any actual show of strength.[32]

After the decline of Egyptian power in the Near East, the Pharaohs Haremhab (1345-1318) and Seti I (1317-1301) had to reconquer the lost provinces. More exact details about these battles are once again preserved for posterity in the victory inscriptions in the temple at Karnak; among other accounts, is that of the conquest of a "fortress of Canaan" which was situated on a lofty mountain, and this is the first time we find this familiar Old Testament name in the Egyptian inscriptions.[33]

During the era of the Ramessides, Egypt was faced by a new opponent in the now recovered Hittite kingdom, which had been active in the Amarna era, extending its military installations from Asia Minor down into Syria. The border of these two spheres of influence was Nahr-el-Kelb, "Dog River," north from Beirut. Ramses II (1301-1234) had two inscriptions cut into the cliffside high above the sea, designating the boundary line. The decisive confrontation in this Hittite-Egyptian quarrel over the possession of Syria and Palestine took place, as it had once before taken place in earlier times, at the fortress of Kadesh on the Orontes (1296 B.C.). Chariot warfare had already been perfected by both sides. The struggle was a bitter one. On both sides there were auxiliary troops. Despite the Egyptian victory, which was a Pyrrhic victory, there was no essential change in the power position on either side. In the year 1280, they made a peace treaty, which was sealed by the marriage of a Hittite princess to the Pharaoh, and thus guaranteed peace in the Near East for seventy years.[34]

---

32. The Standard edition of the Amarna texts is J. A. Knudtzon, *Die El-Amarna-Tafeln,* (1907); a selection appears in *AOT,* 371ff., and in *TGI,* Letters 4-13. Text criticism in W. V. Soden, "Zu den Amarnabriefen aus Babylon und Assur," *Or* 21 (1952), 426-434. K. A. Kitchen, *Šupiluliuma and the Amarna-Pharaos* (Liverpool, 1962).

33. *AOT* 94; *AOB* 95/96.

34. Inscription and illustration of Nahr-el-Kelb in *AOB,* 146-147. G. J. Botterweck, "Der sogenannte chattische Bericht über die Schlacht bei Kades, ein verkannter Brief Ramses II," *BBB* 1 (1950), 26-32.

Ramses II, during the long years of his reign, led the new kingdom to its highest political and cultural development. Under his son and successor, Merneptah (Merenptah 1234-1220) troubles among the sea peoples brought the pharaonic kingdom to the point of destruction. Already at the very outset of his reign, Merneptah had to deal with two Libyan tribes who were threatening to invade the Nile valley from the west, in order to establish settlements on the Nile plains. This Libyan attack was only an advance guard of the wave of peoples which seethed down over the Balkan islands and through the eastern Mediterranean and caused widespread confusion. This movement of the sea peoples coincides with the advance of the Indo-Germanic Illyrians and the Doric migration into the Balkan peninsula.

Among these sea peoples which make their appearance in the inscriptions and battle records of the 19th and 20th dynasties, belong the Shirdana (Sardinians?), who already fought under Ramses II as auxiliary troops; also the Shakalsha (Sicilians), Tursha (Tyrrhenians, Etruscans), Luka (Lycians), Ahaiwasha (Achaeans?) and finally the Peleshet (Philistines).[35]

Merneptah immortalized his victory over the Libyans in the temple at Karnak. The so-called "Israel stele" records an annihilating blow dealt by Merneptah to the Israelites: "Their land is desolate and without fruit."[36]

This powerful movement among the sea peoples, to which even the Hittite kingdom in Asia Minor fell victim shortly after the year 1200, was opposed by Ramses III (1197-1165) before the gates of Egypt. It must be recorded, as this Pharaoh's immortal service in the interest of world history, that Egypt was

---

E. Edel, *Weitere Briefe aus der Heiratskorrespondenz Ramses II;* Fs. A. Alt, *Geschichte u. At* (1953), 29-64.

35. Scharff, *Ägypten,* 162ff. J. Wiesner, *Zur Herkunft der Etrusker FF* 19 (1943), 51-53. Together with the sea peoples, they come to Asia Minor and, around 300 B.C., make their way further into Italy.

36. Israel stele, with the victory song of Meneptah, in *AOT,* 21ff., and *TGI,* 34.

thus spared, for a few centuries, from this invasion which swept away everything in its path.

In the recent era, Egypt no longer had enough power to hold onto her possessions in the Near East. The unhappy political position of Egypt in Palestine and Phoenicia, in the days of the 21st dynasty, is best described in the travel account of Wen-Amon, who was sent from Thebes in order to arrange a supply of wood from Lebanon for the bark of the god Amon.[37]

Such was the world political situation in which the land bridge between Egypt and Mesopotamia was able to function as a middle power. Into this rhythm of world history falls Palestine's occupation by Israel, her consolidation into a kingdom, and its eventual rise to hegemony, the influence of which was felt from the banks of the Nile all the way to the Euphrates. It is true that the Libyan Pharaoh Shoshenk made an attempt to invade Palestine during the time of Solomon, but without any significant success. In the era of the prophets, Palestinian propaganda spoke of the power of the Pharaohs as a proverb and a distant wonder, a power from which salvation could be expected against the Assyrians and Babylonians. But Egypt's impotence is mercilessly unmasked by the prophets: "Egypt is a broken reed of a staff, which will pierce the hand of any man who leans on it."[38]

---

37. Journey account of Wen-Amon in *AOT*, 71-77, and *TGI*, 36-43. W. F. Albright, *The Eastern Mediterranean World About 1060 B.C.* in *Stud.* D. M. Robinson (1952).

38. Is. 36, 6.

CHAPTER IV

THE RELIGION OF THE EGYPTIANS

BIBLIOGRAPHY

G. Roeder, *Urkunden zur Religion des alten Ägyptens,* (Jena 1923[2]), *Volksglaube im Pharaonenreich,* (Stuttgart 1952). – H. Kees, *Totenglaube und Jenseitsvorstellungen der Ägypter,* (Berlin 1956[2]). – *Der Götterglaube im alten Ägypten,* (Berlin 1956[2]). – A. Erman, *Die Religion der Ägypter, ihr Werden und Vergehen in vier Jahrtausenden,* (Leipzig 1934). – H. Junker, *Pyramidenzeit, das Wesen der altägyptischen Religion,* (Einsiedeln 1949). – J. Vandier, *La religion egyptienne,* "Sammlung Mana," (Paris 1949[2]). The introductory section offers an extensive bibliography on the history of religion in general and an exhaustive study of the literature on the individual areas of the Egyptian religion. Cf. also "Bibliographie analytique des religions de l'Egypte," zehn Artikel über den letzten Stand der ägypt, Religionsgeschichte, *RHistRel,* (Paris 1944/50). (Special printing: *Religions egyptiennes antiques,* Paris 1952). – J. H. Breasted, *Geburt des Gewissens,* (Die Entwicklung des moralischen Verhaltens im kulturgeschichtlichen Verlauf Altägyptens), (Zurich 1950). (Evolution of Religion!) – H. Kayser, *Göttliche Tiere,* (Hildesheim 1951). – H. Junker, Die Religion der Ägypter, in *Christus und die Religionen der Erde II* (1951), 565-606. – H. Bonnet, *Reallexikon der ägypt,* Religionsgeschichte, (Leiden 1952). – G. Thausing, *Die Religion der Ägypter,* Eine Betrachtung ihres Wesens, WZKM 52 (1953-55), 7-26. – H. Frankfort, *Ancient Egyptian Religion, an Interpretation,* (New York 1948). – H. Kees, *Das Priestertum im ägyptischen Staat vom Neuen Reich bis zur Spätzeit* (Probleme der Ägyptologie I), (Leiden-Köln 1953). – R. Anthes, *Egyptian Theology in the Third Millennium B. C.,* JNES 18,

(1959), 169-212. – E. Drioton, "Die ägyptische Religion," *Die Religionen des Alten Orients,* (Aschaffenburg 1958). – S. Morenz, *Ägyptische Religion,* Die Religionen der Erde, Vol. 8, (Stuttgart 1960). – G. Röder, *Die ägyptische Religion in Texten und Bildern. Vol. I: Die ägyptische Götterwelt* (1959). – Vol. II: *Mythen und Legenden um ägyptische Gottheiten und Pharaonen,* (1960). – Vol. III: *Kulte, Orakel und Naturverehrung im alten Ägypten,* (1960). – Vol. IV: *Der Ausklang der ägyptischen Religion mit Reformation, Zauberei und Jenseitsglauben,* (Zürich-Stuttgart 1961).

WHEN we enter the Egyptian pantheon, we are faced by a chaos of the most divergent divine figures. Even professional Egyptologists speak of the ancient Egyptian religion as an almost incomprehensible phenomenon.[39] But this sphinx is easiest understood if we attempt to solve the riddle of its historical development. The history of Egyptian religion has nothing of what appears to be the eternally impassive calm of the pictorial representation of the gods, who never abandon the flat surface of the pictures and inscriptions to enter into the perspective of time. But if we learn how to read correctly, we shall soon discover that a grandiose historical drama is unrolling behind the scenes of this apparent immobility; a drama which we might better call a tragedy, since its theme involves the descendancy of the sky god in favor of beasts and animals. Already in the prehistoric cliff inscriptions[40] we find gods represented with animal heads, belonging to the North-African-Hamite culture cycle.[41] The choice of a particular animal seems to have been dictated by the circumstance of the place. The uniformity of the Egyptian landscape implies a certain narrowness of choice in this respect. It is natural that in Upper Egypt it should be primarily the predatory animals and the beasts of the desert which make their way into the cult: jackal, desert dog, falcon, hawk; on the border of the

---

39. E. Drioton, *La Religion égyptienne dans ses grandes lignes,* (Cairo, 1945) – "La vieille religion égyptienne passe souvent, même aux yeux d'égyptologues, pour quelque chôse d'á peu près *incompréhensible*" (p. 1).

40. Frobenius, *Tierköpfige Götter auf Felsbildern,* (Leipzig, 1937).

41. Scharff, *Ägypten.* Kapitel uber "Älteste Göttervorstellungen," 18-21.

desert were encountered antelope and gazelle. Nor is it surprising that the crocodile, the strongest and most dangerous water animal alongside the hippopotamus, was particularly venerated wherever rocky cliffs or islands or sand bars in the river imperiled the sailor's progress. Along the wadis at the desert's edge we find the cult of the ravening lioness. Among the domestic animals, bulls, cows, cats, goats, and rams all enjoy divine honors. The list further includes the sycamore and pomegranate tree, shield and arrow.[42]

The religious picture presented by ancient Egypt is a manifold one. Every independent organization, every city, every province had its own divinity, which it honored in the figure of animals, plants, or inanimate objects. Most ethnologists explain the roots of this animal cult in terms of totemism.[43] These totems were magic signs of relatedness and belonging together; they could be either animals or inanimate things. It was from these totems that the Egyptian provincial insignia developed. It might be true that elsewhere in the history of religion the totem did not enjoy any religious cult, but it seems to be proved with reasonable certainty that ancient Egypt had made the step from totem to divine cult.[44] On the basis of this totem cult as the foundation of the provincial insignia, the later cult of the Pharaohs can be easily explained; in totemistic mentality, the chieftain or king represents the incorporation of the totem animal.

As soon as Egyptian religion makes its appearance, together with the beginning of historical time, we are already faced with a plurality of gods. The ancient Egyptian term for god (*nṯr*)

---

42. Cf. Kees, *Handbuch der Altertumswissenschaften III,* 1. 3, 1, pp. 11ff.

43. The word totem is derived from the North American Algonquin language and means a blood relative in the sense of brother or sister. Relationship with the totem can be considered as a racial descent from the animal in question or as the consequence of some special connection between an ancestor and the totem animal. Cf. J. Haekel, *Der heutige Stand des Totemismusproblems.* In Festgaben zum 4 internat. Ethnologenkongress (Wien 1952), 33-49.

44. S. Morenz, *Ägyptische Religion,* 26. Erklärung der Götternamen, 22ff.

has not been satisfactorily explained in terms of etymology; it is possible that the concept "power" is one of the factors. The essence of the gods is well described by their names. Thus, Amon means "the hidden," a proper appellation for the invisible god of the air; Khons means "the wanderer," since he is the moon god who wanders his way across the sky; Horus, "the distant one," is the sky god, in the form of a falcon; Neith, "the terrible," is a war goddess, with a bow; Sekhmet, "the mighty," is also a war goddess, and her animal is the lion; then there is Toth, apparently "the messenger"; Isis, "the royal throne"; Hathor, "the house of Horus," that is, the sky goddess who gives shelter to the falcon Horus; Atum, "he who is a totality," and many others. The names of the gods thus refer either to cosmic space or their special spheres of competence. Morenz might be correct when he says that the gods came to life by being given names. Their spheres of activity were personified, and the number of the gods was thus increased. According to the ancient Egyptian conception of things, the gods all came into being. And just as they once came into being, they will once again pass away. In connection with the Biblical account of creation, we shall have occasion to take up this thought once again. Despite this fact, it is hardly possible to share the opinion of G. v. D. Leeuw that "God is a latecomer in the history of religion."[44a] Quite the contrary! Already in the most ancient texts we see clear evidence of a belief in the one supreme God, the creator and preserver of the world, and the other gods. No matter how much this figure is caked over by various myths, this one supreme God is always recognizable behind the plurality of gods. It is hardly possible to speak of an original Egyptian monotheism,[45] since this involves the retrospective projection of Christian articles and

---

44a. *Phänomenologie der Religion,* Second edition, 1956, 103.

45. The chief proponent of Egyptian monotheism must be considered the Vienna Egyptiologist, Hermann Junker. His works: *Götterlehre von Memphis* (Berlin, 1940). "Der blinde und der sehende Gott," Sitzungsbericht der bayr. Akademie der Wissenschaften, phil-hist. Abt. (Munich, 1942), Part 2. *Pyramidenzeit, das Wesen der ägyptischen Religion* (Ein-

concepts of belief into ancient times, but we are justified in speaking of an ancient Egyptian belief in one supreme God.

The essence of this world God can be deduced from his name. A very ancient name is "the great one," "wĕr"; a particularly frequent name is the title "the great God, the lord of heaven." In ancient Heliopolis, he was called Atum, the "god of all," the "lord of all." He says of himself: "All things belong to me." Equivalent in meaning to this title "god of all" is the name "Nenwen," "that which is," a title whereby God is designated as the original source and bearer of all existence and being. As a further name, he bears the title "lord to the very end."[46]

Among the images in which this "lord of all" is pictured, there is one which seemed most effective and remained in use from the very beginnings of Egyptian religion down to the time of its final collapse: the conception that the figure of God filled the whole expanse of heaven, and that sun and moon are his two eyes with which he watches over the earth and its inhabitants day and night. This sky god, even in the most ancient times, was called: "he in whose countenance are two eyes."[47] In the New Kingdom he was praised with these words: "You are the god who was at first, when no god had yet arisen, when no thing's name was yet named. When you open your eyes, it is light for everyone."

---

siedeln, 1949). His approach is similar to that of Drioton, "Le monotheisme de l'ancienne Ègypte," *Cahiers de l'Histoire d'Égypte* (1948), 149-169. Drioton, *La religion égyptienne dans ses grandes lignes* (Cairo, 1945). "Egypte la plus ancienne a pratiqué une religion du ciel!"... he speaks further of a "tradition monothéiste depuis les plus ancien temps" (p. 3).

46. On the other names of God cf. Junker, *Pyramidenzeit* 29ff. Also "The Living One," an appellative of God. (cf. Gen. 16, 13), *Bibl* 36 (1955), 261. "'Der Lebendige' als Gottesbeiname in den Personennamen des Alten Reiches," *AnzphilhistKl der östAkW* 12 (1954), 169-191.

47. In Egyptian this God has a double name: *Mhnti-irti*, "he whose face has two eyes," and *Mhnti-n-irti*, "he whose face does not have two eyes." This is a reference to day and night. For greater detail, consult Junker, *Der blinde und der sehende Gott.*

It is true that we encounter many titles such as the "great god," "lord of heaven," "only one," in the case of other divinities as well; their eternity is also stressed. But it is precisely in this area that the historical evolution of Egyptian religion is visible. Aspiring local gods, in an effort to substantiate their claim for unique validity and honors, are equated with the god of all. In the evolution of Egyptian religion, politics has an important position. Thus, in ancient times, the tribe which fought under the tutelage of the falcon god, Horus, had managed to subjugate the entire country from the fourth cataract to the Mediterranean Sea. The falcon god became the god of the kingdom. Corresponding to the realm over which his power now spread, he was elevated above the other gods and, as "Horus," was made equal to the supreme sky god. He is already represented from the time of the first dynasty as the falcon who fills the sky, his wings stretched out in protection over the whole earth, and his sparkling eyes, the "Horus eyes," are the twin stars of day and night.

In the 5th dynasty, the history of Egyptian religion entered upon a new stage. The Horus religion was dissolved or, to put it better, was united with the sun religion of the sun god Re at On (in Greek: Heliopolis). This interior commingling is recognizable in terms of the external representation: the solar disk is placed between the falcon's wings. This winged sun enjoyed great popularity. The sun god Re was now identified and united with the ancient local god Atum, who is once again an incorporation of the "god of all," in the god Re-Atum. The Pharaoh was now not primarily an incarnation of Horus, but rather a son of the sun god Re. The priesthood at Heliopolis developed a theological system of their own, in an effort to unite all these different divinities; a theology which found its most telling expression in the "great nine of the gods."[48]

During the time that Memphis was capital of the kingdom, the Heliopolitan theology was transformed into a Memphitic

---

48. For a more explicit discussion of theogony and cosmogony, cf. p. 252.

system. Since the 12th dynasty, however, it was the local god of Thebes, Amon, who enjoyed hegemony in the heaven of the gods. He was mingled with the sun god Re, so that from that time on Amon-Re was the most frequently venerated god of Egypt. It was in his honor that the Pharaohs built the great temples of Luxor and Karnak, the history of whose construction extends from the Middle Kingdom into the Ptolemaic period. We might well ask in astonishment how these transformations among the gods could take place so easily. The simplest answer is the fact that, side by side with the political pressure, there was still a trace of monotheism to be found in all these supreme gods. The god Amon of Thebes is also an ancient sky god. His azure blue throne is a reference to the color of the sky.[49] But this belief in one god was heavily overlaid by myths, so that it necessarily led to a religious reaction. This reaction made its appearance under Pharaoh Amenhotep IV (1377-1358), the "heretic on the throne of the Pharaohs."

The verdict of history on this man oscillates between ideal reformer and sickly scion of a tired line.[50] An objective appraisal of his career immediately establishes the fact that Amenhotep chose the throne name "Neferkeperu-Re Ua-en-Re" – "beautiful to look on is Re, the Only One of Re!" in an effort to re-establish the ancient belief in the sun in its pure form. In this ambition he quickly met with the opposition of the priesthood. He abandoned Thebes and established a new capital, Akhetaton, "horizon of the solar disk," further to the north. In Thebes, he inaugurated an iconoclasm in which he had everything that recalled Amon destroyed. While the sun religion of Ikhnaton does not represent anything typically new in the history of Egyptian religion, there

---

49. Wainwright, "The Sky-Religion in Egypt" – derives the name of Amon from the Libyan "aman," "water." H. Kees, "Ein Sonnenheiligtum im Ammontempel von Karnak," *Or.* 18 (1949), 427-442.

50. Ghaliungui, "A Medical Study of Echnaton," in *Annales du Service des Antiquités de l'Égypte,* 47 (1947), 29-47.

50a. M. Doresse, "Les Temples atoniens de la région thébaine," *Or.* 24 (1955), 113-135.

is one new element in the fact that it is the solar disk (Aton), as abstracting from every animal and human figure, which is the object of veneration. The official divine image now becomes the solar disk, beaming its rays in every direction. Where these rays are directed towards men, they generally end in human hands, which offer mankind the ancient symbol of life, the ringed cross. Corresponding to this reform, Amenhotep IV also changes his Amon name to Ikhnaton, that is "he who is well pleasing to Aton." The most famous religious document of this time is the hymn to the sun, the work of Pharaoh Ikhnaton. Upon the death of this reformer on the throne of the Pharaohs, his reform entirely collapsed. His stepson TutanKhamon ("perfect is the life of Amon") returns to Thebes. Amon re-enters his supreme position in the Egyptian pantheon, a position which he will hold until the Recent Era.[51]

Side by side with these various manifestations of the sun religion, since the time of the first interim era, in which the collapse of the pharaonic power was experienced in the most unsettling manner, the Osiris religion came more and more into prominence. There is no uniform opinion as to the origin of Osiris. But at any rate, Osiris was a king of the most ancient times, who was murdered and who, after his death, rose to the rank of god of the dead. Later history joined this concept with motifs of the Nile inundations and fertility, and finally astral elements were incorporated into the figure, so that Osiris takes on the form of a universal god.[52]

The judgment of the dead is also bound up with his image. Osiris, the ruler of eternity, the prince of the "western ones" (that is, the dead who were buried on the west bank of the Nile, the side of the setting sun), sits on his throne; before him stand the four sons of Horus and beside him squats a monster with

---

51. J. Spiegel, *Soziale und weltanschauliche Reformbewegungen im Alten Ägypten* (Heidelberg, 1950); "über das ägyptische Aufklärungszeitalter," pp. 57-79. C. Desroches-Noblecourt, *Tut-ench-Amun. Leben und Tod eines Pharao* (1963).

52. H. Junker, *Die politischen Lehren von Memphis* (Berlin, 1941).

the body of a hippopotamus and the head of a crocodile, the "gobbler," to whom the souls of the wicked are cast in prey. From the right hand side the souls of the departed are led before the goddess of justice. Between both groups, in the middle of the picture, is the balance upon which the heart of the departed is weighed against a symbol of truth. This weighing is presided over by Anubis and Horus; Thot, the secretary, stands to the side, entering the proceedings on his papyrus. All around the hall are sitting the 42 judges, who represent the 42 Egyptian provinces. The departed soul now turns to face the tribunal and pronounces the "words which are spoken upon entering the hall of the two truths, in order to separate this N.N. from all sins which he has committed, so that he may look upon the countenance of all the gods."[53]

These texts from the *Book of the Dead,* with their vivid representation of the judgment of the dead, can be adduced as testimony to the high state of Egyptian ethics, which was firmly anchored in conscience and the will of the deity. When a man dies, he and all his deeds beside him are exposed to judgment. But Egyptian ethics suffered the same fate as Egyptian belief in God. While the ancient sky god was gradually desecrated into the form of animals, ethics too fell into the hands of magic and superstition. It was precisely by this fact that the judgment of the dead was despoiled of all its ethical power. In the last analysis, the judgment could be decided not on the basis of what the man had done, but on the basis of who had the greater powers of sorcery and magic. Thus some departed souls are provided with texts which contain only a so-called "negative confession," in which no sins are mentioned, but only their good deeds, in an effort to deceive the judge of the hereafter; by reciting these texts it was possible to achieve power over the judge and influence the verdict.[54]

---

53. *ANET* 34: "Ägyptisches Totenbuch." Translated and annotated by G. Kolpaktchy (Munich, 1955). A. Champdor, "Le Livre des Morts." Papyrus d'Ani, de Hunefer, d'Anhai, du British Museum (1963).

54. On Egyptian ethics, cf. especially H. Junker, *Pyramidenzeit,* 76ff.

On the basis of this historical evolution of Egyptian religion, it is possible to understand and explain many elements which would otherwise be an insoluble puzzle. Are we not, perhaps, justified, looking back on the history of religion, in speaking of a *mysterium iniquitatis*? On the one hand we see a cultural development without parallel and on the other hand, the idea of the original sky god is clouded over more and more. There are magnificent ethical concepts which, however, never come to their full expression. When we leave behind us these ancient classical cultures and make our way into the land of the Bible, we find it only twice as difficult to answer a fundamental question: how was it possible that precisely here in Palestine, in the people of Israel, exposed to the manifold influences of the Ancient Near East on right and left, monotheism was preserved in its purest form, and the concept of Messianism grew apace?

THE PRINCIPAL GODS OF THE EGYPTIAN PANTHEON

Amon: God of Thebes, represented in human form, sitting on an azure throne, two feathers on his head; identified with the sun god, he is called Amon-Re. *Anubis*: a jackal, honored in Lykopolis, god of the dead. *Atum*: original god of Heliopolis, later equivalated to the sun god, represented as Pharaoh. *Bastet*: the cat goddess of Bubaste. *Hathor*: cow from Dendarah. *Horus*: the falcon god from Edfu, equivalated to the sky god. *Isis*: female consort of Osiris. *Khnum*: ram god from Aswan. *Khons*: moon god from Thebes. *Mont*: war god, a falcon or a steer, patron of Hermonthis. *Mut*: hawk, female consort of Amon. *Osiris*: god of Busiris, god of fertility, represented as a mummy on a green throne. *Ptah*: god of Memphis, represented as a mummy with smooth-shaven head. *Re*: sun god.

Breasted, in *The Birth of Conscience,* presents valuable material, but explains it in an evolutionistic sense, thereby prejudicing his work. In the later Egyptian era there was an effort to combat this polytheism. The many gods were to be considered merely as the various apparitions of the One God. Cf. E. Otto, "Zum Gottesbegriff der Ägypt. Spätzeit," *FF* 35 (1961), 277-280.

Sebek: crocodile god in Fayum. *Sekhmet*: lion goddess of Memphis. *Seth*: god of Ombos, whose animal was apparently a wild boar. *Thot*: god of Hermonthis, in the form of an ibis or ape.[55]

55. E. Drioton, *La religion égyptienne dans ses grandes lignes* (Cairo 1945). There is also a table of illustrations of the divine images, reprinted in *ANEP*, 1954, No. 573.

SECTION TWO

THE PEOPLES OF THE NEAR EAST

LITERATURE

The following outline of selected literature is designed only to serve as background positions, leading the way to further study and the creation of an independent sense of judgment.

a) General Works on the History of the Ancient Near East: With proper critique, the extensive work of E. Meyer can still be used today: *Geschichte des Altertums,* Vol. I, 1: Einleitung und Anthropologie, I, 2: Die ältesten geschichtlichen Völker und Kulturen bis zum 16, Jh. v. Chr. (1926[5]). – II, 1: Die Zeit der ägyptischen Grossmacht, (1928[3]). – II, 2: Zeit bis auf die Perserkriege, (1931). – III: Der Ausgang der altorientalischen Geschichte, Neu hrgb. von E. Stier, (Stuttgart 1937). – B. Meissner, *Babylonien und Assyrien, Ninive und Babylon,* (Bielefeld 1926[4]). – A. Moret, *Histoire de l'Orient,* 2 Vols., (Paris 1929 & 1936). – L. Delaporte, *Le peuples de l'Orient méditerranéen,* Vol. I: Le proche Orient asiatique, (Sammlung Clio, Paris 1948). – Geschichte der Babylonier, Assyrer, Perser und Phöniker, Geschichte der führenden Völker, Vol. 3, (Freiburg i. Br. 1933). – G. Contenau, *La civilisation d'Assur et de Babylon,* (Paris 1937). – Fr. Hrozny, *Die älteste Geschichte Vorderasiens,* (Prag 1940). – K. Bittel, *Grundzüge der Vor- und Frühgeschichte Kleinasiens,* (1950[2]). – H. R. Hall, *The Ancient History of the Near East, From the Earliest Times to the Battle of Salamis,* (London 1950[11]). – F. Cornelius, *Geschichte des Alten Orients,* (Stuttgart-Köln 1950). – Geschichte und Kultur der semitischen Völker, (Stuttgart 1955[2]). – A. Moortgat, "Geschichte Vorderasiens bis zum Hellenismus," In: *Weltgeschichte in Einzeldarstellungen*: *Ägypten und Vorderasien im Altertum, von A. Scharff* & *A. Moortgat,* (Munich 1950). – "Grundlagen und Entfaltung der sumerischen und akkadischen Kultur," *HM II* (1953), 224-260. – G. Furlani, "Babylonien und Assyrien," *HM II* (1953), 261-330. – H. Schmökel, "Geschichte des alten Vorderasien," *Handbuch der Orientalistik, Vol. II*: *Keilschriftforschung und alte Geschichte Vorderasiens,* 3 *section.* (Leiden 1957). – *Kulturgeschichte des Alten Orients,* (Stuttgart 1961). – S. Moscati, *Die Kulturen des Alten Orients,* (Munich 1962). – R. Pittioni, "Der urgeschichtliche Horizont der historischen Zeit," *PropWG I,* (1961), 227-322. – W. von Soden, "Herrscher im Alten Orient, *Verständliche Wissenschaft, Vol.* 54, (Berlin 1954). – "Sumer, Babylon und Hethiter bis zur Mitte des 2, Jahrtausends v. Chr.," *PropWG* I, (1961), 525-609. – A. T. Olmstead, *History of Assyria,* (Chicago 1960). The older work, *The Cambridge Ancient History,* 3 vols., (1923-25), can still be used, especially for its maps, illustrations, and copious bibliography.

b) Archaeological literature: C. Contenau, *Manuel d'archéologie orientale,* 4 vols., (Paris 1927-47). – V. Christian, *Altertumskunde des Zweistromlandes von der Vorzeit bis zum Ende der Achämenidenherrschaft,* 2 vols., (Leipzig 1940). – A. Parrot, *Archéologie mésopotamienne,* Vol. I: *Les étappes;* Vol. II: *Technique et problèmes,* (Paris 1946 & 1953). – E. Forrer, *"8000"* im *Alten Orient* nach den letzten Ausgrabungen und neuesten Erkenntnissen, (Zürich 1947). – L. Woolley, *Middle East Archaeology,* (Oxford 1949). – The Art of the Middle East, (New York 1961). – *Mit Hacke und Spaten, Die Erschliessung versunkener Kulturen,* (Leipzig 1950). – H. Th. Bossert, *Altsyrien;* Kunst und Handwerk in Cypern, Syrien, Palästina, Transjordanien und Arabien von den Anfängen bis zum völligen Aufgehen in der griechisch-römischen Kultur, (Tübingen 1951). – G. Grosvenor, *Everyday Life in Ancient Times;* with 215 Illustrations, 120 Paintings by H. M. Herget, (Washington 1953). – H. Schmökel, *Ur, Assur und Babylon, Drei Jahrtausende im Zweistromland. Grosse Kulturen der Frühzeit,* (Stuttgart 1955[2]). – M. Riemschneider, *Die Welt der Hethiter,* Grosse Kulturen der Frühzeit, (Stuttgart 1955[2]). – A. Parrot, *Mari, documentation photographique,* (Neuchâtel-Paris 1953). – J. Finegan, *Light from the Ancient Past.* The archaeological background of the hebrew-christian religion, (London 1959[2]). – M. A. Beek, *Bildatlas der assyrisch-babylonischen Kultur,* (W. Röllig und W. von Soden) (Gütersloh 1961). – H. Gressmann, *Altorientalische Bilder zum Alten Testament, – AOB,* (Berlin-Leipzig 1927). – J. B. Pritchard, *The Ancient Near East in Pictures relating to the Old Testament; ANEP,* (Princeton, New Jersey 1954). – J. A. H. Potratz, "Einführung in die Archäologie," *Kröners Taschenbuchausgabe* Vol. 344, (Stuttgart 1962).

c) Introduction to the texts: The study of the history of the Ancient Near East is inconceivable without source texts. That is why it is essential to offer some suggestion as to how these ancient texts can be acquired. This outline is restricted to collections, while in the discussions that follow, special studies are occasionally referred to.

Under the direction of E. Schraders, from 1889-1900, appeared the 6 vol. *Keilschriftliche Bibliothek* (*KB*). I-II: Assyrian texts; III: Babylonian texts; IV: Juridic and economic texts; V: El-Amarna correspondence; VI: Religious texts. The *Vorderasiatische Bibliothek* (*VAB*), proposed to include 20 vols., is to include all the written material discovered to date. The cuneiform text is given in transliteration and in German translation. Particularly noteworthy are: Vol. I: *Die sumerischen und akkadischen Königsinschriften,* by Fr. Thureau-Dangin, 1905; Vol. II: *Die El-Amarna-Tafeln,* by J. Knudzton, (1915); Vol. IV: *Die neubabylonischen Königsinschriften,* by S. Langdon, (1912). – D. Luckenbill, *Ancient Records of Assyria and Babylonia,* 2 vols., (Chicago 1926-27). – E. Ebeling - B. Meissner - E. Weidner, *Die Inschriften der altassyrischen Könige,* (Berlin 1926). – These older editions have been surpassed by a new undertaking, *Handbuch der Orientalistik.* In vol. 5 there is a new view of the cuneiform literature.– R. Borger, *Einleitung in die assyrischen Königsinschriften, Das zweite Jahrtausend vor. Chr.,* (Leiden-Köln 1961). – The numerous texts discovered in the excavations at Mari have been edited, beginning with 1950, in *Archives royales de Mari,* (Paris). – The Asia-Minor-Hittite documents can be had in *Keilschrifttexte aus Boghazköy,* vols. 1-6, (Leipzig 1916-23; vol. 7, Berlin 1954). Also: *Keilschrifturkunden aus Boghazköy,* vols. 1-27, (Berlin 1921-53). – A selection of this no longer negligible literature is to be found in Gressmann, *AOT* and Pritchard, *ANET.* – The most important texts for reading are offered in German translation in K. Galling, *Textbuch zur Geschichte Israels* (Tübingen 1950). – An English parallel is D. Winton Thomas, *Document from Old Testament Times,* (London 1958).

d) Among the periodicals which give an "orientation" in the Ancient Near East, the following must be mentioned: *Orientalia* (Or), published by the Pontifical Biblical Institute since 1932 – *Zeitschrift fur die Kirche des Morgenlandes* (WZKM), Vienna, since 1887, – *Zeitschrift der Deutschen Morgenländischen Gesellschaft* (*ADMG*), Leipzig, since 1847, – *Zeitschrift des Deutschen Palästinavereins* (*ZDPV*), Leipzig, since 1878 – *Der Alte Orient* (*AO*), Leipzig, since 1903 – *Revue Biblique* (*RB*), Paris since 1892, (organ of the French Dominican Bible School in Jerusalem), – *Biblica* (*Bib.*), Rome, since 1919 (Organ of the Pontifical Biblical Institute) – *Bulletin of the American Schools of Oriental Research* (*BASOR*), Baltimore, since 1919 – *Palestine Exploration Quarterly* (PEQ), London, since 1869 – *Vetus Testamentum* (*VT*), Leiden, since 1951 – *Internationale Zeitschriftenschau für Bibelwissenschaft und Grenzgebiete* (*IZBG*), since 1951, edited and produced by Fr. Stier, Tübingen: attempts to include and briefly outline all pertinent articles, an indispensable tool for a speedy orientation. There are countless other worthwhile publications which are mentioned, from time to time, in the footnotes to the discussions that follow.

e) THE PEOPLES of the history of the Ancient Near East are the inhabitants of quite different regions: the peoples of the Syro-Arabic desert, Canaan, the Phoenician coast, the mountain countries of Asia Minor, the land between the rivers Euphrates and Tigris down to the Persian Gulf, and into the mountains and plateaus of Iran. The history of the Ancient Near East does not bear the stamp of one single ethnic group, such as the Semites. The area of the "fertile crescent" is a meeting ground for peoples who are as basically different in blood, descent, and language, as the lands they inhabit; the only thing they have in common is their effort to take possession of the fertile parcel of land between the desert and the mountains, where, for the first time, around 3000 B.C., in the land of Sumer, a high form of culture was developed.

The peoples of the Syrian desert belong to the Semitic family, while the mountain peoples belong predominantly to the Indo-Germanic group, which concentrated particularly in the Near East during the 2nd and 1st millennia.

All these peoples, whether they are mountain nomads, desert bedouins, or permanently established farmers and city-dwellers, live in a perpetual cultural exchange and standing enmity with each other; and it is this interplay that determines the form of Ancient Near East history. Ancient Near East history is thus the result of the confrontation of a complex of peoples which have all been welded together into a supra-national organism, similar to that found in the West during the Middle Ages.[1]

These racial, ethnic, cultural, and geographical data are further complicated by the addition of the essentially new and history-making factor of God's revelation. God did not reveal himself in an abstract situation, devoid of history, but in the actual and often very confusing rhythm of Ancient Near East history. The

1. A. Moortgat, *GVA* 204: "Die Träger der Geschichte, übervölkischer Komplex."

statement that "the Word became flesh" makes it even more imperative to confront the historical realities of that era. It is only against the real background of Ancient Near East history that "the humility and grandeur of God" are visible in new dimensions.

f) THE LAND BETWEEN THE TWO RIVERS: in terms of history and culture, the most important territory is the land traversed by the great twin rivers Tigris and Euphrates, a territory which stretches from the Armenian mountain ranges between the Zagros Mountains and the Syro-Arabic desert. Tigris and Euphrates belong together in terms of their origin, since the Tigris rises very near to the sources of the Euphrates; they also are associated in their courses, which, flowing in a south-easterly direction, are aimed at the same eventual goal; at one point, in fact, in the neighborhood of Babylon, they are within 50 km. of each other, only to separate further again, but not so far apart as in the northern sector of their course. They finally reach a confluence, and for some 150 km. they form a single stream, at present-day Shatt-el-Arab.

Despite their common characteristics, each river has its own individual traits. The Euphrates (Purat, from the Israelite word for "the great river" or "*the* river"), is not so long, in terms of direct route, from origin to mouth, although in its actual course it is much longer than the Tigris. Its direct route covers some 1,120 km. while its direct course covers 2,600 km. The Euphrates first turns towards the west, but is then forced towards the south and southeast, and makes its way in countless bends and turns. After breaking its way through the southern Taurus chain, it enters into the level plain at Carchemish, where it exchanges its rapid mountain flow for the slow and lazy pace adapted to the plain country.

From the west, the direction of the desert, the Euphrates receives little water, at least today; there are, however, several valleys which lie in its direction (wadis), which in the remote past, may easily have contained brooks or rivers. To the east, the proximity of the Tigris leaves no room for tributaries. Tributaries are to be found only where the two streams diverge, west of Ninive and Assyria primarily. There we find the Balikh, running in a southerly direction parallel to the Euphrates at that point; the famous crossroads city of Haran lies along the Balikh. From the same region comes the most important tributary of the Euphrates, the Khabur, which rises in the neighborhood of Edessa. The Tigris (Diglat in Sumerian and Akkadian) is much more direct in its principal direction, and thus only half as long as the Euphrates and – since it flows through more mountainous country from which it receives numerous tributaries (for instance, the Greater and the Lesser Zab) – also presents a more rapid course, which, at some points, is a veritable torrent.

During the rainy seasons, both streams take on a great quantity of mud from the mountains, which they deposit partially along their course, by inundation of their banks, and partially only after emptying into the sea. Thus, they have not only produced a rich humus of exceptional fertility in the countryside through which they flow, but they have created new cultivable land by the alluvium they have deposited along the Persian Gulf. That is why the two rivers have, in the course of time, managed to unite in a single stream, whereas, at an earlier date, they emptied into the sea as independent rivers.

The natural fertility of the soil, effected by this inundation, would never have been productive without the exceptional energy of a very active people; the terrible heat and dryness which prevails for the greater part of the year turn the area into a desert, while the inundations in spring and fall practically turn it into a sea, from which only unhealthy pools and morasses remain behind. These natural disadvantages, however, were overcome by the process of canalization, and made serviceable for the population. An extensive net of countless canals crossed almost the entire plain, bringing water from the rivers, swollen by the melting snow in the mountain ranges and by the torrential downpours, into the most remote sections of the country, thus making possible an irrigation which was adapted to the climate.

Several canals joined the two streams together in such a way that in the north the water of the Euphrates could be diverted into the Tigris, and in the south water could be diverted from the Tigris into the Euphrates. Such a project, which is unparalleled in its age, could only have been undertaken by a population which was as numerous as it was energetic, and under the direction of a very enlightened government. Unfortunately, modern times have witnessed the destruction of large sections of what was formerly inhabited country; this is largely due to the fact that the two streams have been pushing their mouths further and further into the sea and thus turning ancient ports into inland cities. There is also an increase in the salt content of the arable land, within historical times, which necessarily leads to the depopulation of the country. A people who were strong enough to undertake such a gigantic enterprise must also have been capable of other works. Actually, this country gives evidence, even in very ancient times, of magnificent architectural projects, a lively scientific endeavor, the cultivation of art and literature, and, more particularly, a truly astounding development of statecraft.[2]

2. Ä Schöpfer, *Geschichte des AT.* Sixth edition (1923), 40-42.

CHAPTER V

PREHISTORY AND EARLY HISTORY

THE excavations of prehistoric sites undertaken in the Near East within recent years enable us to trace the course of human development here back into the shadows of prehistory. The following chart shows the most important excavation sites and periods of culture.[3]

EXCAVATION SITE – Barda Balka / CULTURE – Old Stone Age settlement with the oldest stone implements yet discovered in the land of the two rivers: hatchets, scrapers, stone knives; Acheuléen; c. 50,000 B.C.

EXCAVATION SITE – Hazer Merd / CULTURE – Cave Dwellings, Middle Paleolithic, Mousterien - Levalloisien.

EXCAVATION SITE – Palegawra / CULTURE – Cave dwelling of hunting people; flint instruments, Microlithic.

3. A. Pohl, "Forschungen und Funde," *Or.* 21 (1952), 254. M. A. Beek, *Bildatlas der assyrisch-babylonischen Kultur* (1961), 41. The number of years in these lists are only to serve as an approximation; they vary considerably in different authorities.

EXCAVATION SITE – Shanidar / CULTURE – Cave dwellings, most ancient skeletal finds, a child and three adults, Neanderthal type; carbon dating: c. 34,000 B.C.

EXCAVATION SITE – Karim-Shahir / CULTURE – An open settlement of short duration; first attempts at agriculture and domestication of animals; no pottery as yet, stone instruments in Microlithic, between c. 7000 and 6000.

EXCAVATION SITE – Jarmo / CULTURE – The earliest village in the Ancient Near East; 15 successive strata established: transition from food-gatherers to food producers; carbon dating – 4857.

EXCAVATION SITE – Hassuna / CULTURE – Transition to agriculture; in all 6 strata evidence of burned pottery; transition from one room to a house with several rooms; c. 5000.

EXCAVATION SITE – Samarra / CULTURE – Village settlement with distinct Samarra pottery; c. 4000.

EXCAVATION SITE – Halaf / CULTURE – Village settlement with distinct Halaf pottery; c. 4000.

EXCAVATION SITE – Obed / CULTURE – Transition to city settlement with market and temple; earliest stages in Eridu; c. 3600 to 3200.

The above depicts the evolution of ancient man in the Ancient Near East. In Barda Balka (some 45 km. east of Khirkuk) an excavation yielded an old Stone Age settlement in which cattle hunters (an abundant find of animal bones) maintained themselves side by side with stone workers. The bones are the remains of wild horse, wild bull, wild goat, elephant, etc. This settlement probably owed its origin to the last of the interim periods in which man could settle in the open with a favorable climate.

At the approach of the Ice Age, he once again had to withdraw into the protection of the caves. The hunter life continued, as the caves of Palegawra (65 km. east from Khirkuk) clearly show; they were inhabited by a group of hunters who lived on wild horse, gazelle, and venison. At the withdrawal of the Glacial Age, man once again ventured out of the caves and gradually took up the practice of agriculture, as the stone hatchets and stone sickles of Karim-Shahir (c. 2 km. from Jarmo) clearly evidence. Between 7000 and 6000 B.C., the transition from agriculture to the domestication of animals occurred. Men also learned how to build houses; eloquent testimony of this is to be found in the 50 huts constructed of pressed clay in Jarmo (55 km. east of Khirkuk). This was an introduction to village culture, properly so-called. The chronology of Jarmo, as established by carbon dating,[4] is 4857 B.C.; but this can only serve as an average approximation.

In the course of the later Stone Age, the picture of human development grows clearer. Albright places it in the year 8000 to 4500 B.C.[5] The locations of this culture were no longer only in the mountain land; man descended into the valleys and plains. The recent Stone Age culture is the product of the last hunters and the first sedentary farmers. These settled wherever they found tillable soil, particularly in the alluvial land in the Persian Gulf.

---

4. R. I. Braidwood, "From Cave to Village in Prehistoric Iraq," *BASOR* 124 (191), 12-18. The earliest culture seems to be the Shanidar caves discovered in the Zagros Mountains in 1952. Carbon testing, applied to the bone tools, yielded an age of more than 34,000 years. *Or.* 24 (1955), 321.

5. The present position of stone age investigation in the Ancient Near East is well and readably summed up in the work of the great American scholar F. W. Albright, *From Stone Age to Christianity. Monotheism and Historic Fact* (Münich, 1949). The excavation material is catalogued and described in V. Christian, *Altertumskunde des Zweistromlandes.* Vol. I: Text 1. Die Landschaft und ihre Besiedlung. 2. Die Ruinen und ihre Erforschung. 3. Die Denkmäler: Vorzeit und Frühzeit (Leipzig, 1940). K. Bittel, *Prähistorische Forschung in Kleinasien.* Istanbuler Forschungen. Vol. 6, 1934. K. Bittel, *Grundzüge der Vor-und Frühgeschichte Kleinasiens,* 2nd edition (Tübingen, 1950). Anton Moorgat, "Die Entstehung der sumerischen Hochkultur," *AO* 43, 1945, with 28 illustrations and 32 tables, a richly illustrated account of the transition from neolithic into early history. A. M. Beek, *Bildatlas,* 41: Prehistoric Times. With maps of the sites, and abundant illustrations.

Together with stone tools, they already made use of clay vessels baked over an open fire, for a great variety of purposes. Thus, we must picture the Ancient Near East, towards the end of the Late Stone Age, as a vast district which, in its mountainous sections, was populated primarily by hunter peoples, and by tent-dwelling shepherd nomads in the Syrian desert regions, while the fertile lands between the rivers were gradually taken into possession by individual agricultural tribes, who had perhaps already been organized in villages, peoples whose agricultural instruments and animal industry were not yet sufficiently developed to make hunting entirely superfluous. The complete transition from the hunter stage to the sedentary farmer took place in the course of the 4th millennium. Archaeological finds for the culture development of the Recent Stone Age were yielded by excavations in Tell Halaf, Tell Hassuna on the Tigris, and Tepe Sialk, in Iran.[6]

In the Orient, there is an early transition from the Recent Stone Age, with the invention of copper working, into the Chalcolithic Age, the Copper Stone Age (c. 4500-3000).[7] In the excavation yields, this is characterized by the appearance of colored pottery work together with the discovery of copper tools. A variety of colors have been worked on a bright background. There also is evidence of a new firing technique. The pottery was no longer

---

6. A good orientation on Tell Halaf is to be found in Max von Oppenheim, *Der Tell Halaf, eine neue Kultur im ältesten Mesopotamien* (Leipzig, 1931). The standard account of the excavations is to be found in the two volume work of M. von Oppenheim, *Tell Halaf*: I, *Die prähistorischen Funde* (Berlin, 1943), edited by H. Schmitt, treats the development of pottery from the ancient monochrome technique down to painted pottery and glazed work; describes the figurines, the squatting female figurines, post idols, painted animals, stamps and flat seals, etc., and concludes with an exhaustive account of prehistoric culture in Tell Halaf. II: Rudolf Naumann, *Die Bauwerke* (Berlin, 1950). These include the temple palace with the scorpion gate, the vaults, the city walls. There is also an abundance of map material. The account of the excavations at Sialk can be found in R. Girshman: *Fouilles de Sialk près de Kashan* (Paris, I, 1938; II, 1939).

7. H. Quiring, "Die Älteste Geschichte des Kupfers." *FF* 19 (1943), 57-59.

baked over an open fire, but in potter's ovens, which could be regulated. On the basis of difference in the pottery, this era of history is divided into the early, middle, and late Copper-Stone Age. Important finds were made, in addition to Tell Halaf and Tepe Sialk already mentioned above, in Samarra on the Tigris, north of Baghdad, and primarily El-Obed, 7 km. from Ur in Chaldea, an ancient settlement on a natural hill in the middle of the marsh district. For the Assyrian district, it is the excavations in the mound of Tepe Gawra, northwest of Nineveh, which are decisive.[8] Tell Halaf and Samarra belong to the early Chalcolithic Age (c. 4000). Both areas give evidence of marked difference in the style of their pottery work. Tell Halaf was fond of the double ax, the bull's head, rosettes, and Maltese crosses – religious symbols – which were classically copied in stone and clay. A basic motif of the Samarra was the swastika (fylfot), with animals (birds, ibex, fish) or, less frequently, men rotating about it. The Samarra style seems to have come from Iran. The figure of the mother goddess was particularly venerated in this early agrarian culture. Many clay figurines of naked women, not to mention numerous bulls' heads and figurines, point in this direction.

The middle and late Chalcolithic Age (c. 3600) has received the name Obed Era, for the whole of Mesopotamia. Important discoveries fall into this era: the potter's lathe, metal casting, and seal engraving. It is the seals, with their variety of artistic representations, which now begin to form a valuable source for the knowledge of these old cultures. The science of architecture was also making its first attempts, as witnessed in the temple sites in Tepe Gawra in Assyria, and in Eridu in southern Babylonia. We might ask where these new impulses came from, and surmise that between 4000 to 3200 there must have been some population shifts in the Ancient Near East. The harsh and minimal

---

8. Ernst Herzfeld, *Die Ausgrabungen von Samarra,* Vol. V. Die vorgeschichtlichen Töpfereien (Berlin, 1930). H. R. Hall and G. H. Woolley, *Ur-Excavations,* Vol. 1: Al-'Ubaid (Oxford, 1927). E. A. Speiser, *Excavations at Tepe Gawra,* Vols. I-VIII (Philadelphia, 1935).

conditions of life in the desert steppes and in the mountain countries could hardly have fostered anything like consistent periods of peaceful tenure.[9]

Towards the end of the 4th millennium, Sumer takes over the cultural leadership of the Ancient Near East and, in advance of Egypt, develops the first semi-historical classical culture. This step takes us from the stage of prehistory into ancient history.

9. W. v. Soden, *PropWG* I (1961), 531ff.

CHAPTER VI

THE SUMERIANS

1) PEOPLE AND LANGUAGE

SUMER, or Shumer, is, in itself, not the name of a people; it means simply: "cultivated land" as opposed to the uncultivated steppe and desert.[10] The inhabitants of cultivated land can belong to the most divergent peoples, languages, and races. But, already in the 3rd millennium, the language of south Babylonia was called Sumerian, and the first cultural people were called the Sumerians. Their ascendancy in Babylonia was preceded by periods of unrest and cultural descendancy, which probably coincided with the immigration of new peoples. Our information is incapable of greater precision here. That is why we do not know where the Sumerians came from and to what race they belonged. At all events, they were not Semites. Their language, to the present day, remains completely isolated. Scholarship has not advanced beyond its first faltering attempts here. Some

10. The word Sumer is explained in Deimel, *Sumerische Grammatik* (Rome, 1939), Sumerian *ki-en-gi-ra,* in keeping with the laws of phonetic change, becomes the Akkadian *sumer*. The Sumerians called their country often merely *kalama,* "land, country," as opposed to *kur,* "foreign territory."

opinions hold that there are related characteristics in the languages of the Caucasus or in the Dravidian languages of India, or even Tibeto-Burmese.[11] The Sumerians may have made their way into the south Babylonian plateau by crossing the high country of Iran or by way of the sea. Their origins are lost in the shadow of antiquity; and thus the creative power of this new people shines out all the brighter.[12]

Sumerian ceased to be a spoken language already in the course of the 2nd millennium before Christ; but, just like the Latin of the Middle Ages, it maintained an authoritative position in liturgy and science up to the end of Ancient Near East history. In the Golden Age of the Sumerian culture, literary works were composed in this language which left a deep impression upon the intellectual life of the Semitic peoples who followed. For the Semites took over not only the Sumerian script but also their religious and literary works. Since Sumerian, after dying out as a spoken language, was still extensively used in divine service, it was necessary to develop a system for learning the sacred language. Thus we have vocabularies and translations, and it is precisely from these bilingual school texts that the long-forgotten language of the Sumerians was once again taken up and deciphered by scientific scholarship, thereby restoring a portion of sunken history to light.

---

11. V. Christian, "Die Herkunft der Sumerer," *FF* 35 (1961), 50: Migration along the sea route from the territory between Brahmaputra and Jhindwin; linguistically related to Tibeto-Burmese. K. Oberhuber, *WZKM* 52 (1953-55), 81-89: related to the language of the "mountain peoples." W. von Soden, *PropWG* I (1961), 535: because of relationships with India, a migration across South Iran is most probable today.

12. H. Schmökel, *Das Land Sumer* (Stuttgart, 1950). H. Lenzen, *Die Sumerer* (Berlin, 1948).

13. The best introduction into the mysteries of the Sumerian language is offered by the work of A. Deimel, *Sumerische Grammatik,* second edition (Rome, 1939), with an historical introduction on Sumer. Also, Deimel's great *Sumerische Lexikon,* third edition (Rome, 1947-1950). The last volume contains the "Pantheon babylonicum."

2) CUNEIFORM

The Sumerians are the inventors of writing. Originally, the object to be written was simply pictured, or "drawn." This picture writing developed into a phonetic and syllable script. It was not only the consonants that were written, as in the hieroglyphic script and in Hebrew, but also the vowels. Under the influence of the writing material (the Sumerians wrote with a hard stylus on soft, fresh clay, which was then baked), curved lines had to be avoided and straight strokes with corners were preferred. Later on, a stroke in the form of a wedge was adopted as the single element of the script, and every individual sign was formed by a composition of such horizontal, vertical, and oblique wedges: this gives rise to the name cuneiform (*cuneus*, in Latin, "wedge"). The clay which contained this writing was in a tablet, cylinder, or prism form.

Since baked clay offers extremely great resistance to the process of weathering, and at the same time is practically indestructible, entire archives and libraries of cuneiform tablets have been preserved in the ruined cities. Since cuneiform writing made its way throughout the entire Near East – it was adopted by the Semites and later also by the Hittites in Asia Minor – these written records are to be found from Asia Minor to the Persian Gulf. The Egyptians also made use of this cuneiform script in their diplomatic relations with these various foreign powers, as the archaeological finds of El-Amarna in Upper Egypt indicate. The knowledge of the cuneiform literature is thus synonymous with the knowledge of the history of the Ancient Near East. The earliest written accounts are concerned with the affairs of commerce: delivery and payment of oil, grain, etc. These commercial documents make up an extensive part of the literature. Next come the historical documents which are concerned with constructions and wars and the negotiation of treaties. Hand in hand with these we find the religious texts, formulas for magic and conjuring, psalms and hymns to the gods. Then comes the recording of the great myths of creation and the great epic poems of antiquity. In the shadow of the temples, the first schools arise, in which every possible form of knowledge was pursued, from the learning of cuneiform script itself up to the rites of religious initiation.[14]

The excavations in Ras-Shamra on the Syrian coast, ancient Ugarit, present sufficient texts in which the step from syllabic writing to an alphabetic cuneiform had already been made.[15] Still, it seems that this alphabetic cuneiform was not widely spread, since, in the meantime, the much simpler Phoenician alphabet had already begun its triumphal procession over the whole world.

3) THE SUMERIAN CLASSICAL CULTURE

The development of the Sumerian classical culture was dictated by the geography of the country itself. Prosperity and misfortune in this low land between the two rivers was inexorably bound up with the inundations of the Tigris and Euphrates. If the farmer was to have any success in such a region, he must necessarily join with other farmers in a village community, in order to harness the river, complete the canal system, and provide for sufficient irrigation as a communal project. These village cultures developed into the theocratic city which has left its characteristic stamp on the whole Sumerian period. The land belongs to the divinity. It was the temple which distributed work, clothing, and nourishment to each individual. This theocratic-socialistic economy did manage to produce some individual accomplishments of considerable magnitude, such as the con-

---

14. The novice will be filled with enthusiasm for the study of cuneiform texts in reading the book: *They Wrote on Clay* by E. Chiera, 1941 (second edition). The very largely Sumerian historical texts are assembled by Fr. Thureau-Dangin, "Die Sumerischen und akkadischen Königsinschriften," *VAB* I, 1 (1907). G. Barton, *The Royal Inscription of Sumer and Akkad* (New Haven, 1929).

15. H. Th. Bossert, *Altsyrien* (1951), 62: Ugarit alphabet.

struction of the Ziggurat,[16] the "Tower of Babel," but by attempting too much it bore within itself the seeds of its own decay. Thus we find evidence of decay, revolution, and social reform. Side by side with the principal divinity of a given city, there were also other gods together with their temples and economically dependent communities; in Lagash, for example, there were 20, directed by an "ensi," who was subordinate to the city god. Finally, there were also private economic communities, which cultivated a part of the land and were obligated to military service in times of war. Since there is neither wood nor stone in the southern part of the land between the rivers, and both commodities have to be supplied from a great distance, such accomplishments were possible only by the establishment of a well structured community.[17]

4) HISTORY

a) The early Sumerian classical culture (c. 3000-2800): This period is also called the Uruk (Erech) Culture, after its principal site. Strata VI-IV date back to early history. The village has now been definitively replaced by the temple city. But in this connection the concept of "city" is to be taken rather as a temple or monastery property. The land belonged to the divinity: the representative of the god was the *lu-gal,* the "great man," that is, the priest-king. We already find here the same economical structure that is so clearly marked in the historical period. The new impulse is evidenced first of all in the field of architecture. Side by side with the traditional high-terraced temples, we now see the construction of monumental temple buildings on the flat ground. The masonry was supplied partially

---

16. Woolley, *Ur-Excavations* Vol. V: "The Ziggurat and Its Surroundings," (New York, 1939). A. Schneider, *Die sumerische Tempelstadt, Plenges staatswissenschaftliche Beiträge.* Part 4 (1920). H. Lenzen, *Die Entwicklung der Zikkurat* (1941).

17. For greater detail on the economic life, see H. Schmökel, *Kulturgeschichte des Alten Orients,* 46-84.

by purely indestructible concrete work. The bricks, or tiles, were square in form. These were used to construct the mighty walls of triple naved temples, whose longitudinal axes measured as much as 80 m. The loam coating of the walls was imbedded with countless clay cones, producing a mosaic effect along the walls.[18] A further innovation is to be recognized in the technique of seal production; seals had been used from very ancient times as a sign of private property, stamped into the fresh clay before it was baked. Now the cylinder seal is discovered, which, with its pictorial representations, presents the best source for our knowledge of the intellectual world of this early era. The greatest accomplishment of the Early Sumerian Era consisted, however, in the invention of writing. The idea of writing arose from the demands of commerce. The most ancient written records are, in fact, commercial documents. Available to the writer of this early age were some 2,000 picture and symbol signs. The beginning of writing actually inaugurated a new era in the history of mankind. The Uruk culture comes to an end around 2800 B.C., with a great catastrophe which annihilated the architectural achievements of the generation which first invented writing.

b) THE JEMDET-NASR ERA (c. 2800-2600): this cultural division gets its name from the small mound near Kish, not far from Babylon. While the Uruk culture remained confined to southern Babylonia the traces of the Jemdet-Nasr culture[19] can be followed throughout the whole of Mesopotamia and down into Egypt (Naqada II). This might well have coincided with the establish-

---

18. E. Heinrich, *Kleinfunde aus den archaischen Tempelschichten in Uruk* (Leipzig, 1936). H. Lenzen, "Die Tempel der Schicht Archaisch IV," *ZA, NF* XV, 1-20. The excavations at Uruk are being carried on by the Deutsche Archäologische Institut and the Deutsche Orientgesellschaft. In the *Abhandlungen der Deutschen Orientgesellschaft* the "Vorläufigen Berichte über die Ausgrabungen in Uruk-Warka" appear as a regular feature. In the winter of 1958-59 I was privileged to take part in the excavation work as a guest, and study the ancient history on the spot.

19. Greater detail in W. von Soden, "Die Dschemdet-Nasr-Kultur," *PropWG* I (1961), 538ff.

ment of an early Semitic kingdom. Uruk arose slowly from these blows. The temple structures are now much more modest; they are built once again in high terraces. The marble head discovered in Uruk in 1939,[20] which clearly belongs among the greatest masterpieces of art in the Ancient Near East, is perhaps a representation of the mother goddess Inanna – or perhaps a priestess. In Tell Ukair, in northern Babylonia, archaeologists discovered impressive remains of a great secco painting with animal figures and cult scenes. Cylinder seal technology and the art of stone cutting developed to the point of mastery. The best evidence of this is the alabaster vase from Uruk,[21] a religious vessel one meter tall. The relief ornamentation provides a rich source for understanding the intellectual development of the times. In the foreground, at the bottom, we see a line of waves, which represent the fecundating foundation waters. The next strata shows five pairs of sheep, and above them is a procession of nine naked men walking in file and bearing sacrificial gifts. At the very top stands the mother goddess Inanna, receiving the gifts. The picture of the king is, unfortunately, broken off. On other representations, however, the king is represented as the keeper and shepherd of the flock, as protector against the wild animals. The identification of this shepherd king of pictorial representation with Dumuzi, the beloved of Inanna, which is regarded as certain by many authorities, is actually quite dubious.[22]

c) THE EARLY DYNASTIC ERA (c. 2600-2360): As sources for this era we have royal lists and poetic sagas at our disposal. The royal lists can be used only cautiously, however, since they give impossible regnal numbers, as much as 625 and 1200 years for a single ruler. But in the sagas there is always some evidence

---

20. Illustration: *PropWG* I (1961), after page 540.

21. Illustration *ibid;* see also *ANEP* No. 502; Meek, *Bildatlas,* No. 92.

22. The spread of the Tammus faith is contested especially by A. Moortgat, *Der Unsterblichkeitsglaube in der altorientalischen Bildkunst* (Berlin, 1941). The specialists in Sumerology, however, maintain that something more is being read out of the pictures than what they mean, and are able, to say.

of an historical nucleus. Sumer, like ancient Greece, was divided into individual city-states, each with its own prince (ensi). From this Early Dynastic Era the history of the city-states Uruk, Ur, and Lagash, becomes more and more prominent. It is only to be expected that rivalry and warfare broke out among these neighboring city-states. Strong personalities could easily become tyrants. Such a one was Gilgamesh. The epic[23] recounts of him that he imposed so much forced labor upon his people that they begged the gods for deliverance. The excavations in Uruk showed that this point of the epic is true. A city wall was unearthed there, 9.5 km. in length, with 900 semi-circular towers. This helps to date the reign of Gilgamesh in the neighborhood of 2600 B.C.

The Early Dynastic Period in Ur was established by the unearthing of the royal tombs[24] and achieved world-wide fame as a great sensation. Some 2000 graves were opened, covering a period of some four centuries. Most of them date back to the times of the dynasty of Mesannapaddas, whom many scholars identify with Mesilim of Kish (c. 2600-2500). Among the artifacts discovered in the graves are some artistic masterpieces. To us today it seems incomprehensible that the king's whole retinue should have followed him in death. Was this, perhaps, despite its splendid cultural achievements, still a barbaric age? The answer to this question is to be sought in the divinization of the kings. By the process of a sacred wedding ceremony[25] the king was elevated to the rank of the gods. Thus, his death meant a transition to a higher mode of existence. Obviously, the men who followed their king into the realm of death all hoped to share this higher form of existence.

The founder of the dynasty of Lagash is called Urnanshe (c. 2500). He built the temple and the city walls. Under his

---

23. A more explicit treatment of the Gilgamesh Epic in connection with the deluge story.

24. C. L. Woolley, *The Royal Cemetery. Ur Excavations II,* (Oxford 1934). Also: *Ur of the Chaldees,* (London, 1950).

25. On the divinization of kings, see page 75.

grandson Eannatum, there must have been a military confrontation with the neighboring city of Umma in a quarrel over the district of the Gu-edin. The peace treaty was recorded on the "hawk stele,"[26] a limestone slab, 1.5 m. in height, 1.3 m. in width, and 11 cm. thick, inscribed on both sides. The divinity is represented as a man, in more than life size, while the king is on his war chariot as if attacking the enemy. The dead on the victor's side are buried, while the enemy are left to the birds of prey. Eannatum not only made war on the city of Umma, but he also struck Elam and extended his power far upstream, so that in truth he succeeded in establishing dominion over the whole of Sumer. But his work did not survive his death.

It is not until Urukagina[27] had carried out his reforms, establishing "freedom" and doing away with "slavery," offering protection to widow and orphan, that the Sumerian theocracy is once again firmly established in Lagash.

His great rival is Lugalzaggisi (c. 2360), the ensi of the neighboring city of Umma. This prince seized political power, made Uruk his capital, and established the first world empire in Asia, extending from the Persian Gulf to the coast of the Mediterranean. This he was able to accomplish only with the help of his warriors, who were "as numerous as the weeds in the field." In his own people, and in the priesthood, he certainly found no support. The Sumerian theocratic city is incapable of supporting the tension of world hegemony. The establishment of "a kingdom of the four corners of the earth" was reserved for the younger nation of the Semites.

Under the leadership of Sargon, the Semites approach their confrontation with Sumer. Lugalzaggisi is conquered and Sargon establishes the united kingdom of Sumer and Akkad. The relationship between the two kingdoms can be compared to that existing between Rome and Greece. While Rome managed to conquer

---

26. For an illustration of the Hawk Stele see *ANEP*, 298-302.

27. W. von Soden, "Urukagina von Lagasch, der erste soziale Reformer," Herrscher in *AO*, 8-15.

Hellas with the weapons of war, it always remained subject to the spiritual and cultural hegemony of its captive. Thus, the Semites took over the political leadership in the united kingdom, but spiritually and culturally it was Sumer which long retained the upper hand.

CHAPTER VII

SUMER AND AKKAD

THE original home of the Semites was, insofar as it can be established at all, the Syro-Arabian desert. Throughout the entire course of the Ancient Near East's history, historically demonstrable with certainty only beginning with the Jemdet-Nasr Period, they began to abandon the meager existence of their desert home and force their way, sometimes friendly and sometimes hostile, into the crescent of fertile countries. The political weakness of the outlying districts, as well as the sheer force of excess population frequently brought the ethnic reservoir of Arabia to the point of overflowing. In the history of the Ancient Near East, there are three such Semitic population explosions which – to treat them in a rather coarse schematic outline – fall within the 3rd, 2nd, and 1st millennia before Christ. The naming of these ethnic elements is somewhat difficult. The first Semitic empire-builders, in the 3rd millennium, are generally called Akkadians. These can be spoken of, properly, only after the establishment of the city of Akkad, approximately 2350 B.C. But this same Semitic ethnic element had been leaving traces in Babylonia for a long time; it was not until the foundation of the united kingdom of Sumer and Akkad that it attained its full maturity. After the year 2000 B.C., a new nomadic ethnic element began growing in significance; in the technical literature it bears a variety of names. The stock is described as west-Semite, Canaanite, east-Canaanite, Amurru or Amorite, and even Hebrew. In the present discussion we favor the name Amurru-Bedouins, or Amorites, a decision which will be substantiated below. The 3rd Semitic migration, that of the Aramaeans, had already encompassed the whole Fertile Crescent by the year 1000 B.C. In the course of the 1st millennium, the whole Semitic Orient had become completely Aramaean. This was followed by a millennium of quiet, until, in the explosive Arab seizure of power, the Semitic element experienced the zenith of its power and development.

1) THE WORLD EMPIRE OF AKKAD (2350-2150)

Contemporary with the Sumerian dynasties in Ur, Lagash, and Uruk, north Babylonia was already being ruled by kings of Semitic descent. One of them, Sargon of Kish, seized the reins of political power and completely reshaped the face of the Ancient Near East. The Akkad period[28] seems to have been only a short period (2414-2233 according to the middle chronology, and 2350-2150 according to the low chronology), but it was this period that first realized the united kingdom of the four ends of the earth, which from that time on formed the dream and ideal for every future age.

The territorial extent of the Akkadian kingdom is one neither in population nor in language.[29] It embraces almost the whole

---

28. W. von Soden, "Das Grossreich von Akkade," *PropWG* I (1961), 547-552. A. Moortgat, *GVA* 256ff. Also: *HM* II, 250ff. H. Schmökel, *GAV* 39-51.

29. Akkadian belongs to East Semitic; under the influence of the basic Sumerian population it has undergone an independent development, and thus it gives evidence of considerable variations in phonetics and vocabulary when compared to the West and South Semitic languages. Among other features, it has largely lost the hard gutturals, including the h, while, on the other hand, it has retained the old case endings and the short final endings. It is possible to distinguish two dialects: Assyrian in the North

of the then known civilized world, from Iran to Asia Minor and down towards Egypt. The theocratic-federative Sumerian state has turned into a centralistic state, administered by official appointees, entirely governed by a king who, because of his unheard of exploits, was now raised to divine dignity. The Akkadian world empire is the work of a generation of rulers who were endowed with genius.

The founder of the kingdom is Sargon (Akkadian: *sharru-kin*, "the king is legitimate"). His ancestry is veiled, in order to substantiate his divine origin. His real father was the Semite La'ipu. But in the chronicle it is recorded that Sargon's father was unknown. His mother, however, was one of those brides of the gods who had obligated herself never to have children. When, despite this fact, she was delivered of a male child in the city of Azupiranu, she placed him on a reed basket in the Euphrates. There he was discovered by the "water-pourer," the gardener Akki, who took him home and raised him. Thus Sargon became a gardener and grew up until the goddess Ishtar fell in love with him just as she had previously fallen in love with Gilgamesh and Tammuz. It was by her favor that he achieved political control over the "black-heads," the Akkadians, and established the "kingdom of the totality of the lands" (*šarrût kiššat mâtâti*).[30]

Sargon next took over the supremacy of his native city Kish. Military confrontation with the Sumerians was now unavoidable. It took place under Lugalzaggisi and resulted in victory for the Semites. The decisive element in the battle might well have been the introduction of new weapons. The Akkadians were armed

---

and Babylonian in the South. The Akkadians took over cuneiform writing from the Sumerians. Since it was the Assyrian royal inscriptions that were best known among the monuments of the Akkadian language, the entire language was originally called Assyrian (hence also: Assyriology). Cf. A. Ungnad, *Grammatik des Akkadischen* (with an exercise book in transliteration) third edition (Munich, 1949). Dr. Delitzsch, *Assyrische Lesestücke* (Leipzig, 1912). *Assyrisches Handwörterbuch,* 1896. A. Deimel, *Sumerisch-Akkadisches Glossar* (Rome, 1924). *Akkadisch-sumerisches Glossar* (Rome, 1937). W. von Soden, *Akkadisches Handwörterbuch* (Wiesbaden, 1959).

30. *ANET* 119: "The Legend of Sargon."

with bow and javelin in their contest against the heavy Sumerian phalanx, which was equipped only with axe and lance. One Sumerian city after the other fell into the conquerer's hands, until Sargon was able to wash his bloody weapons in the waters of the Persian Gulf.

As first Oriental ruler, Sargon chose a new capital city for himself in Akkad.[31] From there he built his empire of the four ends of the earth. He made his way as far as the silver mines of Taurus, the cedars of Lebanon, in fact, all the way to the "land of the setting sun, all the way to the end" (probably Cyprus). His ships made their way into the territory of the Indus.[32]

For half a century this giant managed to keep his kingdom together. His son Rimush had to subjugate it anew, and put down the uprisings. He was followed by his brother Manishtusu, who reigned for 15 years, before yielding the throne to Naramsin who ruled for almost four decades and brought the kingdom of the Akkadians to its cultural zenith. It was he who first assumed the title "king of the four margins of the world" (or "shores of the world"). What he apparently meant was the coasts of the Mediterranean and the Persian Gulf, as well as the mountain heights of Armenia and Iran, at any rate, the whole of the then known world. His ships made their way to Oman, the land of the precious diorite. In addition to this there were commercial relations with India. In Mohenjo-Daro, in the Indus Valley, archaeology has discovered Akkadian wares and, on the other hand, the Akkadian settlement of Eshnunna has yielded typical

---

31. The location of this North Babylonian city of Akkad has not yet been clearly established by the excavations; probably it is in the vicinity of present-day Abu Habba, the Sumerian city of Sippar.

32. E. Weidner, "Das Reich Sargons von Akkad," *AFO* VI (1952), 1-25; treats the geographical extension of Sargon's empire. J. Nougayrol, in *RA* 45 (1951), 169-183, published a tablet put together from seven fragments, containing a poetic historical novel on Sargon of Akkad: description of a military expedition against an uprising, the king's throne speeches, address before the battle. The rest is missing. Cf. *Or.* 21 (1952), 255. W. von Soden, *PropWG* I (1961), 549.

Indus seals. Naramsin's soldiers made their way beyond the Zagros mountains, deep into Iran, as witness the famous Naramsin stele.[33]

The last rulers of this dynasty of titans bore the presumptuous title Shar-kali-sharri, "king of all kings." During his reign the "mountain peoples," who had been conquered and held in check by his great predecessors, made a counter attack from the north, annihilating both the capital and the kingdom of Akkad.

THE GODKINGS OF AKKAD. The Akkadian kings prefixed their name with the sign for divinity, whereas this was not the case for the Sumerian kings, excepting for A-an-ni-pad-da (JRAS 1928, 627). Thus, this usage must have been introduced by the Semitic kings. In the late Ur-III period (2070-1960), in addition to the king, other men and women were also "divinized." Their statues were exhibited in the temples, and they were offered sacrifice.

This divinization is intimately connected with the "sacred wedding ceremony." The rise and development of this marriage custom can be traced back to times of crisis, and it has its root in magic. It was believed that the marriage act of fecundation, performed in sacred rites, would emanate upon the whole land, and work a blessing on man and beast, field and meadow. This marriage ceremony was a union of the god of the city and his female consort. The king is the representative of the god.

The rite is taken from that of the profane wedding ceremony. The ceremonies are introduced by a mutual exchange of gifts. The bridegroom gives the bride a precious belt, or a living animal, perhaps a captive lion. The bridegroom wears the sacral tasseled robe. The priest is entirely naked, as we can see on the pictorial representations between the years 3000 and 2500.

The bride is also adorned; she is first bathed in the river or in the natrium, then anointed with cedar oil, and adorned with earrings and arm bands. On her finger she wears a ring, and on her head the horned crown as the symbol of divinity, on her feet shoes as a sign of royal dignity; she wears a precious dress, which is cinctured with the belt of the seven oracle stones, which she can also wear about her neck.

The bride is brought to her bridegroom in an ox-drawn chariot or on a ship. The bridegroom's symbol is the ear of grain, while the symbol of the bride is a palm branch.

When bride and bridegroom meet each other, they embrace; then they proceed into the temple, together with many other gods and goddesses,

33. Illustration: *PropWG* I (1961), after page 552. *ANEP*, No. 309.

who are borne in procession. The guest divinities all remain in the "*ubshukinakku,*" the "hall of decisions," the oracle hall; bride and bridegroom enter the wedding hall "*gigunu.*" The only witnesses are Ishara, the goddess of birth and intercourse, and the officiating priest. This wedding hall is to be found in a secluded part of the temple; in the ziggurat it had been built into the uppermost story.

Originally, during this ceremony, a reed hut was constructed for the bride and groom, adorned with green branches. Hence the name "gardener" for the bridegroom and "verdant garden" for the bride.

Upon the completion of such a "sacred wedding ceremony" the kings had their statues erected in the temples, and to these statues sacrifice was now offered; they remain men, they beg for the favor of the gods, they are the mightiest intercessors, since, by their wedding ceremony, they have entered into the ranks of the gods.

2) THE INVASION OF THE GUTAEANS (2150-2070)

Invasions of Babylonia and Assyria from the harsh mountainous heights of west Iran were not infrequent. The influx of the mountain peoples from the north runs parallel with the inroads of the Semites from the southern steppes and deserts. The goal of all these invasions was the fertile farm land in the middle. Towards the end of the Akkad period the mountain countries once again became restless.[34] From Hurru (probably Azerbaijan) groups of people made their way into northern Mesopotamia, where they established a state in which they attempted to write the Hurrian language in cuneiform. An inscription of King Tishari from Urkesh has been preserved. We have no way of knowing how long this first Hurrian settlement lasted. But from that time on, the Hurrians represent an important ethnic element in the Ancient Near East, an element which would achieve much greater significance a few centuries later.

South of Hurru lay the district of Gutium, apparently northern Luristan, populated by warlike tribes. They attacked the civilized land and destroyed the imperial capital Akkad so thoroughly that from that time on it completely disappeared from history. Even today, its precise location is unknown. The Gutaeans,

---

34. W. von Soden, *PropWG* I (1961), 553.

in the chronicles of this era, are referred to as the "dragons of the mountain ranges, who have torn away the bride from her husband and the children from their parents, and taken away the royal power from Sumer, up into the mountain lands." They live on in the memory of the Ancient Near East as plunderers and temple violators. They were able to maintain their ascendancy for approximately one century (2233-2130 / 2190-2065). Since they never established a kingship by succession, but chose their leaders every three years, they were unable to create any lasting order and the native powers managed to regroup in a fight to regain their lost freedom.

3) THE NEW SUMERIAN KINGDOM (2070-1960)

The Sumerians must have endured this catastrophe with resignation. The fight for freedom was led by Utuhegal of Uruk. He struck the Gutaeans a devastating blow and made himself king over all Babylonia. But the liberator soon lost his position of power to Urnammu, the founder of the 3rd dynasty of Ur. The full blossom of the ancient Sumerian empire seemed to have returned. Historians speak of the Sumerian restoration. Urnammu completely reformed the machinery of political administration and the jurisprudence. In the Urnammu Code we read that he disposed of the dishonest officials, introduced just and incorruptible measures, and did not allow the widow and the orphan to be the prey of the mighty.[35] His son and successor, Shulgi, had himself divinized by undergoing the "sacred marriage ceremony." The lively architectural achievements and the flourishing commercial life of this epoch are amply attested to by the excavations of the 3rd level in Ur, so that this whole era is spoken of simply as Ur-III.[36]

The best known figure from this new Sumerian era is Gudea of Lagash (c. 2050), "the greatest prince whom the Sumerians

35. S. Moscati, *Die Kulturen des Alten Orients*, pp. 30, 48.

36. N. Schneider, "Die Geschäftsurkunder der Reichshauptstadt Ur zur Zeit der dritten Dynastie," *Or.* 21 (1952), 67-74.

ever had, a ruler whose quiet and thoughtful image is preserved for us in many statues, and whose countless inscriptions bear witness to his works for posterity."[37] Gudea was not a warlike figure, but rather a venerator of the gods, a temple builder, and the shepherd of his people.

The fall of the 3rd dynasty of Ur (c. 1960) marked the definitive end of Sumerian control over Babylonia. Sumerian control was followed by two Semitic dynasties, that of Larsa with 14 kings and that of Isin with 12. Seen as a whole, these two centuries (20th and 19th) were a time of decline. Individual rulers did indeed attempt reform. In this respect we must mention the code of law of king Lipit-ishtar of Isin (c. 1950).[38] In the introduction we read that this king restored freedom to all the enslaved citizens of the Babylonian cities. The laws which have been preserved deal primarily with property, slaves, family, work for wages. These laws, which apparently had some influence on Hammurabi, have assured Lipit-ishtar of a name that will survive the centuries. The fall of the dynasty of Isin made possible the rise of the previously small state of Eshnunna in the eastern Tigris country. In 1945 a law code was excavated here too,[39] which was at first attributed to king Bilalama, but which actually owes its origin to Dadusha (c. 1850). The paragraphs which prescribe punishment are formulated much more leniently, and the death penalty is prescribed much less frequently, than in the later Code of Hammurabi. It must be noted that in several places attempts were made to codify the law, a step which had never been undertaken throughout the whole course of Egyptian history.

In the labile balance of power, it was no difficult matter for foreign elements to be assimilated. From the Arabian steppes the Amurru had begun a quiet infiltration of the land between

---

37. M. Lambert and R. Tournay, "Le Cylindre A et B de Gudea," *RB* 55 (1948), 403-437; 520-534. Illustrations by Gressmann, *AOB* 4, 44, 47 and *ANEP* 430-435, 511, 513, 749. Texts *ANET* 268/69.

38. Texts *ANET* 159-161: "Lipit-ishtar Law Code."

39. Texts *ANET* 161: "The Laws of Eshnunna."

the rivers. Clever sheikhs began seizing power in various locations, without at first attempting the formation of an empire. The same thing was being attempted by the Elamites, from the east. They came, not as foreign rulers, but as the protectors of the ancient Sumero-Akkadian heritage. One day Kudur-Mabug set aside the tired dynasty of Larsa and put his own son, Waradsin, "servant of the moon god Sin," on the throne. He then took the title "king of Sumer and Akkad." After his untimely death, his brother Rimsin, "wild bull of the moon god Sin," energetically continued the work that had been begun. He subjected one city after another and extended his empire as far as Babylon. Whether or not he managed to subjugate Ashur as well, is not certain. But at any rate it seemed that the kingdom of Sumer and Akkad had risen anew under the Elamite banner. Still, Rimsin was not the typical conqueror; he dug canals, the life arteries of the land, built temples, and gave life and peace to the inhabitants. The Elamite sovereignty was not destined to endure. From Babylon a new ethnic element made itself felt; the Ammuru had grown strong enough to seize political power and reshape the face of the Ancient Near East.

CAPPADOCIAN TRADE COLONIES. After the expulsion of the Gutaeans the Akkadian tradition of empire lived on in Assyria. The royal names of the Assyrian dynasties are pure Akkadian. Of king Ilushuma we read that, around 1850, he conquered large parts of Babylon and the east Tigris country. In his inscriptions he boasts that he has restored "freedom" to these countries. But it remained for the excavation at Kultepe near Kaisari in eastern Turkey to show that ancient Assyria cultivated a lively commercial relationship with Asia Minor. The ancient name of the city was Kanish. In the year 1925, B. Hrozny began excavating here. At a depth of 2-2.5 m. he found numerous clay tablets which belonged to commercial records which, judging from the name of the merchant's family, must have extended over five generations.[40]

---

40. J. Lewy, "On Some Institutions of the Old Assyrian Empire," *HUCA* 27 (1956), 1-79 is of the opinion that these are not merely trade colonies, but evidence of a direct annexation of large territories which were subject to an Assyrian viceroy. But since we have too little knowledge of Asia Minor during this era, the opinion can be considered only as a

In the winter 1948-49, the Turkish government permitted further excavation. This time the digging penetrated to the cultivated ground at the depth of 7.5 m. At this foundation level of the site, it was possible to distinguish four levels of settlement. Level III was so completely surprised by the destruction that one firm did not have enough time to open the 800-1000 letters which were discovered intact and which now form a precious insight into the widespread commercial relationships of the old Assyrian kingdom. A total of some 3000 tablets have now been discovered, primarily commercial correspondence, contracts, and receipts. The language is pure Assyrian, and the dating is also in terms of the Assyrian annual eponyms, high Assyrian officials after whom the individual years were named.

But it is impossible, on the basis of the existence of these Assyrian trade colonies, to conclude to a political dependence of eastern Asia Minor upon the Assyrian empire. It is obvious that the Assyrian empire enjoyed sufficient prestige for its trade colonies to be tolerated even in foreign countries. The sudden destruction of the trade colonies is connected with the violent invasion of the Hittites (c. 1780 B.C.).

---

working hypothesis. Excavation accounts in B. Hrozny, "Les Fouilles de Kultepe," *Syria* XVIII, 3. B. Landsberger, "Assyrische Handelskolonien in Kleinasien," *AO* 24 (1925).

CHAPTER VIII

THE POLITICAL FORMATIONS OF THE AMURRU-BEDOUINS

TOWARDS the end of the 3rd millennium, a new Semitic population element comes into sight in the Fertile Crescent, both in Syria and in Mesopotamia; an element for which there is no one name in the technical literature. We speak of east-Canaanites, or Canaanites, in order to stress the similar characteristics in both east and west; they are also referred to as west-Semites, Amorites, or Amurru; the proposal has even been made that they be referred to as Hebrews.[41] Of all the proposed names, the term Amurru (plural: Amurri) or Amorites has been preferred. At first when we hear this name we are inclined to think of one definite people; but this is only half of the truth. Sumerian Martu, Akkadian Amurru, means literally "people of the desert," and thus, in our own language, Bedouins.[42] The

41. W. von Soden, *PropWG* I (1961), 568 decides for Canaanites. H. Schmökel, *GAV* 73ff., for the West Semites. A. Jespen, *Die "Hebräer" und ihr Recht, AFO* 26 (1945-46), 54, for Hebrews. S. Moscati, *Die Kulturen des Alten Orients* (1962) passim, for Amorites.

42. A thorough and new investigation of this question in: G. Dossin, Les Bédouins dans les textes de Mari. *StudSem* 2 (1959), 38 and 42.

inhabitants of the cultivated land looked down in contempt upon the Bedouins, living in tents along the highlands of the steppe, nomadic and hungry for land: "The Amurru digs for fungi at the foot of the mountain, eats raw flesh, calls no house his own, and has no grave after death."[43] After the collapse of the kingdom of Akkad, the way was free for the Amurru-Bedouins to make their way into the cultivated land. They took possession of the country in both a peaceful and a warlike manner. The nomadic shepherds became at first partially, and then completely, sedentary. After they had already become established in the country, a powerful sheikh seized political control in one city and sought to expand his power. From among the successive land seizures of the Amurru-Bedouins in east and west, we can distinguish three individual forms which set a new stamp upon the Ancient Near East.

1) THE OLD ASSYRIAN KINGDOM UNDER SHAMSHI-ADAD I (1749-1717)

THE new Amorite Bedouins had forced their way into the territory settled by the Assyrians. The sheikh Ila-Kapkapu seized royal power and thereby established the Amorite dynasty in Ashur. His son Shamshi-Adad took up the old Akkadian royal traditions and called himself "king of the world" (*šar kiššati*). He was the true forger of the Old Assyrian Kingdom. A victory stele proclaims his conquest as far as Lebanon; he fought in the east against Elam, built temples in Nineveh, Ashur, and Terka. He sought primarily to extend his power against the kingdom of Mari. When the king Yahdun-Lim was murdered in a palace revolt, he seized the opportunity to make his son Yasmah-Adad king in his place. But he was not cut from the same pattern as his energetic father. We learn of the developments that followed from approximately 130 letters of Shamshi-Adad which

43. Quoted *ibid.*, 42.

have been preserved and discovered in the archives of Mari.[44] The Old Assyrian Kingdom was the personal work of the great Shamshi-Adad. Upon his death, the empire he had constructed fell into ruins. In Mari, the old dynasty under Zimri-Lim came back into power. The rivalries which now began between the two proved favorable to the rise of a figure who is greater than both of them, Hammurabi of Babylon.

2) THE KINGDOM OF MARI UNDER ZIMRI-LIM (c. 1700)

Just as in Ashur, it was an Amorite Bedouin sheikh who seized political power in Mari on the Euphrates and took the fate of this city in his hands. In the 18th century, we discover here the Amorite dynasty of Yagit-Lim, under whose rulers Mari became one of the most powerful cities in Mesopotamia. The excavations which have been in progress since 1933 brought to light a state archive of 20,000 cuneiform tablets; 15,000 of them are business and government tablets; 5,000 contain diplomatic correspondence and offer us an insight into the correspondence of the king of Mari with the then significant political centers of the Ancient Near East.[45]

In Mari, the best preserved palace of the Ancient Near East was excavated, 200m. long, 120m. wide, with 250 rooms. The royal palace had modern accommodations, with plumbing, underground canalization, bathrooms with cold and warm water, and school quarters for the instruction and development of scribes (diplomats). The rulers of Mari furthered the pursuit of agriculture by a system of irrigation ditches and a new kind of plow. Sheep breeding and trade brought wealth into the country.

---

44. *Archives Royales de Mari.* Part I: *Correspondence de Samsi-Addu.* Compiled by G. Dossin (Paris, 1950). A plausible characterization of Shamshi-Adad is drawn by W. v. Soden, *Herrscher im Alten Orient: Schamschi-Adad I von Assyrien, Soldat und Prinzenerzieher*, pp. 23-33.

45. The excavations began in 1933 were interrupted in 1938 and taken up once again in 1951. The first accounts were published in the journal *Syria*. An over-all view is presented in W. von Soden, "Das altbabylonische Briefarchiv von Mari, ein Uberblick," *WDO I* (1948), 187-204. The texts appear in *Archives Royales de Mari* (ARM) (Paris, 1950).

Zimri-Lim entered into alliances with Cyprus, Crete, and the Phoenician cities. Together with international politics, there were also provisions for the private entertainment of the ruler: lion hunting was a royal privilege. The ice for the refrigeration chambers had to be brought from 100 to 200 km.; the king preferred to have white horses for his war chariots, which were very difficult to obtain.

All of the Ancient Near East was, at that time, divided into tiny states, living in alliance or enmity with each other. The Mari correspondence, apart from the less significant principalities, yields the following names: the *Kingdom of Elam,* which Zimri-Lim at one time supports with auxiliary troops, and later makes war against; the land of *Eshnunna,* east of the Tigris, which was coveted by both Ashur and Mari because of its copper; *Gutium,* north of Eshnunna, in the Zagros mountains, which was, for a time, ruled by a queen; *Larsa,* the Sumerian metropolis, now under the Elamite rule of Rim-Sin; Larsa gradually achieved sovereignty over the rest of the Ancient Near East and proved to be the most energetic opponent of Hammurabi of Babylon; then there was the principality of the commercial city *Carchemish* on the upper Euphrates; *Zalmakum* with its capital city Haran, in whose territory the tribe of the Binu Yamina pitched their tents; finally the Syrian states of *Yamhad,* with its capital city of Halab (Aleppo), which developed into a very strong military power, and *Catanum* in southern Syria, which maintained very close relations with Assyria.

Zimri-Lim of Mari gives the best description of the world politics of his day: "There is no king who would be strong enough for himself. Together with Hammurabi, king of Babel, stand 10-15 kings; together with Rimsin of Larsa, the same; with Ibal-pi-el, king of Eshnunna, the same; with Amut-piel, king of Catanum, the same; with Yaram-Lim, king of Yamhad, 20 kings." [46]

---

46. The texts have been made available in G. Dossin, *Archives Royales de Mari*: I. "Correspondence de Samsi-Addu et ses fils." II. "Lettres diverses" (Ch. F. Jean). III. "Correspondance de Kibri-Dagan gouverneur de Terqa" (J. R. Kupper). (Paris, 1950).

This manifold balance of power was directed into new channels by Hammurabi of Babylon, also an Amorite. In the 31st year of his reign, he overcame the coalition which had gathered about the Elamite Rimsin of Larsa; in his 34th year (1695 B.C.) he destroyed Mari so completely that it could never again rise as a rival of Babylon.[47]

3) THE OLD BABYLONIAN KINGDOM UNDER HAMMURABI (1729-1686)

On the middle Euphrates, Amorite Bedouins, who honored the god Marduk, took control of the previously insignificant village of Babilla, which the Semitic newcomers interpreted as *Bab-ili,* "gate of god." The Sheikh Sumuabum (c. 1830) must be regarded as the founder of the dynasty. He fortified Babylon, built temples, extended his sovereignty into the neighboring districts, and thereby entered into the power politics of Mesopotamia. Some 100 years after his death, Babylon, under Hammurabi, succeeded in maintaining a world empire. Before the Mari finds, attention had been focused too exclusively upon Hammurabi in his solitary genius. The Mari texts allign him properly within the contemporary power politics of the many states, principalities, and kingdoms of the Ancient Near East. By adroit politics and successful wars he succeeded in encompassing the centrifugal tendencies into one great whole and thereby advanced the Sumerian-Akkadian idea of world empire to a new reality. His kingdom represents a synthesis between Akkadian world empire and the god-given shepherd's office of the Sumerian kings. Hammurabi's empire looms before us – inso-

---

47. The excavations of winter 1951-52 show that Hammurabi did not completely destroy the city of Mari. He was content with destroying the city walls and he spared the inhabitants. He left a strong garrison to serve as guard. In an effort to please the people, he even had the Temple of Dagan adorned with frescoes and pictures. It was only under the Hittites, led by Mursillis I, that Mari was completely destroyed. Cf. A. Parrot, "La dernière campagne de Mari 1951/52" *Or.* 21 (1952), 501 and 366.

far as we can recognize it — as a centralistic administrative state, in which there were, in addition to the king, a great multitude of government officials, administrators of great estates and provinces, as well as tiny cities with their councils of elders and a merchant guild under a "head merchant," who might also have been a royal agent. In the cities there was an urban element of free artisans, while in the country several farmers worked together to cultivate the land of the large estate owners. A special social class was composed of imperial soldiers, generally from the ranks of the Amorites, who were provided with a small feudal property and had to supply military service. Next to the king, the temples were the greatest land-owners. It was into this manifold complexity of life that Hammurabi sought to bring order by his famous Code.[48] He made Babylon the political, intellectual, and religious focus of the Ancient Orient.[49]

Politically, it was the Amorites, the Bedouins of the Syro-Arabian desert, who conquered in the 18th century; but in the intellectual and religious domain, they were faced with the ancient Sumero-Akkadian heritage. Sumerian long remains the language of liturgy; Akkadian is the language of literature and diplomacy, while the Amorite language maintained itself for a while as the popular speech, and then yielded to Akkadian-Babylonian.

Just as the kingdom of Akkad fell before the stormy inroads of the mountain peoples from Gutium, the world empire established by Hammurabi proved to be, in time, a victim of the mountain peoples who forced their way inexorably into the lands of the "Fertile Crescent."

---

48. A more thorough evaluation of the Code of Hammurabi will be found in connection with the Sinai legislation, Vol. II.

49. On the Babylon excavations, cf. R. Zehnpfund, "Babylonien in seinen wichtigsten Ruinenstatten," *Der Alte Orient* 11 (1910). St. Langdon, "Ausgrabungen in Babylonien seit 1918"; *AO* 26 (1926). Andre Parrot, *Archéologie mésopotamienne. Les étappes* (1946). Koldewey, *Das wiedererstandene Babylon* (1925). E. Unger, *Babylon, die Heilige Stadt* (1931). G. Contenau, *La vie quotidienne à Babylone et en Assyrie* (Paris, 1950).

THE BEDOUINS OF THE MARI TEXTS[50]

The Mari texts indicate that the Amurru, founders of the empire, were threatened by new waves of Bedouins, from the territory of the Syro-Arabian desert. These were the Sutu or Sutaeans, the Channaeans and the Benjaminites. The Sutaeans were lords of the desert. The Sheikh Hammiurku assembled 2,000 Sutaeans and made a great raid in the land of Catanum. With 60 others he attacked the oasis of Tadmur (Palmyra). They even attacked the flocks of the king of Mari. Thus, Sutu takes on the meaning of plundering Bedouin in this era. The Channaeans had already entered upon the process of civilization. They make up the body-guards for the king, act as a desert police, and are always ready to enlist in military campaigns. The Channaean tribe thus evolved into the professional soldier. The great tribe of Benjaminites (*maru-* or *binu- Yamina*) had already embarked upon the stage of land-possession. They are subdivided into four subsidiary tribes: Ubrabu, Amananu, Yahruru and Yarihu. The pasture lands of the steppe had become too narrow for them; that is why they forced their way across the Euphrates and tried to penetrate above the Khabur. The position is well described in a letter written from an outpost to the king of Mari: "Because of the Binu-Yamina, concerning whom I have already written my master, I have sent a man into their cities, in order to clarify the situation. When they were asked, they answered: 'There is no more pasture land, and we are traveling towards the higher country.' This is what they told me. My security troops are strong. Every one of the Binu-Yamina who tries to make his way from the low country into the high lands. will be captured and then thrown into prison."[51] The Assyrian king Shamshi-Adad first threatened heavy punishments, but eventually preferred to buy the friendship of these Bedouins by gifts of money, against the event of war. On the other hand, Zimri-Lim of Mari dealt them a devastating defeat at the mouth of the Khabur at Zaragatum – without lasting effect. The Benjaminites were under the command of a king; in addition to this office, we also find the title of *dawidum,* which was first translated by "chieftain" or "general," but whose real meaning is not yet clear.[52]

The appearance of the Benjaminites in the Mari texts naturally gave rise to the question of a possible connection with the Israelite tribe of

---

50. The leading work for this era is J. R. Kupper, *Les Nomades en Mésopotamie au temps des rois de Mari* (Paris, 1957). D. O. Edzard, *Die "Zweite Zwischenzeit" Babyloniens* (Wiesbaden, 1957). G. Dossin, "Les Bédouins dans les textes de Mari" *StudSem* 2 (Rome, 1959), 35-51.

51. *ARM,* No. 102.

52. The problem is discussed in G. Dossin, *StudSem* 2 (1959), 51.

Benjamin. It was supposed that they had been expelled from their homeland in the north, migrated towards the south, and established themselves in Palestine. The name of the city Jericho is supposed to have affinities with the Benjaminite tribe of Yarichu. But it is impossible to achieve more than speculation in this respect. The name Binu-Yamina means literally "sons of the right hand," and figuratively "sons of the south," thus, southern tribes. In north Syria there were also the Binu-Sim'al, "the sons of the left hand," that is, the northern tribes. Tribal names based upon the direction of the territory they inhabit are not unfamiliar. They make their appearance in various places without there being evidence of any racial relationship.

CHAPTER IX

THE "MIDDLE AGES" OF THE ANCIENT NEAR EAST

AROUND the year 1500 B.C. – an approximate date which is subject to considerable fluctuation – a deep-seated structural change developed in the history of the Ancient Near East. Prior to the epoch introduced by this date, the Egyptian and Mesopotamian powers had represented the decisive powers in history. Now the picture changes. The mountain tribes, which encircled the north-eastern part of the Ancient Near East, and somewhat later the desert peoples (Aramaeans) which form its southern boundary, accentuate their centripetal movement, forming strong states and entering combat on equal footing with the powers of the river valleys. There are three mountain peoples who establish strong states in the Ancient Near East around the middle of the 2nd millennium B.C.: in southern Mesopotamia the *Kassites,* in northern Mesopotamia the *Hurrians,* and in Anatolia the *Hittites.* For all these peoples, national history had begun much earlier, but it is not until around 1500 that they make their first active impression upon the history of the Ancient Near East. At first it seems that the older cultivated lands along the rivers were being overrun by barbarians, somewhat similar to the

Roman Empire and its fate at the hands of the Germans. But, in a gradual melting-pot process, these new peoples appropriated the elements of the older cultures for their own. Thus the resultant culture knows neither victor nor vanquished. Like the Rome of the Middle Ages, Mesopotamia enjoyed the triumph of its culture, together with its political descendancy, in the age of the mountain peoples.[53]

1) THE KASSITES

As the Semites, wave after wave, penetrated from the Syro-Arabian desert into the fertile civilized land between the two rivers, sometimes by the friendly avenue of immigration, and sometimes by the warlike avenue of conquest, there was also, and at the same time, a gradual but steady penetration of Mesopotamia by the mountain peoples, who were making their way down into the valleys and plateaus. There are no written records for the warlike conquest of Babylon by the Kassites.[54] Hammurabi's successors already speak of the "hordes of the Kassites." The commercial documents of the time make frequent mention of more and more Kassite names, men who were taken on as harvest workers. All this points to a peaceful immigration. The immediate homeland of the Kassites is in the mountain ranges of present-day Luristan. The few remnants of the language that have been preserved, especially the names of divinities preserved in personal names, point back further to the Caucasus. Names of individual divinities like Shuriash, which has been identified – correctly enough – with the Indian Sun god Suria, Maruttash (Indian, Marut), or Buriash (Greek, Boreas), make it obvious that the Kassites had come into contact with Indo-Germanic elements, and that the ruling class had been composed partially of Indo-Germanic elements. But the conquer-

---

53. S. Moscati, *Die Kulturen des Alten Orients,* 147ff.

54. G. G. Cameron, *History of Early Iran,* Chapter V, 89ff. Treats people, origin, language, and the first migration period of the Kassites. W. von Soden, *PropWG* I (1961), 595ff.

ing class is quickly assimilated into the original population, just like the Amurru who penetrated from the desert. Still, they do succeed in establishing a Babylonian dynasty, which ruled over Babylonia for almost four centuries (1600-1200). The era of Kassite hegemony is clothed in a peculiar shadow. Only a very few written documents have survived to cast some light upon what was, proportionately, a rather long period. The first kings, Gandash, Agum, and Kashtiliash, once again assumed the ancient royal title "Ruler of the four ends of the earth, King of Sumer and Akkad, King of Babylon." In the Amarna-era there was a lively intercourse with Egypt. Kassite princesses find their way into the harems of the Pharaoh. In keeping with the practice of the Ancient Near East, Kurigalzu built a residential city for himself, Dur-Kurigalzu.[55] With respect to the history of commerce, the so-called *kudurru* are the most obvious characteristics of the Kassite era; they are more or less regularly worked stones, which are conceived of as sacred boundary stones, and were entrusted as fiefs by the king to highly placed officials, priests, or temples, making them tribute-free.[56]

If the Indo-Germanic element can be established only sparingly in the Kassite immigrations, it comes up much more clearly in the second group of mountain dwellers.

2) THE HURRIANS

The Hurrian problem is still very much in flux.[57] What we can safely say, up to the present time, is this: It is possible to distinguish two stages in the Hurru immigration. The first wave

---

55. The city was excavated in Aqar Quf, a few kilometers north of Bagdad. For the excavation account, see Taha Baqir, "Iraq Government Excavations at Aqar-Quf." *Iraq VIII* (1946), 73ff.

56. Illustration in *ANEP* No. 519-521.

57. Cf. especially the works which present an entirely new picture: R. T. O'Callaghan, *Aram Naharaim* (Rome, 1948) with a rich bibliography. C. Contenau, *La civilisation des Hittites et des Hurrites de Mitanni,* (Paris, 1948). An introduction to the linguistic problem is presented in E. A. Speiser, *Introduction to the Hurrian* (New Haven, 1941).

of Hurrians occurred from the 22nd to the 20th century, apparently together with the invasion of the wild Gutaeans, who put and end to the empire of Akkad; it was during the time of the Gutaean rule over Sumer and Akkad that the principal Hurrian god Kumarbi was taken into the Babylonian pantheon.[58] This presupposes a significant influence on the part of the Hurrians. The names of the 3rd dynasty of Ur also give evidence of Hurrian elements (c. 2000 B.C.). In Mari, too (1700) there are also Hurrian texts. The oldest traces, the tables of the kings of Tisari (24th to 23rd century) in the Hurrian language, and a Sumerian mythological poem,[59] all point beyond northern Mesopotamia, into the Zagros mountain range, as the point of origin for the Hurrian infiltration of Mesopotamia. From 1700 to 1500 B.C. there are no sources at all. In this dark age the second principal immigration of the Hurrians must have taken place. After 1500 B.C. they have already taken Assyria and established the powerful kingdom of Mitanni, in which they represented a majority of the population, while the political rule lay in the hands of an Indo-Arian ruling class. About the same time we find a Hurrian trade center in the city of Nuzi[60] east of the Tigris; even in the Hittite capital of Hattushash, in Asia Minor, Hurrian gods are venerated. The Hurrians penetrate throughout Syria and into Palestine and Edom. In the Bible we find them under the name Horite.[61] Whether or not they are the people whose pressure

---

58. H. G. Güterbock, *Kumarbi. Mythen vom churritischen Chronos aus den hethitischen Fragmenten zusammengestellt, übersetzt und erklärt.* Istanbuler Schriften No. 16 (Zurich-New York, 1946).

59. W. von Soden, *PropWG* I (1961), 533. The tribal territory of Hurrum identified with the modern Azerbaijan. Following page 576 there is a map of the districts settled in this epoch.

60. Excavation account in *Harvard Semitic Series, Vol. XV*: *Excavations at Nuzu* (1955). Archives of a business firm with details of management and legal texts, extremely important for understanding the patriarchal age.

61. In Palestinian place names it is still possible to recognize the traces of Hurrian settlement. Cf. B.S.J. Isserlin, "Hurrian and Old Anatolian Place Names in the Semitic World," *PEQ* 88 (1956), 141-144. Die Stadtnamen Saruhen (Fürstenfeld"), Megiddo, Lakisch belongs here.

triggered the invasion of the Hyksos into Egypt is a question which cannot yet be definitively decided.

Mitanni is the name with which we designate a widely extended state between the Zagros mountains and the Mediterranean Sea (1480-1330 B.C.), from Van-See to Ashur and Arrapha, in which developed the Hurrian nation and the Hurrian power to its cultural zenith. Even Assyria was subject to the king of Mitanni. Shausshatar had a door of gold and silver brought from Ashur to have installed in his palace in the capital city of Mitanni, Wasshukanni. But the autonomy of the Mitanni state was broken by the resurgence of Assyrian power under Shalmaneser I (1272-1243), and the Hurrian element was gradually assimilated into the general population.

The most peculiar phenomenon of the history of the Ancient Near East is to be found in the fact that the power of the Hurrians was most intimately connected with an Indo-Arian ruling class, the names of the Mitanni kings are pure Indo-Arian, for example Artamasura (Indian: *rtasmara* – he who preserves the memory of the holy law), Matiwaza (Indian: *mati-vaya* – his victorious power is prayer), Shausshatar (Indian: *sauk-sastra* – son of the Suksastra), Tushratta (Indian: *tvis-rata* – he who possesses the shiny war chariot), etc. In a treaty with the Hittites, the Mitanni king calls upon the Indian gods Mitra, Indra, and Varuna, to witness the keeping of the treaty. Moreover, there are many expressions, dealing with the breaking and training of horses, which are Indo-Arian. The ruling class bears the Indian name Marianu (young man, warrior). Amenhotep II makes this statement in a victory inscription: "His majesty's booty on that same day: two generals, six m-r-yy-na together with their war chariots, horses, and weapons."[62] In the Rig-Veda, these Marianu are mentioned in connection with war chariots and the war god.

Thus, it would seem that an Indo-Arian tribe, after learning to train horses (apparently in the course of the 18th century) and after the discovery of the war chariot, had managed to establish sovereignty over large sections of the Ancient Near East, based on cavalry and war chariots.[63]

---

62. Newly discovered inscription, 2.85m. high, in 34 lines: recounts an expedition of Amenhotep II against Syro-Palestine (Retenu). Cairo museum. Further texts in Galling, *TGI*, 29f.

63. Probable point of departure in South Russia. Cf. Fr. Hancar, "Ein nordisches Streitwagenbild im östlichen Kaukasus," *FF* 19 (1943), 26. From Nuzu come the oldest texts on the breeding and training of horses: the technical expressions are Indian or Hurrian. H. Kronasser, "Indisches in den Nuzitexten," *WZKM* 53 (1957), 181-192.

When the Egyptians of the New Kingdom, after the expulsion of the "Hyksos," made more and more serious advances on Syria-Palestine, they found an energetic adversary in the kingdom of Mitanni, which is called Naharin in the Egyptian sources. When the Assyrians threatened Mitanni from the north, it had already shrunk to a tiny territory which the Assyrians called by the ancient name Hanigalbat. All three names, Mitanni, Naharin, and Hanigalbat, refer to the same historical state which sought to postpone its eventual demise by acting as a buffer state in the battle between the Assyrians and the Indo-Germanic Hittite state of Asia Minor, and eventually completely disappeared.

3) THE HITTITES

In the strict sense of the word, the name Hatti is proper only to the original Asia Minor people who preceded the empire-building Hittites. This "pre-Hittite" population did not belong to the Indo-Germanic period. It venerated the sun god of the city Arinna. Its language had already died out in the 14th century, in the Hittite capital Hatushash. But many expressions were adopted from the conquering Indo-Germanic element. Most of all, they gave their conquerors their own name: Hatti, or Hittite.

When we speak of the Hittites today,[64] we generally understand it to refer to the Indo-Germanic conquerors who, from 1900 B.C., gradually overcame all of Asia Minor. Since everything that we know of the Hittite language, its structure and its vocabulary, places it in relation with the west Indo-Germanic languages, it was generally accepted that the Hittites must have immigrated from the west, when they took possession of what was later their tribal land, the high country of eastern Asia Minor, which is encompassed by the Halys in a wide arc, coming perhaps from the Balkans over the Hellespont and Bosporus.

---

64. Exhaustive presentation of the Hittite history and culture: M. Riemschneider, *Die Welt der Hethiter. Grosse Kulturen der Frühzeit*, second edition (Stuttgart, 1955). A. Goetze, *Hethitische Kulturgeschichte. Kulturgeschichte des Alten Orients*, Vol.: *Kleinasien*. second edition (1957). H. Schmökel, *GAV* 119-153. W. v. Soden, *PropWG* I (1961), 605-609; II (1962), 48-57. H. Otten, *Das Hethiterreich. Kulturgeschichte des Alten Orients*, published by H. Schmökel (Stuttgart, 1961), 311-446.

But the division between east and west Indo-Germanic elements must have taken place much earlier. More recent scholarship tends to substantiate the fact that the Hittites, like the other Asiatic Indo-Germanic elements, penetrated into Asia Minor across the district between Pontus and the Caspian Sea.

The Hittites were not an ethnic unity; like the Greeks, they are composed of different tribes, such as the western and eastern Luvians in Cilicia and northern Syria, and the Palaic-speaking tribes in Paphlagonia. One tribe managed to seize political control. This first Hittite empire foundation (c. 1800) is described in the Anitta cuneiform tablet, the oldest known witness to the Hittite language. Anitta was the prince of Kussara, whose location is still unknown. He conquered the city of Nesa, and treated the population in a friendly manner. But the city of Hatushash, which had offered resistance, was starved into submission, then destroyed and cursed. The extent and duration of this first empire are not yet known. Labarna (c. 1600) is considered as the founder of this old-Hittite kingdom; his name, in the form Tabarna (cf. Tiberius) was later assumed by all succeeding kings as an official title, something like "Caesar." Hattushilish I, that is, "he who is from Hattushash," seems to have rebuilt Hattushash after its destruction and raised it to the dignity of a capital city. The excavations at the modern Turkish village Boghazköy, situated along the east of Ankara, have restored the sunken glory of the Hittite kingdom into the light of history.[65] The concept

---

65. The city had been built on a mountain overhang; the "great mountain" Buyukkale is separated from the other city by a ravine; hence the Turkish name Boghazköy, "ravine town." A city wall, 6m. in length, enclosed the city area of 168 hectares. The very first excavations, in 1905 and 1907, already unearthed cuneiform archives. The further excavations, 1931-39 and from 1952 onwards, were carried on by the Deutsche Archäologische Institut. The approximately 20,000 cuneiform tablets have been published in the "Keilschrifturkunden aus Boghazköy" (*KUB*): the juridic texts are the work of E. Neufeld, *The Hittite Laws* (London, 1951). These ruins were visited in November, 1958; Hittite history studies on location; quarters with a Turkish peasant; unforgettable sunset through the Lion Gate in the city walls.

of king which we discover in the Hittite mentality is something quite different from what we have met with in the rest of the Ancient Near East. There are many similarities with the early German kingship of the Middle Ages. The Hittite king is leader in war and peace, controlled by the nobility as a class. He receives his lofty office from the hands of the Panku, the council of the nobles, not like a god as in Egypt, not like the representative of a god as in Sumer, nor as a divine mandate for the service of humanity, as in the case of Hammurabi, nor is it like a divinized humanity, as in the rulers of Akkad.

Labarna built the old Hittite kingdom into a world state, reaching to the sea in both north and south, and pushing deep into the west. His son and successor, Hattushilish I, set out against Syria, but did not succeed in subjugating Halab (Aleppo). It was his son and successor, Murshilish I (c. 1540-1510), who succeeded in seizing the hegemony in the Ancient Near East. In a fantastic campaign reminiscent of the Roman campaigns of the Emperors in the Middle Ages he advanced to Babylon, where he deposed the last successors to the dynasty of Hammurabi, and thus legitimized his claim to supreme lordship over the four ends of the earth.

Since the Hittite kingship was an office that was highly desired by the various noble families, the Old Empire soon collapsed as a result of the internal struggle for power. It was not until after the reform of the laws of succession to the throne, under Telepinu, around the year 1480 – the nobility renounced its claim to royal dignity but retained its prerogative of passing criminal sentences – that the New Hittite Empire (1400-1200) could arise. Tudhaliyash II, probably the "King Tid'al of the Gentiles," who is named in Gen. 14, set out against northern Syria, conquered the city Halab-Aleppo, and thus laid the foundation for Hittite supremacy in this region. He thereby set a limit to the Egyptian advance under Thutmose III. Under his two successors Hattushilish II and Tudhaliyash III, the empire declined so completely that Shupiluliuma (1380-1346) had to begin all over again. He developed the Hittite empire to the rank of a world power. Egypt was then in the Amarna period, experiencing an era of descendancy, and had completely lost its political influence in the Ancient Near East. Thus, Shupiluliuma was able to penetrate into Syria, all the way to Lebanon, and shatter the Mitanni Kingdom, which he reduced to the position of an Hittite vassal state by arranging a marriage between his daughter and Mattiwaza, the leader of the Mitanni. It was also his accomplishment to have transformed the loosely structured Old Hittite feudal state into a strictly administered bureaucratic state. With the reawakening of Egypt, in the New Kingdom, under Ramses II, the battle for supremacy in Syria had to be decided. The decision took place in 1296 in the battle at Kadesh. The Egyptian accounts tell of a great victory. The Hittite sources, on the other hand, tell of the pursuit of the enemy all the way to Damascus by king Muwatalli (1315-1290). The fact of the matter is that Egyptian power, from this time on, never spread beyond the Lebanon. Between these two powerful opponents, an "eternal peace" was concluded. This peace treaty was the greatest political event of the 13th century; it guaranteed peace to the civilizations of that age.

The work of Shupiluliuma, Murshilish II, and Hattushilish III withstood pressures from all directions, for several decades, down to the end of the 13th century. Hattushilish III was even invited by Ramses II to make an official visit to Egypt.[66] The visit never materialized, however, since new dangers made their appearance on the political horizon. The greatest danger threatened from the west, where the Ahhiyawa and the Arzawa lands [67] began pounding more and more strongly against the gates of the empire. Our sources suddenly grow mute, like the voice of a man who

---

66. E. Edel, *Der geplante Besuch Hattusilis III. in Ägypten. MDOG* 92 (1960), 15-20.

67. F. Cornelius, *Historia, Zeitschrift fur alte Geschichte,* XI (1962), 112: The Ahhiyawa identified not with the Achaeans, but with the Argives. On the subject of Arzawa lands, cf. H. Otten, *Das Hethiterreich,* 365ff. These are the first reports on the West and Southwest of the Asia Minor peninsula.

is struck down by a mortal blow. New Indo-Germanic migratory tribes, breaking their way from the Balkans across Greece and the Aegean islands into Asia Minor and Egypt, and new Semitic tribes, forcing their way upwards from the south, out of the desert work together to reshape the face of the Ancient Near Eastern world. They make their appearance with unheard of manpower, armed with the weapons of the Iron Age.

After the collapse of the Hittite Empire on Asia Minor territory (c. 1200), the Syrian possessions hold out for a while. Among these late Hittite principalities we must count Kue (Adana-Karatepe) in eastern Cilicia, with which King Solomon trafficked in horses; then the powerful city states of Carchemish, Halab-Aleppo, Arpad, and Bit-Agusi.[68] The Hittite population passed over into the inrushing Aramaeans, but continued to retain the Hittite name, as a monument to a great bygone era. It is in this sense that the Bible speaks of Uriah, David's general, as a Hittite (2 Sam. 11, 4).

The Hittites must have taken over cuneiform writing from the Semites at a very early period; but, side by side with the cuneiform, the older Hittite hieroglyphic was also in use. Since this was generally written on wood tablets, few monuments have survived.[69]

The advance of the sea peoples was broken at the gates of Egypt, and turned towards Palestine. Remnants of this migration are the Philistines (cf. next section). As a counter balance against the hordes pouring out of Asia Minor and the Aramaeans penetrating from the Syrian desert, there arose the new Assyrian kingdom, which was to determine the fate

---

68. Schmökel, *GAV* 140ff.

69. The thorny story of the decipherment of the Hittite hieroglyphs is presented concisely by J. Friedrich, *Entzifferungsgeschichte der heth. Hieroglyphen,* 1939. I. J. Gelb, *The Contributions of the New Cilician Bilinguis to the Decipherment of Hieroglyphic Hittite* (Chicago, 1950). H. Th. Bossert, "Die phönizisch-hethitischen Bilinguen vom Karatepe," *Oriens 1,* 163-192. R. Werner, *Die Entzifferung der heth. Hieroglyphen,* Anthropos 46, 260-268. J. Friedrich, *Hethitisches Keilschrift-Lesebuch.* Indogermanische These are the first reports on the West and Southwest of the Asia Minor *Hethitisches Wörterbuch. Ibid* (1961).

of the Ancient Near East for half a millennium, until the time in which, after the brief interlude of the new-Babylonian Empire, the Indo-Germanic Medes and Persians were to take over the hegemony of the East.

Since the historical development of these kingdoms is intimately connected with the history of the kingdoms of Israel and Judah, a more thorough discussion of their history will be reserved for the corresponding section of Israelite history.

4) THE ARAMAEANS

The origin of the Aramaeans is, like every origin, not clearly determined.[70] The kingdom of Mitanni had been shattered by the combined forces of Hittites and Assyrians. Shortly afterwards, the sea peoples annihilated the Hittite Empire, and the Egyptian supremacy in Syrian territory was dissolved. It is no wonder that the desert Bedouins made their way into this empty territory, in search of *Lebensraum.* Towards the end of the 12th century, strong Aramaic tribes in east and west have already begun their advance. Their home territory lay on the Jebel Bishri between the Euphrates and the oasis of Tadmor (Palmyra). From this central point they possessed the right bank of the Euphrates down towards Babylonia; at the same time they penetrated into Syria, as far as the Antilebanon. At this time in history, they crossed over the Euphrates at the mouth of the Khabur and firmly established themselves in Upper Mesopotamia. Here the city of Gozan and the crossroads city of Harran became their most important settlement centers. The whole territory

70. According to Amos 9, 7, Yahweh called the Aramaeans out of Kir; according to 1, 5, he will drive them back to Kir again; the same is true of the Aramaeans of Damascus (2 Kings 16, 9). Since the identification of Kir with any known city has not yet proved satisfactory, and the texts clearly imply that Kir must be the original home of the Aramaeans, ḳîr could well be connected with the Sumerian ḫur, "mountain, highland, desert." On the Aramaean question, cf. A. Dupont-Sommer, *Les Araméens* (Paris, 1949). O'Callaghan, "Aram Naharaim, "A Contribution to the History of Upper Mesopotamia in the II. Millennium B.C." Rome, *AnOr* 26 (1948). H. Schneider, "Aram und die Aramäer in der Ur-III-Zeit," *Bib 30* (1949), 109. S. Moscati, *Die Kulturen des Alten Orients* (1962), 184ff. W. F. Albright, *HM II* (1953), 361ff.

was called by the name Paddan Aram or Aram Naharaim, "the fields of Aram," or "Aram of the rivers."

The Assyrians were hardly able to offer resistance against the intruders. Tiglath-pileser I, in the year 1112 B.C., led a campaign against them and threw them back across the river. But, as might be expected in the case of the Bedouins, such strikes from the Assyrian army were meaningless. Tiglath-pileser I has left reports of 28 such campaigns. As soon as he turned his back, the Aramaeans made their way back into the country and tried to establish a permanent settlement.

When, at the end of the 12th century, the Aramaeans had already made great inroads all along the Fertile Crescent, they must already have spent several centuries in the process of becoming a nation. Since the name Aramaean, as referring to the Bedouins who were penetrating from the Syrian desert, first appears in the cuneiform texts of Tiglath-pileser (1112),[71] their forebears are perhaps best designated as Proto-Aramaeans. The Assyrian documents refer to them as Ahlamu. This is still not the name of the people; Ahlamu is the plural of hilmum,[72] "friend, comrade," and thus synonymous with "company." Ethnically, the various companies of Bedouins who invaded the cultivated land might well have belonged to different groups; at the end of the 12th century these Ahlamu-companies were synonymous with the Aramaeans (ahlame-armaia). Their penetration into Syria is also mentioned in the Ugarit texts. A recruitment list mentions a *bn army,* an "Aramaean" who had two bows and a sling as his weapon.[73] A gift pronouncement[74] of the king Ammistamru of Ugarit, at the beginning of the

71. The name Aram does occur already on one of the cuneiform tablets of Naram-Sins and on a votive tablet from Puzuris-Dagan (Drehem); but its reference to the Aramaeans is certainly not established. These texts have been more closely examined by M. McNamara, "De populi Aramaeorum primordiis," *VD* 35 (1957), 131-136.

72. R. de Vaux, *Die hebräischen Patriarchen und die modernen Entdeckungen* (1959), 52.

73. *UM,* Text 321, III, 22.

74. McNamara, *VD 35* (1957), 137.

13th century, already mentions the "fields of Aram" (*eḳlat A-ra-mi-nu*). Thus it appears that we must date the beginning of the Aramaean migration, not in the 12th century, but much further back. The Aramaean migration is thus nothing more than the continuation of the migrations of the Amurru-Bedouins already mentioned in the Mari texts. While the Amurru established empires in their path, the Aramaean tribes managed only to set up a few principalities in Mesopotamia and Syria, and even these were annihilated by the new advances of the Assyrians. Their later history is closely bound up with the early royal period in Israel, where it is treated more explicitly. In Babylonia, the Aramaean Adad-apal-iddina had managed to seize political power already in the first half of the 11th century. It was not until half a millennium later that the Aramaean Chaldaeans were active in establishing an empire here. We might thus say that the Chaldaean dynasty of the new Babylonian kingdom since Nabopolassar (625-605) is the expression of the centuries-long Aramazation of Babylonia, just as much as the Hammurabi dynasty was the political and cultural product of a centuries-long infiltration by the Amurru-Bedouins. Even though the Aramaeans of the west achieved no great military significance, they did enjoy an ethnic and linguistic victory, so that in the middle of the first millennium before Christ the lands of the Fertile Crescent were Aramaeized. After the decline of the Chaldaean kingdom, the Aramaean language assumed international importance even under the Persian hegemony, as "imperial Aramaic." [75]

5) THE INDUS CULTURES

After the excavations in the Indus valley and the "Indian" finds in the land between the rivers, recent decades have witnessed a steadily maturing appreciation of the fact that the newly discovered Indus culture deserves a place of importance equal to that of the river cultures on the Nile and the Euphrates-

75. For a good presentation of Aramaean studies, cf. *Handbuch der Orientalistik*, Vol. III, Sec. 2 and 3. (Leiden, 1954).

Tigris. The settlement of the Indian continent, just like that of East Asia and the Indian island, extends back to the era of the glacial and pluvial periods. Skeletal remains of the ice-age inhabitants of India have not yet been discovered, but the presence of stone instruments clearly demonstrates the existence of early man in this region.

The shadow which veils the prehistory of India is first penetrated in the extreme northwest. In the highlands of Iran and Beluchistan, already in the 4th millennium before Christ, the first Late Stone Age cultures and settlements had existed. Just as in Egypt and Mesopotamia, there was an attraction for the river plains, since they offered a better potential for development. Around the year 3000 B.C., the transition from Stone Age to Metal Ages had already been completed in most of the territory of the northwest highlands. Between 2500 and 1500 B.C., a marvelously advanced culture developed in the Indus valley; its discovery is closely linked with the excavation of the cities of Mohenjo-daro and Harappa. Mohenjo-daro is situated on the northwest shore of the Indus (*sindhu, "stream"*), some 400 km. above its mouth; Harappa lies on the Ravi, a tributary of the Indus, about 550 km. northwest of Mohenjo-daro. During this millennium, the entire river district of the Indus, from the Arabian Sea up into the foothills of the Himalayas, presented a unified culture. Whether or not any attempt was made to unite the individual city states into a great empire, similar to that of Sumer and Akkad, is a question beyond the limits of our present knowledge. At any event, we do have evidence of conscious and deliberate planning in the area of social administration and city organization. The city plan of Mohenjo-daro boasts a regularity which can only be the result of officially controlled building. A network of precisely parallel main streets, crossed by other parallel streets at right angles, divides the city into large blocks, some 400 m. long and 200 to 300 m. wide. Within these blocks the houses stood in regular lines and rows. Structures of a more particular nature lay on a mountain-like elevation. Here a bath was discovered, consisting of one large, rectangular basin, with steps leading to it on both sides, and several smaller bathrooms. Many private houses also had wells and bathrooms; an extensive canal system served for public hygiene.

Even though the excavated ruins still testify today to the magnificence of this early Indian culture, we are still without the key to understanding the spiritual and intellectual life of the Indus people. The sign language written by the Indus people on countless seals and seal impressions, which have come down to our modern times, is completely undeciphered. If we could succeed in this challenge, it would be possible to rescue the Indus culture from its present state of isolation.

Around 1500 B.C. the Indus cities were the victims of a warlike invasion. On the ruins of the highly advanced culture, the barbarian people now built their primitive dwellings. In Mohenjo-daro we can still see skeletons of the former inhabitants who were cut down in their bedrooms, along the corridors, and in the streets. At about this same time the "mountain people" made their inroads into the lands of the Fertile Crescent. The same migration of peoples made itself felt in India. Thus the destroyers of the Indus culture are the Arians, who established their possession of the land between the years 1500 and 1200 B.C. The pride of the conquerors is evident even in their name; Arya, Arian, means "hospitable, noble," and thus "noblemen"; the non-Arians, on the other hand, are called "ungracious" (Dasyu), "inhuman," mere barbarians. For the knowledge of the early-Arian or old-Vedic era (c. 1500-1000) we have religious and court literature texts at our disposal. The court epics of Mahabharata and Ramayana have preserved reminiscences of the most ancient times; but later elements were so widely superimposed that the ancient traditional data can be established only with the greatest difficulty. On the other hand, the most ancient sections of the Vedas – etymologically, a derivation of the root *vid,* to know – go back to the period between 1400-1200, when the land was being conquered. The Vedas are not so much poetical creations as they are rhapsodies of songs, sacrificial formulae, and magic spells, composed by priests for their later use in ritual ceremonies; they are thus the sum total of sacral "knowledge." Their present form dates from approximately 1000 B.C. – thus, in the same period at which the Bible began to develop. For more than a thousand years they were passed on orally from generation to generation, and only after the beginning of the era were they fixed in written form.

Even though India appears only on the distant eastern horizon of the history of the Ancient Near East, even in ancient times the bond between east and west must have been much more intimate than the sparse results of excavation might lead us to surmise. At any event, together with the Indo-Arian chariot-warriors of the Hyksos and Mitanni eras, the gods of the Indian pantheon were introduced into the lands of the Bible.[76]

---

76. Chr. von Furer-Haimendorf, "Altindien. Die vorgeschichtlichen und primitiven Kulturen bis zum Einbruch der Arier," *HM II* (1953), 464-498. L. Petech, "Indien bis zur Mitte des 6. Jh," *PropWG II* (1962), 353ff.; following page 360 is a color photo of the storage chambers of Harappa. On the religion of the pre-Vedic and Vedic Indians, cf. J. Gonda, *Die Religionen Indiens. I: Veda und älterer Hinduismus* (Stuttgart, 1960), 48-102.

CHAPTER X

THE RELIGIONS OF THE ANCIENT NEAR EAST

LITERATURE

In addition to the historical works already mentioned, which also contain a more or less explicit treatment of the development of the religions, there is also a specialized body of literature which treats primarily the essence and history of the religions of the Ancient Near East: E. Dhorme, *Les religions de Babylone et d'Assyrie,* Collection, (Mana, Paris 1950). Particularly stimulating are the discussions following each chapter, in which the most recent contributions to the history of religion are evaluated. – Fr. König, *Christus und die Religionen der Erde,* (Vienna 1951), Vol. II, 383-440. – N. Scheider, *Die Religion der Sumerer und Akkader,* Vol. II, 441-498. – Liagre Böhl, *Die Religion der Babylonier und Assyrer.* – The problem of prehistory and early history is treated by F. W. Albright, *From Stone Age to Christianity,* (1949). For the specifically Sumerian religion, cf. Charles F. Jean, *La religion sumérienne d'après les documents sumériens antérieurs à la dynastie d'Isin* (circa 2186), (Paris 1931). Treatment of local divinities, then a description of the Sumerian pantheon and, in the second part, a conspectus of sacred places, times, and persons, as well as the effect of religion on life. – A. Ungnad, *Die Religion der Babylonier und Assyrer,* (Jena 1921). Arranged according to categories: myth and epic, prayer and song, magic and ritual texts. There is also the earlier work of M. Jastrow, *Die Religionen Babyloniens und Assyriens,* 3 vols., (1905 to 1912). Among the Italian works, from the great religious collection of Raffaele Pettazoni we might mention: Guiseppe Furlani, *La religione babylonese ed assira*: Vol. 1, *The Gods*. Vol. 2: *Myths and Religious Life*, (Bologna 1928 and 1929); an extensive bibliography! – On the etymology of the names of the gods, consult A. Deimel, *Sumerisches Lexikon*, IV, 1: *Pantheon Babylonicum*, cuneiform catalogue of the Babylonian gods' names (1950), Part 2, edited by F. Gössmann, *Planetarium Babylonicum*, the Sumerian-Babylonian names for the stars, (Rome 1950). – K. Tallqvist, "Akkadische Götterepitheta," in *Studia Orientalia* VII, (1938). – B. Landsberger, *Babylonisch-assyrische Texte*. In E. Lehmann, *Textbuch zur Religionsgeschichte*, second edition, (1922). – A. Falkenstein - W. von Soden, *Sumerisch-akkadische Hymnen und Gebete*, (Zürich 1953). – J. A. van Dijk, *Sumerische Götterlieder*, Second part, (Heidelberg 1960). – "Le antiche divinità semitiche," The ancient Semitic divinities, *Collection*, published by S. Moscati, *Studi Semitici*, (Rome I, 1958). – G. Conteneau, "Die alten Religionen des Vorderen Orients," in *Die Religionen des Alten Orients*, (1958), 63-120. – S. H. Hooke, *Babylonian and Assyrian Religion*, (London 1962).

The oldest traces of religious expression go back far into the shadows of prehistory.[1] Small finds, such as the terracottas of female idols or statues of bulls, prove that the veneration of a great mother divinity goes back to the very beginnings of rural village culture. Side by side with these smaller finds, the temple structures offer clear testimony of the veneration of a god. The temple of Ea at Eridu goes back to this prehistoric time; this is the first example of the ziggurat form. In prehistoric times there were already two great temple structures in Uruk IV, a temple of the great mother divinity and a temple with high terraces, the so-called "White Temple" of the sky-god Anu.[2] As soon as the Sumerian people enters into the full light of history and begins to leave written records of its religious convictions, we recognize a well characterized pantheon.

The divinities of the Ancient Near East evidence a confusing number and variety. The Sumerians describe the number of

1. The pre- and early historical archaeological material is briefly summarized in Albright, *Von der Steinzeit zum Christentum* (1949), 123ff. W. v. Soden, *PropWG I* (1961), 531ff.

2. On the subject of Anu-Ziggurat and the White Temple, cf. E. Heinrich, *Vorläufige Berichte über die Ausgrabungen in Uruk-Warka* VIII, 190; IX, 19ff.; X, 21ff.

their gods as 3,600 (60 x 60) and this is not a particularly great exaggeration.[3] The great lists of gods from the library of Ashurbanipal numbers 2,500 gods. A. Deimel, in the *Pantheon Babylonicum,* catalogues 3,300 and K. Talquist, in the *Akkadischen Götterepitheta,* lists 2,400 divinities. Their number has been considerably increased by the more recent discoveries in Ugarit, Mari, and Asia Minor. But these numbers can create a certain amount of misunderstanding, since they have been drawn up on the basis of different times and places. Actually, no more than 25 divinities were ever venerated at one given time. From Mari, for example, there is a catalogue with the names of 25 divinities.[4]

When we pass from this manifold variety of divinities as recorded in history, and go back into the Sumero-Semitic early periods, we find a much simpler picture. The Sumerians practically always venerated one particular god who took on the character of a universal god. Thus we can speak of a Sumerian monolatry,[5] the veneration of one supreme being together with a more or less numerous catalogue of subordinate divinities. In the case of the Semitic nomads, who penetrated into the civilized land in the course of the 3rd millennium, it is quite incorrect to speak of a pantheon. They venerated El (*ilum*) as supreme god. The fact that sun, moon, and stars all appear as formative elements in the ancient personal names, does not permit us to conclude that these were venerated as divinities together with the god El. Today we can consider it a demonstrated fact that the Semites brought a well developed faith in a supreme deity into the land they overran. It is only when they established permanent settlements and built their cities that the divinities began to multiply.[6] Archaeology and ancient Semitic philology

---

3. W. von Soden, "Die sumerische Kultur, Religion und Literatur," *PropWG I* (1961), 560.

4. M. J. Dahood, *StudSem I* (1958), 65ff.

5. M. Lambert, "Polythéisme et monolatrie des cités sumériennes," *RHR 157* (1960), 1-20.

6. Three studies must be mentioned here which investigate the three Semitic areas of settlement: Mesopotamia, Syria-Palestine, and Arabia,

thus confirm the story of the development of religion as it is presented in Biblical prehistory.

Since the Sumerian and the Semitic culture finds were already beginning to interpenetrate in the earliest era at which we can examine them, and since the Sumerian pantheon had been taken over to a great degree and further enlarged with new names by the Babylonians, we shall treat the Sumero-Babylonian pantheon as a unit. But we must always bear in mind the fact that the individual divinities have undergone a considerable but varying degree of development over the course of the two or three millennia that we are privileged to examine. But in the era in which the Old Testament began to make its presence felt in the religious discussions of the Ancient Near East, the pantheon was full and definitively set.

THE SUMERO-BABYLONIAN PANTHEON

The cuneiform sign for god is a star, in Sumerian *dingir,* in Akkadian *ilum.* Whenever anyone wanted to designate an indescribably great being, he would point to heaven. Correspondingly, the supreme god bears the name Anu, "sky," in Sumerian. The Semites designated their supreme being by the word El (*ilum*). Despite the most varied lines of attack and interpretation, the meaning of this name cannot be established. Most probably, it seems to be derived from the root *'wl,* "to be strong, to be leader"; in this explanation, El would mean "leader," in the sense of "lord." But with the elaboration of the pantheon, this name which originally designated the supreme god came to be used as a generic term for the proliferation of divine beings.[7] God was thought of in human terms. The gods might indeed be

---

in terms of their most ancient conceptions of divinity: J. Bottéro, "Les divinités sémitiques anciennes en Mésopotamie." M. J. Dahood, "Ancient Semitic Deities in Syria and Palestine." W. Caskel, "Die altsemitischen Gottheiten in Arabien." These appear in *StudSem I* (1958), 17-118.

7. M. J. Dahood, *StudSem I* (1958), 74ff.; published with illustrations, edited, "Zeuge," unedited, "Fremdling."

called bull, lion, etc., by way of comparison, and they might have a given animal in their retinue when they are pictured; but still they are never themselves represented in the form of an animal, as are the gods of Egypt. Even the demonic "mixed creatures" have a human face. The animal element gives rise only to symbol, as, for example, when the god's crown is always recognizable by the presence of a bull's horns.

Since the gods were thought of as more sublime human beings, a human mode of life was also attributed to them. They need food and drink, have wives and children, live in a house, or in a temple. The temple is not the congregating place for the faithful, but primarily the dwelling place of the gods. In the cella (the most sacred room) of the Ishtar temple in Ashur, in front of the cult relief along the inside of the shorter wall stood an incense stand and an altar, while at the right and left, along the longer wall, the images (each seated on his own bench or standing) of the devotees were portrayed in an attitude of perpetual adoration. Originally these must have been only the consecration statues of the kings and the princes, but later people of lower rank were also admitted to this intimate form of divine worship. Since the principal gods were thought of as kings, they were also given a royal court with ministers and retinue. The gods, thus, do not live within a timeless remove; they have fates just like men, and the divine myths tell this story.

At the end of the 3rd millennium, since it is only then that the theological conceptions are clearly to be grasped, we mark the appearance of a pantheon, arranged in triads.[8] Cosmic space was the realm of *Anu,* lord of the sky; *Enlil,* was lord of the earth, and *Ea* was lord of the water. Then there is the astral triad of *Sin,* moon, *Shamash,* sun, and *Ishtar,* morning-evening star, also formed with the storm god Hadad. This second triad bears clear marks of Semitic origin. Then there are the lesser gods of natural phenomena, such as fire, river, grain, etc. The rise and fall of the individual divine powers is intimately con-

---

8. J. Bottéro, *StudSem I* (1958), 54.

nected with the ascendancy and descendancy of the political powers. Thus, in the Sumero-Babylonian pantheon we can distinguish cosmic gods, astral gods, nature divinities, and national gods.

1) THE COSMIC GODS

The Sumerian sky god *An* (Semitized as Anu or Anum) always occupies first place in the pantheon, even though later a local god comes to the fore. It is Anu who gives Hammurabi the kingship; he punishes the evil and rewards the good. He is first in time and space. He is called especially "sky god" (*il-šamê*), "sky king" (*šar-šamê*), or simply "sky father" (*ab-šamê*).[9] He is the king of gods and man, just like the Olympian Zeus. Sceptre, diadem, and shepherd's staff are his insignia in heaven. That is why kingship is derived from heaven. In primeval days it came down from heaven. Anu originally had no goddess for a consort. But in order to make him resemble the other gods, he was given Antum (feminine form for An – heaven, sky) for his consort, who does not, however, have any personal characteristics. In the figure of Anu we can clearly recognize the original supreme deity, which he always basically remains. The principal seat of Anu's cult was in Uruk, where stood his temple E-anna (-house of the sky); however, his cult spread through all Sumeria and Akkadia, and later also Assyria.

The ruler of the space of the universe is *Enlil,* whose name is simply the word for rule, sovereignty (*ellilutû*), a meaning which is also expressed by the Babylonian supreme god Marduk. In speaking of the Old-Sumerian god, his devotees spoke simply of the "old lord." He was originally the "lord of the wind," and since the wind brought rain and water, he is also "lord of the flood." Since the wind comes from the mountain, he is called simply the "big mountain." As god of the tower of Nippur, his

---

9. The Babylonian divine epithets, which are the best source for determining the nature of the divinities, are compiled and examined in K. Tallqvist, *Akkadische Götterepitheta* (1938).

principal place of worship, he bears the title Kur-gal (big mountain), from whom the gods themselves seek refuge at the time of the great flood. His temple in Nippur is called E-kur (house of the mountain). His consort, who gave him 8 children, is called Nin-khur-sang (consort of the mountain). Enlil is thus the lord of the earth, the four directions, all lands and peoples. Since he is borne along in the storm winds, he is also called "wild warrior" or "wild bull" (*rîmu*). His favorite son is Ningirsu, the brave warrior of Enlil, city god of Lagash.

The realm of the abyss and the ocean is subject to En-ki, "lord of the earth." His second name Ea, which, according to the Sumerian, is interpreted as "residence of the water" or "in the water" might also be of Semitic origin.[10] En-ki's temple in Eridu is called E-apsu, "house of the primeval flood," the Okeanos of the Greeks, which surrounds the globe of the earth. Even though the ancient Sumerians attempted to interpret the word Apsu as "wisdom of the father" or "father of wisdom," it is obviously a Semitic word, meaning "end, boundary." En-ki was venerated particularly as a god of magic and of occult knowledge. It is he who put a spell on the primeval flood and lulled it to sleep, so that it could be overcome. It was he who gave the Babylonian Noah the advice that he should seek refuge in a ship, upon the waters, from the hostile earth. Thus he is considered as a friend, in fact as "creator of man" (Nu-dim-mud). His consort was called Nin-ki, mistress of the earth or Dam-gal-nun-na, great bride of the prince (Ea) or also Dam-kian-na, mistress of heaven and earth.

Lord of the underworld is *Nergal.* As a god of darkness he is not accepted into the luminous cosmic triad. The realm of his power is expressed only in the euphemistic words "land without return" (kur-nu-gi-a) or simply as the "great land" (Ki-gal), into which all men must enter at the time of their death. His proper name is derived from Ne-iri-gal, "lord of the

---

10. J. Bottéro, *StudSem I* (1958), 37, refers to the name attested in the Mari literature, Iâ-il, "Yah is God."

great city," that is, the underworld. Nergal is both a god of the dead and a god of pestilence. And since catastrophes could be interpreted as punishment from the gods, he is also an avenging god. Nergal's identification and veneration as divinity of the underworld might well be connected with the Akkadians. At his side stands his consort *Nin-ki-gal,* mistress of the great land, that is, the kingdom of the dead. As such she has a role to play in mythology. It was she who invited all the gods to a banquet. When her herald Namtâr (fate) appeared among the gods, they all stood up, excepting for Nergal who remained seated. Then Nin-ki-gal (–Ereškigal) desired his punishment. Upon Ea's advice, however, Nergal takes seven demons with him in his battle against Ereškigal. He is victorious. She offers to marry him and he thus becomes lord of the underworld. His animal is the lion. The conception of the "devil" as a lion is still evident in the Epistle of St. Peter (1 Pet. 5, 8): "He goes about like a ravenous lion, seeking someone to devour." – The principal site of his cult is the city of Gutu, whose inhabitants were transported to Samaria by the Assyrians (2 Kings 17, 25).

2) THE ASTRAL GODS

Side by side with the cosmic triad Anu – Enlil – Ea (Nergal, as god of the underworld, does not belong to this triad), there is the astral triad of sun, moon, and evening star, recognizable throughout the whole of Mesopotamia. The astralization of the Sumerian cosmic religion is to be attributed to the influence of the Semites, who came in from the desert where they had formed a first-hand acquaintance with the starry skies. The Sumerians called the moon god simply *Na-an-na,* "man in the sky." The waxing and waning of the moon were interpreted as a fight with demons. His symbol was the bull's horn, the bull's head with blue beard, or a skiff which glides across the sky. His consort is called simply Nin-gal "the great mistress." But it was under the Semitic name, Sin, that the moon god achieved his greatest triumph. It is true that the Sumerian theologians attempted to interpret this foreign name as Zu-en or En-zu, "lord of wisdom," but this does not alter the originally Semitic character of the moon god Sin.[11] We have here a further evidence of how the Sumerian and Semitic theologies fused with each other at a very early date. The principal site of the moon cult was Ur in Sumer, and Harran in Upper Mesopotamia.

Just as the day proceeds from night, the sun also proceeds from the moon. The south Semites venerated the sun as a goddess,[12] but in Mesopotamia, perhaps under Sumerian influence, it was the masculine conception which prevailed. The sun god (Sumerian: Utu, Semitic: Shamash) was considered as the son of the moon. He was presented in human form, either sitting on a throne or on the steeds of the sun. His epithets are "he who gives life" or "he who awakens the dead." Since he conquers over the powers of darkness, he is *the* hero *par excellence.* As god of light, he also becomes god of legislation and divination. The principal sites of his cult were Larsa and Sippar. His temple was called E-Bab-bar, "white house" that is, "house of the rising sun." His consort is called A-a or Aya, "sky bride."

Particularly great significance under the symbol of morning and evening star, "Venus," attaches to the Sumerian Inanna, the "mistress of the sky."[13] She corresponds to the Babylonian Ishtar, the west-Semitic ʿAštarte. Apparently, under the influence of the Sumerian "sky mistress," the evening star appears as a goddess, whereas the west-Semites and the Arabs venerate it

---

11. J. Bottéro, *StudSem I* (1958), 44-47.

12. W. Caskel, *ibid.,* 108.

13. For the divine epithets, cf., under Inninna and Ishtar, Tallqvist, *Akkadische Götterepitheta* (1938) and A. Deimel, *Sumerisches Lexikon IV.* A special grouping of ideograms. 1. *Pantheon babylonicum or Keilschriftkatalog der babylonischen Götternamen.* (1950). I. J. Gelb, "The Name of the Goddess Innin," *JNES* 19 (1960), 72-79. A marble bed discovered in Uruk (Erech) in 1939, one of the greatest masterpieces of art from the Ancient Near East, is perhaps a representation of the mother goddess Inanna – or a priestess? Illustrated in *PropWG I* (1961), 540.

as the masculine god 'Attar.[14] Just like her star, which appears as both a morning and an evening star, the goddess herself has two faces. She is, on the one hand, the goddess of love, the "mistress of love," the "queen of joy." Her city Uruk was a "city of courtesans, harlots, and strumpets." In her temple sacred prostitution was practiced. Istar is the successor to the mother divinity familiar from prehistoric times, the understanding helper of expectant and nursing mothers. Thus she is addressed by the moving and maternal epithets: "Goddess, lady, mother of mercy, who comes before the angry gods and appeases them." She was so loved by the people that she gradually replaced Antum, the wife of the sky god Anu, and finally assumed the essential traits of the supreme god himself, whereupon she was invoked as "goddess of goddesses, queen of all gods, mistress of heaven and earth!"

As evening star, Istar is the goddess of love, but as morning star she is the goddess of war. Her animal is the lion or the wolf. As war goddess, she falls in love with, for example, Sargon of Akkad, and makes him a military hero and world ruler. The favorite sites of the Istar cult were Uruk, Babel, Kis, and later Arbela; she was frequently invoked simply as "*Akkaditu*," "the lady of Akkad," or "the lady of Uruk," etc.

Among the other stars, the Pleiades were venerated as gods of second rank, the "seven" (*Šibî*). Then the planets, the "wild sheep of the sky," and in this sequence: Jupiter, Venus, Saturn, Mercury, Moon, and Sun. The fixed stars were the noble sheep shepherded by Orion, the *Sib-zi-an-na*, "the good shepherd of the sky." The twelve signs of the zodiac were first definitively established in the 5th century B.C., although their origin can be traced back into the 12th century. In later times, the expression Chaldaean is equivalent to astrologer and star-gazer. Still, we must reject the theory which holds that this astral cult or astral science was the foundation of Babylonian religion. It was not

14. J. Bottéro, *StudSem I* (1958), 40-42. M. J. Dahood, *ibid.*, 87f. W. Caskel, *ibid.*, 105f.

until during the course of the 1st century B.C. that the connection between gods and planets was more firmly established, and only in the recent era does astrology play a decisive role. The ancient times were under the rule of the cosmic gods, together with the nature divinities who enjoyed a special veneration.

3) THE NATURE DIVINITIES

From earliest times, simple man was exposed to the terrifying spectacle of the thunder storm. Thunder is God's voice, and lightning is the expression of his wrath. Whereas the Sumerian storm god Iskur has a rather insignificant role to play within the Sumerian pantheon, Hadad, the thunder god of the Amurru, becomes so important, since the time of Hammurabi, that he takes his place among the principal gods. He is a destructive element; he produces the floods and ravages the harvest. Because of his warlike character, he also belongs in the ranks of the war gods. His epithet is "horned wild bull" or "wild bull of the heaven and the earth." He is represented as standing upon a bull with a sheaf of lightning bolts in his hand. His principal cult site is Ashur, whose kings particularly like to name themselves after him. As Ba'al he makes his way into the highest rank of the Canaanite pantheon. As Jupiter Heliopolitanus of Baalbek in Lebanon, he achieves world significance even in the Roman era.

Beside the storm and thunder god, there were also several gods of fire; in fact, every river, every brook, every canal and mountain was accorded its own divine being. Among the nature divinities, those who are connected with the growth and decay of vegetation made the strongest impression. Thus there is Nin-giš-zi-da, the "lord of the true tree (of life)," Geštin-anna, "vine of the sky." Most widespread of all was the Tammuz cult. The ancient sources on Tammuz, the Sumerian Dumuzi, however, have been made to yield more information than they actually contain. Originally, Dumuzi may have been a god-king of the city Badtibira, in the fabled era before the flood.

Since the Jemdet-Nasr era, we frequently find the king represented as the "guardian and keeper of the flocks," as a fighter against the wild animals who threaten the flocks. The identification of this shepherd king with Dumuzi is, however, very uncertain. Dumuzi's fate is, at any event, closely connected with the descent into hell of the goddess of fertility, Inanna. Upon her arrival in the underworld, Inanna is completely disrobed and murdered by the mistress of the underworld, Ereshkigal. This results in the cessation of all fertility on earth. Upon the urgent request of Inanna's herald Ninshubura, Enki, king of the underworld, lets Inanna return to life. She is allowed to leave the underworld, however, only if someone can be found to take her place. Faithlessly, she chooses her formal royal beloved, Dumuzi, who must take her place and go down into the realm of the dead, where he becomes one of the princes in the underworld. This Dumuzi is often described as an annually dying and resurrecting god,[15] but in the Sumerian tradition there is no support for this view.[16] That it is his death and return which are annually celebrated at the spring New Year's Feast, in the ceremony of the "sacred wedding," is a view which had been frequently asserted, but not yet substantiated.[17]

4) THE NATIONAL GODS

It is in the evolution of the national gods that the development of Babylonian religion can best be followed. Whenever a city succeeded in asserting its supremacy over other cities, this was not only a political victory, but also a religious triumph. The ascendancy of the world empires is also an ascendancy

---

15. Thus primarily A. Moortgat, *Tammuz. Der Unsterblichkeitsglaube in der altorientalischen Bildkunst* (1949). "Grundlage und Entfaltung der sumerisch-akkadischen Kultur," *HM II* (1953), 224-260. H. Schmökel, *GAV* 12, 22, 168, 241. F. R. Kraus, *WZKM* 52 (1953), 36ff. maintains that this position is untenable.

16. W. v. Soden, "Die sumerische Kultur, Religion und Literatur," *PropWG I* (1961), 562.

17. *Ibid.*, 557.

of new gods. Thus, in the new Sumerian era (Ur III), the moon cult achieved its greatest spread and significance, but was then forced to yield its position by the Akkadian Ishtar cult. With the rise of the Amurru under Hammurabi, Marduk, the city god of Babel, ascended to the height of the pantheon. The Assyrian armies bore the banner of the god Ashur into every country, and finally, in the new Babylonian kingdom, Marduk's son Nabu was ruler of the world.

Marduk seems originally to have been a local god, but the political rise of Babel made him a universal god. The interpretation of his name has not yet been clarified.[18] Written in its Sumerian form AMAR.UTU, he was represented as "the young bull of the Sun god," that is, as son of the sun. The derivation *Mâr-du-ku,* "son of the pure abode," that is, the place where the fates are determined, already presupposes his ascendancy and is thus secondary. In his greatest period he was considered as the supreme god, determining the fates of gods and men alike. The Marduk temple in Babel was, accordingly, regarded as the center of the cosmos. The temple tower bore the name *E-temen-an-ki,* "house of the foundation of heaven and earth." This divine claim to power reached such proportions that Marduk eventually absorbed all the gods into his figure. In the Enuma-eliš epic, he has 50 names. The individual gods are only apparitions of the one great Marduk, *the* "lord" (*bêl*) *par excellence.* His consort *Ṣarpanitum,* the "silver shining," (reference to the moon?), is also invoked as "my mistress" (*bêltiya*). Marduk's animal is the Babylonian dragon, a mixed creature with the head of a serpent, the paws of a lion, and the tail of a scorpion, generally red in color.

---

18. J. Bottéro, *StudSem 1* (1958), 57ff. G. Dossin, *StudSem 2* (1959), 38, makes the very convincing proposal that Marduk entered the settled land together with the Amurru-Bedouins; this much is evident from his name alone. Marduk is to be divided *Mardu-ku,* with the honorary epithet *gu-dibir. Mardu* (Sumerian) and *dibir* (Semitic) mean "steppe, desert"; *gu-ku* means land, territory. Marduk is the God of "The desert country," and thus simply the God of the Amurru-Bedouins.

In the new Babylonian kingdom, it is Nabu, son of Marduk, who achieves such importance that he gradually forces his father from his position as one supreme god, and eventually takes over the leadership of the gods himself. His name is interpreted as "the shining one," and his star is Mercury. The new kings particularly like to name themselves after their god; for example, Nebuchadnezzar, Nabonidus; his temple stands in Borsippa, a few kilometers south of Babel. Originally, he was only the scribe among the gods, the inventor of writing; but gradually he became the god of wisdom and learning, and eventually god of the empire.

In Ashur, the same process takes place with the city god of Ashur who bears the same name, Ashur. His temple bears the presumptuous name *E'Sar-ra* (house of the omnipotence). The political changes also effected changes in theology and mythology. The heroic deeds which were recounted of Anu in the Sumerian era are now told of Marduk in the Babylonian period, and of Ashur in the Assyrian epoch.

The Mari texts have cast new light on the figure of the god Dagan, the "king of the lands." Originally, he seems to have been a west Semitic local fertility god. With the penetration of the Amurru, he managed to appropriate for himself the ancient territories of Babylonia and Assyria. The name is also attested to among the Philistines and Phoenicians. Even though he is here represented with a human head and a fish body, he must have had nothing to do with fish (*dag*) originally. The derivation from "grain" (*dagan*) also seems to be secondary.[19] At any event, he belongs to the new gods who were borne to the head of the pantheon by the new peoples.

The Indo-Arian ruling class of the Hurru venerated the Indian primary deities *Mithra, Indra,* and *Varuna,* as we can see from their personal names and later treaty texts; apparently they also venerated the storm-god *Vaya,* the sky-god *Sva,* and the lawgiver

---

19. M. J. Dahood, *StudSem I* (1958). 78-80. The hypothesis that the Greek Poseidon is to be derived from Dagan is not immediately obvious. His name would thus be compounded of *pot-*, "powerful" and *dôn-daon-dagon,* that is, the exclamatory form: "Mighty Dagan!"

Rta. The principal figure of the Hurrian pantheon was the storm-god *Teshup;* his consort was called *Hepat.* His sacred animal was the bull; his chariot is drawn by bulls who bear the names *Sheri* and *Hurri,* "day and night." His weapon is the thunderbolt. Sheaves of lightning bolts and battle axes are part of his normal array in pictorial representations. A further primary figure in the Hurrian pantheon was *Shaushga,* many of whose traits are reminiscent of Ishtar. Her sacred animal was the lion. The Hurrian pantheon is extraordinarily colorful, since Babylonian gods were also adopted.[20]

The interpenetration of many peoples and ethnic groups has left its stamp upon the Hittite pantheon. There is mention of the "thousand gods," a vast host of powers allied for offense and defense, but never properly subordinated into an orderly pantheon. Since only a few myths have come down to us and the small number of extant prayers does not express much that is characteristic about the individual gods, the great mass of Hittite divinity names remains colorless for us. Among the state divinities, the sun goddess of Arinna, taken over from the pre-Hittite population, was venerated most. Also worthy of mention is the fertility god Telepinu, likewise pre-Hittite, whose name was also borne by a king. The most valuable monument of Hittite religion is the rock relief of Jazilikaya near Boghazköy, on which the gods, standing upon animals, are represented in a procession.[21]

The religious picture of the Ancient Near East is thus a manifold and changing one. Syria-Palestine is precisely the district in which not only the political but also the religious interests of the varying peoples intermingle and interpenetrate. It is only against the background of the religions of the Ancient Near East

---

20. H. Schmökel, *Kulturgeschichte des Alten Orients,* 431. R. Dussaud, *Les religion des Hittites et des Hourites, des Phéniciens et des Syriens. Sammlung "Mana"* (Paris, 1949). W. v. Soden, *PropWG II* (1962), 55.

21. Bittel-Naumann-Otto, Yasilikaja, "Architektur, Felsbilder, Inschriften und Kleinfunde," *WVDOG 61,* 1941. M. Riemschneider, *Die Welt der Hethiter. Götterwelt und Religion.* Second edition (1955), 68-92. *AOB,* No. 337. *ANEP,* No. 537.

that the individuality of the Old Testament can really be appreciated. But since the comparison between the gods of the pagans and the one God of Israel is a confrontation that was made on Palestinian soil, it must be Palestine, in its pre-Israelite population and religions, that next will occupy our attention.

APPENDIX

ANCIENT NEAR EASTERN CHRONOLOGY

Since our knowledge of the Ancient Near East has been unbelievably advanced by the excavations of recent decades, it is important to establish a secure basis for the accompanying chronology.

1) Chronology by excavation levels (stratigraphy): The general establishment of chronology is aided by archaeological finds in various strata. When excavations in different places yield the same material, we are justified in concluding to the contemporaneity of these archaeological strata. The best point of departure for the historical identification of such strata is offered by the pottery finds. According to the manner of preparation, baked over an open fire or in a potter's oven, made by hand or turned on the potter's wheel, according to the kind of painting and the preferred motifs, we can already determine a chronology in its broader outlines.[1]

In order to determine this strata chronology more precisely, we must turn to written chronological sources, and calculations based on astronomy.

---

1. The indispensable and monumental work on this aspect of chronology is Cl. F. A. Schaeffer's *Stratigraphie comparée et chronologie de l'Asie occidentale* (*IIIe-IIe Millénaires*), 70 maps, 324 illustrations (London, 1948). P. Van der Meer, *The Chronology of Ancient Western Asia and Egypt,* second edition (Leiden, 1963). J.A.H. Potratz, *Einführung in die* Archäologie (Stuttgart, 1962): "Relative und absolute Chronologie," 154-227. A very comprehensive introduction to the chronological problem.

2) The royal lists: Berossus (Babylonian: Bêl-ussur-šu – may Bel protect him!), priest of Bel-Marduk in the principal temple of E-sag-ila in Babel, born c. 340 B.C., wrote a great historical account of his people in three books, with the title: *Babyloniaka.* The first book treats of the Babylonian cosmogony, the second presents the chronological succession of the Babylonian kings, beginning with the ten fabled kings before the flood, and ending with Alexander the Great. The work is dedicated to King Antiochus I Soter (280-260), the restorer of the Babylonian temple of Bel. In his chronology, Berossus did not make use of any cuneiform sources. His work is preserved only in fragments, in the Jewish historian Flavius Josephus, who makes frequent use of it in establishing the sources of Biblical history, and in the early Christian Church historian Eusebius. The Berossus chronology has recently been subjected to a most thorough investigation by F. Cornelius,[2] according to whom the regnal dates of Hammurabi are to be reckoned between the years 1728 and 1686 B.C. Berossus' work is written in Greek. Recent excavations, however, have unearthed many cuneiform texts, and the construction of the Ancient Near East chronology will owe much to their interpretation.

Since the peoples of the Ancient Near East had no fixed point of origin for determining their chronology (such fixed points were to be found in later history, in the various eras: Seleucid era, from 312 B.C.; Pompeian era in the individual Near Eastern cities established by Pompey; in Rome, reckoning from the foundation of the city, etc.), they needed to search for some constant point against which to reckon the passage of time.

These are the royal lists, in which the regnal years of the individual rulers were preserved. For Babylonia, there are two such lists, generally referred to as A. and B., which mutually complement each other, beginning with the first Babylonian dynasty under Sumu-abum and continuing to the year 626.[3] These lists, however, are not complete. Furthermore, it is not always clear whether or not the kings described ruled after each other or simultaneously with each other. Together with these royal lists, some of the more important events have been preserved in chronicle style. The most important document of this kind is the "Babylonian Chronicle."

---

2. The Berossus fragments have been published in collected form by C. Müller, *Fragmenta historicorum Graecorum* (Paris, 1849), pp. 495-510. A newer reworking by P. Schnabel, *Berossos und die babylonisch-hellenistische Literatur* (Leipzig, 1923), pp. 250-275. F. Cornelius, "Berossus und die altorientalische Chronologie," *Klio* 35 (1942), 1-16. "Die Chronologie des älteren Orients," *FF* 20 (1944), 75.

3. The material for the royal lists is most concisely summarized in Schmidtke, *Der Aufbau der babylonischen Chronologie* (1952). Published in a second edition, *AOT* (1926), 332. *ANET* (1955), 265.

We take one step forward in chronology with the Assyrian royal lists, which, because of their synchronization with the Babylonian kings, make it possible to arrive at a more precise identification of years. The Assyrians reckoned according to eponyms (Assyrian *limu*), that is, high government officials after whom the year was named. Since the Assyrian eponyms from 911 to 648 B.C. are known,[4] the first millennium of Ancient Near Eastern history can be considered as chronologically established. The uncertainty and fluctuation of several centuries begins in the 2nd millennium. The farther back we progress, the greater the uncertainty. The more recent discoveries have yielded a firm foundation for the chronology of the 2nd millennium. Two new Assyrian royal lists and the cuneiform texts of Mari have brought new direction to the problem.

The royal lists of Essad-Nassouhi,[5] so named after their discoverer and translator, present a complete catalogue of the Assyrian kings, beginning with Puzur-Ashur I (c. 2000 B.C.), down to the destruction of the Assyrian kingdom in the year 606 B.C. The Royal lists of Khorsabad (Dûr-Sharrukîn)[6] which were discovered at the excavations of the "Oriental Institute of the University of Chicago" in 1932/33, contained 117 Assyrian kings down to Ashur-nirari (763-746). For 79 kings the regnal years are given. On the basis of these lists, we can now date the regnal period of the great west Semitic ruler on the Assyrian throne, Shamshi-Adad I, between the years 1749 and 1717 B.C. In this calculation there is still a possible fluctuation of up to 20 years, since the regnal years of Ashur-nirari are not given, and they can be reckoned in various ways. The reign of Shamshi-Adad I is the fixed point for the Ancient Near East chronology of the 2nd millennium. The cuneiform texts of Mari [7] have succeeded in bringing this royal personage into the full light of history. He is a contemporary of the Babylonian ruler Hammurabi, and he came to the throne, not 20 years after Hammurabi, but even before him (c. 1700 B.C.).

3) Astronomical calculations: The data presented by the royal lists can now be largely confirmed by astronomical calculations. The Baby-

---

4. On the eponym lists, cf. *Reallexikon für Assyriologie II* (1938), pp. 412-457. *ANET* (1955), 274. Furthermore see E. F. Weidner, "Die assyrischen Eponymen," *AFO* (1941), pp. 308-318.

5. Essad-Nassouhi (Stambul): "Grande liste des rois d'Assyrie," *AFO* 4 (1927), 1ff. Furthermore see E. F. Weidner, "Die neue Königsliste von Assur," *AFO* 4 (1927), 11-27.

6. On the Khorsabad lists, cf. E. F. Weidner, *AFO* 14 (1944), 362 to 369. E. Cavaignac, "A propos des listes de Khorsabad," *RA* 40 (1945 and 1946), 17-26; 149-150.

7. On the chronology of Mari, cf. W. von Soden, "Das altbabylonische Briefarchiv von Mari," *WO* 1 (1948), 187-204.

lonians very early learned to observe the changing sky, not so much from a purely scientific motivation, but rather on astrological and religious grounds. The astronomical data transform our relative chronology into an absolute one. The solar eclipse recorded for the 10th year of the Assyrian king Ashur-dan III has been calculated as occurring on June 15, 763. Thus we have another fixed point of reference for the 1st millennium. For the 2nd millennium, it is the Venus tablets of King Ammizaduka, the second last ruler of the Hammurabi dynasty, a grandson of Hammurabi. These tablets record the early and late rising of the morning and evening star (Venus), for the eighth year of his reign. As we succeed in fixing this year astronomically, the relative chronology of the 2nd millennium will also be absolutely fixed by astronomy.

Since, however, the stellar configurations repeat within definite rhythms, there are also several points of departure for the Venus tablets. St. Langdon and J. K. Fotheringham, on the basis of their calculations, have established Hammurabi's regnal dates for the years 2067-2025. On the basis of the astronomical cycle, A. Ungnad proposes a number that is 275 years smaller and thus computes Hammurabi's dates as 1792-1750 B.C. But since this date contradicts the latest discoveries, Albright [8] has recently proposed a second diminution of the figures, in a secondary cycle of 64 years. According to this, Hammurabi would be dated 1728-1686 B.C. Since F. Cornelius has arrived at the same result on the basis of the Berossus lists, this newer chronology can be considered as definitively established, with the addition of a very small coefficient of uncertainty.[9]

These solar and stellar observations are further corroborated by the lunar observations. These are juridic texts which present the phases of the moon for the sake of precisely dating the beginning of the month.[10]

On the basis of these foundations in the 2nd millennium, it is possible to make some further progress into the 3rd millennium, and even to the

---

8. W. F. Albright, "Stratigraphic Confirmation of the Low Mesopotamian Chronology," *BASOR* 144 (1956), 26-30. M. B. Rowton, "The Date of Hammurabi," *JNES* 17 (1958), 97-111 decides in favor of the middle chronology.

9. The literature on the Venus Tablets: St. Langdon and J. K. Fotheringham, *The Venus-Tablets of Ammizaduqa* (Oxford, 1928). A. Ungnad, "*Die Venustafeln und das* 9. *Jahr Samsuilunas,*" In: *Mitteilungen der altorientalischen Gesellschaft XIII*, 3; 1940/17. K. Schubert, "Die altorientalischen Dynastien zur Zeit Hammurabis," *WZKM* 51 (1948), 21-23. Th. Böhl, *King Hammurabi of Babylon in the Setting of His Time* (*About 1700*) (Amsterdam, 1946).

10. J. Schaumberger, "*Die Mondfinsternisse der dritten Dynastie von Ur.*" In: *Zeitschrift für Assyriologie N. F. XV*, p. 50.

more remote past; the element of uncertainty, however, grows in proportion to the length of time involved.[11]

Since the decision on the credibility of the available data is, ultimately, a matter of scientific conscience, and since a date which seems certain to one scholar will appear questionable to another, there is still much confusion of dating in the presentation of Ancient Near East history. The following rule of thumb should be kept in mind: "Begin with the low chronology and then add 64 years on the basis of the Venus periods, in order to arrive at the date of the middle chronology. By adding another 56 years, you arrive at the dates for the high chronology."[12] Our presentation is based on the low chronology.

4) THE ATOMIC OR RADIO-CARBON CALENDAR: The progress of atomic physics has opened new possibilities for establishing chronology. The measuring of time is based on the radio-active decay of carbon. From cosmic radiation, neutrons are constantly entering our atmosphere. Here they strike upon nitrogen atoms (N-14) and alter them. This gives rise to a radio-active carbon atom, with an atomic weight of 14 (C-14), an isotope of the normal carbon (C-12). Passing through the atmosphere, this carbon enters into plants which absorb the normal carbon gasses and give off oxygen in return. This process continues as long as the plant is alive. But at the moment the plant dies, the carbon-14 begins to dissipate into radiation. This decay proceeds in accordance with regular laws. After the course of an ascertainable period of time, only half of the original material remains; this is the so-called "half life." For C-14, its duration is 5,360 years. Now if, for example, we were to ascertain the quantity of C-14 present in a piece of wood that is discovered at an excavation, it is possible to compute the "day of death" on which the ultimate decay first originated. Obviously, the problem is hampered by many factors which make for uncertainty. The radiation grows weaker over the course of the years. The outside limit must now be set at 20,000 years; by refining the technique, scientists hope to push this figure to 40,000 or 50,000 years.

---

11. E. Weidner in *AFO XV* (1951), 85-102, examines the whole of the chronological material, and with respect to the erroneous positions taken during the last three decades, he can only warn against a too hasty fixation on any chronological system. The question is still very much in flux. Weidner presents a new list of the Babylonian, Assyrian, and Hittite kings, and gives Hammurabi's dates as 1704-1662, the lowest estimate to date.

12. J. A. Potratz, *Einführung in die Archäologie*, 211. W. v. Soden, *PropWG* I (1961), 530, however, is shifting from the low chronology he formerly represented, to the middle, in his new presentation of Old Testament history.

Even though there has been much objection against this method – the numbering that resulted sometimes contradicted the archaeological facts – it still points out the way along which the uncertainties of our chronology can eventually be established on the basis of admissible evidence.[13]

---

13. A. Libby of Chicago is regarded as the inventor of the carbon test; there are also several other methods for determining dates: the fluoride test, dendro-chronology, guano chronology, pollen analysis, examination of radiation curves, etc. Cf. J. A. H. Potratz, *Einführung in die Archäologie* (Stuttgart, 1962), pp. 172-227.

SECTION THREE

CANAAN AND ITS INHABITANTS

THE middle section of the Fertile Crescent, in the course of Ancient Near East history, presented neither a political nor an ethnic unity. As might be expected from its central position, the most varied spheres of interest all crossed here. In times of strength, Egypt reached up from the south and penetrated into the Asiatic territory; from the Syro-Arabian desert came constant new waves of Bedouins into the settled land; from the north it was the Assyrians, Babylonians, Hurrians, and Hittites who sought to take possession of this land in the middle. There was already a history of several thousand years behind this country when, in its southern sector, the "land of the Bible" gradually began to form as a clearly defined picture. In the back and forth of power politics, there was a constant change of boundaries, territories, and even names. The middle section of the Fertile Crescent was, so to speak, the potter's wheel of the Ancient Near East. It can hardly be an accident that it was precisely here, this intersection point between two continents, that witnessed the revelation destined for all peoples.

CHAPTER XI

THE LAND OF THE BIBLE

LITERATURE

A chronological catalogue of the literature that refers to the geography of the Holy Land, from the year 333 to 1878 A.D. is to be found in the always valuable work of R. Röhricht, *Bibliotheca geographica Palaestinae,* Berlin 1890. Enlarged and republished by D. H. K. Amiran. 1963.

The whole Palestine literature, in systematic order, with authors and contents, from 1895-1924, is collected in P. Thomsen, *Die Palästinaliteratur. Eine internationale Bibliographie,* Leipzig, from 1908. Vol. VI (1953) continues the literature up to 1944.

Important for the knowledge of the Bible lands is the 6 vols. work of G. Dalman, *Arbeit und Sitte in Pálästina,* Gütersloh, from 1925. Also: *100 Deutsche Fliegerbilder aus Palästina,* 1925. *Jerusalem und sein Gelände,* 1930. – H. Guthe, *Palästina, Land und Leute,* 1927. – P. Karge, *Rephaim, Die vorgeschichtliche Kultur Palästinas und Phönikiens,* 1926. – R. Köppel, *Palästina, Die Landschaft in Karten und Bildern,* 1930. – M. Blanckenhorn, *Die Geologie Palästinas nach heutiger Auffassung,* 1931. – A. Bonne, *Palästina, Land und Wirtschaft,* 1933. – P. Abel, *Géographie de la Palestine,* 2 vols. 1933, 1938. – R. Gradmann, *Palästinensische Urlandschaft,* ZDPV 57 (1934), 161-185. – M. Noth, *Zur Geschichte des Namens Palästina,* ZDPV 62 (1939), 125. *Die Welt des Alten Testaments,* Berlin 1953. – Cl. Kopp, *Die heiligen Stätten der Evangelien,* Regensburg 1959.

BIBLICAL ATLASES

H. Guthe, *Bibelatlas,* Leipzig 1936. – G. E. Wright and F. V. Filson, *The Westminster Historical Atlas to the Bible,* London 1946. – J. Bright, *Biblical Geographies and Atlasses,* (Outline of biblical geography and cartography), *Interpretatio* 2 (1949), 324-336. – H. G. May, *A Remapping of the Bible World,* (Nelson's New Bible Maps), (New York 1949). – R. Köppel, *Die grosse Reliefkarte von Palästina* (in 3 Plates). – H. Bengtson and Vl. Milojcic: *Grosser historischer Weltatlas,* 1. *Part: Vorgeschichte und Altertum,* Munich 1953. Rand McNally, *Historical Atlas of the Holy Land,* edited by E. G. Kreaeling, New York. – H. G. May, *Oxford Bible Atlas,* London 1962. – *Atlante Storico della Bibbia,* edited by P. Lemaire and D. Baldi, 1955. – *Bildatlas zur Bibel,* edited by L. H. Grollenberg, Gütersloh 1958. – The student who can read Hebrew will profit from the *ATLAS YISRAEL, Atlas of Israel, Cartography, physical geography, history, demography, economics, education,* Jerusalem 1956. – M. du Buit, *Géographie de la terre sainte,* Paris 1958. (With 18 geographical maps as a supplement). – G. Eichholz, *Landschaften der Bibel,* Neukirchen 1963. (Countless color photographs.)

TRAVEL GUIDES

R. Boulanger, *Moyen-Orient, Liban-Syrie-Jordanie-Irak-Iran,* Les Guides Bleus, Paris 1956. – Elian-J. Finbert, *Israel,* Les Guides Bleus, Paris 1955. – Th. F. Meysels, *Israel,* Schwann Reiseführer, Düsseldorf, 1959. – Zev Vilnay, *The Guide to Israel,* 5th ed., Jerusalem 1962.

1) NAMES AND TERRITORIES [1]

a) THE LAND OF RETENU: In the Egyptian sources for the Middle Kingdom, the Asiatic sphere of influence is called the land of Retenu (*rtnw*) and its population are called *Amu.* Both names remain to be explained. Many scholars believed that Retenu originally referred to the city of Lod on the Palestinian coastal plateau, and was gradually extended to include the mountain country lying inland. Thus, the first city with which the Egyptians came into contact would have given its name to the whole district. In itself this could be possible; but it does not sound entirely convincing. It is more probable that the Semitic

1. Cf. the detailed article "'äräs jisra'el" in *EncMikr* I, 607-616.

root *rzn*, "prince," is the basis for the word *rtnw;* Retenu then refers to the land of the Semitic "principalities and sheikhdoms." On the basis of the Egyptian execration texts, not only Palestine on both sides of the Jordan, but also the Phoenician coast together with the Syrian hinterland are part of this territory. East of Retenu there is the land Khedem, the "eastland" of the desert dwellers. In this very ancient time it is already regular practice for the land of the Bible to be mentioned in connection with a larger geographical unit.

b) THE LAND OF THE HURRIANS: In the New Egyptian Kingdom the reference Retenu is replaced by "land of *Haru*," land of the Hurrians (Biblical: Horites). In connection with the Hyksos' coming into power, Palestine too had been invaded by Hurrian tribes who were so strong that the Egyptian war-Pharaohs simply named the country after them. According to the Anastasi papyrus the "land of the Hurrians" reached from the borders of Egypt to above Damascus.

c) THE LAND OF CANAAN: From the 15th to the 13th century, the Egyptians called their Asiatic province Canaan. The most ancient source for the occurrence of the name Canaan in the form *ki-in-a-nim* is the inscription on the base of a statue of King Adrimi of Alalah in northern Syria, towards the end of the 15th century. In the Amarna texts, we find the form *kinaḫu* or, augmented by the Hurrian local suffix *-na*, *kinaḫ-na*, *kinaḫ-ni*. The meaning of the word is not yet established. In any event, Canaan cannot be derived from *kana'* in the sense of "lowland," since the Canaan known to antiquity was, preponderantly, mountainous country. Possibly it was the purple trade, so actively carried on in Phoenicia, which gave the whole coastal strip together with the hinterland the name "purple land." [2]

---

2. On the derivation of the name, see J. Lewy, "Studies in the Historic Geography of the Ancient Near East" *Or 21* (1951), 403. The basic element *kina* related to *uknû,* lapis lazuli, blue purple. S. Moscati, however, thinks that Canaan is a non-Semitic word which originally was intended as a mockery of this meaning. *IZBG VII*, No. 1368. On the inscription of Idrimi, cf. *Bib* 33 (1952), 160, and *Or* 20 (1951), 381.

According to the Egyptian-Hittite peace treaty of 1280, Canaan formed a clearly defined political magnitude. It referred to the Egyptian province on Asiatic soil. The precise boundaries are still preserved in the Book of Numbers (34, 1-12). It is not the boundaries of the Davidic kingdom which are handed down here, but rather the boundaries of the Egyptian province of Canaan. Its northern boundary is described as a line from the Mediterranean Sea (about 50 km. north of Beirut) to Mount Hor, presumably a foothill or peak in the Lebanon range; from there the boundary runs eastward across Lebo-hamath in the valley depression between the two Lebanon ranges, as far as Hazar-enan ("fountain courts"), on the edge of the desert. The territory north of these boundaries belonged to the Hittite sphere of influence. The eastern boundary ran along the edge of the cultivated land towards the south, embracing the entire district of Damascus and Bashan. Following the Yarmuk, the boundary curved along the Jordan and ran downstream towards the south end of the Dead Sea. The southern boundary ran from the Dead Sea through the wilderness of Sin across the oasis Kadesh-Barnea, to the River of Egypt. The western boundary was formed by the Great Sea. Thus, the territory of Canaan embraced not only Palestine, but also Phoenicia, large sections of Syria, and territory east of the Jordan.

It is in this sense that the Bible also uses the name Canaan (Judg. 4, 2, 23; 5, 19; 2 Sam. 24, 7; Is. 23, 11; Prov. 31, 24). Accordingly, in the table of nations (Gen. 10, 15ff.), Canaan is called the father of many cities and many tribes. His first born was the city of Sidon, the powerful Phoenician commercial city on the coast. It follows, therefore, that the land of the Bible belongs to the territory of "greater Canaan," but is not identical with it.

d) Palestine: The original "Palestine," that is, the "Philistine land," embraced the coastal strip between Jaffa and Gaza, together with the district of the five Philistine cities. During the whole Biblical era, the name Palestine is never used to designate the land of the Bible; it rather refers to the land along the seashore, outside the tribe of Israel. It was not until the Romans, after the collapse of the Bar-Kochba revolt (135 A.D.), in an effort to eradicate the Jewish name, annexed the former province of Judea to Syria, and called it Syria-Palestine, that is, Palestinian Syria, as distinguished from Greater Syria. The Christian authors used the name Palestine for the Bible land only from the beginning of the 4th century. Jerome still speaks of the "land of Judea, which is now called Palestine." [3] This has been preserved as the common name down to our modern day, and it will no doubt continue to be used in the scientific literature, even though the land of the Bible is now divided between the states of Israel and Jordan.

e) THE PROMISED LAND ISRAEL: God already promised the Patriarch Abraham the land that he was traveling through. Hence we speak of the land of promise, or the promised land. The boundaries of this land far surpass the more narrow limits of Palestine. It reaches from Egypt to the great river, the Euphrates, and thus embraces the whole middle of the Fertile Crescent. The land of Israel in the more narrow sense, was understood, in the times of the kings, as the territory that extends from "Dan to Beersheba," a relatively small country which is only some 240 km. in length. Measuring the distance from the Mediterranean Sea to the outermost inhabited margin of the Syrian desert, we arrive at a distance of 150 km. The territory in which the greater part of Old Testament history was enacted thus embraces an area of only 34,000 square kilometers.

In this tiny territory there are great contrasts, with respect both to climate and landscape as well as history. Crossing the country at the geographical latitude of Jerusalem, from west to east, we find at the Mediterranean Sea a fruitful plain, blessed with abundant precipitation, which almost abruptly passes into a rolling hill country, reaching a height of more than 1,000 meters in the Ephraemite Mountains. Towards the east, the mountain range falls off abruptly towards the Jordan trench,

3. *EncMikr* I, 614.

which, at Jericho, reaches a depth of 250 meters below sea level, with almost tropical climate and vegetation. The land east of the Jordan is essentially a plateau, which, because of the precipitous descent to the Jordan valley, gives the impression of a mountain range. Proceeding from northern Palestine towards the south, we encounter the same contrasting landscape. Even from the lake of Gennesaret we can see the snowcapped peak of Mt. Hermon, with its alpine character. Progressing further to the south, we see the mountain range sinking, turning into plains and valleys, and, in the south, eventually emerging as a steppe. The character of this basic Palestinian landscape essentially dictates the course of its history. Their geography forces the individual parts of the country to develop in different directions. Only a towering royal personality like David succeeded in forging a unity of this country, from the Great Sea to the east Jordan steppe, from Hermon deep into the desert of Juda, and creating a united state. When this crystalization point was lacking, the individual tribes each began to pursue their private interests, and the territory fell back into its original form.

2) THE GEOLOGICAL EVOLUTION OF PALESTINE [4]

The foundation of the Palestinian continent is formed by the sea depositions which belong to the Jura and Cretaceous group. The lowest stratum, which is evident in the Jordan trench, belongs to the Jura. This is followed by the Nubian sandstone, which belongs to the Cretaceous, and is visible in certain areas of the Jordan valley (*Nahr-ez-Zerqa* – the blue river).

The primary element in the Palestinian mountain ranges is formed of the strata of upper Cretaceous, chiefly the mighty stratum of Cenoman, 600 meters on an average, a hard limestone

4. For the study of Palestinian geology, there are many excellent maps available. For the Jordan area, cf. the three large pages in wall-map format published by A. M. Quennell, *Geological Map of Jordan.* An accompanying key in *A Handbook of the Geology of Jordan* (Jerusalem, n.d.). For the Israelite section, the large *Atlas Yisra'el* III, 1-2; maps with elevation lines and ten cross-section pictures (Jerusalem, 1956).

which the flowing water has carved into deep, canyon-like valleys.

Above the Cenoman rests a stratum of Turon and the uppermost stratum of the Cretaceous formation, the Senon, which lies exposed in large areas of Palestine, on the eastern slopes of the Judean and Samaritan Mountains. Senon is a blinding white limestone, very soft and ripply, with strata of flint imbedded in it.

In the Tertiary Era (Oligo-Mio-Pliocene), the volcanic disturbances of the Pliocene covered the Palestinian landscape (*Gebel ed-Druz*) and the northern third of the land east of the Jordan with a stratum of basalt. The volcanic lava, at the southern end of the Lake of Gennesaret, also penetrated across the Jordan furrow towards the west.

Syria-Palestine owes its present form to the great tectonic catastrophe of the Tertiary Period, in which meridional depressions, folds, dislocations, and fractures combine to produce the present features of the landscape.

One of these depressions split the Lebanon Mountain range, so that today it presents the appearance of a double range, whose western branch, Lebanon proper, reaches a height of 3,089m in its northern peaks, whereas the Anti-Lebanon, running parallel to it in the east, attains its highest elevation in the great Hermon 2,814m, to the south. The two mountain ranges are separated by a valley settling, Coele-Syria (*Beqa'*)[5] which reaches its highest elevation at Ba'albek which thus forms the watershed. This is the source of two rivers, one of which, the Leontes (*Nahr el-Litani*), forced into a deep gorge, flows towards the south, then turns at right angles and breaks through the neighboring mountain range, to enter into the sea somewhat north of Tyre. The other, the Orontes (*Nahr el-Kebir* – the great river), maintains its northerly direction along a much longer course, with considerable meandering, then, before mouthing

---

5. E. de Vaumas, "La fracture syrienne et le fossé palestinien," *RB* 54 (1947), 370-387. J. Angénieux, *Le problem structural de la Beqaa. A propos de la "Réinterpretation du fossé syrien" par E. Vaumas.* Mélanges de l'Université St. Josef Beyrout 27, 153-166. E. Bikermann, "La Coelé-Syrie. Notes de géographie historique," *RB* 54 (1947), 256-268.

on the sea, also turns towards the west where it receives the waters of the Apri (*Afrin*) descending from the Taurus, and empties into the sea south of Seleucia.

At the southern end of the Anti-Lebanon (at the Great Hermon), begins the second depression, which is much more characteristic. It forms a crevasse which runs in an almost perfect southerly direction, and which has borne the plateau downward, deep under the sea level of the Mediterranean; at the present-day Dead Sea, it reaches its greatest depth – the lowest spot on the entire continent – then, in the course of its further extension towards the south, rises to a height of 240m above sea level, from which point it once more begins to sink and eventually passes into the Gulf of Aqaba on the Red Sea.

This crevasse was at one time joined to the Mediterranean Sea, as the various stratifications clearly indicate, so that the Palestinian Mountains towered up like precipitous cliffs and islands from the sea. When the face of the land later changed, this connection with the Mediterranean Sea was broken off, and the Jordan depression now forms only an inland sea which, however, since its water intake did not counterbalance the evaporation, grew smaller and smaller. This is how the Jordan valley came to its present form and features.

3) THE GEOGRAPHIC DIVISIONS OF PALESTINE

The geographical divisions of Palestine are determined by its geological evolution. The Jordan Trench cuts the land into two sharply divided sections, east of the Jordan and west of the Jordan.[6]

---

6. Cf. Aemilian Schöpfer, *Geschichte des AT*. sixth edition 1923, 26ff.: "Schauplatz der biblischen Geschichte, Palästina und seine Nachbarländer." M. Noth, *Die Welt des Alten Testaments. Geographie Palästinas,* second edition (1953), 1-82. M. du Buit, *Géographie de la Terre Sainte*. 18 maps (Paris, 1958).

A) *The Land West of the Jordan*

a) THE MOUNTAIN AND HILL COUNTRY: A cursory examination of the map of Palestine shows that Galilee belongs to a spur of the Lebanon mountain range. Next, comes the Plain of Jezreel or Esdrelon, south of which the mountain recommences. With reference to the territories settled by the old tribes, we speak of the mountains of Ephraim and Judah, or the mountains of Samaria and Judaea.

The mountains of Galilee present two distinct sections on the basis of differences in physical appearance; the northern part forms a more closed mountain chain, containing the highest mountains in the country, while southern Galilee forms a more hilly landscape. In lower Galilee is situated the city of Nazareth, built into a gentle valley like an amphitheater, with the great Mount Tabor (probably: "heights, hill") rising majestically to the southeast.[7]

The two mountain ranges situated south of the Plain of Jezreel are not sharply separated from each other; the mountains of Samaria are, to a certain degree, a northern continuation of the mountains of Judah. In Judah, the mountain ridge runs in an almost southerly direction, much closer to the Jordan than to the sea coast. Precipitous and deeply eroded ravines run in the direction of the Jordan and the Dead Sea, while, in the direction of the Mediterranean, the mountain range sinks more gently and in slow degrees down into the plain. The mountains of Samaria do not have this regularity of formation; the mountain ridges run in different directions; between the mountains there are occasional deep basins from which the water cannot find an outlet.

The mountains of Samaria, also called the Mountains of Ephraim after the tribe of that name, are divided into a northern and southern section, the boundary between them being the valley of Schechem, so that Ebal and Gerizim, can be considered as

---

7. D. Winton Thomas, "Mount Tabor, the Meaning of the Name," *VT* 1 (1951), 229.

the boundary pillars of the two mountain chains. In the valley between the two lay the ancient city of Schechem, famous both in the days of the Patriarchs and in the later history of Israel. Schechem was the middle of the first Israelite kingdom, in the days of the Judges; Schechem witnessed the national assembly which led to the split of the kingdom; Schechem was the first capital of the Northern Kingdom; later it became the principal possession of the religious sect of the Samaritans, who had their sanctuary on Mt. Gerizim. On the location of the ancient city, after its destruction, the magnificent city of Flavia Neapolis was built, of which the present-day Arabic city of Nablus is still reminiscent. North of the Schechem valley, on a round mountain hill, in the middle of a fertile valley, lay the city of Samaria, founded by King Omri, and raised to the dignity of capital city of the Northern Kingdom. Since there are no springs on the mountain, the city had to secure its water supply by a system of cisterns. Herod the Great rebuilt this city and named it Sebaste, which still survives in the name of the modern village on that location, Sebastiyeh.

The mountains of Ephraim branch towards the northwest into Mt. Carmel which sweeps down straight to the sea, and towards the northeast into the mountain range of Gilboa.[8] Between these mountains, in the south, and the Galilean hill country in the north, extends the Plain of Jezreel (also called Esdrelon, Plain of Megiddo, or the great plain), in the form of a triangle, watered by the Kishon. This plain was of the greatest strategical importance. It was the crossroads for a number of important routes, including the commercial and military highways between Egypt and Babylon. This area alone, from all of Palestine, offers sufficient room for the development of large bodies of troops and the deployment of war chariots. From the most ancient times, it has been the arena for bloody and decisive battles. The plain gets its name from the cities of Jezreel and Megiddo, two very

---

8. Apparently derived by dissimilation from *gibboa'*, rough, uneven territory": L. Köhler, *ThZ* 2 (1946), 314.

important strategical points of support. The Plain of Megiddo is *the* battle field of Scripture. The Book of Revelations (16, 16) locates the decisive battle in the Apocalyptic war at Armageddon (*har-Megiddo* – Mountain of Megiddo).

The mountains of Judah, proceeding towards the south, can be divided into three sections. The peaks of the southern and northern sections rise to more than 1,000 m., while the middle range, by way of comparison, shows evidence of a certain settling, with an average height of only 750 meters. In this area is situated Jerusalem, since David's time the capital of the kingdom, and two hours south of Jerusalem, in a very fertile region, the city of Bethlehem, David's city and the birthplace of Christ. Seven hours further south is Hebron, made holy by the sojourn of the patriarchs and their family burial grounds. It was here that David, as king of Judah, first maintained his residence, after the death of Saul; it was here that Absalom had himself acclaimed king; later Hebron was one of the capital cities of the Idumaeans and today, after Mecca, it is the greatest sanctuary of Islam. Further to the south lay the border city of Beer-sheba, which means "well of the seven," or "fountain of the oath."

b) THE COASTAL PLAIN: The strip of coast land between the mountains of the west Jordan country and the Mediterranean Sea is divided into two unequal sections by Mt. Carmel jutting out far into the sea. North of Carmel extends the Plain of Acco, which grows constantly narrower as it approaches Phoenicia, until it is abruptly broken by the Ras en-Naqura standing far out against the sea. The plain south of Carmel is flanked by the mountains of Ephraim and Judah, towards which a gently pitched row of foothills gradually rises. From Mt. Carmel to Jaffa, it is called the Plain of Sharon, southwards, towards Gaza it is called the Shepelah (low country). The Shepelah gradually passes over into the Negeb, the "southland," which yields an abundant harvest if it is sufficiently irrigated – there is an adequate water supply.

c) The Jordan valley: The Jordan[9] today, *Sheri'at el-kebire* (the great river), rises from a series of mountain rivers which come from the southern and western slopes of Mt. Hermon. It then flows through a plain which has marshy stretches, and immediately empties into a lake some 6 km. in length, the *Bahret el-huleh* (Lake Huleh), 2 m. above sea level, which is a dry bed today. South of this lake it has to cut its way through a bar of basalt, which has been formed across the Jordan Trench at right angles. After making its way through this bar, the Jordan flows into the "Lake of Tiberias" (*Bahret tabariyeh,* named after the most important Roman city on its shore) or the Sea of Gennesaret (*kinneret* - harp?). It is 21 km. in length; its greatest width is some 12 km. On its western shores there is a small fertile alluvial plain, *el ghuwêr* ("the small lowland"). For the remainder of its course, on its east, west, and northwest sides, it is bounded immediately by the rising mountain range.

Between the southern end of the Lake of Gennesaret, and the northern end of the Dead Sea, a direct distance of 105 km., we have that part of the Jordan Trench which today is simply called *el-ghôr,* the "low place." While the eastern wall of the Ghor is essentially made up of a single, and apparently vertical, geological dislocation line, along which the East Jordan Mountain Range is channeled by the Jordan Trench, the West Jordan Mountain plateau is very irregularly sunken in several levels and rolling ravines as it approaches the Jordan Trench, so that the western wall of the Ghor forms a very fluctuating line. South of the Lake of Gennesaret, the Ghor is only 3-4 km. wide, but then widens 12 km. towards the west, forming the Bay of Beth-Shan (*Tell el Ḫosn*). Approximately half-way between Gennesaret and the Dead Sea the narrowest point is reached (3 km.). Then, immediately south of the confluence of the *Nahr-ez-zerqa,* after a precipitous mountain ridge (*qarn ṣarṭabe*) constricts the Jordan

---

9. "Jordan" is probably not to be derived from the Semitic root *yârad* ("descend") but should be regarded as a name transfer from Crete, and the river Yardanos, which is also not a proper name, but means simply "stream, river": C. H. Gordon, *Or* 21 (1952), 383.

valley, the mountain range recedes and from there to the Dead Sea the Ghor is at its widest, measuring some 20 km. from west to east.

The Jordan twists and turns countless times along its course. A bank of luxuriant vegetation, *ez-zôr,* accompanies the sinuous course of the river. Between the river course proper and the Jordan Plain, the Ghor, extends a section of marly ground, a few hundred meters in width, deeply furrowed by erosions, which the Jordan floods in its annual spring inundations (towards the end of April or the beginning of May). The Jordan Plain itself, towards its southern end, is a desert wilderness for lack of precipitation, containing only a few isolated oases, such as Jericho. Only a very small section of the Ghor, immediately south of the Lake of Genneseret, is arable land.[10]

d) The Dead Sea: The lake into which the Jordan empties is called, in the Bible, the Salt Sea (Gen. 14, 3), "The sea of Arabah" (Deut. 3, 17); the name "Dead Sea" is a later innovation; the Arabs call it the sea of Lot (*Bahr el-Lut*). This remarkable body of water is 76 km. long and 15.7 km. across at its widest point. Its somewhat fluctuating water level lies, at present, some 352 m. below sea level. A tongue of land jutting out from the east divides it into two sections of quite varying size and depth. The larger (northern) section reaches a depth of almost 400 m., while the southern part is only a shallow salt lagoon, ranging in depth from half a meter to, at the most, 4 meters. The water contains much more salt, and much more acrid salts than does the sea water and it is thus also significantly greater in density.

Since there is no exit for its waters, the water carried by the Jordan and its other rivers must necessarily evaporate, while the mineral elements remain behind. The salt content changes according to time and place, but it generally increases in proportion to its distance from the mouth of the Jordan. There is also much salt in the land surrounding the Dead Sea. Thus,

---

10. M. Noth, *Die Welt des AT,* 2nd. ed. (1953), 11ff.

for example, the lowest stratum, some 34 to 35 m., of the *Gebel Usdum,* which lies along the southwest shore, consists of almost pure bluish rock salt, which is protected from being dissolved by rainfall by the gypsum-impregnated Cretaceous marl which has formed a layer above it. On the eastern side of this ridge, 11 km. in length, where the rock salt is exposed, vertical fissures have been formed, together with several stone pillars, which the Arabs call "*bint šēyẖ*" (daughters of Sheikh Lot).

The very peculiar natural phenomenon which the Dead Sea and its surrounding territory displays are all connected with its low position, and, no doubt, also with its evolution. Many authorities were of the opinion that the Dead Sea, together with the whole geological formation of the Ghor, did not develop until historical times (after the destruction of the Pentapolis), by the collapse of the subterranean hollows, which caused an abrupt sinking of the landscape, and thus the Jordan originally found its way to the Red Sea, flowing through the southern Arabah. But the significant rise in terrain towards the south (the watershed of the Arabah is 240 m. above sea level), the direction of the secondary valleys in the Arabah, etc., make it certain that the Dead Sea, and the entire geological trench of the Jordan Valley, already existed in prehistoric times; thus there never was a connection with the Gulf of Aqaba. Geological investigation shows that the entire sinking of the Jordan valley is the result of the formation of several parallel fissures, one long vein gradually settling between them. The various well-defined terraces along the shore, as well as the salt deposits in Gebel Usdum show that the Dead Sea, as a result of the frequently repeated lengthy periods of alternating moist and dry climate (the so-called Pluvial Periods, which correspond to the European Glacial and Inter-Glacial Periods), has contained a varied amount of water.

B) *The Land East of the Jordan* (*Transjordan*)

The land east of the Jordan, a spur of the Anti-Lebanon, is a mountainous strip mixed with high plateaus; it stretches from the great Hermon to the mountains of Edom towards the south. Three rivers, flowing from the east, divide the territory into several sections, which also display a variety of physical characteristics. These rivers are the Yarmuk (*Šeriat el-Menadire*), which gathers its waters from the mountains east of the Lake of Genneseret, maintains a south-westerly course, and flows into the Jordan south of this Lake; the Jabbok (*ez-zerqa*), and the Arnon (*el-Mujib*) which flows directly into the Dead Sea. The southern boundary of the land east of the Jordan is formed by the salt brook which empties into the southern tip of the Dead Sea, separating the country east of the Jordan from Edom. The sections of Transjordan bordered by these rivers have their own names in Scripture; but it is not always the same territory that is meant. The reason for this is to be found in the fact that these names are actually the names of the states and peoples which have changed their territorial location and extension in the course of time. From north to south, we can distinguish three such territories: Bashan, Gilead, divided into north and south Gilead, and Moab.

Bashan occurs first as the name for the country ruled by the Amorite king Og (Num. 21, 33). It is the northernmost section of Transjordan, bounded on the north by the Great Hermon and the Plain of Damascus, and on the south by the Yarmuk. Towards the east this territory has a significantly greater extension than the southern districts, which are hemmed in by the Arabian Desert. Bashan owes its physical characteristics to an immense volcanic activity which built its mountains from basalt and covered the flat areas with streams of lava. This also explains its extraordinary fertility, which is indicated already in its name (*bāšān* - fat). There is great physical diversity; Bashan is a mixture of mountains, plateaus, and plains, and thus contains several sharply distinguished districts.

The northernmost district of the country was Geshur and Maaca, in the neighborhood of the Great Hermon. The western part, modern Golan (*Gaulanitis*), is made up of a mountain range which gradually levels towards the south, dropping down in a series of gentle steps towards the Jordan and the Lake of Gennesaret. Towards the east rises the plateau of En-Nurka (apparently the territory of *Batanaea*). Towards the southwest is the extensive mountain range of Hauran (*Auranitis*), which today is called Gebel ed-Druz. Towards the northwest is the plateau of El-Lega (place of refuge, *Trachonitis*), covered with lava, a region very difficult to reach because of its wild and stony character, and thus feared, from ancient times, because of the robber hordes who made their stronghold there.

South of the Yarmuk rises the land and mountain range of Gilead. The name is used with different meanings. In its broadest sense it means the whole of Transjordan, insofar as it was inhabited by Israelites, and in its narrowest sense it refers to the district between the rivers Yarmuk and Jabbok; most frequently it is used to designate the whole territory from the Yarmuk down to the Arnon and thus also includes a section of Moab. In this sense, Gilead consists of two sections divided by the Jabbok (cf. Deut. 2, 12, 13; Josh. 12, 2). The northern part of Gilead, in the strictest sense, the modern-day *Gebel Ağlûn,* the *Galaaditis* of Greco-Roman times, is a plateau which reaches an elevation of approximately 1,000 m. towards the south; the southern section is called *el-Belqa*ʿ.

The mountains of Moab: the name designates a people derived from one of Lot's sons, and then the kingdom ruled over by the Moabite kings; thus, as the designation of a territory, it is not a fixed area.

Since the descendants of Ammon had settled to the north, and those of Moab to the south of the Arnon, Moab originally signified the territories south of the Arnon to the southernmost point of the Dead Sea, where the land of Edom begins, separated from Moab by the Salt Brook. "For Arnon is the boundary of Moab, dividing the Moabites and the Ammonites" (Judg. 11, 18). Later, however, Moab spread over the Arnon towards the north; even the district across from Jericho is called "the fields of Moab," so that Moab refers to all the country east of the Dead Sea. In this sense, Moab is divided into two sections by the

Arnon River and occupies that section of the high land on the eastern shore of the Dead Sea which belongs to the Arnon River system. The mountains of Moab, in three precipitous steps, rise to a height of 800 to 1,240 m. It is a plateau heavily fissured with ravines that empty into the Dead Sea, a plateau above which the mountains do not extend to any great height. The mountain ridge runs towards the east, barely perceptible where it crosses the plateau.

C) *Palestine's Neighbors on the South*

Edom is the country which extends south from Palestine down to the Gulf of Aqaba. The basin of Arabah divides the district into two parts, an eastern and a western section. The eastern section – the mountain range of Hor, later known as *se'ir* – is a continuation of the Moab range, and thus the southernmost part of the spur which extends from the Great Hermon throughout the whole of Transjordan. But in its physical characteristics, the mountains of Edom are different from the mountains of Moab. Whereas the Moab range falls steeply towards the Dead Sea, the Edom mountains rise towards the west in three fairly broad steppes. Towards the east, on the other hand, and particularly in the southern section, it passes over into the desert in one broad steppe. The western range rises from the Arabah much more gradually, so that its ridge rises farther from the low country than the eastern range. The northernmost section is very fertile (*Palestina salutaris*), while the western section is made up of absolutely unproductive and inaccessible rock, an obvious contrast to the fertility of the Promised Land.

Arabia (*'arab-'erab*), as used in the Old Testament, refers to those districts which border Palestine on the south or southwest; it is the Greek and Roman writers who first use the word to designate the famous Asian Peninsula we know today. The greater part of modern Arabia was unknown to the ancients, and even today Arabia is a proportionately little explored country. The interior of the peninsula is, particularly in the south, a district of shifting sands (*Ruba'el hali* – the empty quarter), and then the hilly countryside *Neğd* and the desert *Nufud* gradually arise, to the north, going over into the Syrian desert east of Palestine. Arabia is thus, for the greatest part, a country of nomad peoples, so that Arab, in Scripture, is equivalent to desert-dweller or steppe-dweller. Urban culture, in Arabia, developed only along the coastal strips protected by marginal mountain ranges, particularly along the southern shore, which witnessed, even in remote antiquity, the activity of tiny, but flourishing, urban centers.

The classical writers distinguish several districts: the Arabia desert (*Arabia deserta*), the Syro-Arabian desert, the fortunate Arabia (*Arabia felix*), the country of Yemen in the southeast; rocky Arabia (*Arabia petraea*), the land which stretches from the Dead Sea towards the south, named after the rock city of Petra (*Sela* - rock). This partly overlapped with the Edomite district; but its continuation is also counted in, the Sinai peninsula between the Suez Gulf (*sinus hieropolitanus*) and the Gulf of Aqaba (*sinus aelaniticus*). The southernmost section of the peninsula is occupied by a mighty mountain range, from which spurs branch out towards the northwest and the northeast, along the coast and the Arabah, between which lies an extensive plateau, the desert of Sur in the west, and the desert of Paran in the east. According to tradition, the mountain of the Ten Commandments, Sinai or Horeb, belongs to this southern range; it is generally identified as the Gebel Musa.

The great significance of Arabia, both in secular history and in the history of religion, lies in the area of ethnography. Arabia is the home of the Semitic peoples; in the course of Ancient Near East history new waves of Semitic immigrants constantly set out from here, flooding over the surrounding cultivated land between the two rivers, and towards the west, and giving the impetus to new periods of history.

CHAPTER XII

THE INHABITANTS OF CANAAN IN PRE-ISRAELITE TIMES

LITERATURE

R. Köppel, *Untersuchungen über die Steinzeit in Palästina-Syrien,* (Rome 1933). – C. Watzinger, *Denkmäler Palästinas, eine Einführung in die Archäologie des Heiligen Landes*: Vol. I (1933), Von den Anfängen in der Altsteinzeit bis zum Ausgang der israelitischen Königszeit (40 Tables, 80 Illustrations); Vol. II (1935), Von der assyrischen Besetzung bis zur arabischen Eroberung. – W. Otto, "Phönikien, Palästina und Kypros," *Handbuch der Archäologie,* (Munich 1939), 797-848. – E. Kalt, *Biblische Archäologie,* (1934). A. G. Barrois, *Manuel d'archéologie biblique,* 2 Vols., (Paris 1939 und 1953). – C. Kopp, *Grabungen und Forschungen in Palästina,* (Köln 1939). – A. Bea, "La Palestina preisraelitica, storia, popoli, cultura, *Bibl 24* (1943), 231-260. – Ch. C. McCown, *The Ladder of Progress in Palestine,* A Story of Archaeological Adventure, (London 1943). – H. Th. Bossert, *Altsyrien,* (Tübingen 1951). Equivalent to a small library, with 1470 illustrations. – W. F. Albright, *Von der Steinzeit zum Christentum,* (Bern 1948). – "Syrien, Phönizien und Palästina," *HM II* (1953), 331-348: "Vorgeschichte, Bronzezeit und Frühgeschichte Israels." – *The Archaeology of Palestine,* (Harmondsworth 1956[2]). – "Die Religion Israels" in *Lichte der archäologischen Ausgrabungen,* (Munich-Basel 1956). – A. Jirku, *Die Ausgrabungen in Palästina und Syrien,* (Halle 1956). – *Die Welt der Bibel,* Fünf Jahrtausende in Palästina-Syrien, Grosse Kulturen der Frühzeit, (Stuttgart 1957). – G. E. Wright,

Biblische Archäologie, (Göttingen 1958). – *An Introduction to Biblical Archæology,* (London 1960). – V. Maag, "Syrien-Palästina," *Kulturgeschichte des Alten Orients,* hrgb. von H. Schmökel, (Stuttgart 1961), 448-475: Vorgeschichte, Bronze und Eisenzeit.

Since the excavations are constantly bringing new material to light which could lead to the correction of interpretations and hypotheses that are currently held, it is indispensable for the serious student to continue his investigations in the periodicals referred to at the beginning of this section.

1) STONE AGE IN PALESTINE

Since France first took the lead with its rich discoveries in the investigation of prehistoric cultures, in recent decades the Ancient Near East, and thus also Palestine, has come to occupy a place of exceptional interest.[1]

In terms of Alpine geology, scholars are accustomed to distinguish four Glacial Periods (Gunz-Mindel-Riss-Wurm) and three Inter-Glacial Periods (Gunz-Mindel; Mindel-Riss; Riss-Wurm). These European Glacial Periods have their counterparts in the Palestinian Pluvial Periods, together with their Inter-Pluvial Periods. Scholars, however, warn against a too schematic interpolation of European concepts into the Near East.[2] The glaciers furnished a yardstick for the European division; though there were no glaciers in Palestine, it is still possible to read the rhythm of the ages in the river terraces (Jordan, Orontes, and Litanni). Up to the present time, however, this method has yielded insufficient results. The most reliable time table for prehistoric Palestine might well be the coastal dunes with their caverns.[3] This line of investigation has demonstrated the existence

---

1. An outline view of the older finds in P. Karge, *Rephaim. Die vorgeschichtliche Kultur Palästinas und Phöniziens* (Paderborn, 1925). A new position is outlined in the article on the Stone Age (together with abundant illustrations) in *EncMikr* I (1955), 667-696.

2. L. Picard, *ZDPV* 55 (1932), 232. On the Glacial Age chronology, cf. J. A. H. Potratz, *Einführung in die Archäologie* (Stuttgart, 1962), 173ff.

3. M. Pfannenstiel, *Das Quartär der Levante. I. Teil: Die Küste Syriens.*

of a strong Pluvial Period corresponding to the Third Glacial Age (Riss); it was followed by a weaker Post-Pluvial Period (corresponding to the Wurm Glacial Age), and gradually passed over into historical time with moderate climatic fluctuations – the greatest aridity occurring in the Middle Stone Age (Mesolithic).

1) OLD STONE AGE: The most ancient artifacts are generally held to go back into the second Inter-Glacial Period (350,000 to 230,000),[4] which lasted the longest. But the history of civilization proper [5] cannot be clearly traced in the Syro-Palestinian area until the time of the last Inter-Glacial Period (180,000-120,000). Discoveries in the open air, such as *coups de poing* and sounding devices of flint, show that man was in a position to move freely in what was then a tropical climate. He lived by hunting and by gathering food from plants. When the climate grew worse, in the last Glacial Age (120,000-20,000), he withdrew into caves. The remains of human habitation in the caves forms the most valuable material for the knowledge of this early age. In the year 1934/35, in a cave at Gebel Qafzeh near Nazareth, skeletal remains of 5 men were uncovered, related to the European Neanderthal type. In 1923, in Wadi 'Amud, the "valley of the pillars" near Capernaum, 10 skeletons of men, women, and children of the same race were discovered.[6] This type of human is characterized by a low, recessive forehead, and protruding

---

1953. Since there were no Glacial Periods in the South, the chronology can be determined on the basis of the fluctuations of the Mediterranean. Drilling, connected with the construction of oil pipe systems, has yielded abundant material. N. Shalem, "La stabilité du climat en Palestine," *RB 58*, 54-74.

4. On the appearance of man in the first interval period, cf. W. F. Albright, *Archaeology* (1951), 51ff.

5. V. Maag, "Syrien-Palästina, Vorgeschichte," In *Kulturgeschichte des AO.* 448ff.

6. R. Köppel, "Das Alter der neuentdeckten Schädel von Nazareth," *Bibl 16* (1935), 58. A. Keith, *Researches in Prehistoric Galilee, a Report on the Galilee Skull* (London, 1927). Published also in *PEQ 63* (1931), 165; 64 (1932), 42.

bone structure above the eyes. The discovery of animal remains testifies to his manner of life. We see him in battle with rhinoceros, hippopotamus, elephant, and aurochs (bison), animals which have continued to live into historical times. The *homo galilaeensis* is very closely related to the Neanderthal type, although he is not so specialized as his European relative. Whether or not this is proof of an immigration from east to west, with developing specialization of the racial characteristics, must remain a question. But at any event, it does point to the bridge function of the Ancient Near East.

In the various caves along the precipitous sides of Mt. Carmel, in addition to the Neanderthal type described above, excavation has yielded skeletons of the Cro-Magnon type, an early stage of the present-day European (c. 70,000). This man is known as Carmel man or *Homo Carmelitanus.*[7] The stone tools are already highly advanced. Side by side with the *coup de poing* we find stone chisels, scrapers, daggers, and knives; there are also lance heads and arrow heads. Pierced sea shells were worn as ornaments or as amulets.

2) MIDDLE STONE AGE: Further south along the coast, some 40 km. east of Tel-Aviv (Jaffa), we find the caves of *Wadi-Natuf.* The lowest excavation levels yield remains of Palestinian Neanderthal man; the peculiar characteristics of the tools in the second level required the formation of a special culture period, the Natufian (c. 8000 B.C.). The stone tools were highly advanced; there were also tools and instruments of bone. Man, at this age, is no longer merely a food-gatherer; he has learned to use cutting instruments, such as stone sickles, with which he can harvest the free growing fruit. In this era man domesticated his first household animal, the dog, whose early ancestors belong to a species

---

7. R. Köppel, "Die neuentdeckten Neandertalmenschen von Athlit," *Bibl.* 13 (1932), 358-362; 15 (1934), 419-436. The standard work on the excavations is Garrod-Bate, *The Stone Age of Mount Carmel, Excavations at Wadi el Mughara,* Vol. I (Oxford, 1937); Vol. II, *ibid.,* (1939), published by A. Keith and Ch. C. McCown.

of jackal which has died out. Natufian man bears the essential characteristics of the later Mediterranean race, doliocephalic and short in stature; he thus forms the basic stock for the later Semito-Hamites, who could hardly have been sharply distinguishable, at that time, either racially or linguistically.[8]

3) THE LATE STONE AGE: It is not only the mountain country of Galilee, the mountains of Carmel, and the Mediterranean coast whose caves have yielded testimony to the life and activity of prehistoric man in Palestine; he has left traces of his fight for existence in the mountain country of Judah and in the Jordan Plateau. The most significant discoveries were yielded by the cave of *Wadi el Khareitûn,* 10 km. southeast of Bethlehem. From the name of the excavations at Tahune near Bethlehem, the whole culture is called Tahunian (6000-4500 B.C.). This "Bethlehem man" completed the step from food-gatherer to hunter and village-builder.[9] The oldest levels of Jericho show the same characteristics: terra cottas of sheep, bulls, doves, as well as phallus, and also the round plan for the temple and its surrounding dwellings, in which wall paintings were discovered — this already determines the basic type of later Palestinian culture. In Jericho, the step from village to city was taken in the 6th millennium.[10] Jericho is the oldest walled city which has been

---

8. The caves in Wadi Natuf were already discovered by Mallon in 1925, who granted the excavation rights to the British School of Jerusalem. Dorothy Garrod has been continuing the excavations since 1928. The excavation account is in *PEQ 60* (1928), 182-185.

9. The excavations around Bethlehem were conducted by the French Consul in Jerusalem, Neuville, under the supervision of the Paris Palaeontological Institute. A concise account in Köppel, *Bibl 15* (1934), 58-73; Neuville, *RB 43* (1934), 237-259; de Vaux, *RB 53* (1946), 99-124. Settlements from the Late Stone Age, prior to the use of pottery, were discovered in the neighborhood of Petra. Excavation account of Diana Kirkbride, *RB 67* (1960), 235-238; *PEQ* 92 (1960), 136-140.

10. V. Maag, "Syrien-Palästina, Vorgeschichte," *Kulturgeschichte des AO,* 453ff. Kathleen M. Kenyon, "Excavations at Jericho," *PEQ* 84 (1953), 81-96; 85 (1954), 45-63; 86 (1955), 108-118. See also my compilations: "Stand der Ausgrabungen in Jericho," *BuL* 22 (1955), 172-176; *Der Seelsorger* 27 (1957), 145-150; *Theological Digest* 1 (1958), 162-167.

excavated to date. One is surprised to note the careful construction which is in evidence here. All the buildings show evidence of carefully constructed floors. A base of stone and clay was covered with plaster, leveled, smoothed, and finally painted. The walls were constructed of clay or unbaked brick, dried in the sun. Particularly peculiar is the manner of burying the dead. The bodies of the deceased were exposed until the flesh had decayed away. Then the skull was filled with clay, modelel in the form of a portrait, and actually set up in the house for veneration — ancestor worship! The strata between 6000 and 5000 offer no evidence of pottery. But immediately afterwards we note the appearance of rough, hand-finished pottery, and after 4000 there is evidence of the potter's wheel.

The so-called megalith people[11] also belong to this Late Stone Age, before the discovery of pottery. By megaliths we understand mighty rock fragments, set up by human hand. In Palestine, such megalith structures are to be found on the margin of the cultivated land in Transjordan, on the mountain ridges of middle Palestine, and on the western slopes of Mt. Carmel. Single-standing megaliths are called *menhirs;* megaliths arranged like the four walls of a room are called *dolms;* clusters of stone arranged in the form of a cross are called *cromlechs.* These names originate from the language of the Bretons, in whose country these phenomena were first encountered. These are all meant to serve as monuments, primarily for burial sites. It is pointless to conclude to the existence of a megalithic race from the magnitude of these monuments. But certainly the sight of such structures might well have kindled the imagination to produce the giants of antiquity. A precise date for the megalithic culture is not possible. Apparently it was sedentary farmers and not nomadic shepherds who erected these monuments.

---

11. V. Maag, *ibid.,* 451. W. F. Albright, H.M. II (1953), 355. R. Pittioni, "Der urgeschichtliche Horizont der historischen Zeit," *Megalithkultur, PropWG* I (1961), 247, 262f., 275f.

4) THE COPPER STONE AGE: In the Near East, the knowledge of copper-working makes its appearance very early, side by side with the continued use of stone tools; thus the transition period of 4500 to 3000 B.C. is designated as the Copper Stone Age. The classical source for this period is the excavations in Teleilat el-Ghassul, 5 km. north of the Dead Sea and 5 km. east of the Jordan, from which the whole period is called Ghassulian.[12] In this era, man lived in closed settlements, not yet fortified. The houses are built of sun-baked bricks, and covered with wood. In the houses there are magnificently colored wall paintings, which show a predilection for geometric designs. The same culture level is evidenced in the excavations at Beth-Shan, Megiddo, Tell-el-Fara, and Haderirah.[13] The Chalcolithic finds at Abu Matar are deserving of special mention, as are those at Safadi and Horvat Beter, in the neighborhood of Beersheba.[14] The carefully constructed subterranean storage rooms yielded lentils and a

---

12. In 1929, P. Mallon noticed the special art of the Mounds north of the Dead Sea at which the Papal Institute of Excavations had just completed work. At first it was thought that the location of Sodom and Gomorrha had been found; these hopes, however, were illusory. Instead, the expedition had found an unexpected layer of the culture of Ghassulian. About the year 2000 before Christ this settlement was destroyed either through fire or earthquake and after that it was not resettled. The excavations were made public by Mallon – Köppel – Neuville, *Teleilat Ghassul* I-II (Rome, 1934-1940). See also *Kurzberichte Bibl.* 12 (1931), 85-89; 16 (1935) 241-225; 32 (1951), 316.

The excavations were again undertaken 1959/60. R. North, *Ghassul* 1960. "Excavation Report," *Analecta Biblica,* 14 (1961) – *Idem,* "Scavi palestinensi sotto bandiera pontificia," *Teleilat Ghassul, BIO* (1961), 86-89. E. Unger, "Die Erde als Stern des Kosmos im 4. Jahrtausend am Toten Meer, *Telielat Ghassul, ZDPV* 77 (1961), 72-96.

13. A small prehistoric library substitutes for the work of Bossert, *Altsyrien* (Tübingen, 1951). No. 993: Murals of Ghassul, the famous star. No. 1049-1061: Small utensils of flint. No. 1223-1230: Drawings on rocks consisting of pictures: horned goats, a large cow and a wildcat. No. 1126-1174: Development of ceramics.

14. Report of the excavations: J. Perrot, "The Dawn of History in Southern Palestine," *Archaeology,* 12 (1959), 9-15. M. Dothan, "Excavations at Horvat Beter (Beersheba)," *Atiqot,* 2 (1959), 1-42.

variety of grains. The dwelling places were also built into the mountain slope, chamber-like, so that the impression of cave-dwellers could easily arise.

5) THE BRONZE AGE: As in the river countries, the transition from the Copper Stone Age to the Bronze Age took place in Palestine around the year 3000 B.C. Since writing was invented at about the same time, it is in this millennium that history in the proper sense actually begins. Prior to this date, the historian was referred, of necessity, to the interpretation of mute relics; but now man begins to speak of himself in written documents, haltingly at first, but then with greater and greater assurance.

The Bronze Age is divided into three parts: the Early Bronze Age from 3200 to 2200 B.C.; this is further subdivided into Early Bronze Age I: 3200-2800; Early Bronze Age II: 2800-2500; Early Bronze Age III: 2500-2200 B.C.; Middle Bronze Age: 2200-1600; Late Bronze Age: 1600-1200 B.C. Around 1200 B.C. the Israelites immigrate into Palestine and this initiates the Iron Age of Palestine. This chronology is established primarily on the basis of pottery remains. The oldest pottery remains go back to the Late Stone Age (5th millennium). They were baked over an open fire. The method is gradually perfected and refined. Eventually the potter's wheel and the potter's oven were invented. The external forms become more elegant and were adorned with a greater variety of painting, both of which elements are characteristic of the type in any given epoch.[15]

2) CANAANITES AND AMORITES

Concerning the language and racial stock of the inhabitants of Canaan in the Late Stone Age we can make no definite statement, since there are no written documents at our disposal.

---

15. The first impetus to the chronology of the pieces of earthenware or shards was given by Fl. Petrie, *PEQ* 22 (1891), p. 68. His position was at first strongly criticized. The decisions of the time or provenance to which the shards belong, differed among the explorers by several hundred years. Today this branch of archaeology has reached such precision that

In the course of the 3rd millennium, in the early Bronze Age, the Semites make their appearance not only in Mesopotamia, but also in Syria and Palestine. In Mesopotamia this early Semitic population element is called Akkadian; for Palestine there is no corresponding name, for lack of historical records. The most ancient names of mountains, rivers, and cities, such as Lebanon ("white" mountain), Sharon, Carmel, Tabor, Gilboa, Jordan, Yarmuk, Arnon, etc., are already Semitic. Even the Phoenician port cities of Tyre, Sidon, and Beirut have Semitic names. Thus we can conclude that in the course of the 3rd millennium Semitic Bedouins, coming from the area of the Syro-Arabian desert, made their way peaceably or in war towards the west, where they took over the existing villages and cities and also founded new settlements. The Semitic ethnic element then succeeded in winning the upper hand, in the course of the Early Bronze Age, so that the land from that time on appears to be Semitic. The individualities of the early Bronze Age ethnic dislocations and racial mixtures are, however, almost completely beyond our ken. The one point that we can clearly establish is that after a golden age in the 3rd millennium, some catastrophe must have occurred around the year 2,000, which spelled the end of the Early Bronze Age culture. Many cities, such as Ai ("ruin") and Jericho, simply sank in ruins.[16] It seems that new waves of Semites inundated the land in great strength.

---

the provenance of findings, their definite time, or era of culture can be determined with only small margins of difference.

For a knowledge of Palestinian ceramics read Heinz Otto, "Studien zur Keramik der mittleren Bronzezeit in Palästina," *ZDPV* 61 (1938) 147-277. G. E. Wright, *Pottery of Palestine* (New Haven, 1937). J. G. Duncan, *Corpus of Dated Palestine Pottery* (London, 1930). E. Rosenthal, *Pottery and Ceramics,* Pelican Books (London, 1949). H. Salmang, *Die physikalischen und chemischen Grundlagen der Keramik* (Berlin, 1951, 2nd ed.). J. A. H. Potratz, *Einfuhrung in die Archäologie* (Stuttgart, 1962), p. 147: "Keramik-Dünnschliffe."

16. For further work on the bronzes of Palestine see W. F. Albright, *HM II* (1953), 337ff. and for names: *Idem, Archaeology of Palestine* (1951), p. 179. S. Moscati, *Die Kulturen des Alten Orients,* p. 187.

Comparisons with the history of Mesopotamia make it obvious that these new Semites were none other than the Amurru-Bedouins. In the east they achieved the foundation of empires, in Babylon, Ashur, and Mari; in Syria they established a few city states; in Palestine they became the bearers of the classical Bronze Age culture. Since Amurru, as we have already explained, means simply "Bedouin," the Canaanites, with whom this second Semitic immigration is most simply identified, were sedentary Amurru-Bedouins. Both names, Canaanites and Amorites, settled wide districts of Palestine, so that the "land of the Canaanites" or "land of the Amorites" came to be used almost without distinction.[17]

The Canaanites are the builders of the fortified cities, which must be compared not with our own residential cities, but rather with the fortress cities of the Middle Ages, meant to serve as refuge in times of war or crisis. (Jerusalem comprised an area of only 5 hectares, Jericho 2.5 ha., Gezer, 9 ha.). The city walls were generally very massive (4-8m. thick, often a double belt) and thus prevented the rain from washing away the remnants of destroyed cities, so that the Tells (ruin mounds) which are so characteristic of Palestinian landscape generally go back to this Bronze Age settlement of the Canaanites. The Canaanites never succeeded in establishing one united empire. The physical characteristics of the country made this impossible. The form

---

17. In this respect, the Amurru-Amorites have a wide span of significance. Only the Amorites of the Egyptian province of Canaan can properly be called Canaanites, while there were also Amorite kingdoms and settlements in Transjordan, such as the kingdom of Og of Bashan and Sihon of Heshbon, both of which were annihilated by the Israelites upon their entry into the country. In North Syria between Lebanon and the Nasaerian Mountains, during Amarna periods there was a buffer state called Amurru, which was swept away by the inroads of the sea peoples. We must be careful not to restrict the significance of the Amurru by a too narrow interpretation of their activity. Bo Reicke - L. Rost, *Biblisch–historisches Handwörterbuch* (Göttingen, 1962), 84: article: "Amorriter." A wider view is taken in an article on the Amurru, *EncMikr* I (1956), 440-446.

of state characteristic of the Canaanite settlement was the city kingdom and, in times of war, the league of cities, in which one of the more powerful kings took over the leadership. This was also the situation which the Israelites had to confront when they took over the country. The Israelites never succeeded in possessing the fortress cities of Dor, Gezer, Megiddo, Beth-Shan, etc.; they first took possession of the Palestinian mountains and attempted to assert their mastery over the Canaanites from this point of vantage. The Israelite tribes in Galilee and in the Judaeo-Samaritan mountain country were separated by two Canaanite wedges in the terrain of Esdrelon and by the Canaanite block of settlements around Jerusalem. In the battle at Megiddo (Judg. 4, 24) the fate of the Canaanites was decided. From that time on they pass over, as a race, into the Israelite people, although they exercized an unwholesome effect in the area of religion. It was King David who overcame the last Canaanite remnants in the fortress of Jebus, erecting his new capital, Jerusalem, on the site of the old Canaanite fortress. Under Solomon the old Canaanite cities became mostly the seats of viceroys, in an effort to shatter the old tribal structure and facilitate the formation of a centralistic state.

The culture of the Canaanites is familiar primarily from Egyptian sources. The Pharaohs of the Middle Kingdom sought to annihilate their Asiatic enemies even before taking the field against them, by curse and charm. From the 19th and the 18th centuries, we have the so-called "Execration texts." [18] The names of the foreign princes and cities were written on clay figurines or simple potsherds; these were then shattered, in the hope that by shattering his name the enemy would also be shattered in a form of magical telekinesis. In these execration texts we find the names of many Canaanite cities which are known from later history but which, unfortunately, are nothing more than names. A more colorful picture of Canaan is presented by the story of

---

18. Text in *ANET* 328-329. A. Goetze, "Remarks on some Names occurring in the Execration Texts," *BASOR* 151 (1958), 28-33.

19. See above p. 25.

Sinuhe, mentioned above.[19] In addition to these Egyptian texts, we have the archive discoveries in Mari, Nuzi, Babylon, and Boghazköy. The sources become more abundant in the golden age of the New Kingdom. The diplomatic correspondence from the archives of Amarna throws a powerful light on the turbulent affairs in Canaan. For north Syria, the archives in Ugarit have become an abundant and not yet exhausted source for new insights into the history of that age.

These literary sources have been enlarged and complemented by the excavations in Palestine, in which the lower strata have proved to be almost entirely Bronze Age. Precisely because Canaan's history meshes so closely with that of Egypt and Mesopotamia, it has been possible to introduce a better chronological system as well. Canaan could already look back upon a rich cultural development when, at the end of the Bronze Age, Israel first entered this sphere of development. Thus it follows that Israel entered the history of the Ancient Near East at a relatively late age.

THE PHOENICIANS: By Phoenicia [20] we refer to the narrow coastal strip from *Ras-en-Nakurah* down to *Nahr el-Kebîr* (Orontes), with the coastal cities of Tyre, Sidon, Beirut, Byblos; but the golden age of Phoenician power also includes the districts to the north, to Mt. Casius, and southwards to Mt. Carmel.

The Egyptian sources make no distinction between Phoenicia and Palestine, but group the entire territory, as we have mentioned above, under the name Canaan. This broader use of the word holds until the time of the Seleucids; on a coin struck under Antiochus IV (176-164 B.C.) the city of Laodicea in Lebanon is described as a "city in Canaan."

Racially and linguistically, ancient Phoenicia does form a unity with Palestine.[21] The Phoenicians are Canaanites. They founded their city-states

---

20. The word Phoenicia is merely the Greek translation of the Semetic Canaan. "Phoinos" means "red, purple"; Phoenicia is "the land of purple." In the summer of 1951 I made a bicycle trip along the Phoenician coast and I began to wonder if perhaps the name of the country might not have come from the red-brown color of the earth. For the derivation see *EncMikr* IV (1962), 196.

21. O. Eissfeldt, "Phoiniker." In *Pauly - Wissowa* XXIII, II, Col. 350-380. *Idem,* "Philister und Phoiniker," *AO* 34 (1930). R. Weill, *La Phénicie*

along the coast, and entered into an active commercial relationship with Egypt. Since the coastal strips are very narrow and access to the interior of the country is extremely difficult, the Phoenicians were forced, by reason of their geographical position, to be a nation of seafarers. The position of Phoenicia in the Amarna era has come to light primarily in the excavations of the coastal town of Ugarit, present-day *Ras-Shamra,* on the northern end of Phoenicia.[22] Ugarit was suddenly destroyed and completely disappeared from history; its excavated temples and palaces, its necropolis, and especially the many texts in the cuneiform library have resurrected this city from oblivion.

After the storm of the sea peoples (12th century) the city of Sidon assumes leadership in the league of cities. About 1000 B.C. it is dissolved by Tyre. King Hiram I (996-936) enters into commercial relationships with David; Ittobal strikes a treaty with Ahab and brings the kingdom of Israel under the religious and political influence of Phoenicia. Under Pygmaleon (820-774) the city of Carthage is founded. Phoenician ships sail as far as Tarshish in Spain and thus make available to western cultures the spiritual and material blessings of the east. It was also the Phoenicians who, apparently in the 9th century, brought the Greeks into contact with

---

et l'Asie occidentale (Paris, 1939). C. Contenau, *La civilisation phénicienne* (Paris, 1949). He treats the geography, history, religion, excavations, etc., very well and fully. W. v. Soden, "Die phönikische Kolonisation," *PropWG* II (1962), 75f.

22. Ras - Shamra, ancient Ugarit, is 12 km. north of Lattakijje, situated along the mountainous stretch of land where the Syrian coast, across from Cyprus, juts out farthest into the Mediterranean. In 1928, L. Albanese, searching in the neighborhood of the harbor of Minet-el-Beida, discovered an ancient grave which subsequent excavations revealed to be part of the necropolis. The excavations were under the direction of Shäffer. He unearthed five levels: V-IV, prehistoric time; III, city around 2000 BC; II, Hyksos era; Ugarit achieved its greatest blossoming and assumed a position equal to Tyre and Sidon and other cities on the Phoenician coast. The inroads of the sea peoples then destroyed the city. There are two large temples. But the most significant find was the library containing cuneiform tablets in Akkadian, Ugarit, Hurrian, and an as yet unknown language. Part of these written records are in the cuneiform alphabet, which probably first developed on Ugarit soil. These mythological texts are important for our knowledge of the Canaanite religion. Most significant is the *Aliyan-Ba'al Myth* and the *Keret Saga.* The excavation accounts have been published in *Syria* regularly since 1929. The monumental work on Ras-Shamra is by Cl. F. A. Schaeffer, *Stratigraphie comparé et chronologie de l'Asie Occidentale, IIIe et IIe Millénaire* (Paris, 1948). See also W. v. Soden, "Ugarit," *PropWG* II (1962), 57-60.

the alphabet script which has since become established throughout the world.

Upon the ascendancy of Ancient Near East empires, the Phoenician cities, after stubborn resistance, lose their autonomy just like the kingdoms of Israel and Judah.

3) HABIRU AND HEBREWS

Whereas the first half of the 2nd millennium can be designated as the golden age of the Amurru-Bedouins, the second half, between 1500 and 1000 B.C., can be called the golden age of the Habiru-Bedouins. The empires established by the Amurru in no way terminated the penetration of new Semitic Bedouins from the district of the Greek-Arabic desert. The two names, Amurru and Habiru, seem to overlap to a large extent. That is why Jepsen[23] has made the proposal that the Semitic immigrations of the 2nd millennium be referred to exclusively as the immigrations of the "Hebrews." His proposal must currently be treated only as a working hypothesis, but by giving such prominence to this name, which is based on the table of nations (Gen. 10, 24) and the more recent text discoveries, it does cast new light on the pre-Israelite situation in Palestine. Against this background, Israel's growth as a people is much more understandable; Israel would thus be considered as only one tribe in the "Hebrew immigration waves." The problem will be taken up again later.

1) The Sources

a) THE "HEBREWS" IN THE BIBLE: Most of the "Hebrew passages" are to be found in the stories of Joseph and Moses; they occur particularly when an Egyptian, thus a foreigner, speaks of the Israelites (Gen. 39, 14, 17; 41, 2; Ex. 1, 16; 2, 6); or when an Israelite addresses the Egyptians, foreigners (Gen. 40, 15; Ex. 1, 19; 2, 7; 3, 18; 5, 3; 7, 16; 9, 1, 13). The word Hebrew is used four times to distinguish the Israelites from other ethnic

---

23. A. Jepsen, "Die 'Hebräer' und Recht," AFO 15 (1945-51), 55-68.

groups (Gen. 43, 32; Ex. 1, 15; 2, 11, 13). Similarly, in the wars against the Philistines the name Hebrew is used only in the mouth of the enemies, the Philistines (I Sam. 4, 9; 13, 3; 14, 11; 29, 3). A special case is represented by the "Hebrew" slaves in Ex. 21, 2 and Deut. 15, 12. There are two passages which can not be classified: in the campaign of the eastern kings, a fugitive reports to "the Hebrew Abraham" what had happened to his cousin Lot (Gen. 14, 13); likewise, when the tempest threatens, Jonah identifies himself as a "Hebrew."

This would appear to determine Abraham's ethnic origins and those of his posterity; they are "Hebrews," that is, they belong to a people of Hebrews. But the question is not so simply solved. According to Gen. 11, 14 ff., six generations before Abraham in the Semite family tree there was a man called Eber (Heber),[24] from which, correspondingly, the Table of Nations in Gen. 10, 21 derives "all the children of Heber," that is, "all the Hebrews." On the basis of the further allusions in the Table of Nations, this also includes some Arabian tribes (Gen. 10, 25 ff.). Thus it is obvious that the word Hebrew includes not only the Israelites, but must be taken in a much broader sense. Text finds from Babylonia, Assyria, and Asia Minor on the one hand, and Syria, Palestine, and Egypt on the other hand, have cast much light on this "Hebrew question" without, however, being able to produce a definitive solution. Every new document can force us to give up the results of our current speculation and search for new possibilities in the solution of the problem. The discussion is, thus, still very much in flux; but the following points must be presented.

b) THE HABIRU[25] OF THE CUNEIFORM TEXTS: In the entire second millennium before Christ, throughout the entire territory of the Ancient Near East, in the cuneiform texts (we must remember that cuneiform was the diplomatic script used by all the various

---

24. Hebrew *'ayin* was transcribed as *h* in Latin, hence *'ébär* – *hébär*.
25. On the writing and pronunciation of this word there is no unity of opinion. R. Borger, "Das Problem 'apiru (habiru)," *ZDPV* 74 (1958), 121-

courts) one word keeps recurring, which is to be read as Habiru according to the syllable script, and according to the picture script (ideogram) as SAGAZ;[26] the word apparently is unclear and fluctuates in meaning.

Apart from the mention of the Habiru in the Legend of Naram-Sin in the Akkadian era (2350-2150), whose formulation goes back to a later time, the Habiru appear first in a text from the time of the 3rd dynasty of Ur (Ur III: 2050-1950). In Asia Minor they are spoken of as prisoners in the 19th century. In lower Mesopotamia they are mercenaries of the kings of Larsa, Warad-Sin (1770-1759) and Rim-Sin (1758-1698). Under Hammurabi they are subject to a royal overseer of their own (1728-1686). The Mari texts from this same time speak of the Habiru as hostile hordes which threaten the cities of Upper Mesopotamia.

The Habiru occupy a very special position in the Tablets of Nuzi. They are described as foreigners who, under certain definite stipulations, sell themselves either individually or in groups as slaves. For the 15th and 14th centuries, the Amarna Tablets from Egypt attest the presence of the Habiru in Syria and Palestine. They are hordes who threaten the civilized land. The Egyptian governors in Palestine and Syria address one plea for help after another to the Pharaoh's court, without, however, receiving any active support. For the 14th and 13th centuries, the golden age of the new Hittite empire in Asia Minor, the Habiru are attested as mercenaries of the Hittite kings, obligating

---

132, thinks that the reading *habiru* should be replaced by *hapiru,* which is derived from *'aparu* "dust, earth"; *'apir,* "covered with dust, dirty degenerate," intended as a mockery of foreigners. H. Cazelles, "Hébreu ubru et *habiru," Syria* 35 (1958), 198-217. The forms hapiru, habiru, ubru, ubaru, 'apiru, 'îbri are explained as mere dialectical developments of the same basic root. R. de Vaux, *Die hebräischen Patriarchen und die modernen Entdeckungen* (Düsseldorf, 1959). The problem of Habiru is on pp. 44-54, M. P. Gray, "The Habiru - Hebrew Problem in the Light of Source Material Available at Present," *HUCA* 29 (1958), 135-202.

26. The identification of Habiru and SA - GAZ is suggested by a Hittite text in which the "gods of the SA - GAZ" and the "gods of the Habiru" are used equivalently.

themselves to military service under the invocation of the "god of the Habiru" or the "gods of the Habiru."[27]

The inscription of King Idrimi of Alalah on the Orontes (end of the 15th century) tells how he fled through the desert of Sutu towards Canaan, but was unable to remain there, and thus spent seven years with the Habiru troops. Similarly, one of the 450 tablets discovered in Alalah speaks of "a house for 1,400 soldiers of the Habiru."

The Ugarit texts (14th century) speak of a whole district in the city of Halab as belonging to the Sag-gaz, who, in the translation, are identified with the Apirim (*prm*).[28] Thus, we appear to have three different words to designate the same ethnic element, three words which must be strictly distinguished: 1. Sagaz, 2. Habiru, 3. Apirim.

The texts quoted above speak of the Habiru in the most varied circumstances. They are mercenaries in the service of a foreign power; wild hordes which threaten the settled land; prisoners of war and even slaves in the midst of a peaceful population. One or another among them may have worked his way up to an important position. Despite these variegated aspects, the Habiru have one common trait: they are foreigners in the world about them, the world in which they appear, sometimes received as friends and assimilated, sometimes received as enemies and rejected.

Is it possible, considering the broad geographical extension

---

27. Documents serving as proofs of the Habiru Text are R. de Vaux, *RB* 55 (1948), 339ff, where the Habiru question is discussed in terms of the 1948 position. A. Jepsen, *AFO* XV (1945-51), 55-68. The classical work on the Habiru question is the volume of essays published by J. Bottéro, *Le Problème des Habiru à la 4 - ème rencontre assyriologique internationale* (Paris, 1954). Enlarged by H. Cazelles in *VT* 5 (1955), 440-445.

28. Text published by Ch. Virolleaud, "Les villes et les corporations du royaume d'Ugarit." *Syria* 21 (1940), 213. Revision of R. De Langhe, *Les textes de Ras Shamra - Ugarit et leurs Rapports avec le Milieu biblique de l'Ancien Testament* (1954), II. pp. 47, 464. New documents on Habiru: *Bib* 33 (1952), 561 and *Or* 21 (1952), 376.

and the centuries of history spanned, that this could be *one people*? This is the basic problem. Before attempting an answer, insofar as an answer is possible in the light of present-day scholarship, we would do well to examine the parallel Egyptian texts.

c) THE APIRU OF THE EGYPTIAN TEXTS: Seven Egyptian texts speak of so-called Apiru: Pharaoh Amenhotep II (1448-1422), after his military campaigns in Palestine, brings home three distinct groups among his prisoners of war: the *Sasu,* that is, the Bedouins, the *Huru,* the common Egyptian name for Canaan, thus prisoners of war from the Canaanite cities; then there is the third element, called the *Apiru.* Who are they?

One century later Seti I (1317-1301), on an obelisk discovered in Beth-Shan, records that the Apiru were threatening the city from the mountains. The account of the capture of the city of Jaffa at the end of the reign of Seti I (?) mentions an Apiru among the Mariannu who fought in war chariots. From the time of Ramses II (1301-1234) a document has been preserved recording his orders to deliver grain to the Apiru who were working with the army. Under Ramses III (1197-1165) the Apiru appear together with the Mariannu as slaves in a temple. And finally, under Ramses IV (1165) the Apiru are mentioned as laborers in the quarries. More recently, tombs from Thebes show them as laborers in the wine-presses.[29]

The Egyptian texts thus are familiar with the Apiru as a foreign element coming from the Near East, clearly distinct from the Canaanite population (*Huru*). They come to Egypt as prisoners of war, are found as temple slaves, work in the stone quarries and in the vineyards.

---

29. Texts: *ANET* 22, 205, 255, 261, 483ff. T. Säve - Söderbergh, "The ʿp r w as Vintagers in Egypt," *Or* 21 (1952), 376.

2) *Habiru, Apiru, and the Hebrews*

What, now, is the relationship between the cuneiform Habiru, the Egyptian Apiru, and the Biblical Hebrews? That the Habiru of the cuneiform texts are identical with those of the Egyptian chronicles can be regarded as certain. The area in which they are active, the manner in which they work – these are the same. But what is their position relative to the Hebrews?

First let us examine the obvious similarities: just as the Habiru in Mesopotamia are attested as hordes, attacking and threatening cities, the "Hebrew Abraham" (Gen. 14, 13) organizes a campaign against the kings of the east; Simeon and Levi attack the city of Shechem with their people (Gen. 34). Furthermore, the Habiru fight as mercenaries, just like the Israelites in the army of the Philistines (I Sam. 14, 21; 29, 3). The position of the Habiru slaves in Nuzu is quite similar with that of the "Hebrew slaves" in the Book of the Covenant (Ex. 21, 2). But the most obvious parallel is the fact that the Apiru were used for forced labor in Egypt (Ex. 1, 11 ff.; 5, 6 ff.).

To sum up, we have the following general characteristics: the Habiru appear on the margin of the Syro-Arabian desert, from Egypt into Mesopotamia, and penetrate the country either in friendship or in war. Many scholars are of the opinion that the available material is sufficient to conclude to the existence of an ethnologically unified group, which is otherwise identified as the wave of "Amurru, East Canaanite, or Proto-Aramaean" Semitic immigration of the 2nd millennium B.C.[30] Other scholars think that this hypothesis is a bit premature. They see the Habiru-Apiru and Hebrews, not as the name for a single ethnic group, but as a general term for the ethnic elements which appear on the margin of the Syro-Arabian desert in the course of the 2nd millennium to disturb the more civilized world, an element which is composed of ethnologically distinct groups. The solution of

30. Jepsen, *AFO* XV (1945-1951), 55-68. A Pohl, "Einige Gedanken zur Habiru - Frage," *WZKM* 54 (1957), 157.

the problem might well involve both elements. Originally the expression *hab/piru*, "Hebrews," meant the "inhabitants of the desert," in general, the Bedouins. Etymologically, *amurru* and *hab/piru* are equivalent in meaning.[31] If we are now justified in referring to the Bedouins who penetrate the settled land from their desert homes in the first half of the 2nd millennium as Amorites, we are also justified in referring to those of the second half as "Hebrews." They are not identical with the 12 tribes of Israel, and thus, in speaking of the time of the patriarchs and the possession of the promised land we must say that the Israelites were "Hebrew" Bedouins, but not all the "Hebrew" Bedouins were Israelites. The fact of the matter is that the name Hebrew, as referring to the people of Israel, disappears from the Old Testament at the end of the Philistine wars. The identification of Israel with Hebrews is a very late product of history. If we want to correctly understand the early history of Israel, we must restore the word "Hebrew" to its original broad meaning of "Bedouin." Thus there is no contradiction when the "Hebrew" Abraham is also called an Aramaean.

3) *The Aramaean Abraham*

At the presentation of the first fruits, every Israelite had to confess: "My father was a wandering Aramaean" (Deut. 26, 5). Abraham's family, even in Canaan, was intimately bound up with Paddan-Aram (Gen. 25, 20; 31, 18 etc.), with Aram Naharaim (Gen. 24, 10); Abraham's great nephew, Laban, Rebekah's brother

---

31. Attempts have been made to derive the word *hab/piru* from the Semitic: *'aphar*, "dust, sand" and thus explain it as "sand-dwellers, Bedouins"; *habar*, "bind, federate," hence, "federated." But the Semitic derivation is unsatisfactory. As with the word Amurru, it is now only the Sumerian origin that is considered. G. Dossin, "Les bedouins dans les textes de Mari," *StudSem* 2 (1959), 47-49. A Sumero - Accadian lexicon gives the Semitic "desert" as *hursag* and *gabiri* in Sumerian. From *gabiri* the word *hapiru*, "dwellers in the desert," Bedouins, is formed. The derivation of the other forms of the word can be corroborated by the history of linguistics.

and the father of Rachel and Lia, is characterized simply as an Aramaean (Gen. 25, 20; 28, 5; 31, 20, 24). What does this Aramaean tradition mean with respect to the ethnic origin of Abraham?

The word *ahlamû* is, as we have already discussed, like the word Habiru, not the name of a people, but the general designation for the Bedouin hordes on the margin of the Syro-Arbian desert who had already become partially sedentary and now constantly threatened the settled land from their desert dwellings. They appeared as enemies of Assyria, frequently as the allies of the Hittites. It was their bands who harassed the diplomatic traffic between Babylon and the Hittite empire. According to general opinion, the Ahlamu are already the same as the Aramaeans from the 14th century. It is very probable that the origins of the Aramaeans go back much further, so that the early Ahlamu can properly be referred to as Proto-Aramaeans. But we thus arrive at the age of Abraham, whose description as a "wandering Aramaean" is thus quite plausible within the framework of the history of the 2nd millennium.

This, however, still does not univocally establish Abraham's ethnic origin among the Aramaeans: for according to the Semitic family tree (Gen. 10, 1), Abraham is not descended from Aram, the son of Shem, but from his other son Arpachshad, whose 8th descendant he is. This corresponds to the data of Ancient Near East history. In Upper Mesopotamia the state of Mitanni was formed by an Indo-Arian noble class. The Indo-Arian word *arpa-kšad*[32] means, freely translated, "noble class," and thus points to the later "Aram of the rivers." The tradition preserved in Gen. 22, 21 puts Aram into a much closer vicinity to Abraham; it is announced to Abraham that children had been born to his brother Nahor in Paddan-Aram, among whom Aram is also mentioned.

No matter how these texts are evaluated, it is very probable that we can establish the fact that Abraham and his kinship

32. A more detailed treatment in the Table of Nations, p. 424.

belong to the Proto-Aramaeans, who wandered with their flocks for an indefinite period as nomads in the Syro-Arabian desert, and whose most advanced elements, since the beginning of the Ancient Near East "Middle Ages," entered into a constantly more intimate friendly or hostile relationship with the sedentary populations in the territory of the Fertile Crescent.

The Israelites retained the memory of having descended from the Aramaeans; they also knew that their race was a very mixed one. In his prophetic sermon, Ezekiel breaks out into these reproaches against Jerusalem: "Your father was an Amorite and your mother was a Hittite" (Ez. 16, 3). It is perhaps this very fact, more than any theological speculation, which explains why the election of Abraham and the people of Israel which proceeds from him did not take place on the basis of racial or national preference, but rather on the basis of revelation and faith.

4) EDOM, MOAB, AND AMMON

The population shifting which is characterized by the Habiru activity also includes the three tribes east of the Jordan, Edom, Moab, and Ammon, which, according to the testimony of archaeology, made the transition to sedentary settlements towards the end of the Bronze Age (end of the 14th to the beginning of the 13th century). Transjordan enjoyed a sort of golden age in the Middle Bronze Age (19th century). Quite extensive districts were settled, as archaeology can still demonstrate. But this period of culture was abruptly annihilated by a hostile invasion (perhaps the Hurrians?), so that in the time from the 18th to the 15th century, Transjordan plays host to culturally abandoned and only nomadic Bedouins.[33] Edom, Moab, and Ammon are thus also "Hebrews" and ethnic relatives of the Israelites.

---

33. The new archaeological progress in our knowledge of Transjordan we owe to the investigations of N. Glueck, *Explorations in Eastern Palestine IV* (1951). "Go view the land" (a condensed view of the last Jordan investigations) *BASOR* 122 (1951), 14-18. *Idem, The Other Side of the Jordan* (New Haven, 1940). G. Lankester Harding, "Recent Discoveries

The Edomites settled in the southernmost part of Transjordan, on either side of the Arabah basin down to the Gulf of Elath. Their principal centers were Elath, Teman, Bosra, and especially the rock city of Sela. Just like Israel, they were divided into 12 tribes. In their inner-political development they were some centuries ahead of Israel, since they had made the transition to a strictly organized monarchy at a very early time, and this provided them with a transitory superiority over Israel in the time of the Judges. The mountainous and partially desert district of Edom had great significance in commercial politics; the great Transjordan caravan routes (the "royal road") passed through this district towards the Red Sea and Egypt. Moreover, in the neighborhood of Elath there were great copper mines, whose exploitation was already undertaken by the Edomites at a very early age. The Egyptian texts (Harris Papyrus) recount that around the year 1300, at the time of a famine, even the Aduma came to Egypt with their flocks, where they were offered a grazing land. Their history thus runs parallel to the early history of Israel.[34]

Linguistically, the Edomite language is closely related to Hebrew. Apart from a few jar stamps, however, nothing of an Edomite literature has been discovered. The Edomites must have been particularly fond of the wisdom literature (Jer. 49, 7). The Bible (Gen. 28, 18; 36, 1 ff.) makes Esau (Edom) a brother of Jacob (Israel), and archaeology seems to have borne out this relationship. The enmity between the two brothers, as recounted in the Genesis narrative (32, 4), predetermines the later course of their mutual history. They refused Moses passage through their district (Num. 20, 14-21), Saul fought against them (1 Sam. 14, 27), David subjugated them after the battle in the Valley of Salt (2 Sam. 8, 13-15). But they kept trying to shake off the Israelite yoke and whenever the occasion was favorable, they launched their attacks.

---

in the Jordan," *PEQ* 90 (1958), 7-18. The settlement has already made the transition to late bronze. On the aerodome at Amman, a temple with rich stores of gold, pearls and ivory (1550-1250) was unearthed.

They are mentioned also in the prophetic threat oracles (Is. 34, 5-7; 63, 1-67). Bordering on the territory settled by the Edomites, between the Zered and Arnon, is the territory of Moab,[35] which is bordered in the north, up to the upper course of the Yabbok, by the territory of Ammon.[36] The popular account in Gen. 19, 30-38 derives the origin of Moab from Lot. The history of both of these territories is intimately connected with the history of Israel. The most important Moabitic literary document is the inscription of King Mesha,[37] which recounts a victory over Israel which he achieved by the help of the god *Kamosh* (c. 840). Linguistically, Moabitic and Ammonitic are closely related to Hebrew.

The principal places settled by the Moabites were Ir-Moab, Aroer, Dibon, and Heshbon.[38] The Ammonites built the city of Rabbath-Ammon[39] (the great city of Ammon) into an absolutely impregnable fortress.

---

34. The history of Edom and its relations with Israel on the basis of Egyptian and biblical sources is presented in J. Prado, "Los destinos de Edom," *EstEcl.* 34 (1960), 557-567.

35. A compact but valuable history of Moab on the basis of biblical, Ancient Near Eastern and archaeological sources is available in J. A. Thompson, "The History of Biblical Moab in the Light of Modern Knowledge," *ABR* (1956), 119-143.

36. The literary sources for the history of the Ammons are very limited. We are dependent upon the archaeological material and its interpretation. G. M. Landes, "The Material Civilization of the Ammonites," *BA* 24 (1961), 66-86.

37. Mesa Text in Galling, *TGI* (1950), 47. Illustrations in *AOB* 1927, 2nd ed., No. 120. St. Segert, "Die Sprache der moabitischen Königsinschrift," *ArOr.* 29 (1961), 197-267.

38. F. V. Winnet, "Excavations at Dibon in Moab 1950/51," (The most ancient constructions unearthed were a square tower and five city walls) *BASOR* 125 (1952), 7-19; 147 (1957), 5-16.

39. O'Callaghan, "A statue recently found in Ammon," *Or* 21 (1952), 190.

5) HURRIANS AND HITTITES

In pre-Israelite Palestine we find important remains of peoples who had their proper center of power much further to the north. On the one hand, the Hurrians, during the time of the Middle and New Kingdoms in Egypt, left such a stamp on the land of Canaan that in the Egyptian sources it is also called the "land of Haru."[40] The cuneiform tablets excavated at Tell-Taanak also display Hurrian names.[41] Syria-Palestine, in that era, was largely under the control of a Hurrian and, in isolated points, an Arian ruling class.[42] The military use of the horse and the war chariot was a prerequisite for the formation of the Hurrian-Arian cavalry and knightly class. This class not only established itself in most of the cities throughout the country, but also founded cities of its own here and there. In these fortress cities a proud and class-conscious life was lived, which acted as a stimulus and spur for both the intellectual and material culture. The Hurrians passed on to the western lands the achievements of the Sumero-Babylonian culture. When the Egyptians, after the expulsion of the Hyksos, reestablished their sovereignty in Palestine and Syria, the province of Canaan, they changed little in the political situation. They allowed the current city dynasties to retain their control and demanded no more than a recognition of Egyptian sovereignty. It is no wonder that in the Amarna correspondence, among the rulers of Canaan, there are some with Hurrian or Arian names. The city king of Jerusalem is called Puti-Hepa,[43] that is, "servant of the (Hurrian goddess) Hepath." David bought the temple property from a man who belonged to the old nobility, and whose Indo-Arian name was Arauna. At the time that Israel entered the Promised Land, nothing much survived of the once

---

40. G. Contenau, *DBS* IV (1949), 128-138.

41. B. S. J. Isserlin, "Hurrian and Old Anatolian Names in the Semitic World: Some Tentative Suggestions." *PEQ* 88 (1956), 141-144.

42. V. Maag, "Syrien - Palästina" in *Kulturgeschichte des AO.* Also H. Schmökel, 458-461, on the Hurrians.

43. Selected letters of Puti - Hepas in Galling, *TGI* 23ff.

glorious rule of the Hurrian-Arian knightly nobility. In the course of the centuries the ruling class had become Canaanized. In the account of the possession of the Promised Land, the Hivites in middle Palestine are especially mentioned. Under the leadership of the city of Gibeon they had entered into friendly relationship with Joshua (Josh. 3, 10; 9, 1; 8, 8; 24, 8; Judg. 3, 5). The Greek Bible has the form Hurrians instead of Hivites (Gen. 34, 2; Josh. 9, 7; Judg. 3, 3). It is unlikely that all these passages are owing to a scribal error - *hurrî* for *hiwwî* - but at any rate, in the Hivites, the Hurrian ethnic element is active for the last time in history.[44] The account which mentions the Hurrians as having settled also in the land of Edom, in the mountain range of Se'ir, is not unhistorical (Gen. 36, 20-22; Deut. 2, 12, 22); the Hyksos ruling class in Egypt was also partially made up of a Hurrian ethnic element.

Not only the Hurrians, but also the Hittites are mentioned as having settled in Canaan. They seemed to have developed a considerable power for a while, since Canaan is also called "land of the Hittites" (Josh. 1, 4). They appear as the spokesmen of the Canaanite population. More particularly, the Hittites are mentioned as inhabitants of Hebron, where Abraham bought a field with a cave as a burial place for his wife Sara; Esau took two Hittite women for wives; Uriah, in David's army, was a Hittite, and Solomon also took Hittite women for his harem. We must think of the Hittites in Palestine, not as the inhabitants of a narrow territory, a single town and its outlying territory; they had made their way into the country during the time of the greatest extension of Hittite power, spreading from Asia Minor southwards, and even after the political collapse of the Hittite empire they had continued to remain in the country, soon exchanging their own language for the vernacular of the country and preserving only the individuality of their population.

---

44. W. F. Albright, "The Horites in Palestine," *From the Pyramids to Paul* (New York, 1935).

6) THE PHILISTINES

According to the Biblical sources, the Philistines settled on the coastal plain between Raphia and Joppa during the time of the Judges. The center of their settlement was formed by the five cities: Gaza, Ashkelon, Gath, Ashdod, and Ekron. They were ruled by princes who bore the title *Seranim* (tyrannoi), were mutually independent of each other, and banded together for common purposes only in the event of war. In the time of the Judges, they pressed hard against the mountain country from the west, so that the Tribe of Dan had to give up its tribal territory and migrate northwards to the sources of the Jordan (Judg. 18, 1 ff.). In the neighborhood of Jerusalem they attained the heights of the mountain range, where they set up their military outposts in Michmash and Gibeah; at the same time they also spread northwards into the Plain of Sharon and Jezreel. Under Saul and David there was a violent struggle for the possession of the country.

According to the Table of Nations (Gen. 10, 14), the Philistines had immigrated into Canaan from the district of Kasluhim east of the Nile delta; according to Deut. 2, 23; Amos 9, 7; Jer. 47, 4, they come from Caphtor, which the Septuagint and the Fathers understood as Cappadocia in Asia Minor. The Assyrian *Kaptara* and the Egyptian *Keftiu* designate either the island of Crete by itself or including the surrounding islands and the coast of Asia Minor as the Cretan sphere of influence; it is perhaps a general name for the Aegean.[45] In the 13th century, the Aegean, Syria, and Palestine were overrun by sea peoples. By land and by sea they penetrated to the very door of Egypt, where they were defeated, in the year 1194 B.C. by Ramses III. In the victory inscription of Medinet-Habu, the armament of the sea peoples is described in terms similar to that of Goliath.

---

45. The Caphtor question has been recently treated in connection with the text discoveries of Ras - Shamra by A. Alt, "Ein Name Agyptens?" *AFO* (1951), 71-74. J. Prignaud, "Caftorim et Kerétim," *RB* 71 (1964), 215-229.

Among the sea peoples, the tribe of *Pršt* (Purušati) - *Peleshet* (Philistines) is also mentioned. But, despite the Egyptian victory, the Philistines were able to maintain themselves along the southern coast land, while the tribe of the Zakari, a related people, held the Plain of Sharon. The battle between the sea peoples and Egypt represents only the final phases of a long development. The migrations of the Philistines, unfortunately, can be traced only in vague outline. Examination of their pottery, however, does point to some recognizable traces. The Philistine pottery apparently developed from the Mycenaean wares of the 13th century. This tends to substantiate the ancient view that the name Philistine, which may have sounded something like Pelast, belongs together with the Pelasgians.[46] Moreover, it seems to be certain that the migration of the Philistines led through Asia Minor. From Cilicia they must have taken control of the Palestinian coastland in several waves.[47] The Philistines were thus not Semites. Together with them we note the entrance of a new racial element into the land of the Bible. They were contemptuously referred to as "uncircumcised" by the Israelites (1 Sam. 17, 28; 18, 25; Judg. 14, 3; 15, 18). For some time it seemed as if Palestine was going to become actually Philistine, as its name implies, and not Israelite.

The Philistines brought with them the weapons of the new Iron Age, and were thus superior to their adversaries. This "iron" advantage they sought to maintain even after the possession of the Promised Land by the Israelites, refusing to allow them the working of iron (I Sam. 13, 19). In religion, the Philistines

46. W. F. Albright, *HM* 2 (1953) 355. V. Georgiev, "Sur l'origine et langue des Pélasges, Philistins, Danaens et Achéens," *JKaF* 1 (1950), 136-141.

47. G. A. Wainwright, "Some Early Philistine History," *VT* 6 (1956), 199-210; 9 (1959), 73-84. The migrations went from Troas across Lydia, Caria, and Isauria towards Cilicia. The Philistine King, Achish of Gat, bears the same name as Anchiser, the father of Aeneas, who led the Dardanians in the Trojan War. The system of "three - man battle" can be established for Greeks and Philistines alike. Thus, the Philistines would be Dardanians of Illyrian descent.

quickly mixed with the local population. They also adopted the Semitic gods. In Gaza and Ashdod, the god Dagon was especially venerated, in Ashkelon, the goddess Atargatis (Astarte), and in Ekron, the god Baalzebub (Aramaic: Beelzebub).[48]

THE PHILISTINES IN THE AGE OF THE PATRIARCHS: The mention of the Philistines in the Patriarchal narratives has posed literary questions and problems in historical criticism. Since the Philistines were supposed to have first come into the country during the migration of the sea peoples, Abraham and Isaac can hardly have struck a treaty with the Philistine king (Gen. 21, 32, 34; 1, 8, 14, 18). Thus the Bible writer must have transferred later happenings into an earlier age. This would be a rapid and easy solution to the problem of literary criticism. But the answer does not seem to be so simple. If the Patriarchs are dated in the Middle Bronze Age – Abraham approximately 1850 B.C. – then the mention of Philistines is completely unhistorical. But if the Patriarchal era is dated at the beginning of the Ancient Near East's Middle Ages, after 1500 B.C., then a confrontation of Abraham and the forebears of the Philistines is quite possible. Proof for this is offered by the excavation strata on Cyprus and in Palestine which give evidence of widespread destruction, allowing us to conclude to several campaigns and invasions of the sea peoples.[49] There is the added possibility that individual groups of Philistines may have served as mercenaries in the various foreign armies long before the Israelite possession of the Promised Land.[50] The penetration of the Palestinian coastland by the products of Mycenaean culture would thus have begun sometime before the actual Israelite possession of the country. The sea peoples were only following out the route that was already outlined for them by history. What earlier scholars were forced to regard as the literary product of a later editor has now, thanks to the tireless archaeological investigation of the Bible countries, been recognized as a piece of actual history.[51]

---

48. A. Bea, *Enc. catt.* (Encyclopedia Cattolica) V (1950), 1332ff. O. Eissfeldt, "Philister" in *Pauly-Wissowa* XXXVII, 2390-2401. *Idem.*, "Philister und Phonikier,"*AAO* 34, 3 (1936). H. R. Hall, "The Keftians, Philistines and other peoples of the Levant," in *The Cambridge Ancient History*. II (1926), 275-295.

49. J. du Plat Taylor, "Late Cypriot III in the Light of Recent Excavations," *PEQ* 88 (1956), 22-37.

50. G. E. Wright, "Coffins and Mercenaries," *BA* 22 (1959), 54-66. Pottery coffins with lids in human form discovered in Palestine and Egypt, are of Philistines who were employed as foreign mercenaries.

51. C. H. Gordon, *Or.* 21 (1952), 383.

CHAPTER XIII

THE RELIGION OF THE CANAANITES

The Israelites came into close contact with the religion of the Assyro-Babylonians only some two centuries after the division of the kingdom; still, the religion of the Canaanites before the Israelite entry into the land of Canaan was of the greatest significance for them. That is why biblical history necessarily devotes some time to the question. Moreover, the prophets never tired of castigating the negative side of Canaanite cults.

The extra-Biblical sources for the Canaanite-Phoenician religion are first of all the *Phoinikika* of Philo of Biblos, who, like Manetho in Egypt and Berossus in Babylon, wrote the history of his people around the year 100 B.C., devoting a significant part of his work to the description of their gods. His work is based on the older work of Sanchuniathon (the Phoenician form of the name, *Sakkunyton,* comes from the Persian era), who, in turn, goes back to the still older *Hierembaal* of Beirut. The work of Philo of Phoenicia is preserved, in fragments, in Eusebius.[1]

1. C. Clemen, *Die phönikische Religion nach Philo V. Byblos* (Leipzig, 1939). R. Dussaud, "A propos de Sanchuniathon," *Syria* 27, 198. O. Eissfeldt, *Sanchunjaton von Beirut und Ilumilku von Ugarit,* 1952. R. Follet, "Sanchunjaton, personage mythique ou historique," *Bib* 34 (1953), 81-90.

For the knowledge of the Canaanite religion of the 2nd millennium, the religious texts of Ugarit[2] present an inexhaustible source of information. But we are immediately faced with the problem of deciding whether the religious belief passed on in the tradition of this north-Syrian city is also valid for the other districts. A comparison with the other available sources shows that the texts of Ugarit reflect a widely spread creed. Thus, it seems, we are justified in reconstructing the Canaanite pantheon primarily on the basis of the Ugarit texts.[3]

The Canaanites actually had the belief that the whole world of gods belongs together in one higher unity. In the epics and myths we find generic terms like *phr ilm,* "the totality of the gods," *mphrt bn il,* "the totality of the sons of El," *dr il,* "the family of El" *'dt ilm,* "the council of the gods," etc.[4] The Canaanite Olympus was the pyramid-like mountain of Saphon which towered up along the north-Syrian coast, the "mountain of the north." The Latins called it *Mons Casius,* which is equivalent to "mountain of lightning." As we have already explained in the historical treatment above, the most diverse peoples have crossed paths in the territory of Canaan. The course of history was not without its influence on the development of religion. The mute witnesses of pre-literary times clearly attest to the presence of religion,

---

2. A. Jirku, *Kanaanäische Mythen und Epen aus Ras Schamra - Ugarit* (Gütersloh, 1962). C. H. Gordon, *Ugaritic Manual. Newly Revised Grammar, Texts in Transliteration, Cuneiform Selections, Paradigms.* Glossaries and Indices. *Analecta Orientalia* 35 (Roma, 1955). J. Aistleitner, *Wörterbuch der ugaritischen Sprache,* published by O. Eissfeldt (Berlin, 1963). H. L. Ginsberg, "Ugaritic Myths, Epics and Legends," *ANET* 129-155. W. F. Albright, *Die Religion Israels im Lichte der archäologischen Ausgrabungen* (Munich - Basel, 1956). V. Maag, "Die syro-kanaanäische Religion," in *Kulturgeschichte des Alten Orients,* published by H. Schmökel (1961), 570-596. G. Pavlovsky, "De religione Canaanaeorum tempore occupationis israeliticae, *VD* 27 (1949) 143-163; 193-205. M. J. Dahood, "Ancient Semitic Deities in Syria and Palestine," *StudSem* 1 (1958) 65-94. R. Dussaud, "Les Religions des Hittites et des Hourrites, des Phéniciens et des Syriens." *MANA* (Paris, 1945).

3. S. Moscati, *Die Kulturen des Alten Orients,* p. 197.

4. M. J. Dahood, *StudSem* 1 (1958), 66.

a belief in supreme beings, and in a hereafter; but the interpretation fluctuates in the conflict of opinions.[5]

Even the historically intelligible Canaanite pantheon displays a confusing uncertainty regarding the essential characteristics and attributes of its divinities. The same duties and privileges are attributed now to one, now to another; the bonds of relationship are easily varied, and even the sex of the divinities is not consistent.[6] Despite this, the following basic points can be made with a fair approximation of certitude.

1) EL, FATHER OF THE GODS

At the head of the Canaanite pantheon stood the god El. He was called *bny bnwt,* "creator of creatures," *mlk,* "king," *tr il,* "bull El," *lṭpn il dpid,* "benevolent and gracious El." Kingly power, in the full sense of the word, was attributed only to El; he it is who shares this kingly power with men, as the Keret epic recounts. His dwelling place is in the remote distance, in the thousand fields and plains, at the source of the two rivers, in the midst of the abyss of the great depths.[7] In this respect we find the name of the chaotic ancient power *tihamat,* who is better known from the Babylonian creation epic. El thus stands in opposition to the chaotic powers which ruled at the beginning of creation. Though no myths regarding the creation of man have yet been discovered, it follows from his epithet *abu-adami,* "father of mankind," that men are also his creation. The whole cosmos, gods and man alike, have their origin in El, and rest in him; he himself stands above cosmos and chaos. In El's chamber there dwells, not a god who needs to stem the inroads of chaos, but a comfortable, venerable, and at the same time, solemn regent,

---

5. On the Stone-Age religion of Canaan, see V. Maag, *Kulturgeschichte des AO,* pp. 563-570.

6. S. Moscati, *op. cit.* 197.

7. "El mabbikê naharêma, qirba apiqê tihâmatêma," *RB* (1939), 597. *bungen,* pp. 87ff.

sure of his dominion. As long as he is there, the structure of the world he founded will abide. It is only within this structure that there is an over-world and an under-world, an awakened and ascending living and a descending dying, oriented towards death. In their ritual life, in their sacrifices, and in the singing of their conciliatory hymns, it is the gods concerned with this cycle of life with whom the men of Ugarit have primarily to deal. On the other hand, all the reverence which is shown towards El is the reverence that the transitory offers to the intransitory, in order to escape the curse of dissolution.[8]

These ancient texts display a very striking and majestic and dignified image of the deity. The controversy as to whether El is simply a generic name for divinity as such or a clearly defined individual person, must be decided in the favor of the person.[9] Comparisons with the other Semitic religions permit us to conclude that El was venerated originally without a consort and throne-partner as the supreme being. If he conveys the impression of a *deus otiosus*, a leisurely and unconcerned god, in the course of the nation's later religious development, this was never the case. El's apparent passivity and withdrawnness is not weakness, but "super-world."[10]

Within historical times, we find, side by side with the only god El, a consort called *Aṣhirat* - Asherah.[11] Her favorite epithet is *aṭrt ym*, "she who strides upon the sea." Is this to be taken as a reference to the primeval sea of origin, above which she is exalted, like El? El's creative powers were also attributed to her. Thus she becomes *qnyt ilm*, "creatrix of the gods"; the gods are *bn atrt*, "sons of Asherah"; they are seven in number, hence the common expression *šbʿm bn atrt*, "the seven sons of Asherah." Even when they begin to rule the world, as fully mature sons of the gods, they still have to suck eternal life from the breast

---

8. V. Maag, *Kulturgesch. des AO*, p. 575
9. O. Eissfeldt, *El im ugaritischen Pantheon*, (Berlin, 1951). M. H. Pope, *El in the ugaritic texts* (Leiden, 1955).
10. V. Maag, *op. cit.* 574.
11. M. J. Dahood, *StudSem* 1 (1958), 80.

of the mother of the gods. The sons of the gods are and remain "sucklings." An echo of this conception of the divinity is to be found in Ps. 8, where God's praise is proclaimed "from the mouth of (God's) children and sucklings," an expression which, in the Bible, must be understood as referring to the angelic beings of heaven.[12] The external form of the goddess Asherah was subject to many transformations; she is even identified with the goddess 'Anat and Astarte. This ready transformability is bound up with the fact that Asherah represents the characteristics of the great mother divinity, already verified in prehistoric times.

2) BA'AL AND THE POWERS OF NATURE

The most widely venerated Canaanite divinity was not El, but Ba'al. It seems that he did not originally belong to the Canaanite pantheon, since he is not considered as a son of El, but as a son of Dagan. But since Dagan was a national divinity of the Amurru, the ascendancy of Dagan's son Ba'al must somehow coincide with the Amurru-Bedouin's ascendancy in the land. There are also certain related characteristics that identify him with the Hurrian storm and thunder god *Teshup*.[13] At all events, Ba'al introduces a new and younger element into the history of Canaanite religion.

The word *ba'lu* means simply "lord," and thus could be used for any number of gods. Since the 15th century, however, it is the storm, rain, and thunder god Hadad who is called simply Ba'al, the "lord (god)." As lord of the sky and of the clouds, he was considered the bringer of fertility. His symbol was, accordingly, the bull. Representation in animal form did not

---

12. Cl. Schedl, "Ugaritisches zu Psalm 8," *FF* 38 (1964), 183-185.

13. M. J. Dahood, *op. cit.* 77. A further point needs to be investigated: whether the ascendancy of Ba'al is connected with the invasion of the Indo-Arians. The Canaanite Ba'al can be interchanged with the Indian god Shim. The bull and fertility cult is still flourishing in modern India. This knowledge was borne in on me during my sojourn in India in the winter of 1963/64.

in any way exclude human and personal characteristics. He is thus represented as a youthful god, with bull's horns, holding a bundle of lightning bolts in one hand, and brandishing a thunderbolt in the other. On other pictures he is standing directly on a bull, again with lightning and thunder in his hands. As a warlike general, he made his way across the clouds in his war chariot. His "sister," beloved, and consort was 'Anat. He meets her hovering in the clouds; but then the mythological picture breaks through: the bull Ba'al copulates with the cow 'Anat. The fruit of this mating of the gods is a divine bullock. Ba'al's essential identity thus fluctuates between divine person and divine animal, brutally incorporating the life-begetting power inherent in every realm of nature.[14] Ba'al's sphere of activity is celebrated in three myth cycles.[15]

a) THE MYTH OF THE BUILDING OF THE TEMPLES: Since Ba'al was the only god who did not yet have a temple, his sister 'Anat interceded for him with the father of the gods El, whereupon El gave his consent to the building of a palace. With the help of the divine court architect, Koshar-wa-Hasis (clever and wise), the construction was completed. Then the "prince Ba'al," that is, the Ba'al zabul,[16] sent his messengers to the gods and invited them to the dedication. Thereupon there was a great drinking-bout, in which the "seventy sons of Asherah" all took part, and the "prince" himself drank from his magnificent goblet. There were also singers and minstrels.

b) THE MYTH OF THE SEASONS: Here the dark and obscure opponent of Ba'al makes his appearance. While Ba'al is reigning, that is, during the time of the rains, and the greening, blossoming, and ripening that follows, Mot is already waiting for Ba'al's fall.

---

14. Illustrations: *ANEP* No. 489-501. A. S. Kapelrud, *Baal in the Ras Shamra Texts,* (Copenhagen, 1952).

15. See also V. Maag, *op. cit.,* 577ff.

16. According to 2 Kings 1, 2, the storm god of the Philistine city of Ekron bore the title *ba'al-zabul,* "Prince Ba'al," but his name could easily be turned into *ba'al-zebub,* "god of the flies," Vol. IV, 88.

Mot is the antithesis of Ba'al. He is the god of dying off and death. Thus, "life" must yield to "death." Ba'al descends into the underworld. The springs dry up, the fields are withered, vegetation disappears, life ceases. "Ba'al is dead! What will happen to humanity? I shall follow Ba'al and descend into the earth."[17] Ba'al's orphaned throne is offered by the gods to Ashtar, a son of Asherah. But Ba'al's throne is too big for him. "His head did not reach the backrest, and his foot was dangling in the air and could not reach down to the footstool." Ashtar himself realizes that he is not at home on Ba'al's throne and renounces the regency, whereupon Mot takes over the throne for the rest of the year, that is, during the dry season. Ba'al's sister-beloved, the "virgin 'Anat," however, never ceases in her search for her brother, trying to hasten his return from the realm of the dead. When she meets Mot along her way, she casts herself upon him like a fury, "she seizes him, thrashes him with the flail, winnows him with the winnowing fan, grinds him in the hand mill. . . ."[18] Thus, his power for this year is completely broken. Now Ba'al can return to his rule again. This he does in a solemn enthronement, amid the jubilation and the homage of the gods who all raise the joyful cry: "Our king is Aliyan Ba'al, our judge, and no one is exalted above him!"[19] Then the cycle of life and vegetation begins anew.

c) THE MYTH OF THE FIGHT WITH THE DRAGON: While the vegetation myth dramatizes the cycle of the seasons, the myth of the dragon fight goes back into the chaotic primeval times. It recounts Ba'al's life and death struggle with the monster in the primeval waters, Yammu. In later Hebrew this word means simply sea. The "sea," against which Ba'al must do battle, is,

---

17. The derivation of the name Mot from *mutu*, *"mature man,"* is contested by M. J. Dahood, *StudSem* 1 (1958), 92. A. Jirku, *Kanaanäische Mythen und Epen*, p. 64.

18. V. Maag, *op. cit.*, 578. Jirku, *op. cit.*, 70.

19. Ba'al's honorary epithet Aliyan apparently means, not "the Exalted One," but "young bullock." Cf. the biblical name Lea, "con." H. Cazelles, *VT.* 10 (1960), 231. Cf. Vol. IV, p. 29.

however, a primordial chaotic being, a horrible dragon with seven heads. This frightening creature, who is also called "Lothan, the primeval dragon before the time of the world, the wounded dragon with the seven heads" (cf. Is. 27, 1; Ps. 74, 13 f.; Job 26, 13), is symbolic of that chaotic force which must first be conquered if there is to be a world and order. No matter how fiercely Yammu attacks Ba'al, Ba'al neither yields nor falters. His final victory means the triumph of the newer element of creation, which is just forming, over the chaotic elements hostile to creation. The victor presents the divine workmaster Koshar-wa-Hasis with two enchanted bronze clubs. Ba'al's sister 'Anat supported her brother in this battle. She furiously attacked Yammu as he lay on the ground, unconscious, and rolled the monster from the sand into the sea. Thus, the figure of the dragon-slayer Ba'al shines like a divine Siegfried in the Canaanite pantheon. On the basis of Biblical echoes, we can conclude that Ba'al's battle was waged not only against the masculine Yammu, but also against the female dragon Rahab (Ps. 89, 11; Job 26, 12). This would also correspond with the duality of the primeval monsters in the Babylonian creation epic *enuma eliš*.

Many characteristics of Ba'al also appear in the image of the god Yahweh; in the last analysis, however, there is certainly no identity between the two, only the prophetic battle cry "Ba'al! Yahweh!" Regarding the other masculine deities we know nothing more than their names, which frequently elude translation. One riddle is proposed by the god Ashtar,[20] who probably symbolizes the morning star, and, as Ashtar-Kemosh, is venerated as the national god of the Moabites. The myth refers to him as "the monstrous one," because children were sacrificed to him. The

---

20. M. J. Dahood, *StudSem* 1 (1958), 85-90. The morning and evening star was venerated both as god and as goddess: as morning star the war god Ashtar, as evening star the goddess of love Ashtarte. This would account for the androgynous character of the divinity in question; however, the point is contested.

Ammonites called their "lord" simply Milkom, "king." The city god of Jerusalem was Shalim, or Shalem, "the god of salvation" (?); the god of Tyre was called Melkart, that is, *malḳ-kart*, "king of the city (of the dead)," that is, the realm of the dead.[21]

3) THE FEMALE DIVINITIES

Among the female divinities in the mythology of Ugarit, we note primarily Asherat - Asherah and ʿAnat.

a) ʿANAT OF THE TWO FACES: ʿAnat has already been mentioned as the beloved sister of Baʿal. In many respects she is similar to the Babylonian Ishtar, particularly in the fact that she shares her ambivalent identity as goddess of love and war. As Baʿal's consort she bears the epithet *btlt ʿnt*, "virgin ʿAnat." In this respect the stress is not on her virginity, in our sense of the word, but upon her eternally blooming and maiden femininity. In the fight for her slain spouse, hints of unmitigated cruelty show through: "She struck the people by the shore of the sea, she annihilates the men at the rising of the sun. Behind her lie heads like balls, above her, hands like locusts, the hands of the warriors are piled up like straws. She went along her way, the heads hung from her back, the hands hung from her belt, she washed her knees in the blood of the warriors, her thighs in the gore of the fighters." [22] ʿAnat also appears as the source of life, by bearing Baʿal the divine bullock; but she also appears as the annihilator of life. Attempts have been made to interpret this figure in terms of philosophy. Her name is supposed to be connected with the Hebrew *ʿet,* the Aramaic *ʿenet,* and the Akkadian *ettu,* which all mean "time, fate." Thus, it would be "time" bearing and devouring all things, which has taken form

---

21. On Schalim see Vol. III, p. 180ff.; on Melkart see Vol. IV, p. 46ff.

22. Text in A. Jirku, *Kanaanäische Mythen und Epen,* 27. Also, J. Aistleitner, *Die Mythologischen und kultischen Texte aus Ras Schamra* (1959), p. 25.

in 'Anat.[23] Place names such as Anathoth – home of the prophet Jeremiah – and Beth-Anoth show that this goddess was also venerated in Palestine.

b) ASHERAH THE MOTHERLY: In the Ugaritic texts, Asherah is El's principal consort, the venerable mother of the gods; she bears the epithet *elat*, "the goddess," that is, "the consort of El." In Palestine, however, she appears as the consort of Ba'al. She is mistress of the furrowed field and thus goddess of fertility as such. As a goddess of life and love, she has appropriated many traits of 'Anat and Ashtarte. Her image overlaps with that of her partners in many respects. In the last analysis, she is probably the continuation of the prehistoric mother divinity. Since men and women dedicated themselves to the mysteries of life by sexual surrender in her cult, her venerators called her by the honorable title *Qudshu* or *Qadesh*, "the holy one," or, literally, "the holiness of Asherah-Ashtarte." [24] For the prophets, this peculiar form of holiness was simply prostitution and adultery. In pictures, this goddess is represented completely nude, with marked female characteristics, frequently standing on a lion, a lily in one hand and two serpents in the other. The lily is a reference to the goddess of love, the serpent to the goddess of fertility.[25]

The texts from Ugarit also celebrate the marriage of the goddess Nikal with the moon god Yerah. Since moon and fertility go hand in hand, this myth fragment [26] is a further evidence of

---

23. M. J. Dahood, *op cit.*, 81. The Indian goddess, Kali, after whom the city of Calcutta is named, bears the same characteristics as the Canaanite 'Anat. She is also bloodthirsty on the one hand – she wears a neckband of skulls – and on the other hand, she is the mother and source of life. The Congress of Orientalists which met in New Delhi in January of 1964 took cognizance of this parallel in the history of religion. Even today Kali is offered blood sacrifices of animals. One gets the impression that the gods of Canaan are still very much alive in India today.

24. W. F. Albright, *Die Religion Israels*, 90ff. In Palestine the feminine conception of the morning-evening star is predominant, and thus, it is the goddess Ashtarte who is venerated, identical with the Latin Venus.

25. Illustrations, *ANEP* 470-472.

26. A. Jirku, *op. cit.*, 77.

the fertility cult. The Canaanite pantheon was a great temptation for Israel of old, especially in its intoxicating fertility cult. A better knowledge of the Canaanite pantheon will cast new light upon this gigantic struggle. In the course of presenting Old Testament history, we shall have to make a more thorough investigation of the particular traits of this Baʿal religion and its cult.[27]

27. Also Vol. IV, 17ff. Pious queen mother and cult of the mother goddess Asherah; Asherah's brand of infamy, stone monuments, and standards, pp. 44ff.

APPENDIX

SCRIPT SYSTEMS IN PRE-ISRAELITE PALESTINE

LITERATURE

The material on the subject of inscriptions is collected in H. Th. Bossert, *Altsyrien* (Tübingen 1951). (Chronological listing of the finds on page 61; illustrations, numbers 294-312.)

H. Bauer, "Der Ursprung des Alphabets," *AO* XXXVI, 1/2, (Leipzig 1936). – K. Sethe, *Vom Bild zum Buchstaben,* (1939). – M. Noth, *Die Welt des AT. Schriften und Schriftdenkmäler,* (Berlin 1953²), 159-177. – M. Dunant, *Byblia Grammata,* Documents et recherches sur le développement de l'écriture en Phénicie, (Beyrouth 1945). – A. Bea, *Die Entstehung des Alphabets,* Misc. (Mercati 1946). – G. R. Driver, *Semitic Writing from Pictograph to Alphabet* (Schweich-Lectures 1948). – D. Diringer, *The Alphabet, a Key to the History of Mankind,* (London 1949). – W. F. Albright, "Alphabetic Origins and the Idrimi Statue," *BASOR 118* (1950), 11-20. – A. Jirku, "Zum Ursprung des Alphabets," *ZDMG 110* (1950), 515-520. – V. Maag, "Syrien-Palästina," *Kulturen des AO,* pub. by H. Schmökel, (Stuttgart 1961), 519-543.

Already towards the end of the 4th millennium, shortly before the beginning of picture writing in Egypt and Mesopotamia, we note the first attempts at picture writing in Syria and Palestine. In an Early Bronze Age cemetery in Byblos, seal impressions on the handles of jars were discovered which bore picture signs and must certainly be interpreted as writing.[1]

Apart from this most ancient form of picture writing there were, at the time of the golden age of Canaanite culture in the second century,

---

1. Albright, *Archaeology of Palestine* (1951), pp. 185-196.

five script systems in Palestine-Syria-Phoenicia, a more precise understanding of which is partially the result of the most recent investigations. As we have already discussed in the section on the relationship between Egypt and the Ancient Near East, Palestine was always the sphere of influence for the Egyptian power. Thus it is only understandable that there should be some hieroglyphic monuments in Palestine, especially in Beth-Shan, which was always an outpost of Egyptian power in Palestine and was well situated to guard the trade routes into Syria.[2] The diplomatic language of the Ancient Near East was Akkadian; in this language the courts of Babylon, Mitanni and Hattusas in Asia Minor discussed their current problems with the Pharaoh in Egypt, and Akkadian cuneiform was also the medium of expression for the petty princes and kings of Palestine and Phoenicia, in the frequent correspondence with which they keep pressing the Pharaoh in Egypt to take a hand in the political situation of Palestine. Rich sources of this Palestinian cuneiform correspondence were discovered in the archives of the Pharaohs in Tell-el-Amarna in Egypt. Side by side with this well developed script system of the great kingdoms, Palestine-Phoenicia, were also discovered new media of written expression. It may have been that in this middle land the difficulties of hieroglyphic and cuneiform writing were felt more keenly than elsewhere, so that an earlier attempt was made to search for a new script.

Since 1929, however, at the excavations in Byblos,[3] inscriptions on bronze tablets and spatulas have come to light — so far 10 inscriptions —

---

2. Beth-Shan was excavated in several stages: 1922-1927 by Fisher in connection with the University of Pennsylvania; he was replaced by Allan Rowe, *Topography and History* (Philadelphia, 1930); *Four Canaanite Temples* (1940); after 1930 the excavations were continued by G. M. Fitzgerald (*Beth-shan Pottery* 1930; *Arab and Byzantine Levels* 1931). Beth-shan is one of the few Palestinian cities which gives evidence of uninterrupted inhabitation from the time of prehistory to the post-Byzantine Era. Level V dates from the time of Ramses III (1198-1167); level VI yielded a monumental temple of Seti I (1313-1292); level VII yielded a temple and fortress tower from the Amarna Era; level VIII produced scarabs and inscriptions of Thutmose III (1502-1448); level XVIII goes back to before 3000 B.C.

3. The script form of Byblos, ancient Gublu or Gebal on the Phoenician coast (modern Gebe'il), is also called Gublitic or pseudo-hieroglyphic. From Byblos we have 64 cuneiform letters, written by the unfortunate King Rib-Addi to Amarna; Byblos was also visited by Wen-Amun, who wanted to purchase wood for the bark of his god (1100 B.C.). The Amarna letters are composed in cuneiform, while Wen-Amun's travel journal is in hieroglyphic.

which, because of their hieroglyphic character, have been known as "pseudo-hieroglyphs," but which were deciphered by E. Dhorme as a distinct gublitic script. Since only a small amount of material was discovered, only 114 signs are known; the total number of signs might well run to 125 - 150. This number of signs is required because each consonant is written differently according to the vowel with which it is joined. Gublitic is thus a syllable script. An interesting note in this discovery is the fact that 17 letters from the later Semitic alphabet are already to be found at this stage, not indeed in the same meaning, but still in the same form, so that we are forced to consider gublitic as a precursor, if not the "mother" of the later alphabetic writing. On the basis of the archaeological level in which the inscriptions were discovered, gublitic script must be dated somewhere around 2000 B.C.[4]

The excavations carried on by Schaeffer in Ras-Shamra, in 1929, in addition to tablets written in the already familiar cuneiform, produced new sources which could not at first be read, but which were very soon deciphered by Bauer as a Ugaritic alphabet. This must obviously have been the conscious invention of an individual scholar who took the cuneiform wedge as the basic element of his writing and formed 30 script signs by various combinations, the cuneiform alphabet of Ugarit. Ugaritic is essentially a consonant script, like the familiar Semitic alphabet; only it has three signs for Aleph, according as it is pronounced *a, i,* or *u.*

The Ugaritic script achieved its highest development and spread in the middle of the 2nd millennium B.C. It is in this script that the myths and the epics of Ugarit literature are written, a rich source for the religious world of ancient Canaan. Discoveries in Palestine (a copper dagger in Tabor and an inscription in Beth-Shemesh) attest to the wide spread of the Ugarit script.[5]

The discoveries of recent times have been pushing the date for the

---

4. Illustrations in Bossert, *Altsyrien,* No. 878. A. Jirku, *Die Entzifferung der gublitischen Schrift durch E. Dhorme. In Forschungen und Fortschritte* 26 (1950), pp. 90-92. H. Schmökel, *Zur Vorgeschichte des Alphabets, op. cit.* 26 (1950), 153-155. E. Dhorme, "Les Textes pseudo-hieroglyphes de Byblos," *RA* 44, 193ff. "Appendice au dechiffrement des pseudohieroglyphes de Byblos," *Syria* 27, 303ff.

5. The Ugarit alphabet is explained in Bossert, *Altsyrien* 62: The basic element of Ugarit script is the wedge: a verticle wedge equals g; two verticle wedges equal sharp s; three vertical wedges equal 1; one horizontal wedge equals t; two horizontal wedges equal p; three horizontal wedges equal h, etc. C. H. Gordon, "The Ugaritic ABC," *OR* 19 (1950), 374. O. Eissfeldt, "Ein Beleg für die Buchstabenfolge unseres Alphabets aus dem 14," Jh. V. Chr. *FF* 26 (1950), 217-220.

development of the linear Semitic (Phoenician) alphabet, "letter writing," from which not only the Greek and Latin, but all modern alphabet systems are derived, farther and farther back into antiquity.

a) THE SINAI INSCRIPTIONS: In the year 1906, Flinders-Petrie, excavating in the old Egyptian copper works on the Sinai peninsula near Serabit-el-Khadem, came across hieroglyphic-like inscriptions which were supposed to be the original type of alphabet writing. They were dated in the 18th or even the 19th century. Alan Gardiner, however, realized that this was really a Semitic picture script, in which the letters were formed according to the principle of acrophony; for example, the signs "ox-aleph" is the expression for the first letter. The 25 inscriptions are written in good Canaanite, and today Albright dates them at about the year 1500 B.C., since similar inscriptions have been found in Palestine proper.[6]

b) INSCRIPTIONS OF THE HYKSOS ERA (1700-1500 B.C.): These inscriptions include a fragment from Geser, a bronze dagger from Lakish (Bossert number 875), which was discovered in a Hyksos tomb, and a plaque of white limestone from Shechem (Bossert number 866). Particular problems are posed by the newly discovered statue of King Idrimi which belongs to the 15th century B.C.[7]

c) THE EXISTENCE OF ALPHABETIC SCRIPT in the 13th and 12th centuries is attested to by a vase with writing found in Lakish (Bossert number 875), an ostrakon from Beth-Shemesh, and a limestone plaque from Byblos (Bossert number 967). The inscriptions are very short, but they still justify the conclusion that the alphabet script already enjoyed widespread use in the second half of the 2nd millennium.[8]

d) FOR THE END OF THE 2ND MILLENNIUM, however, we have more lengthy texts at our disposal: the inscription of Jehilmik (Bossert number 873), the Ahiram sarcophagus (number 872) from the time between 1050-950; the Mesha inscription from the year 840, a black basalt stone, 1.24m. in height, which recounts the erection of a sanctuary in honor of Kamosh, the great god of Moab, and boasts of victories over Israel.[9] It was

---

6. W. F. Albright, "The Early Alphabetic Inscriptions from Sinai and Their Decipherment." (Date from the time around 1500, Semitic slaves, Funeral texts) *BASOR* 110, 6-22.

7. *Idem*: "Alphabetic Origins and the Idrimi Statue," *BASOR* 118 (1950), 11-20.

8. The alphabet was developed between 2500-1500 in the neighborhood of Egypt and perfected along the Phoenician coast, according to G. R. Driver, *Semitic Writings from Pictograph to Alphabet* (1944).

9. *AOB*, 2nd ed., 1927, No. 120.

by way of the Phoenicians that the Semitic consonant alphabet made its way, in the 10th century, to the Greeks, who enlarged it by the addition of vowel signs.[10]

The most important conclusion for Biblical science to be drawn from this summary is the fact that Israel's growth into a nation, in the 2nd millennium, does not take place in an era devoid of writing. In the Palestine of the 2nd millennium five script systems were in use together, one of which, linear alphabet writing, after a long period of evolution which we can follow rather closely, won the ultimate victory. The invention of alphabetic script put the art of writing, which had previously been the monopoly of professional scribes and priests, within the reach of a much broader class of educated people. Solemn texts, destined for public reading, were chiseled in stone. But since this was a very difficult undertaking, a simpler way was generally preferred. Rough stone plates were covered with a thick layer of plaster which produced a smooth writing surface. The writing was then gouged or scratched onto this surface by a chisel or an iron stylus. This was the manner in which Joshua had the law recorded. Moses had commanded them to "set up large stones, and plaster them with plaster" (Deut. 27, 2), and to write the law upon them. Since such plaster withstands the ravages of weather only poorly, it is hardly to be expected that such inscriptions can still be found. For everyday use, writing was recorded on potsherds, wood, leather, or papyrus. The alphabet script, by way of distinction from the complicated hieroglyphic and cuneiform scripts, which only privileged scribes could master, was called simply "common script" (Is. 8, 1), that is, "script of the people."[11]

---

10. G. Klaffenbach, "Schriftprobleme der Ägäis," *FF* 24 (1948), 193-196. According to A. van den Branden, the inventors of alphabet writing are to be sought, not in Syro-Phoenicia, but rather in the area of southern Arabia. It was Arabian merchants who first sketched outlines of a simplified letter-writing, motivated by the demands of commerce. (Oral statement, Beirut, 1959.)

11. V. Maag, *Kulturgeschichte des AO,* 537.

PART TWO

EARLY HISTORY OF THE BIBLE

IT was necessary to present the history of the Ancient Near East at least in its broader outlines in order to avoid an initial error. The Old Testament does not present the most ancient accounts of the first beginnings of humanity. The people of Israel enter the concert of Ancient Near East peoples only at a late date. Thus, the literature of Israel belongs to the more recent literatures of the Ancient Near East. We have grown accustomed to regarding the "Old Testament" as a unified book, and thereby too easily forget the fact that a thousand years have gone into its composition. In order to understand it correctly, it is imperative to return to its original component units, and try to understand them in terms of their historical evolution. Only thus can a book such as this deserve to be called "history of the Old Testament."

A "history of the Old Testament" needs to examine the writings of Old Testament times not only from the point of view of formal literary history – which is concerned with the origin and history of the texts – but also in terms of their content, by attempting to isolate the operative historical forces. Ancient tradition has divided the Old Testament writings into three groups: 1. Law (*torah*),[1] Pentateuch,[2] 2. Prophets (*nebî'îm*),[3]

---

1. The Torah contains not only the paragraphs of the Law; the laws are generally presented in terms of their historical evolution, together with narrative sections. "Torah" means "doctrine" rather than merely "Law," not unlike the Egyptian doctrine (*sbâyet*), which is approximately equivalent to "world philosophy, philosophy of life." (W. F. Albright, *From Stone Age to Christianity,* 1949, p. 269.) Thus, the Torah recounts the ancient Israelite "Weltanschauung" or outlook on the world.

2. The name Pentateuch occurs for the first time in Origen's commentary of John, but it was apparently used already by the Hellenistic Jews of Alexandria, as the Talmudic expression, "the five fifths of the Law" gives us to understand (A. B. Bentzen, *Introduction to the Old Testament,* 1949, II, p. 9). The Greek translation of the names of the first five books of the Bible, the books of Moses, has passed over into our modern languages: Genesis (creation story), Exodus (departure), Leviticus (Priestly Law), Numbers (counts), Deuteronomy (Second Law). In literary criticism, a different set of criteria are applicable. Since the Book of Joshua is recognized as an organic continuation of the five books of Moses, the term

3. Sacred writings (*ketûbîm*).[4] This literary work does not present any compact unity. It is comprised of the most divergent literary genres, and, in terms of content, it attempts to span the immense space from creation to the religious-national uprising of the Maccabean era. The most ancient traditions of humanity, tribal histories, laws for the regulation of religious and national life, wisdom teaching, songs, prophetic preaching, and history books in the narrower sense of the word, – these all go to make up the "colorful tapestry" which we call the Old Testament. When we look at the back of this tapestry, the threads run across each other's paths in many directions, giving us an insight into the bewildering complexity of Ancient Near East history. And yet this manifold book has a higher unity. When we take it up as a book of revelation, we discover it to be a coherent presentation of the history of humanity, which is not so much a "history of humanity" as it is a "history of God with men." The real playwright in this world theater is GOD who is operative in history. He marks the beginning of the world and history; he threatens with the divine judgment of catastrophe and guides the new beginnings along the course of history. It is in his hands to determine beginning and end of eras. These eras are loaded with the most forceful dynamism; each one brings the other closer to fulfillment. Thus, the Old Testament presents a unified plan of history, whose principal phases are the following:

Hexateuch has been coined (six books), to include it. There is even some discussion of Hepta- and Octa-teuchs including the Books of Judges and Kings. More recently, the term, Tetrateuch (four books) has come into prominence, referring to the books of Genesis through Numbers, Deuteronomy being included among the following books as the work of the "Deuteronomist historian."

3. The Jewish canon counts the historical books among the prophets, which are divided into the former prophets (Joshua, Judges, Samuel, Kings), and the latter prophets (Isaiah, Jeremiah, Ezekiel, and the 12 minor prophets).

4. The "Sacred Writings" include the books: Psalms, Proverbs, Job, Song of Songs, Ruth, Lamentations, Ecclesiastes (Qoheleth), Esther, Daniel, Ezra, Nehemiah, and Chronicles. The two books of the Maccabees, Sirach,

1) PREHISTORY (GEN. 1-11): This presents the foundation and basis for all history, by showing that human history is a struggle in which man is faced with a decision between God and demon. The first 11 chapters of Genesis describe mankind's path from Paradise to rebellion against God and to the building of the tower of Babel. This is a climactic episode, and represents a low point. The world has become pagan. If history is to have any further meaning, God must now initiate a new beginning. The horizon of prehistory is universal; it embraces the totality of mankind.

2) THE PATRIARCHAL ERA (GEN. 12-50): With the call of Abraham, universal history narrows to focus on the particularistic family history of the patriarchs. The foundation of a new humanity is now to be laid. Abraham is the chosen one, for the "sake of the many." The universal interest remains in the background, since the "blessing of the seed of Abraham" is to extend to all peoples; but in the foreground of the story we now have only the history of Israel, which quietly in Egypt, is growing into a people of 12 tribes.

3) MOSES AND THE PEOPLE OF THE 12 TRIBES: With the call of Moses and the exodus from Egypt, this family history broadens into the national-religious history of a people. It was not a profane or empty ceremony when the 12 tribes gathered at Sinai to make a covenant with God and thus be constituted Yahweh's people, proceeding from there to enter the land of Canaan, promised to them by Yahweh as their heritage. The dramatic movement of this story is exhaustively detailed for us – though not always in a manner that can be easily penetrated in terms of literary and historical criticism – in the books of Exodus to Deuteronomy, and also in Joshua, Judges, and the Books of Kings. The possession of Canaan is the final crowning of the

---

and Wisdom of Solomon are, in the Jewish and Protestant canon, numbered among the apocrypha, written in Greek and, as opposed to the more ancient tradition, had to make their way into the canon of inspired books.

work of liberation, begun in Egypt by Moses under Yahweh's command.

4) THE GOLDEN AGE OF THE KINGS AND PROPHETS: In their possession of the promised land, the people of God, the 12 tribes, achieved a national and religious climax (world empire of David, temple of Solomon); but in the background always lurked the danger of turning to the gods of Canaan. In this hour of national peril, the prophets arose and sought to save the covenant of Yahweh, and thus the national autonomy. But they spoke to deaf ears. By her defection to the gods of Canaan, Israel had also lost her right to the possession of the land, and was driven from the land of her fathers by the world powers of the Ancient Near East acting as the executors of Yahweh's divine sentence against her. With the loss of her political autonomy now begins a new and final division of Old Testament history.

5) THE FULLNESS OF TIMES: After the return from exile, the process of interior transformation began to set in, giving Israel the national stamp that Jesus of Nazareth found upon his coming. The time had become ripe for him. It was he who burst the confining limitations of nationalism and brought God's salvation history out of the narrow framework of one "chosen people" into the universal world, the world of human history.

The prehistory is to be understood as a universal prelude to the history of Israel. It does not represent any independent literary work; it is rather part and parcel of the great work of history which begins with the story of creation. Genesis itself is not a work of literature in the modern sense either; it shared the fate of other Ancient Near East literary works and assumed its final form only centuries after it was first written. Divergent streams of the most ancient human traditions have all flowed together here, and only then, by the work of an "inspired" hand, enlightened by the Holy Spirit, have they been formed into the artistic pattern of Genesis.

As a guide line for the interpretation of biblical prehistory, we must here quote from the Letter of the Pontifical Biblical

Commission, January 16, 1948, to Cardinal Suhard, of Paris:[5]

"As regards the composition of the Pentateuch the Commission already recognized the decree of June 27, 1906 that one could maintain that in the composition of his work Moses may have used written documents or oral traditions and admit post-Mosaic modifications and additions. There is nobody nowadays who doubts the existence of such sources or does not admit the gradual accretions to the Mosaic laws due to the social and religious conditions of later times, a process that is also shown in the historical accounts.... We therefore invite Catholic scholars to study these problems without prejudice in the light of sound criticism and the findings of other sciences interested in the matter. Such studies will undoubtedly establish the great part played by Moses as a writer and as a law-giver.

"The question of the literary forms of the first eleven chapters of Genesis is much more complicated and obscure. These literary forms do not correspond to any of our classic categories and cannot be judged in the light of Graeco-Latin or modern literary *genres.* Their historicity can be neither affirmed nor denied *en bloc* without unjustifiably applying to them the rules of a literary genre in which they cannot be classified.... To declare *a priori* that the accounts in them do not contain history in the modern sense of the word would easily lead to the misunderstanding that they contain no history in any sense of the word, while relating in a simple and colorful language suitable to the mentality of a not very developed mankind the basic truths underlying the economy of salvation, and at the same time the popular description of the origins of the human race and the chosen people."

---

5. *Acta Apostolicae Sedis,* 1948, 45-48. Translation: *The Teaching of the Church* (Alba House, New York, 1967) p. 82.

SECTION ONE

ORIGIN OF THE WORLD

THE CONSTRUCTION OF GENESIS

THE construction of the first Book of Moses, the Book of Genesis, has long been a source for wonder. "There is nothing casual or accidental about this book; everything is deliberate, well weighed, and precise." [1] In its present form, the book of creation is a work of art, precisely balanced and precisely planned. But what are the underlying principles of organization?

1) TOLEDOT

If we attempt to analyze the structure of the Book of Genesis on the basis of any kind of division, we are immediately struck by the so-called toledot sentences whose regular reoccurrence divides the entire book into eleven sections, in the following outline:

1. These are toledot of heaven and earth (2,4)
2. This is the book of the toledot of Adam (5,1)
3. These are the toledot of Noah (6,9)
4. And these are the toledot of the sons of Noah (10,1)

1. G. V. Rad, *Das erste Buch Mose,* ATD 1950, 36.

5. These are the toledot of Shem (11,10)
6. And these are the toledot of Terah (11,27)
7. And these are the toledot of Ishmael (25,12)
8. And these are the toledot of Isaac (25,19)
9. And these are the toledot of Esau (36,1)
10. And these are the toledot of Esau (36,9)
11. And these are the toledot of Jacob (37,2).

The outline makes it immediately clear that the toledot of Esau are presented twice in the Book of Genesis. Is this the result of editorial oversight? Hardly! It is rather an indication of the book's construction on the literary model of the number 11. In this convention, 11 elements are enumerated, one of them being differentiated from the other 10 by repetition or by some other device, to give the outline of $10 + 1$. This same principle of construction, first clearly evident in the structure of the Book of Genesis as a whole, is also the outline that determines, as we shall see, the creation narrative. According to the most widely held interpretation, toledot is to be interpreted as "generations, origins, family trees, phases of development." Certainly, these toledot passages each marks a division of salvation history. The first five describe the development of salvation from time immemorial down to the building of the tower of Babel; the second five describe the patriarchal era. Since the whole account is concerned primarily with salvation history, it is not difficult to explain the varying lengths of the individual sections. Whatever is not valuable in terms of the subsequent course of salvation history is eliminated. Thus the family trees of Ishmael and Esau are given, but their subsequent history is nowhere presented. Primary interest is concentrated on the bearers of salvation.[2]

The divisions themselves are clearly enough determined: the only real question is whether toledot is to be considered a title to the following section or a subscript to the preceding section.

---

2. W. Möller, *Biblische Theologie des Alten Testaments in heilsgeschichtlicher Entwicklung*. 1934, 65.

The solution involves the Ancient Near East techniques of literary composition.

The "books" of the Ancient Near East were, for three millennia, clay tablets.[3] The cuneiform symbols were pressed into the soft clay with a stylus, and the clay was then baked. The tablets thus achieved a durability which made them proof against the ravages of time and weather; they have survived for many millennia. For smaller texts small tablets were chosen, while larger tablets, or several such tablets, were used for longer texts. Literary texts were entitled by their opening words. The Babylonian creation epic thus bears the name *enuma eliš*, "when up in heaven." The books of Moses follow the same practice. In Hebrew, the Pentateuch is referred to by the opening words of the individual books: "in the beginning" (*berēšît*), "the names" (*šemôt*), "and he called" (*wiyyikrā'*), "in the desert" (*bemidbār*), "words" (*debārîm*). The title thus gives the opening words, without giving any clue as to the contents of the book, as a book title is generally expected to do. Such official titles are found generally only at the conclusion of a work, in the so-called colophon. Thus, for example, the *Codex Hammurabi* concludes with these words: "The just laws which the wise king introduced. . . . My solemn words have I written upon this stone."

The same thing is true of the conclusion of the Books of Leviticus and Numbers: "These are the commandments (*'ēlleh miṣwôt*), which the Lord commanded Moses for the people of Israel on Mount Sinai" (Lev. 27, 34). "These are the commandments and the ordinances (*'ēlleh hammiṣwôt wehammišpātîm*), which the Lord commanded by Moses to the people of Israel in the Plains of Moab by the Jordan at Jericho" (Num. 36, 13).

On the basis of these data, Wiseman claims that the toledot

---

3. P. J. Wiseman, *Die Entstehung der Genesis.* Das 1. Buch der Bibel im Lichte der archäologischen Forschung. Wuppertal 1957. The student of the Ancient Near East here proposes an entirely different line of interpretation. He attempts to deal with the problem of Genesis on the basis of the cuneiform literature. But many of his conclusions simply do not do justice to the complicated literary origins of Genesis.

sentences are not title inscriptions, but rather title colophons, that is, titles summing up the content of the text printed immediately above them. This solution might apply well enough to the Babylonian cuneiform literature; but the Hebrew literature, with its letter alphabet, was written, not on clay tablets, but rather on leather or papyrus. What we are dealing with is accordingly, manuscripts in the form of scrolls.

2) THE ARRANGEMENT OF THE HEBREW MANUSCRIPT

One must not suppose that the ancient manuscripts present simply a chaotic *tohu-wa-bohu* in their arrangement. For the synagogue services, error-free manuscripts must have been selected and preserved. Eissfeldt[4] claims that already in the time of Rabbi Akiba the text of the Old Testament was fixed, down to the very word and letter. We must thus be dealing with a most precise and conscientious text tradition.

The best manuscript available for study today is the *Codex Leningradensis* (L = B 19A), which served as basis for the BIBLIA HEBRAICA (the edition was begun by R. Kittel, and subsequently continued by P. Kahle, A. Alt, and O. Eissfeldt). This author has had opportunity to consult the Leningrad manuscript for some very careful study.

If this manuscript is assumed as the basis for the methodology, the various divisions and sections are immediately self-evident. The individual "orders" (*sedarîm*) are indicated by the letter S written in the margin. It has been claimed that these divisions and their notation are merely something added to the already established form of the text, to serve as a reference guide for reading in the synagogue: but this is a claim that would have to be proved.[5] It could just as easily be true that the needs of

4. O. Eissfeldt, *Einleitung in das Alte Testament*, B 1964, 929.

the Hebrew Bible, New York 1966 (division by Sedarim 32-65).

5. Chr. D. Ginsburg, *Introduction to the Massoretico-Critical Edition of*

the divine service were one of the considerations that originally determined the present form of the Bible text. Only the most careful examination can demonstrate whether the divisions form a self-contained structural unity, or are simply an artificial superstructure on the text. The conclusion is, as subsequent investigation clearly shows, that there is in fact a unified structural principle. From the very beginning of Pentateuchal criticism scholars have been accustomed to pay as little attention as possible to the present-day condition of the text, as if it merited little or no consideration. After the other "Biblical prehistories" have distinguished and divided the text in terms of the usual sources, we must proceed from the working hypothesis that the divisions and arrangement handed down in the manuscript tradition are actually meant to be divisions and arrangement. We can attempt a valid examination of the past history of this text only after we have explained the form and structure of the text as we have it today. In Vol. II, under the subject of "Pentateuchal Criticism," we shall present a much more explicit discussion of this question.

The first "*sedarim* notation" occurs in the manuscript at 2,4: "These are the toledot of heaven and earth," thus clearly indicating that this toledot sentence is meant to serve as a title inscription to the Paradise narrative that follows. The creation narrative itself does not have any *sedarim* notation. This is quite in keeping with the ancient practice of writing a book: the first "chapter" is not numbered as chapter one, but rather as the "*initium*," or proem, the introductory verses to the entire book. Biblical prehistory is thus divided into this proem (1,1 – 2,3) and eight divisions (2,4 – 11,32). Since the division into *parashes*, that is, selections to be read during the annual synagogue cycle, is only secondary (in the Leningrad manuscript), it is a subject that need not detain us here.

3) PRINCIPLES OF STRUCTURE

The Bible text is like a building constructed from the living stones of the word. Just as, in the case of the architectural work, the plan of construction can be precisely grasped in terms of numbers, so too can the architecture of words that make up the literary composition. Since it is a well-known fact that the ancient scribes counted words, sentences, and divisions, let us take up this traditional method of counting for reexamination. First we must determine precisely what is to be counted, precisely where the principles of literary construction are to be discovered.

The principle we shall select is a very simple one. We distinguish various sections of the text, not on the basis of historical sources or strata, but on the basis of their fundamental structure as *a.* narrative account (N), *b.* introduction to direct speech (I), *c.* direct speech (S).

If the numbers that make their appearance here are actually intended to indicate an obvious symbolic value, than we can indeed speak of structural principles in the text. The interpretation of this symbolism, however, cannot be based upon any modern criteria: once again we must turn to the traditional symbolism handed down from ancient times. The proper methodology here is suggested by the work *"sepher yesirah,"* (Book of Creation), which according to the investigations of Gershom Scholem,[6] is not the product of the Middle Ages, but rather the era that saw the foundation of the Jewish community between the two wars (70 and 135 A.D.). If similar symbolic values make their appearance as early as the structure of the Book of Genesis, then the problem of the origins of the Jewish mystique needs to be rephrased. For then it would be clearly demonstrable that there is much more mystique in the Bible too than has been commonly assumed or admitted.

---

6. G. Scholem, "Ursprung und Anfänge der Kabbalah," *Studia Judaica* III (1962), 20ff.

CHAPTER XIV

THE SONG OF WORLD CREATION

PROEM (GEN. 1, 1 – 2, 3)

Statement of Faith:

1, 1 In the beginning God created heaven and earth.

Night of Creation

2 The earth existed as shapelessness and primordial night,
and darkness lay upon the abyss;
but God's spirit hovered over the waters.

I) Word

3 And God spoke: "Let there be light!"
And it was so.
4 And God saw the light, that it was good.
And God divided between light and darkness.
5 God called the light "day,"
the darkness he called "night."
And it was evening
and it was morning: DAY ONE.

II) Word

6 *And God spoke:*
"Let there be a firmament in the midst of the waters,
to separate water from water!"
7 *And God made the solid firmament,*
separated thus the waters that were under the firmament
from the waters that were above the firmament.
And it was so.
8 *And God called the firmament "heaven."*
And it was evening,
and it was morning: DAY TWO.

III) WORD

9 *And God spoke:*
"Let the water under the heaven gather together into one place, and let the dry be visible!"
And it was so.
10 *And God called the dry "land,"*
the gathering of the water he called "sea."
And God saw that it was good.

IV) WORD

11 *And God spoke:*
"Let the earth bring forth green:
plants that bear seed,
and fruit trees that bear fruit according to their kinds,
that have seed within them upon earth!"
And it was so.
12 *And the earth brought forth*
plants that bear seed according to their kinds,
and trees which bear fruit
that have their seed in them according to their kinds.
And God saw that it was good.
13 *And it was evening,*
and it was morning: DAY THREE.

V) WORD

14 And God spoke:
"Let lights arise in the firmament of heaven,
to distinguish between the day and between the night.
Let them be as signs, for festivals, for days and years!
15 Let them be lights in the firmament of heaven,
to shine over the earth!"
And it was so.
16 And God made two great lights,
the greater light to have rule over the day,
the lesser to have rule over the night, and the stars.
17 And God set them into the firmament of heaven,
to shine over the earth,
18 and to rule over day and night,
and to divide between light and darkness.
And God saw that it was good.
19 And it was evening,
and it was morning: DAY FOUR.

VI) WORD

20 And God spoke:
"Let the water teem with countless living creatures!
Let the bird fly over the land,
up over the firmament of the heaven!"
21 And God made the great sea monsters,
and all creatures that live and stir,
with whom the water teems, according to their kinds.
Also the birds with wings, according to their kinds.
And God saw that it was good.

VII) WORD

22 And God blessed them and spoke:
"Be fruitful and increase,
fill the water of the sea;
let the bird multiply on the land!"

23 *And it was evening,*
and it was morning: DAY FIVE.

VIII WORD

24 *And God spoke:*
"Let the land bring forth living creatures according to their kinds:
cattle, creeping creatures, and wild beasts according to their kinds!"
And it was so.
25 *And God made the land animals according to their kinds:*
the cattle according to their kinds,
and the beasts that crawl upon the earth, according to their kinds.
And God saw that it was good.

IX WORD

26 *And God spoke:*
"Let us make man
after our image as our likeness.
They shall rule over the fishes of the sea,
the birds of the heaven, over the animals and over all the land,
and over all the creatures that crawl upon the earth!"
27 *And God made man after his image,*
after the image of God did he make him,
male and female he made them.

X WORD

28 *And God blessed them and God spoke to them:*
"Be fruitful and multiply,
fill the earth and make it subject!
Rule over the fishes of the sea, the birds of heaven,
and over all the animals that stir upon the earth!"

Dietary Commandment (XI Word)

29 *And God spoke:*
"See, I give you all seed-bearing plants,
that are on the whole surface of the earth,
and all trees that have seed-bearing fruit:
let them be for your food!
30 *And for all land animals, for all birds of the heaven,*
for everything that stirs upon earth, that has the force of life in it:
all green plants for food."
31 *And God saw all that he had made,*
and see! it was very good.
And it was evening,
and it was morning: DAY SIX.

Sabbath Prohibition

2, 1 *Finished were heaven and earth and all their multitude.*
2 *On day seven God was finished with the work he had done;*
And God rested on day seven from all the work he had done.
3 *And God blessed day seven and sanctified it;*
for on that day he rested from all his work,
that God had created, so that man would do likewise!

A) STRUCTURAL PRINCIPLES OF THE TEXT

The following table breaks down the text of the creation narrative in terms of narrative (N), which includes execution, introduction to direct speech (I), and direct speech (S):

Gen 1, 1 – 2, 3	N	I	S	Execution	Totals
Statement of Faith, 1	7				7
Primordial night 2	14				
I Word 3-5		2:	2	27	
II Word 6-8		2:	9	27	
III Word 9-10		2:	9	14	
IV Word 11-13		2:	16	26	
V Word 14-19		2:	21	46	
VI Word 20-21		2:	13	23	
VII Word 22-23		4:	9	6	
VIII Word 24-25		2:	10	20	
IX Word 26-27		2:	17	13	
X Word 28		6:	16	–	
Subtotals:	14	26:	122	202	364
XI Word 29-31		2:	44	17	
Sabbath 2, 1-3	35				98
Final Totals	56N	28:	166	219N	
	275N	28I	166S		469

Based on the testimony of the manuscript itself, the creation narrative 1, 1 – 2, 4 forms a self-contained unit. It is composed of 469 words. But where are the principles of its structure to be found? It is possible to explain the total number in any of a number of ways, but all of them would be quite arbitrary. The text itself furnishes the key to the division. The first verse contains the statement of faith in the Creator of heaven and earth. Verse 2 describes the primordial night of creation, a description which, like the following days of creation, is the language of symbol and imagery. In the outline of the seven days of the week, however, we clearly see the over-riding plan of 10 words of creation, followed by an 11th word in the text of the law. In terms of verbal content, the structure is as follows:

1) STATEMENT OF FAITH: The first sentence of the creation narrative, which is, after all, intended to underline the sanctification of the Sabbath, numbers seven words: *b^e^reshît bara' '^e^lohîm 'et hashshamayim w^e^'et ha'áres.* "In the beginning God made heaven and earth." This verse is also characterized as the thematic sentence of the entire narrative, and is obviously pronounced as a confession of faith in the one God of creation. Verse 2 begins something different, the gradual development of the content of the confession of faith which is so monumentally prefixed to the narrative in verse 1. The very first datum of our investigation is thus the clear enunciation of the number seven.

2) THE TEN WORDS: At verse 2 we must once again begin the count from zero. What follows is the narrative of the second through the sixth days. The blessing of fertility, in verse 28, concludes the narrative of the creation of the cosmos, with man standing firmly in the middle. Next there are two commands, one a dietary command (1, 29-31) in the narrative of the sixth day, and the other the Sabbath prohibition (2, 1-3) which forms the conclusion of the entire creation narrative. This division cannot be characterized as purely subjective or something imposed upon the text: it is firmly anchored in the very words of the text itself. Further argument for this position is one of the "Oracles of the Fathers": "By means of ten sentences (*ma'^a^rôt*) was the world created" (Abot V,1). This is an obvious reference to the ten statements made by God, the commands by which he called all being into existence. Eight times we have the simple formula: "And God spoke," and twice the simple formula is amplified into the formula of blessing (1, 22, 28). Now the dietary command also begins with the introduction "and God spoke." This would make 11 "words." But the 11th word is clearly distinguished and separated from the other 10: it is not a word of creation, but rather a law. Here we are faced with the same structural principle that underlines the toledot of Genesis: 10+1.

If we count through from verse 2 to the conclusion of verse 28, we get the total of 364 words, neither more nor less. At first glance it would appear more desirable to have reached the number 365, the normal figure for a solar year. By resorting to the *apparatus criticus* it would have been a simple enough matter to produce the extra word. But it is awkward to simply assume the license of taking liberties with the canonical text. The Masoretic Text, at all events, contains precisely 364 words. The number should occasion no great surprise: it is the number of a jubilee year.

The law for celebration of the jubilee year is to be found both in the Book of Jubilees and in the Book of Henoch. Because of its fundamental importance to this argument, the text is here given in its entirety, as it is written on the heavenly tablets: "thirteen weeks for each individual period; from one (festival) to the other shall your remembrance (go): from the first to the second; and from the second to the third; and from the third to the fourth. And all the days of the precepts are 52 weeks of days, and together they (make) a full year. So is it inscribed and ordered on the heavenly tablets, and there is no transgressing it, (neither) in an individual year, nor from year to year. But do you bid the children of Israel that they must keep the year according to this number: 364 days, and (this) is a full year, and they shall not shorten its time" (Jub 6, 29-32). According to this text the jubilee year is divided into 52 weeks of 7 days each, a total of 364 days. The year is then further divided into four quarters (quatembers) of 13 weeks each, so that each quarter has a total of 91 days. The law of the 91 days is, moreover, explicitly promulgated in the Book of Henoch, chapter 82. Here too the text reads: "The year is completed in 364 days" (82, 6). This is ample justification for posing the question as to whether or not the existence of the jubilee year can be postulated at the date on which the creation narrative was first composed. But there are more things to be counted.

The two precepts which follow the creation narrative proper, the dietary precept and the Sabbath prohibition, count a total of 98 words, that is, a total of two jubilees. By jubilee we mean the period of 7 X 7, or 49 years; 2 X 49 = 98. The entire account bears witness to the deliberate numerical symbolism of its construction: 7 + 364 + (2 X 49) = 469 words. The final total is meaningful only in terms of the individual subtotals that are contained in it.

On the fourth day of creation, the origin of the great luminaries of the heavens is recorded. What is the purpose behind their creation? "Let them be as signs, for festivals, for days and years" (*mo ʿadîm, yamîm, shanîm*). One might well inquire what were the festival and annual cycles that the author had in mind. The answer is furnished by the very construction of the text itself. The theme sentence at the beginning, with its 7 words, already sets the rhythm for the seven-day week, followed immediately by the 10 words of creation with their 364 words, a clear allusion to the year and its 364 days. The two precepts with their 98 words indicate the basic structure of the jubilee festival. Finally, the 52 words of the first day might well enough be an allusion to the division of the year into 52 weeks (verses 1-5). The basic structure of the text thus indicates the fundamental outline of the holy year (7 + 364 + 98).

Since the creation narrative is dated during the era of spiritual and religious reorientation of the Babylonian Exile, as part of the Priestly tradition (P), one must not exclude the possibility that the magnificent conception of the jubilee year also dates from that epoch. The prophet Ezekiel was, at that same period, outlining the plans for the new people, the new Temple, the new priesthood. All that was missing was the outline for the holy year. The whole purpose of this reform movement was the creation of a holy people. But a holy people must be concerned, in the very first place, with keeping the Sabbath holy. But only in the schema of the jubilee year is the undisturbed order of the Sabbath truly preserved. The solar year with its 365 days and the necessary intercalary days "desecrates" this rhythm. Concern for the sanctification of the Sabbath may, accordingly, very well have prompted this outline for the jubilee calendar.

On the basis of verbal structure, the creation narrative would thus belong to the category of legal texts, texts which promulgate a law. The Sabbath prohibition (2, 1-3) closes with the sentence: "and sanctified it (the seventh day); for on that day he rested from all his work that Elohim had done *laʿasôt.*" The relative clause presents some difficulty for the translator. The last word is an infinitive form, and means "to do" or "for doing." In the *Echterbibel* the difficulty is simply passed over by the translation: "that God had made (*das Gott geschaffen hatte*)." Martin Buber, who is generally so painstakingly accurate in reproducing the very essence of the Hebrew original, transforms the infinitive into a participle: "for on that day he kept festival from all his work, which, doing, God made." The translation is meaningless. The two verbs translated as *machen* (do) and *erschaffen* (make) are never linked together in Biblical parlance. If we consult the concordance for all passages in which the form *laʿasôt* occurs, we must necessarily recognize it as part of the vocabulary of legislation. It occurs 45 times in the Book of Deuteronomy, in some such connection as "in the manner that YHWH, my God, has commanded to do (*laʿasôt*)." It is striking to note that this is the precise term that concludes the explicit promulgation of the Sabbath precept in Deut 5, 12-15: "*laʿasôt 'et yôm hassabat,*" – "to *do* the day of the Sabbath." This identical term from the legal vocabulary now closes the Sabbath text in Genesis, in a most symbolic manner. The divine name Elohim, the subject of the relative clause, is frequently transferred to the main clause in our translations. But its position in the relative clause is not simply a matter of mere stress; it is designed to bracket the last sentence of the creation narrative with the first. "In the beginning God made" (1, 1) and "which God had made" (2, 3c) are the pillars which support and enclose the entire narrative. The practical purpose of the creation narrative and its division in terms of a week is achieved by the force of the final word *laʿasôt*: the translation should thus read: "that God had made to do," or, to reproduce the same thought in clearer form, "for man to do it too." The very structure of the words thus promulgates the jubilee calendar.

3) BASIC WORDS AND DERIVED FORMS: The horizontal component thus has a structure of 364 + 105. We arrive at the same values once again if we, so to speak, describe a vertical component as well. The question this time is the number of basic words employed by the author in his text. And how often does he use these basic words in derived forms, that is, how many times are the words used in the text? We thus set up a table of concordances for the chapter. The result is: 105 basic words and 364 derived forms. Critics have always been struck by the fact that the creation narrative is composed of a relatively small number of words, precisely 105, which the author repeats and still varies in a truly grandiose monotony. We can only marvel at the wonderful precision with which the entire text is composed. 105 is, moreover, a frequent symbolic number. Judith's age is given as 105 years. Mathematically, 105 is the sum of the arithmetical series from 1 to 14.

4) THE SMALLER STRUCTURAL ELEMENTS: Not only in the overall outline is there evidence of a deliberate structuring: it permeates even the smallest units of the whole. A really complete presentation must be reserved for a full commentary. Here we can present only a few observations: the 10 introductory sentences for the 10 "words" count 26 words: the 10 "words" can be divided on the principle 6 + 4; the first 6 number 70, while 7 + 9 and 8 + 10 each number 26, a total of 52 words. The 6 sentences "that it was (very) good" contain a total of 26 words, also. Since 26 is the numerical value of the sacred name YHWH, we might say that the text is sealed with the divine name, a very popular mode of thought in the ancient Hebrew mystique. The number of the year, 364, can also be reduced to the name YHWH (14 X 26 = 364).

On the basis of this rather briefly outlined but nonetheless clearly demonstrable structural principle we can surely venture the conclusion that the author of the creation narrative was following a very closely determined model in the structuring of his text, and that he strictly subordinates the individual structural elements to the overall plan. The basis for the creation narrative is thus a cosmic and mystical model: the fundamental orientations towards the holy year and the sacred name of God are easily recognizable.

5) THE NUMBER OF LETTERS: One might well presume that, in a text that has been so carefully constructed, even the letters are to be counted. But only the most rigorous investigation can determine whether there is any real regularity. For the moment, we must rest content with a single and rather striking discovery: the 11 spoken "words" number exactly 620 letters. This number is also quite frequent in the Jewish mystical writings, with special reference to the mystery of the crown of God. The numerical value of the word for crown (*keter*) is 620. It is said that 620 rays of light emanate from this crown, and penetrate the whole of creation.

6) MYSTERY OF THE THRONE OF GOD: The "Book of Creation" (*sepher yesirah*) already quoted above begins with these words: "In thirty-two wonderful ways of wisdom . . . God has inscribed and made his world." These 32 ways of wisdom are arranged into the 10 primary numbers and the 22 consonants of the Hebrew alphabet. But what we are dealing with here are not simply ordinary numbers. These numbers symbolize metaphysical principles of the world, the gradations of creation. Sober numbers are thus made to express a whole theology of creation of the world by the word. The world has been called into existence by the 10 creator words of God. These primordial words are even represented as living numerical entities: "Their appearance is like a lightning, and the boundary they reach is without end. His word is within them, when they emanate from him and when they return. Upon his command they hasten like the stormwind and before his throne they prostrate themselves . . . and one

single lord, God, the true King, rules over them all from his holy dwelling-place" (*Sepher Yesirah* I, 5.6.). It would follow from this that the narrative of the creation of the world is nothing more than a mystical throne of God. That is why Rabbi Akiba counted the Song of Songs and the inaugural vision of the prophet Ezekiel and the creation narrative among the most sacred texts of Israel's heritage.

7) RELIGIOUS HISTORY: The Bible occupies a position of particular prominence in the field of human literature. But if we also consider its essential role as sacral literature, we are immediately cognizant of many cross-ties with the other sacral writings. This does not mean to focus upon the possible influence of contemporary world religions upon the formation of the Bible text of Old and New Testaments, but merely to call attention to some formal elements common to sacral texts as such. For the moment, we shall refer only to some obvious Indian parallels.

First of all, a word on the conception of sacral structures. The building and structure of a temple or more frequently an altar is the equivalent of repeating the creation of the world. The erection of the New Year's altar signifies, not only symbolically, but in actual fact, the establishment of the year itself. The 360 tile bricks in the outer wall signify the 360 nights of the year; the 360 tile bricks of the Yajusmati refer to the 360 days (*Catapatha Brahmana* X, 5, IV, 10). The full year thus counts only 360 days. (The same conception is to be found in the Book of Jubilees and in the Book of Henoch. The number of the Jubilee Year, with its 364 days, is reached by the process of intercalating a "memorial day" at the beginning of each quarter.) Temple and altar are thus really an IMAGO MUNDI, an image of the cosmos. Ezekiel's new sketch for the Temple involves cosmic numbers which are more closely developed in the Talmud, in the tractate of Middot. Since the actual Temple itself was built according to cosmic proportions, these data would appear to deserve more credence than is usually accorded to them.

In the Indian scheme of things, not only the sacral edifice

but also the sacral text are based upon cosmic numbers. The sacred book is also an IMAGO MUNDI, an image of the cosmos. That is why the sacral book is so carefully measured. Thus, the lesser and the greater year, with periods of 16 or 49 years, form the literary structure of the Rig Veda. This numerical conception of the sacral text goes far beyond the words: even the syllables are counted. According to *Catapatha-Brahmana,* the Rig Veda is composed of 432,000 syllables, a number which corresponds to the greater annual cycle (*hazerwan*), which was already known to the Babylonian Berossus. Not only words and syllables, but also metrical accents were counted. The Veda has as many metrical accents as the year has "moments."

This numerical investigation would have to be extended to other ancient sacral texts as well. Then we would be much more certain of our conclusion that the Biblical numerical structure, particularly in the narrative of the creation of the world, is not simply an erratic bloc in the midst of the sacral literature, but that the numerical organization is an essential element of the sacral text. It is only by properly emphasizing the numerical structure that the hidden beauties of the creation narrative are really appreciated. Number here truly becomes the seal of God, the hedge of the law, the IMAGO MUNDI, the image of the cosmos.

B) THE WORLD PICTURE OF THE CREATION SONG

The clearly constructed song, composed in such simple language, really does not need much in the way of explanation. It is obviously a song about the creation of the world. Everything that exists was created by God. God and world are clearly distinct from each other. The fact that the world exists at all is made possible only by God's act of creation. The song thus achieves a closed picture of the world which is fundamentally distinct from the Ancient Near East creation myths, in which the gods themselves are involved in the process of world evolution.

In the Biblical vocabulary, accordingly, the verb *bārā'* is reserved for the creator God alone.[1] The question of the sources of creation, where all this was created from, is not even posed. It is within God's omnipotence to call non-being into existence. The existence of God is thus the only grounds for the existence of the world. The formula of creation from nothing (*creatio ex nihilo*) is the result of later philosophico-theological reflection; it is a concept foreign to the imaginative thinking of this song. The cosmos, in its totality, is from its very beginning the work of the creator God.

In the manner in which the creation of the world is described, the song of creation shows its dependence upon the Ancient Near East milieu. The poet and the thinker were trying to represent the beginning of all things that exist. In the world about them, everything had its own closed form and figure, by which the various essential qualities of things could be distinguished. Now the poet, in his imagination, does away with forms and boundaries and arrives at the conception of a prime element, which we generally call chaos. This word, however, does not exactly reproduce the contents of his thinking, since it evidently implies the element of lawlessness and arbitrariness. This is not the case. Rather, the thought proceeds from the plurality of the present world to the all-one of the beginning. In this primordial all-one, earth and water were still intermingled without distinction. The poet thus refers to the all-one as "shapelessness" (*tohu*); since forms and figures can only be recognized in the presence of light, these first beginnings were cloaked in "primeval night" (*bohu*). Tohu, in other connections, can mean the wildness of the desert, citiless wilderness (Deut. 32, 10; Ps. 107, 40).

---

1. E. Dantinne, *Création et separation,* Muséon 74, (1961), pp. 441-451. Philological investigation of the meaning of the word *bārā',* which originally meant "separate, divide"; since the work of creation involved a series of such divisions and separations, the verb developed the meaning of "create." In the OT the verb *bārā'* occurs some 48 times, always with God as the subject.

Bohu is a distant echo of the goddess of night *Baau* [2] who figures in the Phoenician epic of the creation of the world. Both concepts unite with the "abyss" (*tehom*).[3]

The fact that the all-one actually becomes a world is to be ascribed to the Spirit and the word of God. Some scholars have attempted to translate *rûaḥ 'elôhîm* as "storm of God, mighty storm"; [4] but a storm does not "hover," which is obviously the original meaning of the verb *rāḥāp*. This concept is the basis for the hovering of the Holy Spirit in the New Testament (Mt. 3, 16). The rest of Biblical theology makes it obvious that the Spirit is the power which proceeds from God and produces wonderful things in the world. Accordingly, the Spirit is active already at the beginning of creation. The Spirit is joined by the Word. Spirit-breathing and Word are intimately connected with each other; the Word is borne upon the breath emitted by the mouth. To put it in other words, the world proceeded from the mouth of God, a conception which is also to be found in Egyptian cosmology.[5]

By Spirit and Word, the all-one is organized in space and

---

2. Philo of Byblos, cited in Gesenius - Buhl, *Handwörterbuch zum AT*. In the Jewish philosophy of the Middle Ages, *tohu* was used to designate the *materia prima,* and *bohu* the *forma substantialis*. But these philosophical derivations have nothing to do with the original meaning of the text. F. M. Tocci, "Il commento di Emmanuele Romano al capitolo I della Genesi," *StudSem* 10 (1963), 26f.

3. The word *tehom* was too hurriedly equivalated with the Babylonian *ti'amat;* but the former is masculine while the latter is feminine; *tehom* refers to the whole of the primordial ocean as a unit, while *ti'amat* refers to only portions of it. Thus, we are faced with an independent conception, proper to the Ancient Bible. A. Heidel, *The Babylonian Genesis,* 2nd ed. (Chicago, 1951), p. 100.

4. An overall outline of the various attempts at explaining the passage in J. B. Bauer, "Der priesterliche Schöpfungsbericht," *Theologische Zeitschrift,* 20 (Basel, 1964) 3f. A lexicographical and thematic investigation of *rûah* in M. Miguens, "Spiritus Domini ferebatur super aquas," *FrancLA* 9 (1959), 37-93. The "Spirit" is a reference to the works of creation: Genesis 1 is thus, conceptually, related with Is 40-48.

5. See page 255.

configuration. The calling forth of light changes the shapelessness and primeval night into form and configuration. The abiding shapelessness is the product of night, while form and configuration are the result of day. By the erection of the firmament, which means literally "hammered fast," there is a division between the above and the below. It is by the creation of the heaven that the visible world achieves its closed configuration. Then there needs to be a further separation, between land and sea, and the spaces within the cosmos have their boundaries. The work of division: light – darkness, above – below, sea – land, can now yield to the work of arrangement.

The earth, below, is decked out in an array of plants, the heaven, above, with the two great lights. Light and plant-life are the prerequisites for the existence of living creatures. Next the air is populated with birds, and the sea with water animals. The song of creation is beginning to focus upon its climax, the creation of man. The earth produces the "fullness of land animals," but man is called into existence by a special command of God himself.

The song has covered a lengthy route, from the all-one down to man. But what is man supposed to do in this cosmos? The divine words of blessing express the essential purpose of human existence. Man is destined "to be lord." Man appears as the lord and king of the animal world. God has committed all into his hands. It is on this basis that we can understand what the expression *b^eṣalmô* actually means. It is not to be translated "after his image," but "as his image."[6] For *ṣĕlem* means something concrete, a picture, a statue, or an image of God. Man, as a being composed of dust from the earth and the breath of God, is an image, a supreme sign, in fact, even the incorporation of God within his creation.[7]

---

6. This is the *b^e-essentiae.* See Gesenius-Kautzsch, *Hebräische Grammatik* (1896) p. 373.

7. The same thought is developed already in G. v. Rad, "Genesis," *ATD* 1, 46.

C) THE WORLD PICTURE OF THE TOLEDOT

The first beginnings of creation are now seen through the prism of the sabbath. World and man are, to phrase it rather brusquely, created for the sake of the sabbath. By keeping the sabbath, the pious Israelite becomes a part of the primeval order of the cosmos. What is more, by keeping holy the sabbath, he becomes like to God, since God also rested on the seventh day and set aside this day by blessing and sanctifying it. The sabbath itself thus becomes a cosmic event. There is nothing more sublime that can be said about the sabbath. We can easily understand the strongly religious orientation of the week of creation.

In the original creation account, the week of seven days is not actually mentioned, although it is obviously presupposed. The origins of the week as a measure of time are lost in the shadows of prehistory.[8] The original measure of time was the phases of the moon. The full moon in the middle of the month can be designated as the most striking turning point. In the Assyro-Babylonian calendar [9] the 15th of the month is called *šapattu.* The distance that separates full moon from new moon can easily be divided into two sevens. Hence, the celebration of the first day of the moon (new moon), the seventh day (*sibûtu*), the 15th day, already mentioned (*šapattu*), and the 28th day (*bubbulu*) among the Babylonians. But these were rather dates of particular threat and danger, days on which certain actions were to be done or omitted. All the days remained inseparably bound up with the rhythm of the moon's phases. The peculiar innovation of the Israelite sabbath lies in the fact that the week is now completely freed of its dependence upon the phases of the moon, and the series of weeks continued to run its course independently

8. R. de Vaux, *Das Alte Testament und seine Lebensordnungen, I,* (1960), p. 300.

9. Br. Meissner, *Babylonien und Assyrien,* II, p. 92 and p. 395.

of month and year. As such, the seven-day week is an exception within the time divisions of the Ancient Near East. We cannot be too far wrong in ascribing the introduction of the sabbath week, which was a sign of Israel's covenant, to Moses himself.[10]

Predilection for the number seven has many parallels in the literature of the Ancient Near East. Seven was considered the number of completion and perfection. In the Gilgamesh epic we read that storm and sea were quiet on the seventh day; further, that the ark was buffeted about one day, two days, three days, four days, five days, six days, but on the seventh day came to rest on the mountain.[11] The poets of Ugarit were also familiar with this schematic form. The fire consumed one day, two days, etc., and ceased finally on the seventh day.[12] These and other texts demonstrate the predilection for the seven-outline in the Ancient Near East poets.

It is precisely the free manner in which the devotee of numerical symbolism uses the terms year, month, and day that suggests the conclusion that he does not mean the six days of creation to be taken in the strict and narrow sense of normal days of the week. They are for him rather symbolic days of creation. If this symbolic character is lost sight of, then the discussion wanders hopelessly into a *cul-de-sac.*

A like symbolism must be kept in mind in interpreting the dietary precept. Man and beast alike, at the beginning, were nourished only on food provided by plant life; meat was eaten only at a later stage of development. This is very clearly a midrash, a legendary embellishment. The impetus may have been presented

---

10. N. H. Tur-Sinai, "Sabbat und Woche," BOr. 8 (1951), 14-24 refers to the "fifth of the month" (*ḫamuštu*) in the Cappadocian tablets, in which a month of 30 days is divided into 5 weeks of 6 days each. Claims that the Israelite Sabbath develops from the addition of a day of rest after every "fifth." Hardly credible.

11. See the examples in J. B. Bauer, *Die Biblische Urgeschichte,* 2nd. ed. (1963), p. 25.

12. *Ibid.,* p. 24.

by the prophetic description of the end-time, in which the lion, the bear, and the viper will lie down peacefully with the ox, the lamb, and the child (Is 11, 6-8). This is simply a powerful allegory, designed to describe the perfect peace of the end-time, and not an attempt to describe the nature of the wild animals as such. Thus the peaceful harmony of the animal world existing at the beginning must also be interpreted allegorically. It is simply a delightful image of primordial peace in the world.

It was by this strict attention to form that the ancient song of creation acquired its solemn monotony, which was already wondered at by earlier commentators. The style of the creation account, in their opinion, gives evidence of a striking schematic arrangement. First God's command, then the words "and it was so," and then the statement that the command was literally fulfilled, finally the name-givings and the blessing; then, God looks at his work and finds it good, or very good. "What an opportunity the author must have had here, to describe the colorful abundance of life and to praise the creator of the universe, like the author of Ps. 104, or Job 34, 4. All these inexhaustible wonders the author has spurned, and from this prodigal abundance he has selected only a few, simple, and obvious elements. An explicit description would have lost itself in details; here it is only the outlines that are given, and the effect is all the more emphatic. The style has a certain lapidary grandeur about it, as in the famous words, 'Let there be light!' The author is speaking to us here, by his very silence." [13]

"The same clarity is evident in the internal construction of the creation narrative, which has the stamp of scientific sobriety. First the elements are created: light, sky, earth, sea, and then the individual creatures which are to fill these elements. Thus the direction is from disorder to order, from lower to higher. The

---

13. H. Gunkel, *"Genesis," Göttinger Handkommentar zum AT I,* 1 (1917), 116ff. Gunkel is a master of developing the literary peculiarities of the individual sections. He has much to teach in the way of text observation, without imposing the absolute acceptance of all his hypotheses.

week of salvation presents an impression of the greatest internal compactness. Every creature is assigned to the place that is proper to him alone; the world is a cosmos, a wonderful work of God.

"This scientific sobriety is joined by a solemn tone. It is this tone that bears along the repetitions which give a uniform dignity to the whole. The tone rises towards the climax: the final creation is the highest creation — man. There is a solemn ring to the blessings of the last three days. And with stately measure, telling of God's rest after his work, the narrative comes to a graceful end."[14]

D) THE BIBLICO-THEOLOGICAL CONTENT OF THE CREATION NARRATIVE

The week of creation is placed at the beginning of the Bible like a Credo, and accordingly it contains the fundamental truths of revealed religion on God, man, and world.

1) THE IMAGE OF GOD presented in the creation account stands out in sharp contrast from that of the polytheistic milieu of the age in which it was composed. It is true that such words as "Tehom, Tohu-wa-bohu — brooding of the spirit, mastery of the stars," do have a mythological echo, since they are also used in the pagan mythologies,[15] but in Gen. 1, they have been divested of their mythological character. The de-divinization and the de-demonization of the cosmos is already evident in the sabbath ordinance. The Babylonian sabbath is an unlucky day, a day on which the demons have power. The biblical sabbath, however, is the day of the creator God, who has produced the universe. In this universe there is no room for gods apart from him. The supreme god of the surrounding religions, *šamaš* (sun), *sin*

14. *Ibid.*, p. 117.

15. Echoes of the Graeco-Latin myths are still to be found in the liturgy (cf. Lauds hymn for the dedication of a church: *Alto ex Olympi Vertice*), without anyone's being particularly scandalized by the fact. The mythical word is only a symbol of the new reality.

(moon), and *aštarte* (stars), must all be referred back to their historical confines as lights in the sky. Even the name for God, Elohim, is not a hold-over from polytheism.[16] Even if the "let us" in Gen. 1, 26 is taken as spoken to the angels, this does not take a jot or a tittle from the overwhelming unity of the God of heaven. The monotheism of the Bible stands out in sharp contrast to the polytheism of the world around it.

The positive presentation of the image of God is so deep that it is not surpassed even by later theology. With absolute sovereignty God is opposed to the world which he has called into existence by Spirit and Word. Even though, throughout the course of the Old Testament, there was no clear knowledge of the triune life of God, retrospective analysis, based on the fullness of revelation, can discover a *vestigium trinitatis,* a "trace of the Trinity," in this presentation. In the pagan cosmogonies, God and world overflow into each other. But here there is an insurmountable distinction. God is eternal and, from the overflowing goodness of his being, he inaugurates the world; "God saw that it was good."[17] He is the creator God in the confession of faith.

---

16. In form, Elohim is a plural; in Biblical parlance, Elohim is used of several pagan gods (Ex. 18, 11; Deut. 10, 17), for one pagan god (Judg. 11, 24; 1 Sam. 5, 7), for a goddess (1 Kings 11, 5); in referring to the true God, the article is generally prefixed, *hā'elohîm,* and the verb is always in the singular. The Ancient Near East texts have destroyed all suspicion of a hidden polytheism in this terminology. In the Amarna correspondence, the Egyptian Pharaoh is addressed as *ilani,* "gods"; a single person and a plural form. In the Boghazköy texts, individual gods are also given the epithet *ilani.* This proves that the plural form does not conceal a polytheistic implication. It is evidence merely of a common Semitic mode of speaking, an attempt to stress the majesty of the person addressed: It is an abstract plural form with singular meaning. See O. Proksch, *Theologie des Alten Testaments* (1950), p. 64.

17. W. F. Albright, "The Refrain 'and God saw *kî tôb*' in Genesis." Mélanges bibliques rédigés en l'honneur de A. Robert, (1957), 22-26. According to Semitic usage, the expression *kî tôb* is equivalent to a superlative. "God saw how very well done it all was."

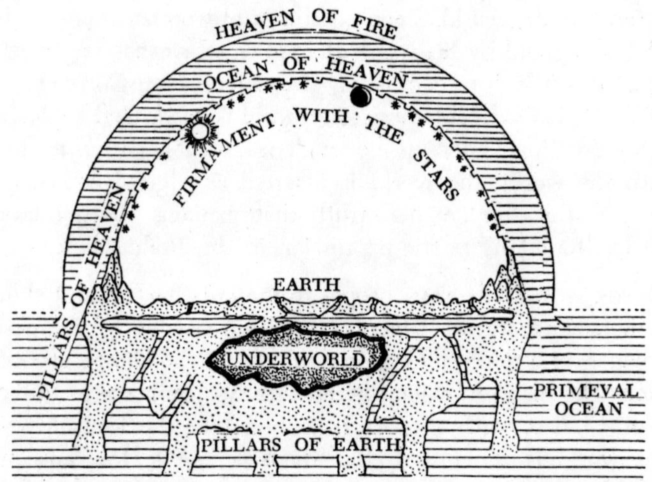

Illustration 1. The World Picture of the Creation Account based on Simon Prado: *Praelectiones Biblicae* (1949), p. 42.

2) THE WORLD PICTURE of the creation account is that of the Ancient Near East. The world is the middle of the cosmos, encircled by the primeval ocean above and below, while the firmament, permanently spread above, keeps the waters above and below apart. The stars are only lamps and lights in the heaven. It is a picture dictated by its times, and, as such, has been completely surpassed by modern science.[18] But this scientifically untenable framework is the vesture for truths which have a lasting validity.

The world is not an immanent whole, closed in upon itself; it is perpetually *open* to God, to whom it owes its origin and towards whom it presses to return after the end of days. The world is so completely dependent upon God that without him it could not exist. Ephraem the Syrian, in his commentary on

18. The Ancient Near East background is well developed in A. Pohl, "Der Schöpfungshymnus der Bibel," *Stimmen der Zeit* 163 (1958/59), 252-266.

Genesis,[19] says that God's countenance has been stamped upon everything in the world, since all things are borne along by his breath and upheld by his word. It follows as a necessary conclusion that this world, so completely dependent upon God's creator word, shares in God's goodness. The world is *good.* God is pleased with his creation. There is no evidence of a negative attitude towards the world; the world is asserted as a good creation of God. It is this fundamental truth that explains the jubilation which has found its poetic expression in the Psalms.

3) THE PICTURE OF MAN proper to the creation account shows the same clear features. It has not yet been vitiated by the pessimistic crisis of a doubting generation. Man is the climax of God's creation. The plan on which the universe was built seems to have been oriented towards him. It is to him that the lordship over all the world is committed. But there is more! He transcends the visible cosmos by the fact that his own inner image is a mirror of God himself. Man has not been made according to the measure of the animals, but – if we might be so bold – according to the measure of God himself, so that he can raise his face towards heaven and speak to God as his Father. To seek man's quality as image of God exclusively in the fact of his spiritual nature would be selling the Biblical reality somewhat short; Biblical psychology must be interpreted in terms different from the philosophy-impregnated psychology of our modern day. The psychology of the Bible is too bound up with physical organs – the seat of the soul is in the intestines, the kidneys, the bones, the heart [20] – for anyone to be able to dissect man into body and soul and say that only the soul is created in the image of God. Man cannot be dissected. It is as a whole, as a being with soul and body both, that he bears the stamp of God.

The division into two *sexes* is also part of the human totality. If there ever was a solid affirmation and acceptance of the reality

---

19. Codex Vaticanus No. 110; a new edition is expected which could do a great service to Genesis exegesis in philological questions.

20. W. Eichrodt, *Theologie des Alten Testaments* (1948), p. 65ff.

of sex, it is in the creation account. God finds his work "very good," and gives his blessing for fruitfulness to the first human couple.

Since man is so completely oriented towards God, it is a logical conclusion that he must keep himself *free* for God, by celebrating the sabbath. Just as the world achieved its final completion in the sabbath rest of God, so man, holding himself free for God on the sabbath, is to confess his awareness of his dependence upon God for existence.

The creation narrative thus ends with a religious appeal. This, in turn, determines the whole character of the account. It is not a question of cosmic and theological knowledge for its own sake, nor is it an appeal to reason, but rather an appeal to the heart, which is the center of the whole man, to take his place, in worship and in homage, within the cosmos created by God. The purpose of the creation narrative is thus entirely religious; the descriptions of natural history are only the word images in which the appeal to man is clothed. In discovering this we have touched upon a fundamental principle that will determine our further biblical-theological exposition.

CHAPTER XV

CREATION NARRATIVE AND NATURAL SCIENCE

LOOKING back today upon the so-called "Biblical question," that is, the comparison between Bible and natural science, over the course of the last century, we frequently get the impression that much effort has been wasted on questions which appear to be a matter of course today. This intellectual battle was, of course, necessary at the time, in order to clarify and differentiate the two conflicting areas. No one could maintain that the Bible lost anything by this; on the contrary, it presents a much more compelling picture to our present generation. Biblical science has learned from this battle, primarily, to better appreciate the fact that God's word is qualified in terms of history. The creation narrative, for example, is located precisely in the Ancient Near East world picture, and in many of its words it speaks a language which we are no longer in a position to decipher to its last detail. Does this imply a betrayal of God's word? Not at all. Quite the contrary, it implies only a fuller admission of the "incarnation of the Word." God's word is not spoken into an unhistorical void, but rather in the concrete framework of human history, so that we can actually feel its pulsebeat. But since it is God's word, it echoes beyond the fleeting metronome of time, dropping the plumb of supra-temporality and eternity into the stream of human time; it is a rock against which the waves of time must break. Unqualified reality within the framework of human conditioning, the measureless within the measure of time, the beatitude of God's kingdom within the poverty of human words – these are the tensions which biblical theology needs to explain and within which it must constantly operate. Its methodology is essentially different from that of the natural sciences. It looks beyond time and sees everything in the light that radiates from above. Its work is to judge everything in terms of "its openness to God." Thus, objectively, there can be no error; error would mean that the light was darkened and God was deceit. Error is possible on the part of the theologian, of course, if he is not completely subordinate to the laws of revelation and is unwilling to properly confront the circumstances in which God breaks through into time, that is, the concrete, historically qualified time and place of revelation. It is only on the basis of a full understanding of the fact that it is qualified in history that the unqualified prophetic imperatives of God's word can be properly recognized.

It was precisely this clarification of the boundaries, the assertion of the Bible as Bible, that was involved in the struggles between Bible and natural history. As the following attempts to explain the creation narrative will demonstrate, both sides were guilty of transgressing their proper boundaries. The fact that one side stubbornly held to the literal truth drove the other side to a complete rejection of the creation text, since the clear evidence of natural science necessarily disproved the literal interpretation. On the other hand, biblical science capitulated far too quickly in face of the "clear findings of the natural sciences," and sought to "save" the Bible by harmonizing and "concordizing." But the word of God does not need any such "saving"; it has its own individual value, independent of any contemporary status of scientific natural history.

The natural sciences also overstepped their boundaries in this conflict, by divesting the Bible of its character of revelation, degrading it into the ranks of Ancient Near East myth, by shutting itself up, autonomously, within the realm of an unending "creation," repudiating any initiative from without, on the part of a revealing God. This illusion of the natural sciences has been burst today by the discoveries of atomic physics. Once again a picture of the world has been recognized as false, and qualified in time, and thus is to be rejected. Astro-physics, in the universe at large, and atomic physics, in the microcosm, have traversed the whole of the universe – it is bounded and measurable in terms of light years – and they have felt their way back to a beginning, which demands a divine imperative, outside the realm of space and time: "Let there be!"

Thus the long intellectual conflict can be considered closed, since an era of new dialogue between Bible and science is now upon us. The Bible scholar must be concerned with "Biblical theology," and the natural scientist must bow before the prophetic word of the Bible, which, in a vesture qualified by time, is still timeless, and thus established as obligatory for every generation.

A) THE MODERN, SCIENTIFIC PICTURE OF THE WORLD

The Biblical student must not be required to be conversant with every branch of science. But still he does have a duty to orient himself on the modern world picture, in order to have a better appreciation of the fact that the eternal validity of the Biblical creation narrative is still determined and qualified by time. It does seem that in the realm of natural science, an era of maximum development has been reached. But neither must we forget that even the explanations by modern atomic-physics of the evolution of the world are nothing more than working hypotheses, which can be once again upset or developed in greater depth by new and more thorough knowledge of the facts. It follows that the human picture of the world, as corresponding to the degree of our natural science, is bound up in constant evolution. The following paragraphs attempt to give a summary outline of our modern world picture.[1]

---

1. A few literary sources: B. Bavink, *Das Weltbild der heutigen Naturwissenschaften und seine Beziehungen zu Philosophie und Religion,* 2nd. ed.

1) CHANGE IN THE WORLD PICTURE: [2] The materials from which heaven and earth, universe and stars are constructed were regarded, at the turn of the century, as having existed "from eternity." Just as the universe itself was considered *infinite,* even so, the stars, as such, were supposed to have had an eternal existence. Thus it seemed that there could no more be a beginning of our cosmic world than there could be an end.

Since that time, physics and astronomy have undergone powerful developments, and our knowledge of matter, which has recently been reshaped by the epoch-making discoveries of atomic physics, has significantly changed, so that the problem of the universe, existing within the scope of time or outside the scope of time, appears in a different form, in the light of modern investigation.

2) THE CONSTRUCTION OF MATTER: The basic elements of all matter in the universe are atoms, whose existence was still doubted towards the end of the last century, though it is well established today; the atom is composed of an atomic nucleus and outer orbits of electrons; the nucleus, once again, is constructed of a positively charged proton and a neutral neutron. It is further recognized that the nuclei are not essentially unchangeable; they can be both split and transformed.

Apart from artificial or violent interference in the atomic structure, science has demonstrated that a great number of our elements are subject to natural mutations by the process of atomic decay, which is the basis of radio-activity. Well-known examples of this kind are radium and uranium. On the basis of uranium decay, the age of the earth's crust can be determined at about 2 billion years. Since the first beginnings of uranium, and thus also the earth, some 3 billion years have passed.

3) CONSTRUCTION OF THE STARS: Modern astro-physics distinguishes between giant and dwarf stars. It was formerly believed that the stars began their life history as massive giant suns, and ended as dwarfs, weak

---

(1952). Idem. *Ergebnisse und Probleme der Naturwissenschaften,* 2nd. edition (Zurich, 1948). Idem. *Weltschöpfung in Mythus, Religion, Philosophie und Naturwissenschaft,* (Basel, 1950). H. Conrad-Martius, *Naturwissenshaftliche und Metaphysische Perspektiven* (Heidelberg, 1949). J. Brinktrine, *Die Lehre von der Schöpfung* (Paderborn, 1956). J. M. Lenz, *Die Himmel rühmen,* 8th. edition (Innsbruck, 1956). The ideals of Teilhard de Chardin, which are finding more and more recognition, are outlined by A. Guggenberger, *Teilhard de Chardin, Versuch einer Weltsumme* (Mainz, 1963).

2. Further explained in D. Wattenberg, "Das Alter der Welt im Spiegel der Atomphysik," *Stimmen der Zeit,* 73 (1948) 141-146. *Neue Sterne Katastrophen im All. Stimmen der Zeit,* 74 (1948/49), 136-147. *Blick ins Weltall* (Berlin, 1947).

in light and shrunken in mass. The greater part of their mass was supposed to have been lost by radiation. But such a process would involve assigning the stars an age which is in contradiction with other astronomic facts.

This conception of things was reversed by the discovery of atomic physics. The real source of the energy which is liberated in the radiation processes of the stars is to be found in the changes in the atomic nucleus. The constant process of transformation from hydrogen into helium, in the interior of the suns, is bound up with such a mighty generation of energy as to guarantee sufficient age for the stars, a date which also concurs with other astronomical facts.

If science can measure the quantitative content of the individual chemical elements in the construction of the stars, especially the proportion of hydrogen and helium, then, on the basis of the assumption that the present helium content evolved, to a large degree, from the original hydrogen, it is possible to determine the time that such a transformation process would require. Such calculations have arrived at a probable age of 4 billion years, for our sun.

4) EVOLUTION OF THE STARS: The age of our sun cannot be immediately presumed for the other stars as well. It does appear to be applicable in the case of those stars which possess an almost identical mass; according to modern cosmological thinking, the distinction of mass, among the stars, is a phenomenon related to distinctions in age, not in the sense (explained above) of mass being lost by the process of radiation and evolution, but in the sense that, in the youth of the universe, only stars with relatively small mass developed, while the more recent past has seen the development of exclusively giant stars, with proportionally greater masses.

This would mean that the dwarf stars were originally dwarf stars, and thus represent chronologically the oldest generation of the universe, a generation to which our sun also belongs, whereas the giant stars, some of which are 40 or 50 times the mass of our sun, incorporate the more youthful citizens of the universe.

For the B-stars, which are very hot and have a large mass, made up almost exclusively of hydrogen, the rather low figure of 20 million years (hardly a hundredth part of the age of the earth) has been determined, making it quite probable that even today new stars are evolving in the universe. Applying the same standards to the meteorites, we discover that none of the meteors is older than 3 billion years, while the youngest among them are only 500 million years old.

5) THE AGE OF THE COSMOS: Within the mighty spaces of our universe we recognize the Milky Way, a spiral-shaped cosmos of some 50 billion stars, which rotates about its own center every 220 million years. In the interior of the Milky Way system, there are considerable variations with respect to distribution of mass, making it probable that since the origin

of the Milky Way world not many rotations have taken place, since they would have produced a more balanced distribution of mass; the age of the system can thus be only a relatively small multiple of its revolution period, a few billion years.

6) EXTENT OF THE COSMOS: The billions and trillions of world systems which fill our space as spiral nebulae, outside the Milky Way system, show, on the basis of measurements in their spectrum, that they are flying out into space with the greatest velocity. The farther distant they are, the greater is the velocity of their flight. The measurable value of this velocity, in the members of the nebula in the constellation of the Big Dipper, is 42,000km. per sec., and in the furthest removed spiral nebula yet discovered, almost 100,000km per sec.

This property of the spiral nebulae, which can be determined by the displacement of the red line in their spectrum, leads to the undeniable conclusion that the universe is undergoing a continuous expansion, a constant growth of world space.

This conception of space has very appropriately been compared to the example of an exploding hand grenade, together with the hypothesis that the total mass of the universe, which today is split into stars and world systems, was once originally grouped into a single primordial star, and that some billions of years ago a powerful cosmic explosion burst this star and hurled the broken elements out into space with incalculable force, so that even today we find them progressing outwards from the center of the universe in headlong flight.

7) "POINT OF ORIGIN" FOR THE UNIVERSE: This very dramatic and remarkable fact (the expansion of the cosmos) has suggested the further hypothesis that the universe is expanding at the speed of light. This would mean that the radius of the world is expanding some 300,000km. every second. If this is the case, then the world must once have looked essentially different and been essentially smaller.

If we assume, as a present radius for our world, some 6 billions of light years, then, measuring backwards into terms of the constant expansion of the universe at a speed equal to the velocity of light, we can calculate that, 6 billions of years ago, the universe must have been compressed practically into a mathematically definable "point." The development of the cosmos must have taken place in the interval elapsed from this original point.

8) CONTINUOUS NEW CREATION: It is, however, inconceivable that the amount of matter present in the world today, some 2 x 10 to the 55th power grams (a 2 with 55 zeros) could, at the beginning of the world, have possibly been compressed into a point without extension (or even into a small star). These difficulties can be obviated only by assuming that matter has been constantly developing, in the form of individual

neutrons at first, and finally in the form of neutron clusters of progressively greater dimension, whose total mass was in proportion to the gradual expansion of growing space.

This would obviously mean that this increase in mass, with respect to the present state of expansion in the universe, must still be going on today in the continuous birth of new stars, and must find its visible expression in the occasional appearance of a "supernova."

9) THE ELEMENTARY ACT OF CREATION: All these considerations point, essentially, to one and the same fact: some 6 billions of years ago, both matter and stars, and thus also world systems, came into being by a world-generating elementary act; or in terms of physics — by the materialization of imponderable matter into neutrons and neutron clusters — there was a creation.

At the same time, the question of a "cosmic prelude," existing before this elementary act described above, is without object; since there simply could not have been such a "prelude." It must also be pointed out that astronomy and atomic physics are in a position today, with the help of cosmic physics, which considers both the world of the stars and the world of the atom, to arrive at a chronology of the universe which represents the cosmos as a complex qualified in terms of time.

10) "IN THE BEGINNING GOD CREATED. . . .": We are once again faced with the elementary statement of the creation narrative: "In the beginning God created heaven and earth." The inquisitive human mind can make its way as far back as this fact; but the ultimate clear assertion comes from this open position, from a personal and speaking God, unbounded by time and space, a God who has called the ancient cosmos into existence by his word of creation and, by his word of revelation, through the agency of prophetically endowed men, has, in the dimensions of time, made known this fundamental fact that stands beyond the confines of space and time. Where the natural scientist has to set aside his tools — for the natural sciences are bound up with the measure of the cosmos — it is the theologian who sets to work and, guided by the light of divine revelation, illuminates them, after the measure of God, to behold the marvelous work of the universe, proclaiming the praise of its creator (Ps. 18 / 19: The heavens declare . . . .).

B) EXPLANATIONS OF THE WEEK OF CREATION

Our discussion would not be complete without an historical retrospect on the various attempts at interpreting the account of creation.[3] It might

---

3. Survey by P. Heinisch, *Geschichte des Alten Testaments* (Bonn, 1950), p. 9ff. K. Fruhstorfer, *Weltschöpfung und Paradies nach der Bibel,* (Linz, 1927).

be called absolutely tragic that the interpretation has been concerned primarily with a point which seems only secondary today, namely the interpretation of the "days." The countless hypotheses on this subject can be divided into two groups. The one group took the Biblical account literally as a precise description of the origin of the world, in all its phases; the others got farther and farther away from the literal interpretation, in an effort to vindicate the symbolic meaning.

1) ATTEMPTS AT LITERAL INTERPRETATION: The 6 days of creation (*hexaemeron*) were considered as days of 24 hours each. This is the opinion maintained by the scholars of the Ancient and Middle Ages' Church and synagogue, down to the modern age. With the rise of natural sciences, however, this view was faced with more and more objections, so that scholars were forced to reconcile the literal meaning of the text with the clear data of natural science.

Thus, some scholars ascribed the origin of the geological strata to the flood (deluge theory) and placed the work of the 6 days before this era. Obviously, the deluge could not have produced such powerful changes, since it could have lasted only a fraction of the time required for the formation traceable in these periods of earth formation.

In order to save the letter, other scholars appealed to the angels. The first verse of Genesis was supposed to describe the world as something complete. It was angels who were supposed to have inhabited the earth at that time. But, when they were forced to leave the earth, as a result of their defection from God, they turned the earth into a desert and left it in a state of chaos. Thereupon, God is supposed to have restored order to the world in six days of 24 hours, the so-called restitution hypothesis. But actually the description of primeval chaos in Gen. 1, 2, does not offer any basis for such speculation. The other interpretations of this order keep getting further and further away from the literal conception of the word *yôm* as day.

2) THE CONCORDANCE THEORIES: Attempts were made to re-establish the harmony (*concordantia*) with natural science by interpreting "*yôm*" no longer simply as "day," but as an era, a period of earth formation. In the week of creation, it would thus be periods of the earth's formation which are described, periods in which the evolution of the universe took place. The stricter theory equated the 6 days with the 6 geological periods, which could be different in length. The work of the 4th day is supposed to mean that God made the stars visible, after having created them earlier. The more moderate position was content with the assertion that the Bible meant only to describe the results of these periods of evolution, without making any statement as to their precise delimitations.

3) THE IDEAL THEORIES: Other scholars completely separate the creation narrative from the realm of natural science and attempt to interpret it on the basis of interior grounds. They dissolve the temporal succession of the works of creation and explain the 6 days as "ideal days," pivotal moments of the divine activity which are to be distinguished only logically from each other. The primary accent is on the week, with the divine day of rest being the clear type and image of the human sabbath. The precise time and sequence in which the divine ideas are realized in actual creation is, as they maintain, of no religious significance. It is wrong to expect any enlightenment on this fact in the Bible. The works of creation could just as well have been achieved all at once. The concept of simultaneous creation was taught by Philo (*de opif.* m. 13) and Origen (*de princ.* 4, 16).

Among the ideal theories, the most significant is the vision theory (Hummelauer, Hoberg). This point of view explains the 6 days as visions of Adam. God allowed our first parent to envision the origin of the world in 6 tableaux, so that he could describe them to his posterity. But who could conceive of such an account of Adam's vision, remaining unchanged over the course of millennia?

St. Augustine's [4] explanation of the week of creation deserves a special mention in this context, since it shows that it was not our modern age which first managed to get away from a slavishly literal interpretation of the text in Genesis. In his work *De Genesi contra Manichaeos,* St. Augustine maintains that God did indeed create the world of matter in the temporal sequence described in Genesis. Several other Scriptural passages, especially the words in Ecclus. 18, 1, "he who lives forever created all things at once," as well as the difficulty of harmonizing this conception with other truths, led him to present a different point of view in his mature work *De Genesi ad litteram*: God did not create the world in 6 days, but in one day, that is, all at once.

By world, in this context, he understood not the present universe as we know it, but the four elements of which it is composed; more particularly, he thought of the earth as covered with water (which he was even willing to admit might be largely steam). The development of the still misshapen mass into the cosmos that we are familiar with did not take place by a new immediate intervention of the divine omnipotence, but rather by the activity of the natural laws and powers which God had created in the world of matter, and thus it took place over the course of time required for such laws to be operative.

Not even for the development of life does Augustine demand a new creative intervention. According to his thinking, at the very first act of creation, God had sown the seeds of life (*primordia, primariae omnium*

4. See also A. Schöpfer, *Geschichte des AT,* 6th edition (1923), 102ff.

nascentium, causales rationes) and along with it the impulse to evolve into organic life.

With such an explanation, Augustine could obviously not conceive of the 6 days in a literal sense, but he did manage to arrive at an explanation all his own. He connected the 6 days of creation with the knowledge of the angels: the day of creation is the angels' knowledge of the particular work of a given day, so that the 6 days are simply the angels' knowledge of creation taking place in 6 phases.

The angels have a two-fold knowledge of every work of creation, corresponding to the divisions of each day into morning and night. By their morning knowledge (*cognito matutina*), which is sharper and earlier, they know things in God and in his eternal ideas; by their evening knowledge (*cognitio vespertina*) they know things in themselves.

Still, St. Augustine does not conceive of the 6 days of creation in such a way that the angels contemplate the works of God in this two-fold light in a temporal succession. Just as creation occurred all at once, the angels also understand it all at once. The created things are arranged in such an orderly relationship that those which are named first are the prerequisites for what is named later, not in terms of time, but by precedence of nature and cause (*non temporali, sed causali ordine*). The story of creation has been presented in terms of the division and sequence described, that is, in terms of the 6 phases of angelic knowledge, so that its popular presentation would be better adapted to the weakness of our human mind.[5]

4) MYTHOLOGICAL INTERPRETATION: This interpretation maintains that the author of the creation account presents a monotheistic reworking of an ancient polytheistic myth; the very first verses already betray a "veritable mythological treasure house" (Gunkel). Whereas the interpretations already examined all hold to the revelation character of the text, the mythological interpretation classifies the creation account as part of the history of Ancient Near East literature, on a par with every other part. The days no longer present any problem, since the whole account is viewed as religious and tendentious (sabbath!) poetry.[6]

5) PROPHETIC INTERPRETATION: This interpretation attempts to arrive at a new understanding of the creation account in terms of prophecy.[7] The most characteristic element of prophecy is the so-called prophetic perspective. By the inspiration of God's Spirit, the prophet sees things

---

5. Augustinus, *De Genesi ad litteram,* IV, 24n 41; V, 5n 13, 15; VI, 33n 52.

6. However, G. V. Rad says, "It is thus incorrect to reckon with something like archaic and half-mythological rudiments in this connection – even only on given points – rudiments which must be regarded as ven-

which will not take place until the distant future, or even at the end of time. In this vision, events are intermingled that are actually some centuries apart from each other. Thus, in the description of the last judgment, the images of the destruction of Jerusalem and the end of the world are intermingled. The destruction of Jerusalem is the point of departure for the whole description. It is this event which provides the images for the description of the end-event. It is the task of the scientific historian to distinguish the historically qualified terms, which refer only to the fall of Jerusalem, and thus isolate the kernel of the end-prophecy.

The creation narrative is thus to be considered as a prophecy, not of the end-time, but rather of the beginning-time. The primeval events are seen and described from the point of view of the narrator. Thus if we are to understand the whole truth of the narrative, we must adopt the point of view of the prophetic writer. Geology, palaeontology, archaeology, etc., must all contribute to exposing the temporally qualified vesture, and isolating the timeless prophetic kernel.

6) THE BIBLICAL-THEOLOGY INTERPRETATION OF THE CREATION NARRATIVE: It is not necessary to postulate a retrospective prophecy in order to correctly interpret the week of creation. There is no prophecy in the account, but only a simple and straightforward credo of faith in the one, almighty, and eternal Creator of the world. This credo has been fused into the Ancient Near East picture of the world, qualified in terms of time. The world picture changes, but the faith remains the same.

"The historian is certainly not surprised to discover that the natural science data of Genesis does not coincide with the results of our modern knowledge; in fact he presupposes this fact: in those days, natural science was in its first beginnings, people thought of the earth as standing still, the heavens as a real firmament, in which God had set the stars. Nothing was then known of the long periods of earth formation; seven days seemed to be

---

erable, and rich in theological symbolism, but less binding for all that .... The concepts contained in verse 2 are outside any mythological connection; in Israel they had long hardened into cosmological catch-words that belonged to the indispensable properties of priestly learning." ("Genesis, Das erste Buch Mose" *ATD* (1950), 36-38.

7. I. Schildenberger, *Vom Geheimnis des Gotteswortes* (1950), pp. 261ff.

enough. No matter how sharply the religious spirit of the week of creation stands out against the cosmogonies of the other ancient peoples, Israel's worldly knowledge was no more elevated than that of her neighbors. Only a very unhistorical attitude could undertake the attempt of bringing the week of creation into harmony with the data of modern science."[8]

The week of creation is a grandiose religious poem, which is imperishable in its religious content. And every open mind, even today, will be able to experience and appreciate the peculiar fragrance of this Ancient Near East religious poetry, without barbarously picking everything apart and attempting to strip away what is untrue. From the religious standpoint, every sentence is still true, no matter how many times the world picture of natural science has changed in the meantime. There is no deeper truth that we can express, than to say that God created heaven and earth, separated light from darkness, divided sea and earth, formed plants, animals, and birds, and finally established man as the lord and master of the whole cosmos. Every sentence is steeped in this credo and thus the light it sheds is one and imperishable.

---

8. H. Gunkel, *Genesis,* 4th edition (1917), p. 130.

CHAPTER XVI

ANCIENT NEAR EAST COSMOGONIES

THE Biblical creation narrative is not an isolated phenomenon standing in an extra-historical position. Corresponding to the characteristics of "a word made flesh," it has also assumed the historical qualifications of space and time. Thus, in order to have a complete historical understanding of the Biblical creation account, we must have at least a cursory knowledge of the Ancient Near East myths on the origin of the world. At the time in which the Ancient Near East cultural world was rediscovered, in the previous century, the great joy of the discovery led scholars far beyond their proper bounds. The great Assyriologist Friedrich Delitzsch, in his book, *Wo lag das Paradies?* (1881), already represented the view that the Bible is only a purged, monotheistic edition of the Babylonian creation myths. This thesis was widely publicized in his three theses on *Babel und Bible* (1902-1904). Bold, categorically phrased statements, and brilliant style bore the Babel-Bible controversy into the widest circles, and gave rise to intensely emotional attitudes and positions on both sides.[1] The Babylonists were primarily concerned with investigating the dependence of Biblical prehistory upon Babel. Hugo Winckler and Alfred Jeremias, in fact, went so far as to attempt the derivation, not only of the religion and culture of Israel, but also that of the other Oriental peoples, even the Chinese in the furthest Orient and the Mexicans in the West, from Babylon. Since they saw Babel as the measure of all things, their school is called the Panbabylonist.[2] These positions quickly provoked a strong literature of defense.[3]

Today we are able to speak much more peacefully and objectively about the relationship between Bible and Babel, and we owe this fact to the intellectual battle described above, which clarified new aspects on both the Babylonian as well as the Biblical side. Babel's influence upon the Ancient Near East is certainly not to be underevaluated; yet, newer discoveries have demonstrated the fact that the Babylonian Semites were not the only people who were creative in the realm of religion. They took over religious ideas, together with the cosmogonic myths, from the older Sumerian civilization, and adapted them to their world and language. For the defenders of the Bible, we might point out one fruit of the argument in the fact that

---

1. For general orientation: Keil, *Zur Bibel- und Babelfrage* (1903). Döller, *Bibel und Babel oder Babel und Bibel?* (1903). Hoberg, *Babel und Bibel, ein populärer Vortag* (1904). E. König, *Bibel und Babel, eine kulturgeschichtliche Skizze* (1902). Ottli, *Der Kampf um Babel und Bibel, ein kulturgeschichtliche Vortrag* (1902). A. Jeremias, *Im Kampf um Babel und Bibel. Ein Wort zur Verständigung und Abwehr* (1903).

2. The Babylonian school is represented by Jensen, *Die Kosmologie der Babylonier* (1890). H. Gunkel, *Schöpfung und Chaos in Urzeit und Endzeit* (1895). Zimmern, *Biblische und babylonische Urgeschichte* (1901). H. Winckler, *Himmels- und Weltenbild der Babylonier als Grundlage der Weltanschauung und Mythologie aller* Völker (1903). A. Jeremias, *Das alte Testament im Lichte des Alten Orients.*

3. The works of Fr. X. Kugler, *Sternkunde und Sterndienst in Babel* (1907 and 1909). Im Bannkreis Babels. *Panbabylonische Konstruktionen und religionsgeschichtliche Tatsachen* (1910). "Auf den Trümmern des Panbabylonismus" in *Anthropos IV*, 477ff.

they now recognize a more imperative need to orient the Biblical world into the world of the Ancient Near East. In fact, we should be inclined to wonder, and perhaps even to doubt the historical character of revelation, if traces of the Ancient Near East world picture were not constantly occurring in the Bible. The Bible is, once and for all, a book of the Ancient Near East! But despite these clearly recognized similarities between Bible and Ancient Near East, we are faced with an even more burning problem: how are we to explain the individualities which set off the Bible against all the other Oriental myths about the origin of the world? Was not Israel, and her religious world, faced with precisely the same processes of culture fusion as the other related Semitic tribes, who all assimilated their religious and even their linguistic individualities to the sedentary population upon their transition from the wilderness into the cultivated land, and eventually passed over into the native population?[4] On the basis of purely immanent historical principles, the same thing must have happened also to Israel; for, during the whole time of her history in Palestine, Israel was always on the road towards paganism. That Israel did not succumb to this influence towards paganism is to be ascribed only to the constant and powerful intervention of the Spirit of God. It is only against the background of Ancient Near East history that the revelation character of the Bible is clearly recognizable. Here the yardsticks of the historian lose their validity; it is here that other, suprahistorical powers manifest their presence.[5]

---

4. A. Jepsen characterizes the Semitic immigrations as follows: "They come at first in proportionally small numbers into the land. They bring no culture of their own, nor do they create one; they pass over completely into the culture of the country. In addition, they soon assimilate the culture of the country. . . ." *AFO* XV (1945/51), 68.

5. The Greek cosmogonies must also be taken into account; essentially they are coextensive with the Ancient Near East accounts. For a general orientation cf. H. Schwabl, *Weltschöpfung. Sonderdruck aus Paulys Realencyclopädie der Classischen Altertumswissenschaft* (Stuttgart, 1958).

A) THE EGYPTIAN COSMOGONIES

The manifold and richly variegated political history of Ancient Egypt is mirrored in the colorful and almost impenetrable religious development of the pharaonic kingdom along the Nile. It is a thankless effort to present the Egyptian cosmogonies in anything like a brief form. But despite the religious transformations over the course of the four thousand year history of Egypt, there are principles of a world picture which have remained essentially the same throughout the ages. The selection offered below is chosen with respect to our understanding of the Bible.

The Egyptian man, who was inclined to be reflective upon the first origins of the world, was living in the land of the Nile. Every year he experienced the land rising anew from the inundations. For him, this was a picture of primordial times. In the beginning it must have been so, too. In a primeval water, which was called Nun, the higher stretches of ground were first visible, and this was also the beginning of the world, the "primordial hill, the splendid hill of primeval times." In various places in Egypt these areas were still shown. It was on this muddy primordial hill that the first creatures moved. "Night, darkness, and hiddenness." In this primordial ooze was also found the egg of a water fowl, from which a goose hatched and flew cackling over the sky. This was the sun. According to another version it was a lotus blossom which grew on the primordial hill, from which the sun-child proceeded. According to the third version, it was the cow who swam upon the water; it was upon her that the sun god took his seat, who then begot all things.... The *Sitz im Leben* of these myths is obviously the Egyptian landscape, in which it is easy to see a blossom or a cow swimming in the floods at inundation time.[6] The ancient Egyptian conceived of the beginning as a primordial ocean, from which gods and world alike were produced. This world picture is treated

6. Erman, *Religion der Ägypter* (1934), pp. 61-62.

somewhat differently in the individual mythologies. The conceptions of the three most important theological schools are presented below.

1) THE COSMOLOGY OF HELIOPOLIS: The sun religion of the Old Kingdom ascribes the first place in the cosmos to the god Atum, the "all-god, who exists of himself." From the watery darkness of the primeval chaos, by the process of self-generation, he produced the primeval elements, by "exhaling and spewing out" the first divine pair, Shu and Tefnut (air, void, and moisture). The Egyptian text involves a play on words here; the names are derived from the activity of the god who begets them. From this first divine pair now arise Geb and Nut (earth and sky). These in turn beget the two divine pairs Isis-Osiris and Seth-Nephthys, which already represent the heroes of antiquity and form the bridge to human history. All these gods, together with the creator god of the primordial beginning, make up the "sacred nine" (ennead) of Heliopolis.

The ancient cosmogonies were not produced for their own sake; they have their *Sitz im Leben;* they owe their written form to a concrete religious situation in life. Thus the Atum mythology is found in a pyramid text, which is written on the interior wall of the pyramid of Mer-ne-Re and Pepi II (6th dynasty, c. 2400 B.C.) and is composed in the form of a prayer: "O Atum, you were on the primordial hill, you grew up as a bird, you spewed out Shu and Tefnut. . . . You lay your arms about them like the arms of Ka; for your Ka (life power?) was in them. . . . Lay also your arms upon the king Nefer-ka-Re and upon this construction, upon this pyramid. . . ." The cosmogony is thus built into the prayer formula. What has happened in times primordial is to be repeated now![7]

---

7. The texts have been edited by K. Sethe, *Die altägyptischen Pyramidentexte,* II (Leipzig, 1910), 1652-1656. Excerpts in G. Röder, *Urkunden zur Religion des Alten Ägypten* (1923), pp. 164-168. A new version has been discovered in the 17th Chapter of the Book of the Dead, that is, texts that were placed in the coffin along with the dead person, intended to effect his secure passage into the hereafter. When he approaches the

2) THE COSMOGONY OF HERMOPOLIS: The political power of the Old Kingdom was opposed, in the first interval period, by strong opponents who shook the old structure in its very roots. Correspondingly, the theological system of Heliopolis was replaced by that of Hermopolis. This system is clearly composed as an opposition to Heliopolis. The primeval god Atum does not come into existence by himself; he is a creature of the sacred Ogdoad, composed of four pairs of gods, all of which were found on the primordial hill in the form of serpents and frogs. When these divine names are investigated in their original meanings, we find the presence of primeval elements not unlike those of the Heliopolitan cosmogony; they are primeval water, gloom, darkness, hiddenness. This system succeeded in breaking the religious precedence of the god of Heliopolis. Theology had been enlisted in the service of politics.[8]

3) THE COSMOGONY OF MEMPHIS: When Memphis, the city of the "white walls," the "balance of the two lands," achieved particular importance as capital city of the empire, it too was the scene of an individual theological system explaining the formation of the world, which was now concentrated on the city god Ptah.

The text in which the cosmogony of Memphis is recorded is clearly conceived as a deliberate opposition to the Atum cosmogony. It does indeed refer to Atum as "the god who exists all by himself" and who has brought everything into existence

---

God of the Universe, he calls out the words of the ancient myth, in order to have a share in eternal life: "I am Atum, who alone was in Nun (the primordial ocean)".... Next follows the text on the creation of the Sacred Ennead, and in conclusion Atum once again sums up his essential attributes: "I am yesterday because I also know tomorrow." By the recitation of these texts from the Book of the Dead, the deceased achieves a position for himself in the cosmic rhythm, and thereby feels himself sheltered in the God of the Universe, Atum. The myths were, accordingly, not merely imaginary pictures, they have life value over the domain of death. Texts in H. Grapow, *Religiöse Urkunden* (Leipzig, 1915/17), pp. 4-13.

8. J. Vandier, *La Réligion égyptienne* (1934), pp. 30-65: The theology and the myths.

of himself. Whereas the other divine beings were all begotten by a masculine and feminine principle, the first divine pair was produced by Atum's impregnating and fecundating himself. That this act was literally understood is clearly evident in the pictorial representations which have been discovered. This rather uncouth conception of the original act of creation may have been arrived at by identifying the original supreme god of creation Atum with the fertility god Min of Komptos.[9]

In sharp contrast with this coarse conception of the process of original creation, the Memphitic theology also offers a spiritualized form of this myth in its highest form. The principle of creation is not "semen and hands" (Atum spilling his seed), but rather "lips and teeth," that is, the intellectual decision to create the world which arose from the heart of Ptah and which, by his imperative word, became reality. The text is as follows:

> "Ptah's Ennead is before him in the form of teeth and lips. That is the equivalent of the semen and hands of Atum. Whereas the Ennead of Atum came into being by his semen and his fingers, the Ennead of Ptah, however, is the teeth and lips in his mouth, which pronounced the name of everything, from which Shu and Tefnut came forth, and which was the fashioning of the Ennead.
>
> The sight of the eyes, the hearing of the ears, and the smelling of the air by the nose, they report to the heart. It is this which causes every completed concept to come forth, and it is the tongue which announces what the heart thinks.
>
> Thus all the gods were formed and his Ennead was completed. Indeed, all the divine order really came into being through what the heart thought and the tongue commanded. Thus the *ka*-spirits were made and the *hemsut*-spirits were appointed (male and female divinities) who make all provisions and all nourishment by this speech.
>
> Thus justice was given to him who does what is liked, and injustice to him who does what is disliked. Thus life was given to him who has peace, and death was given to him who has sin. . . .
>
> Thus it was discovered and understood that his strength is greater than that of the other gods. And so Ptah was satisfied, after he had made everything as well as all the divine order."[10]

---

9. See Junker, *Religion der Pyramidenzeit,* p. 24.

10. The text from Junker, *op. cit.*, 23/24, is from the Shabaka Stone, from the year 700 B.C., but it goes back into the very origins of the

According to this cosmogony, the overpowering and sole primeval principle of the world and the gods is the god Ptah, at the beginning of things. Since the heart is the seat of the spiritual faculties, Ptah first outlines the idea of world creation in his heart, and then realizes it by his word. All things are, thus, in their deepest essence, words of god.

"All myths are clearly overshadowed by the figure of the one god of creation. We cannot call enough attention to the presence of such a pure and spiritual conception of God surrounded by such an abundance of individual cults. Nor must we attempt to belittle its significance by maintaining that it presents the reflections of only a small circle and has had little influence upon the general development of the Egyptian religion. There is no proof for such an assertion. Actually, the concept of creation by wisdom and the will of the all-god was already a common conception before this treatise was written. What is more, the effects of this teaching are evident everywhere in the later theology, and their continuation can be traced to the very end of the Egyptian religion.

Old Kingdom and is one of the most important documents of Ancient Egyptian religion. The priests of Memphis preserved an ancient copy in their temple, but it had suffered damage over the course of the years. They asked Pharaoh Shabaka to have a copy inscribed in stone. The stone was later used as a millstone, so that as a result the text suffered damage once again; the essential elements, however, were preserved. The stone is to be found today in the British Museum. It was first published by S. Sharpe, *Egyptian Inscriptions from the British Museum and Other Sources* (London, 1837), I, 36-38. In the evolutionistic enthusiasm initiated by the study of the history of religion, the text was not properly evaluated, since the Egyptian religion was assumed to begin with alogical, animistic preoccupations. There was no room for a text that told about a Creator God and the challenge of conscience. It was the challenge of conscience. It was only in recent years that the individuality of this text was properly appreciated: A. Erman, "Ein Denkmal memphitischer Theologie," *SPAW* 1911, 916-950. H. Junker, "Die Gotterlehre von Memphis," *APAW*, 1939, No. 23 (Berlin, 1940). J. H. Breasted, *The Dawn of Conscience* (New York, 1933), pp. 29-42. H. Frankfort, *The Intellectual Adventure of Ancient Man* (Chicago, 1946), pp. 55-60. J. A. Wilson in *ANET*, 3-7.

"We must however concede the fact that they were not equal to the task of replacing the less lofty conceptions. The reason for this is the ballast of divergent traditions which could not be shaken off, the rivalry of local cults, and the constant alternation of imperial gods" (Junker).

It is precisely these sad facts which can best serve as an example to illustrate the process whereby the image of the originally one god of creation, who is also judge over good and evil, was gradually degraded more and more into the chaotic by the sheer gravity of the powers that make for dissolution, until finally, overgrown by a plurality of gods and myths, he is hardly to be recognized.

The creation of man was conceived of in the following manner: in the book of Apophis, which is also called the "book of the recognizing of the figures of Re and the subjugation of the Apophis serpent," we read of the struggle between the Sun god and the monster who threatens his path every evening. On the occasion of this battle, he sends out his eye. Since the eye tarries a long time, the other eye begins to cry tears of anger (*rîme*); these tears become man (*rôme*); according to a different version, the sun god looks down with pleasure upon the divine pair Shu and Tefnut, and cries tears of joy, which turn into man. Thus we have only an etymological myth, invented by a poet on the basis of the similarity in sound between "tears" and "men" (*rîme* and *rôme*); but it still clearly expresses the divine origin of man.[11]

Side by side with this account, there was another widespread conception in which the sun god ordered the god Khnum to make man out of clay on a potter's wheel.[12]

---

11. The Apophis Book is a Book of the Dead, given to the deceased as a protection against attack by the dragon. Text excerpts in Gressmann, *AOT*, 1-2.

12. Representation of the god Khnum at the potter's wheel: Gressmann, *AOB* No. 303.

B) THE BABYLONIAN COSMOGONIES

Prior to the rediscovery of the Ancient Near East by the various excavations, our knowledge of the Babylonian cosmogonies was dependent entirely upon the fragmentary work *Babyloniaka* of Berossus, priest of Bel in Babel, who lived some 50 years after the death of Alexander the Great, and recorded the religious and historical traditions of his people in order to make them available to the Greek-speaking world. In the first century before Christ, Alexander Polyhistor made a series of extracts from this book, which was later used by the Church historian Eusebius, through whom it made its way into the Christian era (PG 19, 110-117). During Berossus' time, the study of the native literature was widely cultivated in the shadow of the ancient temples, so that it can be considered quite probable that Berossus was able to base his work on the more ancient cosmogonies. Excavations [13] have not only succeeded in unearthing the almost entirely preserved epic of the seven tables (*enûma eliš*), but other more or less well preserved creation texts as well. Jirku, in his *Altorientalische Kommentar* (1923), already presented 14 Babylonian cosmogonies. Their number has since

13. The first account of the Babylonian creation myth was published by George Smith, *The Chaldean Account of Genesis,* 1876. Further excavations yielded the complete text of the seven tablets. English excavations in Niniveh: L. W. King, *The Seven Tablets of Creation,* 2 Vols. (1902). German excavations in Assur: E. Ebeling, "Keilschrifttexte aus Assur religiösen Inhalts," 1915ff. British-American excavations in Kish: S. Langdon, *Oxford Edition of Cuneiform Texts.* Vol. VI (1923). General edition by A. Deimel, *Enuma eliš seu epos b:bylonicum de creatione mundi,* 2nd *edition* (Rome, 1936). Translations: S. Langdon, *The Babylonian Epic of Creation* (1923). E. Ebeling, *AOT*, 108-129. E. A. Speiser, *ANET*, second edition, (1955), 60-72. R. Labat, *Le Poème babyloníen de la Création* (Paris, 1935). A Heidel, *The Babylonian Genesis* (Chicago, 1951). Selections with notes: J. V. Kinnier Wilson, "The Epic of Creation," published by D. Winton Thomas, *Documents from Old Testament Times* (London, 1953), pp. 3-16. F. Schmidtke, "Urgeschichte der Welt im sumerischen Mythos." *BBB* 1 (1950), 205-223.

increased. The texts stem from different epochs, but all go back to one basic type, which can be traced back into the Sumerian era. From the abundance of material, we have chosen to outline the essential features of the Babylonian epic of the creation of the world, *Enûma eliš*. The time of its composition is not yet agreed upon. Speiser[14] dates it in the old-Babylonian era (Hammurabi); von Soden,[15] on the contrary, dates it in the Kassite era, around 1400. Since the epic is not mere poetry, but also represents the solemn liturgy for the New Year's feast, it was immune to the effects of political vicissitude. After the destruction of Babylon by Sanherib (689), the god Marduk, the principal figure in the epic, was replaced by the god Ashur, and the epic was done into Assyrian. The epic has thus survived a long and varied history. But the additions to the original text are easily recognized as violations of the original rhythm.[16] With respect to this original rhythm, we are not left to our own resources. One scribe has marked not only the principal caesuras, in the middle of the verse, but also the quarter-verse, by diagonal lines on his tablet. The rhythm is based on a two-times-two (2 x 2), or a four foot line. The first two lines are as follows:

enûma / eliš // lâ nabû / šamâmu
šapliš / ammatum // šuma / lâ zakrat

When, above, the heaven was not as yet named,
Below, the firm ground as yet bore no name. . . .

The Babylonian epic of the creation of the world received its name from its first two words *enûma eliš*, "When, above." Since we do not yet possess an accurate translation in the rhythm of the original text, the following selections are based on the translation of E. A. Speiser, as published in ANET.

---

14. *ANET*, 60.
15. *PropWG* II (1962), 71, 105.
16. A. Heidel, *The Babylonian Genesis*, 2nd edition (1951), 16.
17. B. Bonkamp, *Die Bibel im Lichte der Keilschriftforschung* (Recklinghausen, 1939).

TABLET 1: FIRST ORIGINS

When, above, the heaven was not as yet named,
below, the firm ground as yet bore no name,
Apsu, the First One, their begetter,
Mummu and Tiamat, who were all born,
their waters were still mixed all together-
shrubbery and bush were not yet sprung up,
reedbeds were not yet to be seen;
when the gods had not yet entered into existence, not one of them –
Then it was that the gods were formed.

As the very first beginning we have a masculine and a feminine principle, Apsu (Greek: *abyssos*), conceived of as the primordial ocean of sweet water, and Mummu-Tiamat, the salt sea. It is from this primordial sea that the first gods arise, Lakhmu (sky of light) and Lakhamu (mother of light-darkness); these in turn give birth to Anshar, the god of the upper universe of heaven, and Kishar, the god of the lower universe of earth. The son of Anshar is Anu, god of the sky, whose son is once again the earth god Enki (also called Ea or Nudimmud).

But the creation of the gods spells the end of the primeval peace. The primeval gods complain over the younger generation and determine upon its annihilation:

By day I have no rest, at night I cannot sleep;
I will destroy them, put an end to their workings.
Peace and quiet shall be once more restored, we shall sleep!

This throws the younger gods into great confusion; but Ea who understands everything, made a powerful holy incantation against Apsu. He spoke this incantation over the water, and Apsu sank into a deep sleep. Then Ea slew him and established his own dwelling upon the slain god. In this tower a son was born him, Marduk. With the slaying of Apsu the first chaotic primordial element is overcome; but Tiamat, Apsu's wife, is bent on revenge.

TABLET 2: TIAMAT'S REVENGE

Furious they are; they make plans, resting neither by day nor by night.
They take up the battle, violent, awesome. . . .
Ummu Hubur (epithets of Tiamat), who fashions all things,
shaped weapons without match, birthed giant serpents
with pointed teeth and merciless bite,

With poison instead of with blood she filled their bodies....
Serpents she set up, dragons with glittering scales,
tempest-monsters, savage dogs, and scorpion-men....
Eleven such monsters she called into existence.
Among the gods, her first-born,
who had all flocked together around her,
she raised up Kingu, made him mighty among them.
To take first post at the head of the army, to lead the thronged men,
to direct the battle, she gave into his hands....
She gave him the tablets of fate, pinned them to his breast.
Irrevocable be his command!
Firm stand the word of his mouth!

These preparations for war greatly disturb the younger gods. They do not trust themselves to take up battle. Then they think of Marduk, the son of Ea, and decide that he might be capable of serving as leader in the battle. He finally declares himself ready for the task, but only under the condition that after the victory he become king of the gods. Thereupon, an assembly of the gods is convoked.

TABLET 3: THE DIVINE ASSEMBLY

They entered before Anshar, they filled the hall
and kissed each other in the assembly...
conversed together and sat them down to the feast,
ate bread and drank date wine.
The sweet drink gave them other thoughts.
They spoke to Marduk:
Marduk, you are our avenger!
We have delivered kingship to you,
power over everything in all of its fullness....
Wreck or create! Command: it is done!
One word of your mouth and ruined is the cloth.
Command once again and the cloth, it is whole!

A garment is brought in and annihilated at Marduk's word; when it is restored, at his word, the gods all worshipped him and cried: Marduk is king!

TABLET 4: THE FIGHT WITH TIAMAT

Marduk prepared himself for battle with arrows, bow, and quiver. He set the lightning before him. Then he made a net in which to en-

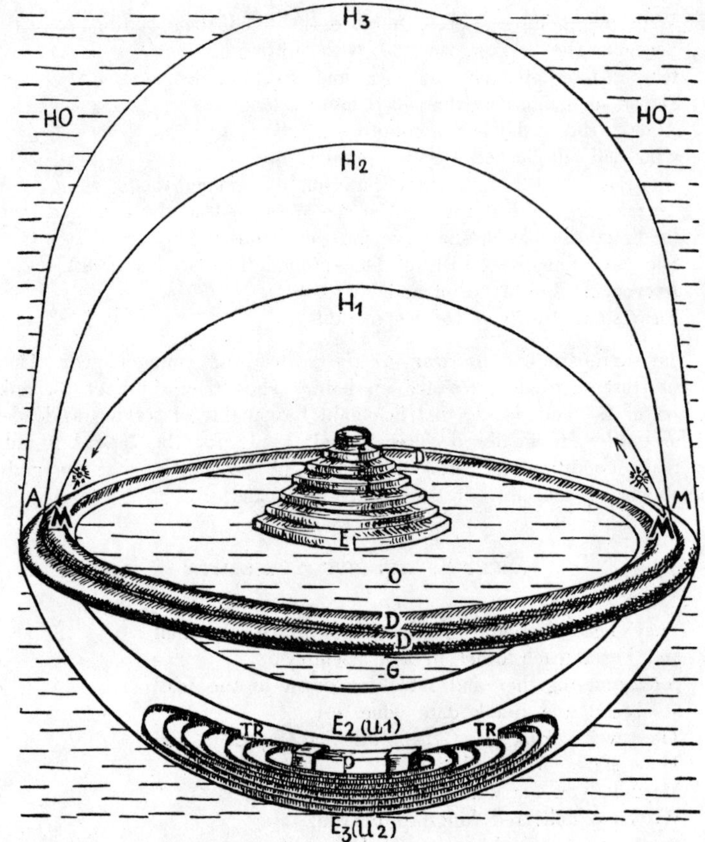

ILLUSTRATION 2: THE BABYLONIAN WORLD PICTURE (after a sketch by W. Schwenzner) published in Bruno Meissner: *Babylonien und Assyrien,* II, 109. Heidelberg – Winters Universitätsbuchhandlung, 1925.

E(1) : Earth (Upper world) O : Ocean of earth
E(2), E(3) : 2nd and 3rd underworld
H(1), H(2), H(3) · 1st, 2nd. 3rd heaven
T, G : Depths and foundation of the Ocean of Earth
A : Evening (West); the two mountains of the sunset
M : Morning (East): the two mountains of the sunrise
D : Dam of the heavens
TR : Seven walls and palace of the realm of the dead

tangle Tiamat. He loosed the winds which he posted beside him: all the hurricanes were enlisted in his service, the four-wind, the seven-wind, the whirlwind, and the destroyer wind.

He mounted the storm-chariot irresistible and terrifying.
He harnessed and yoked to it a team of four,
The Killer, the Relentless, the Trampler, the Swift-Flyer.

Thus equipped, he now sets out against the army of Tiamat. The very sight of him threw the hostile ranks into confusion, but Tiamat was not to be intimidated. Next comes the final word duel before the battle: "Come now, you and I shall do battle!" Then Tiamat gave a terrible cry and the two opponents rushed upon each other.

The lord spread out his net to enfold her,
The Evil Wind, which followed behind, he let loose in her face.
When Tiamat opened her mouth to consume him,
He drove in the Evil Wind that she close not her lips.
As the fierce winds charged her belly,
Her body was distended and her mouth was wide open.
He released the arrow, it tore her belly,
It cut through her insides, splitting the heart.
Having thus subdued her, he extinguished her life,
He cast down her carcass to stand upon it.

With Tiamat dead, her forces were also broken. The enemy sought to flee; but they no longer could, since they were entangled. Then he made them prisoners and shattered their weapons. He likewise shackled the eleven demons. But Kingu, the leader of the enemy forces, he condemned to death. He took the tablets of fate from him and hanged them on his own breast.

Then Marduk divided the dead body of Tiamat, the way a man cuts open a shell-fish. The upper half he made into the vault of the heavens, with the ocean of heaven, and from the other half he made the solid earth and everything upon it.

TABLET 5: THE FURNISHINGS OF THE COSMOS

Hereupon, Marduk determined the dwellings and stations of the great gods, dividing the year and the twelve months among them. Particularly he commissioned the moon (Nannar), to give light at night:

Monthly, without cease, form designs with a crown.
At the month's very start, rising over the land,
Thou shalt have luminous horns to signify six days,

On the seventh day reaching a half-crown.
At full moon stand in opposition in mid-month.
When the sun overtakes thee at the base of heaven,
Diminish thy crown and retrogress in light.
At the time of disappearance approach thou the course of the sun,
And on the twenty-ninth thou shalt again stand in opposition
to the sun.

TABLET 6: THE CREATION OF MAN

After the cosmos had been created, there arose the question of what to do with the prisoners. They could be killed, sold as slaves, or even set free. The divine assembly decided in favor of the last alternative; the only condition was that, in place of the liberated prisoners, other beings should be created who would undertake the service of the gods. But the ringleader Kingu was to be killed. This was Marduk's answer:

Blood I will mass and cause bones to be.
I will establish Lulla (name for the first man)
Verily, savage-man will I create.
He shall be charged with the service of the gods
That they might be at ease!
They bound Kingu, and severed his blood vessels.
Out of his blood they fashioned mankind.
He imposed the service and let free the gods.

TABLET 7: THE GRATITUDE OF THE GODS

In gratitude for the work of liberation, the gods decided to build the temple tower of E-sag-ila. They helped in the construction themselves, and for a whole year they laid brick upon brick, until the structure was completed. They then assembled for a communal banquet. Marduk's face shone for joy. He greeted the gods, his fathers, with this statement: "This is Bab-ili, the seat of your dwelling. Enjoy yourselves here and celebrate a festival." The epic concludes with the 50 names of Marduk.

The present text of the *Enûma eliš* epic is the work of the priests of the temple in E-sag-ila in Babylon. It was presented, according to a ritual which is still extant, at the beginning of the year, on the occasion of the New Year's feast, in the temple.[18] With respect to the creation of man, there are also some other traditions.

---

18. *Ibid.*, 56-69. H. Zimmern, "Das Babylonische Neuyahrsfest," *AO* 25, 3 (Leipzig, 1926).

a) CREATION OF THE MOTHER GODDESS MAMI: The gods press her to create man. She says that she needs blood for that work. Then the moon god Lamga is slaughtered and men are formed from his blood; the monthly waning of the moon could only be explained as killing.[19]

b) CREATION OUT OF MUD: In a ritual text for the reconstruction of a temple, the priest prays: "As Anu created the heaven, Nudimmud the ocean, for a dwelling place, then Ea pinched off some mud from the ocean and with it created the gods and also the men, upon whom he imposed the service of the gods. . . ."[20]

c) SINCE, in the course of the development of religion, Marduk gradually found a place in the series of vegetation gods who annually die and resurrect, other texts recount how it was Marduk himself who was slain and whose blood was then used in the creation of the gods and men.[21]

C) THE PHOENICIAN COSMOGONIES

The Phoenician explanation of the origin of the world is not essentially different from the other Ancient Near East cosmogonies. At the beginning of the world there was primeval chaos, from which gods and men both developed. The Phoenician cosmogony is recorded by Philo of Byblos, in his work *Phoinikika*. Selections of this work were preserved in the *Praeparatio evangelica* of Eusebius (PG 21, 75ff.). He represents the beginning as a gloomy and wet chaos, driven by storm (*pneuma*), from which, by the process of sexual generation, eventually arose the divinity Mot, who bore the seeds of all things within himself. This divinity was conceived of as a moist and slimy mass, which took on the form of a world egg; the splitting of this egg gave rise to an upper half, the sky, and a lower half, the earth. From Kolpia (wind?) and Baau (night?) the first humans were begotten, Aion and Protogonos, who were nourished by the fruit of trees.[22]

---

19. E. Ebeling, "Tod und Leben" (1931), Nos. 37, 172-177. *ANET* 99f.

20. H. Gressmann, *AOT* 25. Also Bonkamp, *op. cit.*, 78.

21. E. Ebeling, "Keilscrifttexte aus Assur religiösen Inhalts." Nos. 143 and 219.

22. This is not the story of Paradise, but rather an account of the development of civilization from its primitive state to the Golden Age of Phoenician culture.

If Philo's cosmogony, even in its external presentation, still expresses the Ancient Near East world picture and thus gives evidence of apparent echoes of the Genesis account, such as "wind over the waters, night, darkness, Tohu-wa-bohu," perhaps also an echo of the name Eve in the name of the first man Aion . . . , its internal thought structure, however, is strictly materialistic, since the concept of a creator god is far in the background.

The old Phoenician or Canaanite conceptions of the origin of the world were considerably advanced by the excavations in Ugarit. Although a creation epic, in the proper sense of the word, has not yet been discovered, on the basis of the already familiar myths, the picture of the creator god El can be clearly recognized, as we have already discussed in the section on the religion of Canaan.[23] This suggests the not too surprising conclusion that the Biblical song of the creation of the world is, in terms of the history of thought and culture, more closely related to the Canaanite than it is to the Babylonian myths of the origin of the world.

D) MYTHOLOGICAL IMAGES IN THE OLD TESTAMENT

Since Gunkel first published his book *Schöpfung und Chaos in Urzeit und Endzeit* (1895), it has been customary to regard several texts of the Old Testament as a precipitate of the Ancient Near East mythology. In the foreground stands the battle of Marduk against the monsters of primordial times. In a somewhat similar manner, according to the Israelite conception, it is Yahweh who overcomes the Leviathan, the Tannin, and the Behemoth.

The Leviathan in the Book of Job (40, 25-41; Vulgate 40, 20-41, 25) is most probably an actual animal, perhaps a crocodile whose fierceness is described by the poet. The Tannin in Gen. 1, 21 refers to the great sea animals, without any reference to

---

23. See above pp. 177ff.

mythology. Similarly, the Behemoth in Job 40, 15 might refer to great sea beasts. But some of the Psalms do pose mythological problems: Ps. 88/89, 10-11 celebrates Yahweh's victory over Rahab: "Thou didst crush Rahab like a carcass, thou didst scatter thy enemies with thy mighty arm." Ps. 73/74, 12-17: "Yet God my king is from of old, working salvation in the midst of the earth. Thou didst divide the sea by thy might; thou didst break the heads of the dragons (Tannin) on the waters. Thou didst crush the heads of Leviathan, thou didst give him as food for the creatures of the wilderness. Thou didst cleave open springs and brooks; thou didst dry up ever-flowing streams. Thine is the day, thine also the night; thou hast established the luminaries and the sun...." [24]

A further mythological reference occurs in Is. 27, 1, when he is speaking of the return from exile: "In that day the Lord with his hard and great and strong sword will punish Leviathan the fleeing serpent, Leviathan the twisting serpent, and he will slay the dragon (Tannin) that is in the sea...." In chapter 51, 9-11 the prophet speaks of the passage through the Red Sea, and refers back to primeval times: "Awake, as in days of old, the generations of long ago. Was it not thou that didst cut Rahab in pieces, that didst pierce the dragon (Tannin)? Was it not thou that didst dry up the seas?"

On the basis of these and similar texts we see that the Old Testament does contain mythological figures, but *no* mythology as such. We are justified in stating that the old myths were known in Israel, which was so thoroughly permeated with paganism, and in constant danger of defection to the Baalim. The prophets and poets make use of this cultural fund in an effort to describe the truly singular power and grandeur of Yahweh.

By way of conclusion, the Biblical creation narrative is at home in the world of the Ancient Near East. It stands above all

---

24. Rahab means, literally, "tossing, rolling," thus a circumlocution for the tossing of the sea. The "helpmates of Rahab" (Job 9, 13) are the sea monsters.

the myths of the origin of the world that have yet been discovered by its clearly characterized belief in one God. This one God is the creator of heaven and earth.

If ethnologists had been able to establish faith in the one God as creator of the world in primitive and ancient peoples,[25] faith existing in a form not yet caked over by myth, this still does not mean that we must conclude to a relationship of dependence. The human mind is capable of concluding from the existence of creatures to the existence of a creator, in every place and at every age (Rom. 1, 19ff.). Thus the coloring of Biblical prehistory cannot be considered merely as a prehistorical coloring;[26] it is and remains Ancient Near East. In itself, it would be possible for a poet and thinker to compose the Biblical song of creation without any particular revelation, since the recognition of the one God on the basis of creation always lies within the range of human reason. But the literary historian cannot cease to marvel at the fact that the image of God was so caked over with myth in the neighboring peoples and so free of myth in Israel. What forces were at work here? The man who believes in a God who reveals himself in history and in word will recognize the breath of God's inspiring Spirit.

---

25. The creation concepts of primitive peoples are best studied in W. Schmidt, *Der Ursprung der Gottesidee*. In Vol. VI there is a summary conclusion on the primitive peoples of America, Asia, and Africa (Munster, 1935).

26. W. Schmidt, "Die Schöpfungsgeschichte der biblischen und ethnologischen Urzeit," *StZ* 134 (1938), 295-305.

SECTION TWO

ORIGIN OF MAN

If we assume the toledot as the principle of division in analyzing the Book of Genesis, then the section 2, 4b-5, 1 must be treated as a literary unit. The Babylonian epic of the creation of the world was known by its initial words *enûma eliš*. Correspondingly, this Biblical section might best be entitled: *beyôm 'aśôt Yahweh*, "on the day that God made." Linguistically, the Hebrew word *beyôm* is a literal rendition of *enûma*[1]. The coincidence of similar initial words could be pure chance, but we cannot entirely dismiss the suspicion that the Biblical author deliberately used the epic title words. The text which begins with 2, 4b is certainly not narrative prose; it is a well constructed and detailed piece of poetry. The content of this poetry would be summed up, by way of supplementary title, in the colophon: *zeh sêper tôledôt 'ādām* (5, 1), that is: "This is the book of the generations of Adam" (or: "this is the book of the origin of man"). Expressing it non-literally, in terms of content, we might translate: "This is the great saga of the origin of man." We call it by the ancient word "saga," since we are dealing with songs which have been handed down and sung from generation to generation, and which contain statements of faith. At the beginning there stands a great poet. Who he was does not matter for the moment. His song sings of the origin of man in Paradise, of his fall and expulsion from the Garden, from the first human murder down to the rise of various vocations and the brutalization of human mores. The essence of man is portrayed in terms of his first origins. Thus, in terms of literary history, we can actually speak of a Biblical epic on the first man.

Passing on now from the greater unit of toledot to the lesser division (in the Leningrad manuscript) in terms of *sedarim* ("orders"), the first *sedar* notation we encounter is at 2, 4a. Order I includes the text of Gen 2, 4 – 3, 21. Here once again we could easily arrive at the premature conclusion that this division is only a later addition by the synagogue liturgy. But we must temper our judgment. Let us examine and see if there is not perhaps

---

1. A. Heidel, *The Babylonian Genesis*, 2nd edition (1951), p. 95.

some unified structural law at work in the formation of this text.

We have already referred to the very simple principle of text division that will be followed here. The text as we have it today consists of three elements: narrative (N), introduction to direct speech (I), and direct speech (S). Occasionally introductory element (i) with new direct speech (s) can be incorporated into the direct speech. Leaving this indirect speech aside for the moment, Order I exhibits the following structural scheme: 5 title + 318 N + 49 I + 217 S = 5 + 584. What do these numbers mean? First we must demonstrate the fact that this is not merely the result of chance, but a clearly developed system of symbolic numbers.

1) TOTAL SUM AND STELLAR YEAR

The 5 words of the toledot title have been isolated as an individual element. The rest of the text totals 584 words. Are we to assume that it is mere chance that precisely these two numbers appear as the very first structural element? The numbers are two very typical Ishtar-Venus numbers. The periodic rotation of the morning-evening star is a cycle of precisely 584 days. This knowledge was familiar to the ancient Babylonians. Vera Schneider presents an extensive treatment of the question in her book[2] *Gilgamesh*: "The zodiac is divided into five equal parts by five successive conjunctions of the Venus star (a phenomenon which occurs regularly every 9½ months). These five points can be joined to form a pentagon and a configuration of five stars."

If such a numerical system of division were apparent only in the general over-all outline of the text, we would necessarily regard it as pure chance. But, as our further investigation will demonstrate, the Ishtar numbers also determine the structure of the text. In addition to the 584 days and the 5 divisions of the zodiac cycle, we also find 15 as a symbolic number for Ishtar. Nineveh, as the city of Ishtar, had 15 gates. In Ashurbanipal's

---

2. Vera Schneider, *Gilgamesh,* (Zurich, 1957), pp. 115-118.

inscription, at one point, we read: "3 X 5 = 15! 15! 15!"[3] Now, Order I contains precisely 15 speeches and 150 words spoken by YHWH-Elohim. We are thus justified in stating that the narrative describing the morning of humanity is symbolically illuminated by the light of the morning star. In the Ancient Near East the morning star is a feminine noun and concept, symbol of the great queen of heaven and mother of humanity. The creation narrative was determined by the jubilee and the solar year. Here it is the astral year that serves as model for the form and structure of the text.

2) NARRATIVE AND MOONLIGHT YEAR

The total of narratives is 318 words. This number is known from the account of Abraham's raid against the Kings from the East (Gen 14, 14) where we read that Abraham mustered his 318 "*hanîk*" (trained men, initiates), pursued the hostile kings as far as Dan, and freed his cousin Lot. On the subject of this number, A. Jeremias has this to say: "The artificial and symbolic value of the number 318 is demonstrated by the Egyptian account of how Kadasmanharve, king of the Kassites, assigned a retinue of 318 men to his daughter upon the occasion of her bridal journey to Amenhotep III, while the sober historical record of this same event, in the Amarna correspondence, mentions only 25 men and 25 women. The same number 318 occurs as the number of Gideon's warriors, according to one textual variant for Judges 7, 16. And in both cases the forces are mystically divided into three parts. Jewish tradition explains the number 318 as the numerical value of the name Eliezer. It is in this mystical sense that we speak of the 318 bishops at the Council of Nicea."[4]

The number 318 is a lunar calendar number. The phases of the moon early provided the simplest measure for reckoning the passage of time, the crescent moon waxing to full moon and then once again waning until it completely disappears at new moon,

---

3. A. Jeremias, *ATAP*, 1930, p. 824.
4. *Ibid.*, p. 310.

a phase which occupies 3 days every month. Over a period of 12 months, this means 3 X 12 = 36 days of new moon or "moon-darkness." If these 36 days are subtracted from the full lunar year of 354 days, the remaining 318 days are the number of days in the year in which there is some moonlight.

The total number of all the words in Order I points to the periodic rotation of the Ishtar-star with its year of 384 days and 5 synods which divide the zodiac cycle into five equal parts. The 318 narrative words now refer to the light portion of the lunar year. The next obvious consideration is whether or not these cosmic numbers have actually set the pattern for the construction of the text.

3) INTRODUCTIONS AND JUBILEES

The total of introduction formulae is the number 49, that is, the value of the jubilee of 7 X 7 days. This arrangement stresses not only the holy week as the fundamental element in the course of the year, but also calls attention to the larger divisions of the holy year. The number speaks for itself and requires no further explanation.

4) THE 217 SPOKEN WORDS

The sum of the 15 speeches can be understood only on the basis of the proportion that is attributed to each of the individual speakers. The number is composed of these elements: 137 YHWH-Elohim + 32 Adam + 22 Eve + 26 serpent = 217 words.

a) THE 137 WORDS OF GOD: In the Paradise section YHWH-Elohim speaks 27 words in 2 speeches, whereas in the temptation story, in 6 speeches, he speaks 110 words. This is a thought-provoking number. The lifespan of the Egyptian Joseph is given (Gen 52, 22) as 110 years. He thus attained what is, to the

Eyptian manner of thinking, an ideal age. There must be some very ancient symbolism involved here; the sage and vizier Ptah-hotpe, whose life is dated in the fifth dynasty (c. 2600), boasts: "My accomplishments upon earth are no slight matter: I have completed 110 years of life which the King has given me."[5] Joshue, too, who carried the remains of Egyptian Joseph into Canaan, is said to have died at an age of 110 years (Josh 24, 29).

The explanation of these numbers presupposes some knowledge of the 22 elements of the world: 5 X 22 = 110. This is the number of perfection as such, composed of time and world together, *chronos* and *cosmos;* the 5 stands for *chronos,* and the 22 for the elements of the world. The number 110 is also the foundation for the structure of the Pyramid of Cheops; the sides each measure 4 X 110 = 440 cubits. YHWH-Elohim, who is perfection *per se,* now speaks precisely these 110 words at a most pivotal juncture in the history of humanity.

There are also the 27 words spoken by God in the first section of Order I: 18 + 9 = 27 = 3^3 words. Both speeches are negative in form: "Do not eat" (2, 16) and "It is not good . . ." (2, 18). The number 27 is the number 3 raised to the third power. It thus expresses the essence of divine perfection.[6]

b) ADAM AND WISDOM: The 32 words assigned to Adam are dictated by the leitmotif of ancient Jewish wisdom mysticism. In the Book of Creation we read: "In 32 wonderful ways of wisdom God has . . . inscribed and created his world" (*Sepher Yesirah* I, i). As we have already described above, in our treatment of the creation narrative, the 32 ways of wisdom are composed of the 10 primordial words of God and the 22 letters of the Hebrew alphabet in which the word takes on form and substance. Adam's conduct can be called anything but wise, but

5. H. Gressmann, *AOTAO,* p. 33.
6. A. Jeremias, *op. cit.,* p. 820.

perhaps this wisdom number was chosen precisely as a counterpart to the folly of his behavior. We must recall, moreover, that wisdom and law are practically synonymous. Adam and the number 32 is already a clear reference to man subject to the commandments of God.

c) Eve and the Elements: Eve speaks 22 words, an obvious reference to the letters of the alphabet. Their relationship with the elements of the world is described above.

d) The Serpent and the Divine Number: The serpent promises Eve that they will be like God (Gen 3, 5). What he urges mankind to attempt he already claims for himself. His words number 26, the numerical value of the word YHWH.

e) The Second Exchange: Four times we have the injunction "Do not eat" in the midst of the direct address, with some sort of introductory formula: first from the serpent (3, 1), then from Eve (3, 3), finally from God at the trial of Adam (3, 11) and at his sentencing (3, 17). This makes a total of 19 speeches. The 4 quotations just mentioned also total: $5 + 8 + 3 + 3 = 19$ words. Once again we have an astronomical symbol. The number 19 was considered as the "golden number" in the astronomical reckoning of the Ancient Near East. On the one hand the synodic year of Venus numbers 19 months ($5 + 584 = 589 = 19 \times 31$), and on the other hand the number 19 expresses the eventual compensatory balance of the solar and lunar years (19 solar years = 235 lunations). For the words spoken by YHWH-Elohim we thus arrive at the formula: $126\ S + 5\ i + 19\ s = 150$, which is a further allusion to the Ishtar cycle.

The above discussion is sufficient to demonstrate the fact that the structure of the text is based upon a cosmic model.

f) Vocabulary and Basic Words: In order to determine how many words an author has at his disposal and the vocabulary he employs it is necessary to prepare a concordance. The text must be read and recorded word for word in columns. When the scholar encounters a word that has been used before, he simply arranges it beside the first recorded usage of the word, in a second column. The first column will then reveal the basic vocabulary. In order to be more precise, we have used the term "basic words" or "basic vocabulary" to describe the list. In the creation narrative we discovered that the author worked with only 105 words. In Order I, on the other hand, we find a vocabulary of 180 words, that is, one half of a cyclic solar year (2 X 180 = 360). This solar symbolism also explains why Order I uses the double form of the divine name, YHWH-Elohim, precisely 18 times. In Babylon the number representative of the sun-god was 20: this also leads to the number 18 in that 360 divided by 20 gives 18.

Particularly noteworthy is the fact that in the narrative of the Fall there are essentially 63 basic words, corresponding to the 63 tractates of the later Talmud. Where we first encounter a story of violation and vindication of a divine precept, we already encounter the leitmotif of 63, the number of tractates on the Law.

CONCLUSIONS: All this leads to important conclusions for the analysis of form criticism. The units have not been put into a longer or shorter form simply in keeping with the exigencies of the particular theme. They are following a rigid principle of overall structural unity. At the very beginning we can see the outline numbers of the words, as well as in the units that are later developed. The process is very much like a metal casting process. First the form is molded and then the words are poured into it. The narrative of Paradise and Fall is, accordingly, actually a well ordered whole, precisely formed and molded, of words, sentences, and units. Not a single word can be removed without disturbing the whole meaningful structure of the text.

This provides a rather clear insight into the methodology and style of the men who produced the final form of the text of the Bible. There was surely a variety of material available for the final casting of the text, strata or sources or traditions to put it in terms of Pentateuchal source criticism, but the authors of the final text treated all this material as independent artists in their own right.

The text of Order I is, today, generally ascribed to the Jahwist tradition. O. Eissfeldt, however, claims that it is possible to isolate a further, "lay" source in the text.[7] G. Fohrer also distinguishes a "nomadic source stratim."[8] It might very well be correct to claim that there is evidence of these older traditions and strata in the text, but, given the present form of the text, they can no longer be adequately defined. Since it is number which serves as the all-pervasive structural outline in even the most insignificant piece of the text, it must be accepted as quite possible that the texts that were once ascribed purely to, e.g., the Jahwist tradition, have been reworked and cast into the later author's structural form. It would thus appear quite impossible to pick out the so-called original or earliest form of the strata that have been incorporated into the present-day form of the text.

This only serves to accentuate the fact that the author of the Paradise narrative was not simply an editor working with the text of a story handed down from ages past, but also a true composer in his own right, reworking the ancient traditional material and filling it with a new sense of form. This complicated structure must obviously be attributed to but a single planner. It is possible, however, that the work was done under his direction in a *beyt hammidrash*, an academy of scribes.

In our elucidation of the theological content of the text we can, accordingly, no longer look back to the origins of the text: they are no longer within our grasp. The only proper objective of Biblical theology must now be to deduce the thought content of the present form of these chapters. Here we once again come face to face with the fact that the formation of the text itself is the only possible key to our proper understanding of the in-

---

7. *Hexateuch-Synopse*, 1962, p. 3ff.
8. *Einleitung in das AT*, 1965, p. 175.

dividual units. The text is to be unlocked only from the point of view of wisdom.

When we broach this term, wisdom, we immediately face the problem as to whether or not this wisdom literature – for that is what we must finally consider this Order I in the text of Genesis – is to be attributed to the first or the second epoch of wisdom literature in Israel. The first era is the Davidic-Solomonic era, with the narratives of Egyptian Joseph serving as the prime example. The second epoch followed much later and did not reach its full development until the post-Exilic era. Any consideration of the artistic formation evident in the text ultimately raises the problem as to whether such a product, thoroughly finished workmanship based upon a structural principle of sacral numbers, could possibly have arisen from the Jahwistic authors of the Davidic-Solomonic era. If the answer is negative, then it follows that one of the true psychological masterpieces of the Jahwist is not really the work of the Jahwist. The very existence of this Jahwist, who figures so prominently in higher Biblical criticism, is eventually called into question. But a whole series of further investigations into the structure of the text must be completed before anything definitive can be concluded on the subject of this very difficult problem.

As the individual treatments that follow all indicate, there are many characteristics that point to a Babylonian origin, so many, in fact, that it once again becomes improbable to attribute the Paradise narrative to the Jahwist of the Davidic-Solomonic era. What is really being put into verbal form here is the great mystery of wisdom and Law, serving as a powerful theme to introduce and organize the whole composition of the Pentateuch, from the very outset. This leads to the necessary further conclusion that what we are dealing with here is not prehistorical and primitive tradition, but rather a deeply theological and mystical and cosmic interpretation of humankind as such.

CHAPTER XVII

THE SONG OF PARADISE

ORDER I, PART 1

GEN. 2, 4-25

SCHOLARS have almost grown accustomed to speaking of a second creation narrative, which is supposed to begin with Genesis 2, 4b. It is obvious that a new style begins with this verse. It is no longer the simple divine name Elohim, but the double form Yahweh-Elohim that is used. God no longer creates his works simply by his word of command, as in the creation songs; he is represented as a man (anthropomorphic). He forms his creation like a potter, he breathes life into it, he plants, he takes a leisurely walk in the garden. Moreover, the sequence of the works of creation is different; in the creation song it is plants, animals, man; but here it is: man, plants, animals, woman.

But a closer examination into the historical style reveals the fact that Genesis 2, 4 is not the beginning of a new creation account; the whole point of interest from now on is concentrated on man. This is not a cosmogony, but rather an anthropogony.[1] In terms of literary genre, the Biblical Paradise account is most

---

1. B. Kipper, Gen. 2, 4b-25, "Una segunda narrativa da criacao" (No second report of creation). *RCB* 4 (1960), 101-105.

closely related to the Sumero-Babylonian culture myths.[2] These myths generally describe first the state of non-existence, in order to present a brighter contrast by letting the culture-creating activity of their god shine out against this dark background. Similarly, the singer's eye, in the song of Paradise, is not on the creation of the world as a whole, but on the rise of the first man. On this basis the expression "second creation narrative" can no longer be justified. The great saga of mankind begins with chapter 2, verse 4. Obviously this must be a very ancient song. This much we can establish on the basis of the double form of the divine name Yahweh-Elohim. What is the meaning of this double form? Tur-Sinai[3] explains this in terms of the procedure customarily used by the cuneiform writer. The proper names of the gods were frequently added as symbols for "divinity" to the text, but never actually read; they had only a graphic character. But since the Biblical texts were not written on clay tablets, this argument has little value. The double form of the divine name is to be understood as a solar symbolism, as explained above.

---

2. M. Witzel, "Texte zum Studium sumerischer Tempel und Kultstätten," *Anal. Or.* (1932). G. Castellino, *Salesianum,* 13 (1951), 334-360 holds that Gen. 3-4 presents a literary unit which is related to the Babylonian creation epic and the other culture hymns, but composed in West-Semetic. The individualities can be explained only on the assumption of basic history. Presentation and coloring are borrowed from the Sumerian tradition. The genus "culture hymn" is exhaustively developed in A. Pohl, "Die alttestamentliche und altorientalische Umwelt. Gedanken zum Paradiesbericht," *StZ* 83 (1958), 241-248.

3. N. H. Tur-Sinai, "JHWH-Elohim in der Paradieserzählung," *Vetus Testamentum,* 11 (Leiden, 1961), 95-99.

A) TEXT: SONG OF PARADISE

(*Gen.* 2, 4-25)

Title Inscription (2, 4a): THESE ARE THE TOLEDOT OF HEAVEN AND EARTH, AT THEIR CREATION

A) *Creation of Man* (2, 4b-7)

4b On the day that God YHWH made earth and heaven –
5 all the shrubs of the field were not yet upon earth,
a all the plants of the field did not yet grow;
for God YHWH had not yet rained upon the earth,
and man was not there to work the ground,
6 and no spring rose up out of the earth,
to water the whole surface of the ground, –
7 then God YHWH formed man of the dust of the earth
and blew into his nostrils the breath of life;
and man became a living creature.

B) *Garden in Eden* (2, 8-9)

8 Then God YHWH planted a garden in Eden in the East
and placed the man he had formed in it.
9 And God YHWH made all kinds of trees grow on
the ground,
lovely to look at and good to eat:
the tree of life in the middle of the garden
and the tree of knowledge of good and of evil.
10 A stream goes out from Eden, to water the garden;
it divides from there and becomes four heads.
11 The name of the first is Pishon.
It circles the whole land of Havilah,
there where the gold is,

12 and the gold of that land is good!
there is resin and jewels.
13 The name of the second is Gihon.
It circles the whole land of Cush.
14 The name of the third is Hiddekel.
It flows eastwards of Ashur.
The fourth stream is the Euphrates.
15 Then God YHWH took man
and set him down in the garden,
to work it and to keep it.
16 *Then God YHWH commanded man and spoke:*
Of all the trees of the garden you may eat, yes eat!
But of the tree of knowledge of good and evil,
of that you shall not eat;
for on the day you eat of it,
you must die, yes die!

C) Creation of Woman (2, 18-23)

18 *And God YHWH spoke:*
It is not good for man to be alone!
I will make him a help as his counterpart!
19 And God YHWH formed out of earth
all the beasts of the field and all the birds of the heaven,
and he brought them to the man,
to see how he would call them.
And whatever the man called all the living creatures,
that is their name.
20 And the man spoke the names for all the cattle,
for the birds of heaven and all the beasts of the field;
for man however he did not find
a help as his counterpart.
21 Then God YHWH let a deep sleep fall upon the man;
as he slept he took one of his ribs
and filled its place with flesh.

22 And God YHWH built the rib
which he had taken from the man, into a woman,
and led her to the man.
23 *Then spoke the man:*
This time it is her!
Bone of my bone,
and flesh of my flesh!
Wo-man let her be called,
for she has been taken from man!

D) Wisdom Oracle (*2, 24-25*)

24 That is why the man leaves
his father and his mother
and cleaves to his wife,
and they become one flesh.
25 The two were naked,
the man and his wife,
and they were not shamed.

In order to present a clearer picture of the words and their division into the various structural elements of narrative (N), introduction (I), and direct speech (S), the following table will be useful:

ORDER I, part one	N	I	S
Title inscription (2, 4a)	5		
A. Creation of Man (2, 4b-7)	54		
B. Garden in Eden (2, 8-17)			
a. the garden (8-9)	31		
b. the streams (10-14)	53		
c. man (15)	10		
d. God (16-17)		6	18 God

C. Creation of woman (18-23)			
a. alone (18)		3	9 God
b. the animals (19-20)	43		
c. the rib (21-22)	26		
d. recognition (23)		2	13 Adam
D. Wisdom Oracle (24-25)	20		
TOTALS	5 + 237 + 11 + 40		= 288 + 5

STRUCTURE

1) THE PORTALS OF THE WORLD: The most important points regarding the structure of the entire Order have already been made. Here we need only take a closer look at the 237 words of the "narrative." The text, 2, 4b, begins with an anacolouthon: *beyôm ʿasôt YHWH-Elohîm ʾéres weshamáyim,* that is, quite literally, "on the day of making by YHWH-Elohim earth and heaven," or, more idiomatically, "on the day that God YHWH made earth and heaven." Now if we count the words in this sentence separately – it serves as a title prefixed to the narrative – we arrive at the number 6 + 231 = 237 words. Once again we are faced with a further mystical symbolism in the numbers assigned to the creation of the world. The decisive text is once again to be found in the Book of Creation: "through 231 portals all things proceed. Thus it happens that all creation and all speech proceed from one name" (*Sepher Yesirah* II, 5). This is what G. Scholem has to say, "Through the combination of the 22 consonants is produced everything that truly exists in the three strata of the cosmos: the world, time, and the human body: in the fundamental realms of all existence. The 231 portals is a figure arrived at by their combinations with two elements each." [3a] In other words, the 22 letters of the Hebrew alphabet produce 231 possible combinations of two consonants each, odd and even, or male and female.

3a. G. Scholem, *Ursprung und Anfänge der Kabbala,* 1962, p. 25.

It is certainly remarkable that this second creation narrative follows the mystical creation number 231. Since this number is, fundamentally, simply the development of the radical elements of the word, we can speak here, as we did in the case of the first creation narrative, of a creation by the word, through the word. In terms of text history this would mean that the two texts are not so far apart from each other as has been generally assumed.

2) THE KINGSHIP OF HEAVEN: The total number of 288 words has a clear analogue in a similar number, raised to the multiple of 100, in the Sumerian lists of the antediluvian kings. The royal lists begin with this statement:

"When the kingship came down from heaven,
the kingship was in Eridu.
In Eridu Alulim was king.
28800 years did he reign."

The first king of Sumerian tradition reigned 288 X 100 years and the Biblical text on the first man Adam numbers 288 words. The correspondence in number is so striking that the critic is forced to admit an acquaintance on the part of the Biblical author with the Sumero-Babylonian tradition. V. Schneider [3b] sees both a cosmic and a musical value expressed in the figure, which must be factored either as 4 X 72 or 8 X 36.

B) INTERPRETATION

1) *Primeval man and Paradise.* In the following analysis we shall concentrate only on the leitmotifs of this song which are of fundamental importance for the history of humanity and for theology.

a) STATE OF NON-EXISTENCE: The Paradise song, just like the Babylonian creation epic, begins with the description of the state of non-existence. There were no shrubs, no plants, no men, only a broad expanse of waterless desert. Why was

---

3b. V. Schneider, *op. cit.,* 1967, p. 188ff.

this so? Our song does not even ask this question. This brief description of non-existence has achieved the necessary tension for the poet to continue: "Then God formed man out of dust." But later Scripture scholars have asked why this is so. At this time the prerequisites for life were lacking, since God had not yet let it rain. Also, there were as yet no men to till the soil.[4] Thus, the song itself first of all describes the void, as a suitable background against which the grandeur of the first man can stand out bigger than life size.

b) THE FORMATION OF MAN: In the formation of the first man we see God at work like a potter. He takes up the dust (*'āpār*) of the waste country,[5] and builds the shape of man, which is still a lifeless figure.[6] In order for man to begin living, God breathes the breath of life into his nose. As long as breath streams from mouth and nose, man is alive. The organic connection between the organs of breathing and human life developed into the concept of "soul" (*nĕpeš*). Originally, *nĕpeš* meant throat, windpipe, and in a transferred meaning, breath, life, soul. It was only by the divine breathing that this figure of dust became a living creature (*nĕpeš ḥayyâ*). Thus the origin of man – the song sings only of man generically (*'ādām*) – is attributed immediately to God. Man is formed by God's hands and vivified

---

4. In the text is explained a further reason why nothing as yet was growing: no canals. The Sumerian loan-word *'ed* is supposed to mean canal. Instead of "rise up" we are to read the hiphil "lead out," and thus the passage restates the negation of the preceding verse. See also A. Bea, *De Pentateucho*, 2nd. edition (1933), p. 148, and *Bib.* 34 (1954), 262-263.

5. "From the dust of the earth" (*'adamah*).

6. In terms of the history of civilization, the image of the potter presupposes the invention of pottery. As a result of the Jericho excavations, we are in a position to form a better idea of the earliest such attempts in human history. See R. Amiran, "Myths of the Creation of Man and the Jericho Statues," *BASOR* 167 (1962), 23-25. In Jericho of the Late Stone Age, statues were discovered whose skeletons were formed of reed stalks, with the human figure shaped around them out of clay. Some scholars believed that the statues were molded around a human skeleton. This type of statue-making might well have suggested the myth.

by God's breath. There is no more grandiose statement that could be made to describe the origin of man. It is a brief summary of the grandeur and misery of the human condition. A creature made of dust, that will return to dust again, and still he breathes the breath of God. We can still almost recognize the imprint of God's hand on his creature man. And thus these verses, rich with their original imagery, represent the noble origins of man. At the same time they are the *locus classicus* of the Old Testament anthropology. It is divided, not so much in terms of body and soul, as in terms of body and life. It is only God's breath, joined with the material body, that makes man a living creature. When God withdraws his breath (Ps. 104, 29; Job 34, 14), man sinks back into dust.[7]

c) THE GARDEN: From the singer's point of view, the Garden was "in the east" (2, 8).[8] From the point of view of Palestine, a great wasteland extends to the east. But somewhere, far off in the land of the sunrise, God's Garden must have existed.

Attempts to locate the Garden have apparently sought to identify Paradise as somewhere in the fertile Babylonian Plain. The words "Garden" (*gan*) and Eden are Sumerian words. The original cuneiform sign for *gan* is a bounded piece of land crossed by irrigation canals. In the most ancient Sumerian texts, *gan* is the normal word for field, that is, for a piece of land that can be made fertile by cultivation. In the broader sense, "garden" could

---

7. G. v. Rad, "Das erste Buch Mose," *ATD* (1951), 61ff. Seligmann, "The meaning of *nepheš mêt*," *StudOr* 16 (1951), 2, holds that *nepheš* means the potency bodies need to live; in itself, it is not part of the body. Just as the power of life comes from God, there is a *vis lethalis* that comes from the demons, bringing sickness and death.

8. An orientation to the ancient world, see J. Lewy, "Studies in Historic Geography of the Ancient Near East," *Orientalia* 21 (Rome, 1952), 417. A man orientated himself by facing the sunrise. "Forwards" (*aḳdamatum*) was East, while "backwards" (*aḥaratum*) was West: "left" was North and "right" was South. In terms of geography, "East" frequently means the territory east of the Euphrates, Mesopotamia; "West" means the land west of the Euphrates. In the Paradise narrative, however, this rather narrow usage had not yet developed.

mean a field of grain, a fruit plantation, or even a reed thicket.[9] The Greek Bible translates *gan* by the Persian loan-word *paradeisos,* which has been taken over into our modern languages. But if we once again translate it as garden, we have a more obvious expression of the fact that the prosperity of this piece of land is totally dependent on human industry and work.

This garden is located in Eden. The Sumerian script sign for Eden is a large earthen vessel, suitable for the preservation of water, milk, grain, and oil, all products of a cultivated land. *E-din-nu* designates the cultivable flat country, the steppe, or even the wilderness.[10] Thus, the two concepts of *gan* and *eden* should be clearly distinguished. Eden is the broader concept, the landscape, steppe, which yields produce only when it is worked; *gan,* on the other hand, the narrower concept, is the fruit garden located in this flat land, rich in trees, a particular blessing of God, in sharp contrast with the otherwise treeless Babylonian steppe. The word *eden* also occurs in geographical names, without having any relationship with the Eden of primeval times.[11] By way of summarizing this etymological investigation: the song conceived of Paradise as an orchard in the midst of the uncultivated desert. The vocabulary points to the Sumero-Babylonian lowlands.

d) THE RIVERS OF PARADISE: The insertion of the rivers represents an attempt to determine the location of Paradise. But, despite all its precision, the attempt is a failure. Obviously, it is based on the conception that the four rivers of the world have their sources in Paradise. It is only upon leaving the garden that the stream is divided into four "heads" (2, 10). This phrasing is

---

9. A. Deimel, *Sumerisches Lexikon,* (1928), see 105, I. *Ibid.,* "De nomine paradisi biblici," *Verbum Domini* 4 (Rome, 1924), 281. A. Pohl, "Das Alte Testament und die altorientalische Umwelt. Gedanken zum Paradiesbericht," *Stimmen der Zeit* 83 (Freiburg in Br., 1958), 241-248.

10. A. Deimel, *Sumerisches Lexikon,* (1929), 168.

11. A stretch of country in the neighborhood of the city of Lagash was called *Gu-edin;* in Northern Syria there was a land called Bit-Adini. The word Eden was used as commonly as our "land."

easy to understand on the basis of the ancient irrigation vocabulary. The place along the river at which a canal branches off is called *ka-id-da* in Sumerian, "beginning, head" of the canal. Its further course is, accordingly, described as "tail" (*kun*). The same expressions were taken over by the Semitic Akkadians (*rês-nâri*) and the Arabs (*ras-en-nahr*). Both terms mean "head, beginning of the stream."

One might thus surmise that the account is speaking of four irrigation canals, something that a cultivated garden might well require. But upon closer inspection we realize that we are no longer involved in the geography of Paradise, but in the larger geography of the whole earth. The two rivers Euphrates (*perat*) and Tigris (*hiddekal*) are sufficiently well known. The other two are more difficult to determine. The position of the Pishon is the object of a rather detailed description. It flows around the whole country of Havilah, which was famous for its gold and its resin and its jewels. The name of Havilah comes up in various territories; attempts have been made to locate it in south Arabia, in northeast Arabia, and even in northern Mesopotamia.[12] This is understandable enough, since Havilah means simply "sandy land." Since Havilah is also mentioned as a son of Cush (Gen. 10, 7), we must not exclude the possibility that Havilah here refers to the Nubian Desert, the famous gold country of ancient Egypt.[13]

The Pishon ("spring river") would then be none other than the third great river of antiquity, the Nile. The fourth river,

---

12. Those scholars who identify the Havilah with Arabia explain the Pishon as Wadi-Faisan, which was a river course in ancient times but today no longer deserves the name. Ancient Akkadian texts, the so called Samarra tablets, recount the construction of a temple in the country of the Havilum, which would be located not far from Armenia. This would identify the Pishon with the Phasis which rises in the Caucasus. It was in this neighborhood that Greek legend located the gold country of the Argonauts. But this is most likely outside the horizon of the Ancient Near East.

13. Helck-Otto, *Kleines Wörterbuch der Aegyptologie* (Wiesbaden, 1956), p. 123.

the Gihon, is spoken of as flowing around the whole land of Cush. As we shall discuss later, in the Table of Nations, Cush refers not only to the southern province of Egypt, but also to the kingdom of the Kassites (*kaššu*). The ruling class of the Kassites belonged to the Indo-Arians. Thus we cannot completely exclude the possibility that the Gihon ("river course") is meant to refer to the distant Indus.[14]

The results of this geographical investigation are very meager. Despite the very exact description, we cannot determine where Paradise actually was. The author of the Table of Rivers must, at all events, have conceived of Paradise as a world mountain, with Paradise lying upon its heights, and the four rivers of the world proceeding down its sides, – a conception which strikes us today as purely legendary, which it obviously is. Still, the Bible-theology significance of this section seems to be an effort to substantiate the fact that Paradise is a place on earth and not in fable land. Thus, it must be possible to precisely describe its position; unfortunately the points of reference are insufficient.[15]

e) THE TREE OF LIFE AND THE COMMANDMENT: Man was put by God into the garden. All the trees were freely offered to him for his sustenance. He lived by gathering the fruit of the trees, a fact which, ethnologically, does correspond to the most ancient cultural levels of humanity. But in the middle of the garden stood a tree whose fruit was forbidden him. If he were to eat of it, he must immediately die. There is a question here,

---

14. We must be careful not simply to transpose our modern-day geographical conceptions into the background of the Ancient Near East. See E. Weidner, "Das Reich Sargons von Akkad," *AFO* 16 (1952), 10.

15. The ancient Jewish and Christian authors actually did understand the four rivers of Paradise as Euphrates, Tigris, Nile, and Indus. Many of them located the position of Paradise in Armenia. F. Hancar, *Festgabe zum* IV *Internationalen Ethnologenkongress in Wein,* (1952), pp. 50-82, feels that he can demonstrate the fact that, in the days of earliest humanity, Armenia was one of the most favorable lands for human development. But still the conclusion to our question is the same: we simply do not know the location of Paradise.

as to whether there was only *one* tree, the tree of life, in the middle of the garden, or *two* trees, the second being the tree of knowledge of good and evil. If we examine the criteria of ancient Hebrew poetic art in a purely formal manner, we must decide in favor of only one tree. On grounds of poetic parallelism, the first thought is immediately taken up and more clearly described in the second member of a verse. Thus the words "tree of life" would be explained by "that is the tree of knowledge of good and evil" (Gen. 2, 9). Now, in Biblical speech, the word "knowledge, to know" (*yādā'*) also belongs to the sphere of life. It is the term used for generation of life. Thus, without examining the other texts first, we must isolate Gen. 4, 1 – a text which belongs to the great saga of the first man: "The man knew his wife, and she conceived and bore." The same expression occurs again in 4, 25. If, according to the principles of Scripture interpretation, a word is first to be explained in terms of its immediate context, then it would be strange indeed if the tree of knowledge did not also refer to the mystery of life. Thus, tree of life and tree of knowledge are one and the same thing.

What is meant by all this will be explained more precisely in connection with the sin of Paradise. The naive reader would immediately think of an actual tree, and in so doing he is perhaps not so naive at that. The most ancient cultural level was that of the food-gatherers. In such a stage of human development, the prohibition of a given tree seems quite meaningful. Moreover, we must remember that in Christianity the greatest realities, life and death, are intimately bound up with the mere eating of the bread of life. Whatever the case, the tree of life in Paradise determined the fate of the first man and the whole human race descended from him.

2. *The Creation of the Woman* (*Strophe 4 and 5*)

The "culture hymn" proceeds. Paradise is already established, and the first man is already there, but he is all alone in the magnificence of the garden. In order to alleviate his lonesomeness, God decides to create him "a help, an opposite." He thereupon created the animals. But in the entire world of animals there was no fitting opposite for man. The man gives the animals their names and thereby asserts himself as lord and master. The leading of the animals before the first man shows that man, basically, has no community with animals. From this quarter there is no help to be had. In the meaning of this song, an animal can never be father or mother to a man. Man comes only from man or from God. Despite the manifold variety of the animal world, man remains lonesome in the midst of creation.

God then decides upon something new. He has a *tardemah* fall upon man. This word is the key to understanding the account of the creation of the first woman. This word did not mean merely normal sleep; the Septuagint translates it as "ecstasy." In the narrative of the Patriarch Abraham, the word appears again. The father of the Israelite nation was in such a state of ecstasy when he foresaw the fate of his people (Gen. 15, 12). The *tardemah*[16] is thus equated with the prophetic state of enlightenment. The body, seen from without, appears to lie in deep sleep. But the mind is bright and awake, and beholds unheard of things. A man is overpowered by the force of the vision, and thus *tardemah* can also mean bewilderment, a state of terror, such as lays hold of enemies. What takes place in such a visionary coma is subject to different laws than the normal course of nature. In the vision, something is seen in image form which is otherwise incompatible. In order to correctly understand the meaning of the vision, it is not enough to pay attention to the images; we must make our way into the basic kernel of the vision. This is the key we need to understand the Bible account of the creation of woman.

Wide awake in his mind, sunken into a visionary sleep, the first man experiences the fact that something is happening to him. God took a "rib" from his body and formed it into a woman.

---

16. See also 2 Sam. 26, 13; Job 4, 13; 33, 15; Is. 29, 10; Prov. 19, 15.

Upon awakening from his state of ecstasy, the man realizes something that was never true of any of the animals: "Now this, she is wholly my bone, my flesh and my blood" (2, 23). With this elementary statement, the song comes to a close.

The wisdom literature has enlarged the song by the addition of a principle of life, and a clever play on words. The fact that man and "wo-man" are made for each other is already evident in their very names. Man, in Hebrew, is *'iš,* and woman *'iššâ;* both names, and both essences, are thus joined together. What the word expresses constantly turns to actual fact, as long as there are men on earth: "Therefore leaves man his father, his mother, and follows his wo-man; and they become one flesh" (2, 24). The play on words can also be appreciated in English.

In terms of literary genre, we are here in the presence of a prophetic vision. The meaning of the vision obviously lies in its attempt to interpret the mystery of man and woman. They are ordered towards each other in this world because this law has been set into them from the moment of creation. Man and woman have each entered into existence by God's creator act. Both of them are inseparably distinct from the animal world. The taking of the man's "rib" would thus be a prophetic image and metaphor. The account is on a par with the Gospel parables; in order to understand it we must inquire into its essential content, without stopping at its purely external vesture. The account of the "rib" would thus be a genuine saga; in terms of image, it has something to express about the essence of man. The image is a fundamental one, so much so that Jesus himself uses it in order to substantiate the fact of monogamy as a condition determined by the creation of man: "What God has joined together, let no man put asunder" (Mt. 19, 2-7).

The English translation has generally used the word "rib." There is some question, however, as to whether this is the original meaning of the Hebrew word *ṣēlāʿ*. The word is used in various connections; it can refer to a mountain ridge (2 Sam. 16, 13), the sides of a tent (Ex. 26, 20; 22), the side of the altar (Ex. 27, 2), the ark of the covenant (Ex. 25, 12), the supports for the temple walls (1 Kings 6, 15), the side chambers of the temple (1 Kings 6, 5; 8), the folding doors (1 Kings 6, 34), etc. The word involves the general meaning of side; rib would be only a specialized meaning, since man has ribs on his side. Attempts have also been made to understand the word in terms of linguistic history, with reference to the original cuneiform terms. The Akkadian word *tilu* or *ṣilu,* which means "life," is supposed to have been translated, erroneously, by *ṣēlā‘*, "rib."[17] Now, since the seat of life is in the blood, we must translate as follows: Eve was formed from "Adam's life blood." A further possibility lies in the fact that the Sumerian script sign *ti(l)* can be read in two ways: as *ṣilu,* "rib," and also as *balâtû,* "life." Thus, Eve would have been formed from the "life spirit of Adam."[18] These interpretations all presuppose erroneous readings, which is in itself most unlikely. We do best to hold to the general form of expression "side." This could very easily be a camouflaged expression. The sexual organs were, from the ancient times, surrounded by a protective taboo. They were spoken of only in euphemistic expressions. Thus, "side" could actually mean "Adam's seed." The first man was shaped directly by God; the first woman from the life seed of the man; all other men are begotten and born of both man and woman. Parthenogenesis represents the ultimate possibility; by God's power and overshadowing, life is generated in the virgin without the man's cooperation.

So much for the short song with its five strophes. With its simple and direct language, with its clear images, it has become the song of humanity, a song that every child can understand and still a mystery for every adult. Once again we must stress the fact that, in terms of literary genre, this is religious poetry, the saga of the first man, and not a treatise on natural history. We do the text an injustice if we turn to it for answers in terms of natural science. What does this saga actually have to say

---

17. P. Riessler, *TübQS* 93 (1911), 497.

18. Feldmann, *Das Paradies,* p. 242. B. Bonkamp, *Die Bibel im Lichte der Keilschriftforschung* (1938), p. 99.

regarding the origin of man? Very much, and still very little! The following theses may be formulated as a summary:

a) Man, in his essential being, cannot be derived from the animal world, either as man or as woman.

b) Man, as man, is the direct creation of God, again both as man and as woman.

c) The first men lived in "Paradise," that is, in harmony with God and creation.

d) The first man had to undergo a test, in which he decided his own fate and that of his posterity.

e) Everything else is poetic imagery: garden, formation of man from dust, formation of woman from the rib,[19] tree, eating.

It is the province of the natural scientist to determine what lies behind these images. Just as the song of creation has nothing to do with the transitory hypotheses about the origin of the world, so the song of Paradise is not concerned with transitory hypotheses about the origin of man. Its focus is upon the essential and abiding elements. Insofar as both songs express the fundamental truths of human existence, they are beyond the reach of space and time. They cannot grow old. What greater thing can possibly be said of man than the simple fact that God has created him!

---

19. L. Arnaldich, "La creacion de Eva," *Sacra Pagina* 1 (1959), 346-357. Explains that the narrative of Eve's creation is not part of the fund of faith. It is the essence of marriage that is being explained in the story, not the natural-history development of the first woman.

CHAPTER XVIII

BIBLE AND EVOLUTION

IN establishing the theological content of the Paradise narrative, the task of the Scripture exegete is actually complete. The Bible has something important to say about the origin of man. But since God has committed the world to the human mind for its investigation, it must be a matter of considerable interest to every scholar precisely what the natural scientists have to say about the origin of man. Their genuine discoveries can only serve to bring God's plan of creation into sharper focus, for there can obviously be no contradiction, in the last analysis, between theological knowledge and the clear discoveries of scientific investigation. The two forms of knowledge are not isolated disciplines; they mutually interpenetrate; by proper cooperation, they can alternately lead each other closer to the truth.[1]

1. The following is only a partial list of the literature, intended to serve as basic orientation. First, we call attention to the series: *Naturwissenschaft und Theologie,* published by the Institut der Görres-Gesellschaft (Freiburg/Munich). Part II: Biological Evolution. Part III: The evolutionary interpretation of man's existence. Part IV: Spirit and Body in man's existence. In these fascicles, the reports and discussions of the annual meetings of the Görresgesellschaft are published, from 1957 on. The work of leading scholars is represented. The discussions give the best indications of the

The Biblical account of the creation of the first man presented no problems until it was taken literally. The first man proceeded from the hand of God, both in soul and body, just as the Bible says. But since the tone of the Biblical account is very human (anthropomorphic), Augustine already shied away from a literal interpretation, as being unworthy of God; for we could hardly portray God as a potter, shaping the body of man. According to Augustine, God built the primeval potencies of life into the world, and man developed from them, so that the first man had to pass through the same stages of development as man today, from embryo to mature age (*De Genesi ad litteram* VI c 13-18 n23-28). But this conception of St. Augustine's remained isolated among the "naive" interpretations of Scripture. It was, eventually, the progress of the natural sciences that first focused real attention upon the problem of the Bible and natural science.

1) THE RADICAL THEORY OF EVOLUTION

Darwin, in his work on the origin of species (1859) represented the view that the manifold variety of organic species in the world of his time had developed from only a few (or perhaps

---

present-day state of investigations. M. Grison, *Geheimnis der Schöpfung. Was sagen Naturwissenschaft, Philosophie, und Theologie vom Ursprung der Menschen.* 2nd edition (Munich, 1960). With an appendix (4 pages) of German literature on the question. Another step forward is taken by Haag - Haas - Hürzeler, *Evolution und Bibel. Die biblische Schöpfungsgeschichte heute; der entwicklungsgedanke und das Christliche Welt- und Menschenbild; die Tatsache der biologischen Evolution* (Lucerne-Munich, 1962). On the world picture and philosophy of *Teilhard de Chardin* see J. V. Kopp, *Entstehung und Zukunft des Menschen* (Munich, 1962). An excellent theological and anthropological treatment of the problem can be found in *Quaestiones disputatae* 12/13 by P. Overhage and K. Rahner, *Das Problem der Hominisation* (Freiburg, Basel, Vienna, 1961). An excellent brief outline in J. L. McKenzie, *Geist und Welt des Alten Testaments* (Lucerne, 1962), pp. 135-140: "Der biblische Glaube und die Entwicklungstheorie."

even only one) original forms of life (evolution theory). The basis for the gradual development, from the amoeba to man, was the battle for survival. The weaker species all succumbed, while the stronger asserted themselves. It is in terms of this natural process of selection and improvement that the variety of species has evolved.

Darwin and his disciples also applied this theory of evolution to man, and taught that man, in his totality, body and soul, is bound up in this process of evolution. In this respect, the theory of evolution transgressed the boundaries of a natural science hypothesis and turned into a philosophical position which was diametrically opposed to revealed religion. While the basic principles of the theory of evolution have, as a whole, been somewhat shaken by the results of natural science investigation, this theory, preached as a "gospel," has continued to preserve its religious impact in wide circles.

2) THE MODERATE THEORY OF EVOLUTION

Since natural science's knowledge of the construction of the living cosmos was constantly being clarified, theologians attempted to bring these realities into harmony with the Biblical account. The whole process of evolution, culminating in man, is not something that happened contrary to the will of the Creator; rather, it is perhaps an even more articulate proclamation of the wonderful works of God than the mere creation of the world in one single act would have been. The theory of evolution appears to meet the Biblical account half-way, where it says that "God created man from the dust of the earth. . . ." "The dust of the earth" is thus to be taken as a Biblical expression for the preexisting material from which the first man was formed. This could be an animal body which had progressed far enough in the process of evolution to be capable of containing a human soul – an "incarnation."

The step from the most highly developed animal to the human

being, however, took place not by virtue of the inherent potencies of evolution, constantly spurring on to further development, but by an individual intervention of God, since the spirit soul cannot proceed from an animal substance; it can only be created by God.

In this more moderate version, the theory of evolution was accepted as admissible by certain famous theologians. Man is, after all, a member of creation, and as such, he is subject to the structural plan of all creation. In his body, man is related to the animal; but his soul comes from the breath of God. But even in this moderate form, which attempts to take into account the religious content of the Bible, the theory of evolution is hardly tenable today.

3) OPEN QUESTIONS

a) PALAEONTOLOGY: Palaeontology has managed to make the fossil man articulate, and ask him about his origin. Together with the scanty skeletal finds, it is primarily the discovery of tools that betray the existence of primeval man. But these already testify to the fact that primeval man was a creator, using the power of his mind to transform stones into usable instruments, according to his need; and no animal is capable of this. Insofar as the most ancient men have left traces of their existence, they are proofs of a rational and spiritual endowment which clearly distinguishes him from the world of animals.

The fossil skeletons show that primeval man was much different in appearance from the men of our modern races, but the long sought missing link, which would connect man with the animal world, has not yet been discovered. Man could not possibly have descended from any of the specialized anthropoid apes we know today; we should have to go back some 30 or 50 million years (before the development of the mammals) in order to arrive at a form which is little enough specialized for both man and anthropoid apes to be descended from it. Thus, it is no wonder that the missing link between man and animal has not been discovered.

b) BIOLOGY: Biology has also achieved new insights into the structure of organic life.[2] Scientists are familiar with a certain development within a structurally determined type, but not a gradual transition from one type to another. Homologies, that is, partial correspondences in various organisms, in which homologous organs occupy the same position within the structural makeup of various living creatures, and are thus morphologically equivalent, can be sufficiently explained if they are interpreted as phases of development proceeding from the undifferentiated and general to the differentiated and particular. Morphology, that is, the study of forms, thus explains similarities of different types, not on the grounds of one being descended from the other, but on the grounds of adaptation to a given end. In structurally different types, which have nothing to do with each other, this can result in the same forms. These morphological conclusions are mentioned only as a warning against a too facile acceptance of evolutionistic conclusions.

In the second place, biology has embryological evidence to offer: in his embryological development, the human passes through stages which can apparently be explained only by the fact that they are inherited from close and distant forebears who were different in form, which also represent a repetition of the state of development upon which certain levels of human ancestry were apparently halted for the whole time of their life. But on the other hand, we are faced with the problem of why the ontogenetic development of the human embryo is preordained to transcend these animal levels whose finished form is invoked as the explanation of his being.

It may be that the human embryo, in the course of its evolution

---

2. O. Feyerabend, *Zeilstrebigkeit in der Entwicklung. Um die Ahnenreihe des Menschen*, Universum 4 (1949), pp. 622-628. The cosmos of living things is, structurally (entelechy) ordered towards man, and thus all living creatures, in a certain degree, owe their origin to man.

from the undifferentiated cell to the complete development of his being, passes through stages which are relative, in terms of duration and sequence, to the development process of animal beings of ontogenetically shorter evolution paths; this might also result in macroscopically and also microscopically identical specific images; but it does not explain why the animal has not advanced beyond the stage of development proper to his being, while the human embryo pushes on to his "full incarnation."

Biology itself has not been able to explain the evolution of new types. Various possibilities have been proposed: gene mutation, neomorphosis, ontogenetic deviation, paedamorphosis, etc.

On the subject of whether man appears at various places at the same time (polygenesis) or at one single place (monogenesis), the weight of contemporary evidence is beginning to incline more and more towards monogenesis. The atomic physicist Pascual Jordan has computed a complicated series of figures on the basis of the number Ω_0 and comes to the conclusion that the biological spread and development of phylogeny is essentially influenced by historically unique forward bounds in the quanta.[3]

c) PHILOSOPHY: The works of Teilhard de Chardin have led to a radical re-thinking of the evolution question. The struggle for his intellectual heritage is still in progress, but it can already be said that evolution, the drive towards higher being, belongs to the primary structure of the cosmos. "For philosophy, the transcendence of essence is not an impossibility. Since, on the basis of empirical knowledge, proof of the facts has not yet been arrived at, metaphysics, in this area, is ahead of the (natural science) investigations."[3a]

d) THEOLOGY: On the theological plane, Karl Rahner has directed the problem of evolution along new avenues. The distinction between the radical and moderate theory of evolution

---

3. *Schöpfung und Geheimnis, Antwort aus naturwissenschaftlicher Sicht,* 1970, p. 91.

3a. A. Guggenberger, *Teihard de Chardin. Versuch einer Weltsumme* (1963), 58.

is passé; both are only lazy compromise solutions. The problem is evolution as such. Rahner is primarily interested in a new approach to the relationship between matter and spirit. "If matter and spirit are not simply disparate magnitudes, but if matter is, to a certain degree, frozen spirit, then a development of matter into spirit does not represent an impossible concept."[4] Biblical prehistory has no answer to the question of how the first man arose. The concrete phenomenality is beyond our knowledge.

e) ETHNOLOGY: Finally, ethnology has also demanded a consideration of the question of evolution and ethnic dependence. Ethnology examines the life conditions of primitive peoples who are still living today. According to the Darwinistic theory of evolution, we should expect to find at least some traces of the transition from animal level to human level. But this is not the case. Ethnology has discovered only the full man, not a being who is plodding along through life in a prelogical stage of half-animal and half-human, but humans who are in full possession of their intellectual and physical faculties, as full humans; in terms of religion, in fact, he is frequently more advanced than the "highly developed" man of civilization who has culturally outdistanced him.

The scientific investigation of humanity is the most intriguing of all the sciences, but it is faced with absolutely insoluble questions. Creation is ordered towards man, and man is built into the structure of living beings, but the moment of his "birth" cannot be grasped. Teilhard de Chardin has found the classic formulation for this fact when he says that man has "entered into existence noiselessly."[5] This new being, who will soon assume sovereignty over all the earth, has himself entered into the world so unpretentiously and quietly that we can no longer find his

---

4. K. Rahner, *Die Hominisation als theologische Frage. Quaestiones Disputatae* 12/13 (1961), p. 78.

5. "L'homme est entré sans bruit," cited by F. M. Bergounioux, "Les sens religieux des hommes de la préhistoire," *Naturwissenschaft und Theologie* 4 (1961), 39.

first traces. For hundreds of thousands of years, we know nothing more of him than that he gradually inhabited far removed districts; his traces are to be found everywhere, throughout the entire ancient world. Thus, whether he made his way from the easternmost parts of Asia, or from the south of Africa, the world lay open before him, and he knew no boundaries. Man is comprehensible only as a member of humanity; but his first origins are hidden in the "void of the beginning."

CHAPTER XIX

THE SONG OF THE FALL

ORDER I, PART 2

GEN. 3, 1-21

Once again, the literary genre must be examined. We are dealing with religious poetry. The account of the first parents' sin does not date back to the primeval age itself, in terms of faithful tradition. A poet-theologian has attempted to grasp the concept of original sin. What he offers is not a theological treatise, but rather a song, in which the tragedy of the first man runs its dramatic course. In this way the author succeeds in expressing a much deeper appreciation of the essence of original sin than mere abstract formulas would have permitted. What we have here it a theological image vocabulary. Religious narratives from primeval times, which attempt to interpret the essence of the world or humanity, are properly called myth or saga in the most genuine sense of the word. The fact that we are here dealing with an ancient saga is evidenced by, among other things, the introduction of the dragon (serpent) as a speaking person, as is further developed in the discussion that follows. In terms of literary history, the scene is played on a mythical plane. This is not to say that the narrative is unreal. Myth and saga are capable of grasping a much deeper level of reality than is possible in a mere external recounting of the facts.

A) TEXT: SONG OF THE FALL
(*Gen. 3, 1-21*)

A) *Temptation* (3, 1-5)

1 The dragon was more clever than all the beasts of the field
that God YHWH had made,
and he spoke to the woman:
Has God really *spoken:*
Do not eat of all the trees of the garden?
2 *And the woman spoke to the dragon:*
We eat of the fruit of the trees of the garden!
3 Of the fruit of the tree that is in the middle of the garden
God has spoken:
Do not eat of it!
and do not touch it!
otherwise you will die!
4 *And the dragon spoke to the woman*:
You will not die, not die!
5 For God knows
that on the day you eat of it
your eyes will be open
and you will be like gods,
knowing good and evil!

B) *The Fall* (3, 6-8)

6 Then the woman saw
that the tree was good to eat

and that it was a delight for the eyes,
a tree inviting to be wise.
And she took of the fruit and ate;
and also gave to the man with her and he ate.
7 Then their eyes were open
and they recognized that they were naked.
And they wove themselves fig leaves
and made themselves aprons.
8 Then they heard the voice of God YHWH
walking about in the garden in the evening breeze.
Then the man and his wife hid themselves
from the face of God YHWH
in the middle of the trees of the garden.

C) *Trial (3, 9-13)*

9 Then God YHWH called to the man
and spoke to him:
Where are you?
10 *He spoke:*
I heard your voice in the garden
and was afraid;
for I am naked and I have hidden myself.
11 *And he spoke:*
Who announced to you that you are naked?
Have you eaten of the tree
of which I commanded:
Do not eat of it!?
12 *And the man spoke:*
The woman that you gave me,
she gave me of the tree – and I ate.
13 *Then God YHWH spoke to the woman:*
Why did you do this?
Then the woman spoke:
The dragon deceived me
and I ate!

D) Sentence (3, 14-19)

14 *Then God YHWH spoke to the dragon:*
Because you have done this,
cursed be you among all cattle
and among all beasts of the field!
On your belly shall you go
and dust shall you eat all the days of your life!
15 I set enmity between you and the woman
between your seed and her seed.
He tramples your head
whenever you strike at his heel.
16 *To the woman he has spoken:*
I multiply and multiply the toil of your
child-bearing!
In travail shall you bear sons,
let your longing be for the man
and he shall be lord over you!
17 *And to Adam he has spoken:*
Because you listened to the voice of your wife
and have eaten of the tree
of which I commanded you by speaking:
you shall not eat of it!
cursed be the earth on your account!
In toil shall you eat of it
all the days of your life.
May it bring you thistles and thorns;
and eat the plants of the field.
19 In the sweat of your brow eat your bread,
until you go back to the earth;
for you were taken from earth;
for you are dust,
and you will once again be dust!

E) Conclusion (3, 20-21)

20 And Adam called his wife's name Hawwah;
for she became mother of all the living.
21 And God YHWH made Adam and his wife
coats of skin and clothed them.

STRUCTURE:

Once again we must consider the structure of the text in terms of the basic elements which make it up:

ORDER I, part two	N	I	S	i	s
A. Temptation (3, 1-5)					
Dragon (3, 1)	10	3		4	5
Eve (2-3)		4	9	2	8
Dragon (4-5)		4	17		
B. Fall (3, 6-8)					
Eating (6-7)	34				
Hiding (8)	18				
C. Trial (3, 9-13)					
God (9)		7	1		
Adam (10)		1	9		
God (11)		1	9	2	3
Adam (12)		2	10		
God (13a)		4	3		
Eve (13b)		2	3		

D. Sentence (14-19)						
on the Dragon (14-15)		5	33			
on the Woman (16)		3	13			
on the Man (17-19)		2	40	3	3	
E. Clothing (20-21)	19					
TOTALS	81	38	147	11	19	= 296
			177			

Let us concentrate only on the speech sections. We have already referred to the four speeches repeated in the text of verses 1, 3, 11, 17. The total count for all the speeches is 177 words. This number is typical of the moon and the calendar. 177 is half of a lunar year of 354 days. The number 177 was of the greatest importance for the reckoning of the calendar; for despite the variability in the number of days in the lunar calendar, the days from the first of Nisan to the first of Tizri were precisely fixed at 177.[1] The entire text is thus permeated with the three-fold symbolism of sun, moon, and morning star.

B) INTERPRETATION

1) MAN IN DECISION

The third chapter of the Book of Creation, *the* catastrophic chapter, sets the foundation for the subsequent history of human woe, which, at the very last hour, God turns into a history of salvation. From a purely formal point of view, the narrative of man's first sin deserves first place in human literature for the mastery of its psychological description. Here we see, clearly expressed in this ancient imagery, what every man and every woman experiences. And this fact already involves a fundamental problem: is this merely a question of human existence, as such,

1. C. Schedl, *Talmud-Evangelium-Synagogue*, 1969, p. 152.

being projected back into a primeval age, or does the text actually mean to recount a unique event, occurring at the dawn of human history?

The narrative begins with the representation of a new person, the serpent-dragon; the serpent is not to be taken as a mute animal; he is superior even to the man in mental acumen and sagacity.[1a] His success over the man is owing primarily to this consummate and evil intelligence; he desires the destruction of mankind. Verse 2, 25 involves a fine play on words in the Hebrew text. The first men were "naked" (*'ārôm*), while the serpent was "clever" (*'ārûm*). Naked naivete unsuspectingly enters into conversation with the crafty personification of seduction. Which side of the balance will yield is clear from the outset.

The serpent begins with a question. The one who asks questions always has the advantage. Eve corrects the ignorance of the stupid questioner. The dialogue is a masterpiece of demonic psychology. The serpent: "Did God really say that you dare not eat of any tree?" God's prohibition is twisted into its opposite. The woman corrects and explains: "Of every tree we may eat; only of the tree in the middle of the garden God has told us not to eat. Otherwise you must die the death!" The evil one denies and twists God's command once again. The following sentence [2] contains the actual serpent's bite which poisons the life of humanity: "You must not die the death!

1a. The Hebrew word *naḥaš*, "serpent," is masculine gender; *naḥaš* belongs to the vocabulary of mythology. Isaiah proclaims Yahweh's victory over Leviathan, the wounded sepent (Is. 27, 1). Our understanding of the text is considerably improved if we translate "dragon" or "dragon-serpent." The serpent, as an animal, cannot speak; but speech is regularly attributed to the evil powers which the ancient people saw represented in the dragon creature. See B. Landsberger, *Die Fauna des alten Mesopotamien* (Leipzig, 1934). On pp. 55-66 he treats the various mythological serpent-dragons which symbolized demons. On p. 54 he tells of a multicolored dragon with yellow face and four feet, a reminiscence of authentic dragon lore.

2. Verse 5 numbers exactly fourteen words, a symbolic mockery of holiness.

Elohim knows full well, / if ye eat of it,
then will open your eyes / and ye be like Elohim,
knowing of good and evil" (2, 5).

The serpent plays the role of the well-intentioned friend. He "reveals" the "true" face of God to Eve. God is evil. The countenance of the good God of creation, at this very moment, is distorted in Eve's soul and turned into a devilish caricature. Everything about her, built up in the beauty of Paradise, is nothing more than a beautiful prison, a deceit, intended to keep man little. But the serpent promises man that by eating the fruit he will ascend into the ranks of the immortal Elohim. The tree in the middle, he says, is actually a tree of life and not a tree of death. Eve believes the word of the serpent more than the word of God. At this point the fall is already spiritually and intellectually a fact. What now follows is only the external conclusion.

What was the essence of original sin? Negatively, it consisted in an unwillingness to believe in God's word and commandment. Disbelief and disobedience are the sinful heritage of mankind; only through the faith and obedience of the new Adam, the Messiah Jesus, have they been removed. Positively, original sin consisted in believing the word of the evil serpent-dragon. His word echoed like a great message of salvation: "By your eating you will be like Elohim!" The common translation, "you will be like God," somewhat limits the meaning of Elohim. In the broader context of the narrative, Elohim is certainly used as the name of the one God. But the immediate context makes it likely that the plural is to be understood here: "You will be like gods, who know good and evil." [3] The tree of the knowledge of good and evil would thus be the tree of divinization. By eating it, they would experience a new existence, and turn into higher, in fact divine beings. In the pagan world of that time, sons of gods

---

3. The Septuagint also reads the plural here. Fischer, *BZ* 22 (1934), 323-331 examines 16 passages in which the combination "good and evil" appears. The results are not really satisfying. Cf. the passages: Gen. 24,

were not unknown;[4] and even in the Bible, belief in heavenly beings, surrounding the throne of God, is to be taken for granted.[5] These beings, however, are obviously not gods, but rather angels in the service of the one God.

After the sin, the first man actually did have a new knowledge and experience of their existence. They had not, however, become immortal gods. "Then opened up their eyes, they knew they were naked." The sudden plunge from their divine dream into the naked reality of their mortal existence. If they had followed God's commandments and not eaten, death would have never struck them. But now they had eaten death from the tree of life. The first Adam failed the test of faithfulness and obedience. Everything that comes from him must face the same death.

50; 31, 24, 29; 2 Sam. 13, 22; Zeph. 1, 2. Even though there is an element of moral good and evil in the passages, the primary emphasis, in relationship to God, is salvation and ruin. Cf. H. J. Stöbe, "Gut und Böse in der jahwistischen Quelle des Pentateuchs," *ZAW* 65 (1953) 188-204, for an analysis of the concepts in vital terms. Good is what furthers the power of life and evil is what hinders or hurts it. Now since the disposition of salvation and ruin is in the hands of God, or the gods, an attempt to acquire "knowledge of good and evil" is actually an attempt to arrogate divine prerogatives. The word "know, knowledge" is no more definite in meaning in this context. Cf. the exhaustive analysis of G. J. Botterweck, "Gott erkennen," *BBB* 2 (1951). At all events it is obviously not a purely intellectual term. *Yādā'* can mean "love, be familiar, have experience, know, be able." With reference to man and woman, it implies sexual relationship. In the Qumran writings we find the statement that a man should not marry before the age of 20: "For only at the age of 20 is he capable of distinguishing between good and evil." Thus "knowledge of good and evil" would appear to refer to full sexual maturity. But this is a much later usage and could hardly present the key to interpreting Genesis. G. W. Buchanan, "The Old Testament Meaning of Knowledge of Good and Evil," *JBL* 75 (1956), 114-120. R. Gordis, "The Knowledge of Good and Evil in the OT and the Qumran Scrolls," *JBL* 76 (1957), 123-133.

4. Cf. The treatment of the religion of Canaan, pp. 177ff.

5. In terms of pagan mythology, we should have to maintain that the first humans, by eating this fruit, wanted to become immortal gods and be called sons of the gods. On the term "sons of the gods" in Biblical usage, see my article "Psalm 8 in ugaritischer Sicht," *FF* 38 (1964), 183-185.

The second Adam, Christ, has, by his obedience, established a new tree of life. He who eats of this tree will never taste death, and will live forever.

This is the essence of original sin. Man is not content to be man; he wants to become God. As to the concrete act in which this attempt to seize upon divinity was clothed, there are several opinions. We shall briefly consider only the most important ones:

a) THE LITERAL EXPLANATION takes this story at face value. The tree was a real tree. What kind of tree it was is unimportant. The fact that Adam and Eve made aprons of the fig leaves for themselves, after their sin, does not permit any conclusions regarding the species of the tree of knowledge, but only the country in which the Paradise narrative in its present form was written down. In ancient Mesopotamia there were no fig trees, but there were many in Palestine. The fig leaves are thus a Palestinian coloring.[6] The serpent-dragon, too, was a real serpent, but possessed by the devil and given the power of speech. The sin consisted in the actual eating of the fruit of the forbidden tree. This literal interpretation will always enjoy some attention, not only with respect to the simple living habits of primitive man – Adam and Eve lived by gathering the fruits of the Garden – but also in terms of the body-soul dichotomy in man.

b) OPPOSED TO THIS IS THE SYMBOLIC EXPLANATION: The Paradise narrative, and the story of man's first sin, is an expression of primitive human experiences in parable language. It was primarily the sexual sphere that was always clothed in rather reticent images. The tree of knowledge could surely mean the mystery of life. In Gen. 4, 1, "to know" is the term used for the sexual act: "Adam knew Eve, his wife, and she conceived and bore. . . ." Before the sin, our first parents were naked and not ashamed; after the sin they covered themselves with fig leaves, out of shame. The curse strikes Eve primarily in her womanly makeup; in pain will she bear her children, and still she will desire her husband with body and soul. Finally, it is only after the sin that Adam gives Eve her name: "Mother of the living" (3, 20).

---

6. B. Bonkamp, *Die Bibel im Lichte der Keilschriftforschung* (1939), p. 99. K. Heisig, "Woher stammt die Vorstellung vom Paradiesapfel?" *ZNT* 44 (1952-53), 111-118. From Greek mythology! The apples of the Hesperides! B. Pipal, "Sie machten sick Schurze," *IZBG* 9 (1962-63), No. 251. The fig tree was considered the tree of death. The aprons of fig leaves is thus an allusion to their mortality.

Was original sin thus the premature enjoyment of sexual activity, at a time when the first man and woman, still in the betrothal time of humanity, were supposed to have waited longer? Was it perhaps an unnatural use of the sex faculties? Was there perhaps, on the part of the woman, an unwillingness to conceive? The mythological school [7] sees the story of man's first sin simply as the transition to sexual maturity. Before the sin, Adam and Eve were "innocent children," unaware of the significance of their sexual differentiation; but one day they recognized the purpose of their bisexuality and covered themselves.

Even though a few expressions seem to point to the sexual sphere, the interpretation of original sin as a sin involving sex does not seem to fit within the framework of the narrative; the narrative tells, in a free and open candor, how God created the first humans as man and woman; in fact, Eve is actually shaped by God (2, 18) as a help-mate and a sexual counterpart for Adam. The author of the first chapter speaks of an express blessing on their fertility (1, 28), and described the bisexual nature of humanity as something very good (1, 31). Reluctance to have children is a typical product of a decadent and tired culture. But the Old Testament is vitally concerned with having children (cf. the establishment of the Levirate; Thamar uses trickery in order to have her child). The fact that Eve is cursed in her womanly capacity (3, 16), is explained by the fact that every creature is struck precisely in the natural potential of its kind, man in his work, and woman in her motherhood.

Coppens [8] refuses to consider any of these attempts at explanation; they are all more or less derived from the mentality of a tired European culture; he attempts to understand the story of the fall in terms of the original Canaanite milieu. This, he claims, is the proper *Sitz im Leben* for the song. It was the cult of Baal which represented the greatest peril to Israel's faith. Thus, the narrative was formulated as a warning and deterrent against the Baal cult. The powers of human fertility were venerated on sacred hills and in sacred woods, under trees. The serpent was a sexual symbol, and the phallus was the sign of Baal. The spread of this cult is attested to by the terra cotta serpents of

7. H. Gunkel, *Genesis* (1917), p. 29.

8. J. Coppens, *La connaissance du bien et du mal* (Löwen, 1948). R. de Vaux, *PB* 56 (1949), 300-308, rejects the argument as inconclusive. But Coppens presents new arguments from the Patristic literature, "L'intérprétation sexuelle du Péché du paradis," *ETL* 33 (1957), 193-220.

Beth-Shan and the bronze serpent of Jezer.[9] Then there is the cult of Asherah and the other goddesses,[10] represented as naked female figures with serpents. If we include the practice of "sacred marriage"[11] (*hieros gamos*), then we are face to face with a mentality that was widely spread in the Ancient Near East; by accomplishing the sexual act, it was thought possible to attain, not only fertility, but also divinity. It is obvious that the ancient Israelites were able to understand the narrative much better and much more contemporaneously than we can. It is the story of God's judgment on the Baal cult. The cult promises divinity, but it ends in shame. Hence the opinion that we are dealing here, not with persons, but with religions which are represented by the persons who speak and act in the narrative.[12] On the one side is Yahweh with his moral precept, and on the other side Baal with the fruit of life. The great sin of Israel, defection to the Baal cult, would thus be considered as the original sin. What we have, accordingly, is a projection back into primeval times.

An understanding of this contemporary background does enable us to understand the story of the first fall on a much deeper plane. Despite many opinions to the contrary,[13] we might well say that the story does have a sexual point. Or to formulate it in a more general way: the whole account is concerned with life, life, and life! In the midst there is the tree of life; man and woman are the propagators of life; "to know" is the expression for the generation of life. Our first parents went after higher, divine life, and partook of death. Thus we can say with certainty that the original sin was a sin that dealt with life. The nature of the sin is necessarily veiled in shadows. But the consequences

---

9. F. Hvidberg, "The Canaanite Background of Gen. I-III," *VT* 10 (1960), 285-294.

10. More detail in Vol. IV, 24ff., "the Goddess Asherah."

11. Cf. the account of Hieros Gamos, above p. 75ff.

12. F. Hvidberg, *op. cit.*, 290.

13. H. S. Stern, "The Knowledge of Good and Evil," *VT* 8 (1958), 405-418. Rejects the sexual interpretation.

of original sin are upon each and every man. The worm of death is gnawing at the human tree of life. According to God's plan in creation, man would have been created for immortality if he himself had not partaken of death. Original sin was not an individual act; the decision that was made then is inherited from generation to generation, as long as there are men on earth (original sin).

That is why the story of the first fall is not simply a polemical document in the struggle between Baal and Yahweh; [14] nor is it an etiological saga, locating the original cause of human misery in the first beginnings of mankind; [15] the dream of immortality and divinity, being like to God, which can be found elsewhere in the Ancient Near East, points to a much more ancient level of tradition.

In conclusion, we might also point to the findings of depth psychology, which, though its methodology is quite different from that of the Bible, still produces results that are worth our investigation. The elements of sin and fall appear in every people. Thus, they must be regarded as archetypes. The tree would be the symbol of unattainable good, and the serpent would be the symbol of obstacle. The serpent is the symbol of fertility, immortality, death, and also burial, thus, in a word, the symbol of human life. On the basis of these archetypal elements, we would thus have to conclude to the actuality of these events described as taking place in the beginning of human history.

If we are actually dealing with archetypes here, then the statement is valid not only for the first man but for mankind in general. Wherever the human agent is present we have a new

---

14. A. M. Dubarle, "Le péché originel dans la Genèse," *RB* 64 (1957), 5-34. Not a mythical event, with universal validity, but an actual event in time.

15. L. F. Hartmann, "Sin in Paradise," *CBQ* 20 (1958), 26-40. The fact of evil in the present world, which could only have been created good by God, is explained by the postulate of original sin. J. L. McKenzie, *Spirit and World of the Old Testament* (Lucerne, 1962), 130, sees original sin in the divinization of nature, a much too general conception.

reenactment of the Paradise narrative. Seen from this point of view, the doctrine of original sin takes on a tremendous depth. We do not simply live in terms of an inheritance that occurred once and for all at the very beginning: each individual man and each individual woman is in precisely the same situation that obtained in the very beginning. In each individual conscience there is a tree of the knowledge of good and evil. Each individual person is involved with the business of proving and temptation. Sin, death, and devil make up the infernal trinity that determine the very essence of human sin, from the first to the very last man on earth. For all humanity is bound up with the experience of Adam. What is really the archetypal experience of each individual human being is, in this narrative, compressed into the framework of a single act and carried back to the first beginnings of human existence. Original sin must, accordingly, be accepted as just as historical a fact as is the personal sin of each present-day man on earth. It would be much too comfortable a solution to make the first parents responsible for the entire situation and fact of human sin. We are all of us sinful Adam. A proper understanding of the sentence passed upon this fall from grace necessarily always involves this twofold aspect: historical point of departure and present-day actualization.[16]

The final and conclusive decision regarding the actuality of original sin rests, however, not upon historical and psychological grounds of evidence, but rather upon revelation and faith. When man is alone, everything threatens to crumble in his hands; but in the overall picture of revelation, he can realize that in the saga of man's first fall, the foundations of human and Christian existence have been proclaimed.

---

16. J. E. Bruns, "Depth Psychology and the Fall," *CBQ* 21 (1959), 78-82.

2) JUDGMENT AND PROTO-EVANGELIUM

The first sin was followed immediately by God's sentence. Their bad conscience made the first parents try to hide from God. When they heard God's voice in the Garden (2 Sam. 5, 24), they were afraid. Adam was the first to answer the divine call. He pushed the blame off onto his wife; but she, in turn, made the serpent responsible. The sequence of the sin was completely reversed. Sin had crept from the serpent, through the woman, into the man. The shared experience of sin had not brought the sinners closer together, but actually driven them further apart. Here we find the first word of judgment, which is related to the later prophetic threats of impending judgment. Here too, as in the later threats, the proclamation of the sentence is already bound up with a promise of salvation.

a) THE SERPENT-VANQUISHER: Only the serpent is the object of a direct curse – not the poor animal itself, of course,[17] but the power of the devil which is symbolized by the serpent. The words of the curse "crawl on your belly," and "eat dust" are taken from the serpent's normal way of life; the serpent, according to popular conception, eats dust. In the symbolic language of the Ancient Near East, these are words of deepest humiliation. The vanquished enemy must "lick dust" (Lev. 11, 42; Deut. 32, 24; Is. 49, 23, etc); those who are condemned to hell must "eat dust and earth." These are simply expressions for the conquering and complete annihilation of a hostile power. The serpent thought he had overcome; but God's divine sentence proclaims his definitive annihilation. His defeat comes from the same quarter where his victory began, from the woman and her seed. This is the classical text from the account:

---

17. J. Hofbauer, "Die Paradiesschlange," *Zkt* 69 (1947), 228-231. The curse was aimed only at the individual serpent, not the whole species as such.

"I set now enmity between you and the woman,
between your seed and her seed.
He treads down on your head,
If you strike out at his heel" (3, 15).

The placing of enmity between the serpent on the one hand,[18] and the woman and her seed on the other hand, dates back to primeval times, accomplished through the words of God's own mouth; thus it belongs to the fundamental realities of human existence. As the demonic power of seduction, the serpent lurks throughout human history, from its first beginnings to its final end, always trying to snatch the final victory (Wis. 2, 24; Ecclus. 25, 33; Jn 8, 44; Rom. 16, 20; Rev. 12, 9; 20, 2). In this struggle, man is assured by God's own promise that he will see a final victory.

In the Hebrew text, there is a play on words. The activity described of both the serpent and the seed of the woman is expressed by the same verb *šûp,* but with a very important nuance of meaning. The first time, the word represents the root *šûp I,* "crush, tread down," and the second time the root is *šûp II, šā'āp,* "snap at, strike at, lie in wait for."[19] Explanations which accept only the most obvious interpretation come to a tragic conclusion: "the outlook of the myth is a sad one. It is a struggle without hope, a fight that no heroism can ever bring to victory. This is a genuine curse! The most terrible part about the curse is the very hopelessness of the struggle in which both parties are doomed to wear themselves out in turn."[20] If the curse text were an isolated factor, we might be justified in accepting this pessimistic interpretation. But the entire Bible is taken up with the triumphal chant of the victory over the serpent

---

18. S. Grill, "Der Schlangenzertreter in Gen. 3, 15," *BuL* 23 (1956-57), 292-294.

19. E. Zolli, "Il verbo *suph* nella letteratura anticotestamentaria," *Marianum* 10 (1948), 282-287.

20. H. Gunkel, *Genesis,* 4th edition (1917), 32. G. v. Rad, "Das erste Buch Mose," *ATD* 1, 75.

(Ps. 89, 11), so that we must accept the likelihood that the author deliberately chose a word with two meanings, in order to achieve a much more gripping presentation of the good news of the serpent's demise. If the serpent "strikes out" at the heel of the "seed," he is trodden upon.

But who is this seed of the woman who is to win the victory over the serpent? Seed is obviously a general term for posterity. This would mean that mankind as such will overcome evil. In the messianic prophesy (2 Sam. 7, 14ff.) however, this general word "seed" is concentrated more and more strongly upon the individual person of the coming Messiah. It is hardly correct to play one interpretation against the other. Here the typal character of the prophetic proclamation of salvation breaks through. The Messiah is never viewed merely as an individual; it is always the people of the Messiah who are bound together with him. This mutual inter-relationship is well expressed by the term "corporate personality."[21] These words spoken to the serpent have generally been referred to as the Proto-evangelium. It is thus a gospel of mankind's victory as such over the serpent, and more particularly a gospel of the serpent-vanquisher in person. The scene is riveted on the decisive moment of final victory. At the very moment in which the serpent strikes out against the Messiah's heel, his head will be crushed. The two members of the sentence are causally and temporally related.[22] On the one hand, the person of the wicked enemy is clearly visible, while on the other hand we have the figure of the Messiah and serpent-vanquisher. The fact that the mother of the hero

---

21. J. de Fraine, *Adam und seine Nachkommen. Begriff der "korporativen Persönlichkeit" in der Heiligen Schrift* (Cologne, 1962). The leit-motif here is the statement of Kierkegaard: "Adam is both Adam and his race."

22. J. Haspecker and N. Lohfink, "Gen. 3, 15: Weil du nach der Ferse schnappst," *Scholastik* 36 (1961), 357-372. Stresses the prophetical genre, citing parallel Ugaritic texts, conclusive evidence for understanding the language.

is also mentioned is in perfect accordance with the type of messianic prophecy.[23]

The Septuagint translation already concentrates the narrative on a definite messianic figure. Victory will be achieved by the seed of the woman (the *sperma*), which, in and of itself, could be taken collectively; but in the following sentence it does not say "*it* (that is, the *sperma,* the posterity) will tread down on your head," but more explicitly, "he" (*autós*). The Septuagint is here thinking of the Messiah to come, the serpent-vanquisher. In this translation, the Greek Bible is faithful to the original Hebrew, which also reads a masculine form: *hû,* that is, "he" (the seed). The old-Latin translation followed the same reading with the words "*ipse conteret. . . .*" It was the Vulgate translation (Vetus Latina already in part, and the Vulgate itself not with absolute clarity) which first referred the "treading down on the head" to the woman (*ipsa*), a reading which can also be substantiated by the original Hebrew text, which does allow a certain latitude: in the Genesis account, the masculine "*hû*" can also be read as a feminine "*hî*" – although this would create a discord with the masculine form of the verb which follows.

These rudimentary philological observations make it clear that the Proto-evangelium is primarily concerned with the Messiah to come, who will fight the end-battle with the serpent, and is only secondarily concerned with the woman whose seed will achieve redemption. The Christian tradition sees this woman (*hā'iššâ*) not only as Eve, and the world of womankind, and all humanity for that matter, which descends from her; in Christianity, the woman of Proto-evangelium is a type of Mary, the mother of the Messiah; many scholars go beyond the merely typical interpretation and affirm that this Proto-evangelium is directly referable to the Blessed Mother.[24] Just as the figure of

---

23. Position of the "Great Lady" and Mother of the Messiah, cf. Vol. IV, 17ff.

24. A mere outline survey of tradition is enough to show how many opinions are represented in the interpretation of the Proto-evangelium. The Christological – Marian conception, which seems almost obvious today,

a savior-messiah already shines over the very first beginnings of lost humanity, the same is true for the figure of that woman who was to be his mother. The Immanuel prophecy of the prophet Isaiah, and the prophecy of the virgin birth, is only a more accurate concretization of this proto-evangelium which dates back to times primeval. This first, original proclamation (protology) points to the end-proclamation (eschatology). Both are possible only by the saving hand of Yahweh, powerfully at work directing the course of human history. The contention that not only the end-time, but the whole time of "humanity" as such, is both Christological and Mariological in its form and force, can well be substantiated on the basis of the Proto-evangelium.

Moreover, the history of religion encounters the motif of a fight with the serpent (or dragon) in many ancient and more modern peoples. In the Bible, accordingly, we might say that a primeval human concept has been taken up and interpreted in terms of salvation history.[25]

---

was not always the most widely favored view. In late Jewish and early Christian exegesis, the most common interpretation was the general moral explanation, a battle between good and evil. Cf. J. Michl, "Der Weibessame in spätjüdischer und frühchristlicher Auffassung," *Bibl.* 33 (1952), 371-401; 476-505. In the same line of a moral battle between woman and Satan, in the opinion of the Syrian commentator Išo'dad of Meru, cf. *Bibl.* 29 (1948) 313-320. It is only in the post-patristic era that the Mariological conception comes more and more into prominence. See T. Gallus, *Interpretatio mariologica Protoevangelii tempore postpatristico usque ad concilium Tridentinum* (Rome, 1949). – Scholion ad Protoevangelium. For the most explicit Mariological interpretation, cf. *VD* 28 (1950), N. Palmerini, "Mulier Protoevangelii Gn. 3, 15 secundum contextam orationem" (An absolute must on Mary) *VD* 28 (1950), 147-152. P. Bonnetain, "Immaculée Conception," *DBS* (1949), III, 240-254; 263-269. P. Hitz, "Le sens marial du Protévangile," *Etude Mariales* (1947-48), 35-83. For the most explicit Mariological interpretation, see M. Brunec, "De sensu Protoevangelii Gen. 3, 15," *VD* 36 (1958), 193-220.

25. Among other heroes, the Apollo of Delphi was venerated as victor over the Python dragon. In the German Siegfried saga the original dragon-combat motif has been refined and stylized. In the various legends of Saint George, there is a strong echo of this motif. The whole question is explicitly treated by M. Vereno.

We could point to many cosmic elements in the structure of this text. The number of words in Order I points to the bright morning star. But one further point must be alluded to. Babylonian astronomy was already familiar with the *'atalu,* the dragon of the heavens. Jewish mysticism is also familiar with him as a cosmic reality. The upper realm of the cosmos is assigned to him as his sphere of activity and power.

If we consult an ancient celestial map, we find, in the polar region, the constellation of the dragon, one of the most stable configurations of stars which is always visible in the northern hemisphere. The dragon is grasping towards the pole, but also maintains a hostile attitude towards another constellation, which is identified with the Babylonian Gilgamesh or the Greek Heracles. Gilgamesh is thrusting his foot, powerfully and victoriously, against the head of the dragon who is snapping at him with open jaws.

This is not a question of introducing some later conception of things into the Biblical text. The author of the Proto-evangelium in particular and the Paradise narrative in general, and we must presume that he was in Babylonia, was well acquainted with these ideas. Just as he gives mankind a cosmic proportion, even so it is perfectly natural that he should see the dragon battle which he has established in the human sphere also shining out as a constant reality in the sky. If it is true that the heavens declare the glory of the Lord, then these two constellations, the dragon and the dragon-slayer, proclaim the Proto-evangelium of Genesis.

b) THE PAINS OF THE WOMAN: Whereas the serpent is cursed directly by God, the man and the woman are touched only indirectly in their life powers. The sin was a sin against life. As a result, the generation and maintenance of life are now condemned to pain and weariness. Passing on the gifts of life, bearing children, in a word, motherhood as such, must always represent the highest fulfillment of the woman, her purest and most intense happiness. But why is all this bound up with suffering and pain?

The singer of this poem can find no other satisfactory reason than to explain it in terms of God's own doing in days of old. In verse 3, 16d, the woman's self-contradictory relationship to her husband is presented as an example. Even though the woman is under man's domination, she still longs for him. The woman desires her own slavery.[26] This statement about the woman's longing seems to presuppose that the woman has a stronger sexual drive than the man; it also follows that she will be the one who seduces him. This concept explains the source of the woman's misery. Contrary to God's original commandment, she had eaten of the fruit of the tree of life, and she was thus struck in her innermost essence as "mother of life."[27] She cannot bear children for eternal life, but only for death.

c) THE TOIL OF THE MAN: The man is also struck in the essence of his life. He must wrest the means of life from the earth. The earth, however, will produce only thistle and thorn. With all his mighty effort, he can succeed only in maintaining life, not in achieving it. Eventually, he himself once again turns into dust and earth from which he was first shaped.

This completes the circle of the great saga. It is wholly bound up with the mystery of life. Man is struck in the very heart of his living. Without some misstep, dating back to times primeval, the present condition of humanity is an incomprehensible riddle. Human nature is thus to be interpreted only in terms of its first origins.[28] The gift of life has been wasted; death, as the executor of the divine sentence, enters into its royal dominion (Rom. 5, 14).

---

26. H. Gunkel, *Genesis,* 4th edition (1917), p. 22.

27. J. Heller, "Der Name Eva," *ArOr* 26 (1958), 636-656. The name "mother of the living" was a reminiscence of the cult of the great mother goddess. But in the Bible her figure is demythologized.

28. J. L. McKenzie, *Spirit and World of the Old Testament* (1962), p. 128.

3) EXTRA-BIBLICAL PARADISE NARRATIVES

a) *The Dilmun Paradise:* In his Ancient Near East texts on the Old Testament, S. K. Kramer has recently published the Enki-Ninhursag myths, with the subtitle "Paradise Myths."[29] The text in question is a Sumerian text from the second half of the second millennium, written in a cuneiform text in six columns, a text which does indeed describe conditions proper to a Paradise, but can hardly be considered as a serious parallel to the Biblical narrative.

The *Sitz im Leben* of this text is not a primeval event which dates to the beginning of humanity, but the everyday diseases and sicknesses which are each to be healed by its own respective divinity. The myth is an echo of the rhythm of life. It falls into three parts: blessed original state – loss of vital strength – healing! The atmosphere of the myth is pregnant with vital and sexual overtones.

Blessed Time Past: "O holy land of Dilmun! The land of Dilmun is holy, the Land of Dilmun is pure. . . . The place where Enki (earth god) lay with his wife; the place is pure, the place is holy where he lay with her. . . . The lion tore no one, the wolf stole no lamb, and the wild hound stole no little lambkin. . . . Widowhood was unknown. . . . The sore eye did not say: I am sick! . . . . The old man did not say: I am old! . . . ."

The great goddess Ninkisilla complains to the god Enki that the islands have no fresh water; he created water and canal, so that the island became a fertile land. In this Paradise land, the impetuous life force of the god Enki now comes to eruption. He impregnated his spouse, the goddess Nin-hur-sag; after nine days, instead of nine months, and without labor pains, she gives

---

29. The text was discovered in the excavations at Nippur and first published by St. Langdon: "Sumerian Epic of Paradise" . . . in Publication of the Babylonian Section. University of Pennsylvania, X, Pt. 1 (1915). Further excavations yielded a more complete text. S. N. Kramer, "Enki and Ninhursag, a Paradise Myth." *ANET* (1955), 36-41.

birth to a daughter, the goddess Nim-mu. When the daughter matures, Enki has relations with her; she gives birth, again without labor pains and in nine days, to another goddess; this goddess, too, is impregnated by Enki, as is the one that follows. This is too much for Nin-hur-sag. Upon her instigation, her great-granddaughter gathers up Enki's seed and scatters it over the countryside. From the seed, eight plants spring up. When Enki sees them, he desires to "know their heart" and devours them one after another. Then Nin-hur-sag, the great goddess, is angry and leaves the island.

Drought: the departure of the great goddess of life resulted in Enki's pining away with disease. The cunning of the hawks, interceding with the sky god Anu, achieves the return of Nin-hur-sag and produces healing; Nin-hur-sag alludes to the birth of the healing goddesses. "My brother, where does it hurt?" — "My tooth hurts." — "Behold, that is why I had the goddess Ninsutu born." — "My brother, what hurts you now?" — "My rib hurts." — "Behold, that is why I had the goddess Nin-ti born," etc.

Even this brief examination of the contents is sufficient grounds for rejecting any closer comparison with the Biblical account of Paradise. These are two quite different worlds.

b) *The Adapa myth:* The nucleus of this myth is once again the problem of life. The god Ea, the wise one of Eridu, had, in those days, in those years, created the "primeval man" Adapa, and endowed him with wisdom and many gifts, although he did not bestow the blessing of immortality. His first office was the service of the god Ea. With his own hands, he prepared the bread for the sacrificial table, and without his hand the table was not prepared.

Then one day he sets out far onto the sea, to fish. The south wind, however, disturbs him at his work. He shatters the wings of the wind, and is thus called to account by Anu, the sky god. On the way to the hearing, Ea advises him that if they offer him "the water of life and the bread of life" up there, he should refuse it; but if they bring him oil, he should anoint himself with it. As it turns out, he is offered the bread and water of life. He rejects them and thereby also rejects the gift of immortality. Upon observing such folly, the sky god has him thrown out; he must return to earth. The rest of the text has been destroyed.

Adapa is obviously a man in decision; but still the background of the myth is quite different from the Paradise narrative.[30]

c) *The tree of life:* The story of the first fall was, at an earlier date, thought to be illustrated by pictorial representations on cylinder seals, but today their significance is better understood than at the time of their first discovery. The picture is generally the representation of a tree, with a fruit on the left and on the right. On either side is sitting a fully clothed person, a woman on the left, and a man on the right, a man with horns, the characteristic mark of a god.

In the plain of Babylonia, with its sparse vegetation, a group of trees, or even a single tree, presents a widely visible landmark. Trees indicate the proximity of water, they give shade, they are useful for their wood and for their fruits. Thus it is only to be expected that, under the influence of the nature religion, the tree should become an object of religious awe, and eventually have some significance in the religious cult. Trees were never the direct object of any cult, however; as the symbol of fertility, they were connected with the cult of certain gods.[31]

Representations of trees on cylinder seals are found from the most ancient to the most recent times. Only the date palm can be identified with any degree of certainty. In mythical representations, this tree is generally strongly stylized in its representation. In the imaginary tree generally called the tree of life, which was particularly popular in Assyria, in the first millennium, elements

---

30. The Adapa myth was found among the Amarna tablets in Egypt. Text in J. A. Knudtzon, *Die Amarna-Tafeln* (1915), pp. 965-969. E. Ebeling, *AOT,* 143-146. Further texts discovered in the Assurbanipal library at Nineveh, *ANET* (1955), 101-103.

31. *Reallexikon für Antike und Christentum*: *"Baum,"* (1951), with copious literature references. Revised by Fr. Schmidtke.

of date palm and pomegranate are mingled. Frequently a winged sun is hovering above the tree. The figures to the right and left are either tutelary deities or human worshippers, venerating the mystery of life. These tree pictures, accordingly, belong to the vegetation cult, and have nothing to do with Adam and Eve.[32]

d) *The Paradise of the primeval peoples:* Up to the present time, no clear parallel for the Paradise narrative has yet been discovered in the Ancient Near East milieu of the Old Testament. Ethnology, however, has some valuable material to offer from the religious worlds of the most ancient peoples.

The ethnologically oldest peoples have always preserved the memory of an original era in which God lived together with man. In like manner, there is some knowledge of a positive commandment of God's, and its transgression, whereupon God felt himself obliged to withdraw from human company. The nature of this prohibition differs according to the tradition. According to the pygmies of Gabon, God himself had reserved the eating of the fruit of a certain tree; if men ate it they turned into animals. Among the Ituri pygmies, it is a pregnant woman who urges her husband to bring her some of the forbidden fruit to eat. Among other tribes, sin consisted in the fact that a very curious woman wanted to see God on any terms, while God, under threat of the most severe punishment, preferred to work in his hut.[33]

In order to present a clearer picture, we shall briefly examine the Paradise narrative of the Bambuti, a pygmy tribe of central Africa, which belongs to the ethnologically oldest cultural stratum of Africa. According to the myths and traditions of the Bambuti

---

32. A. Jeremias, "Das Alte Testament im Lichte des Alten Orients," *ATAO*, 92 derives Bibel from Babel, which cannot any longer be maintained.

33. Cf. W. Schmidt, *Der Ursprung der Gottesidee*, Vol. II, 129; Vol. IV, 42; Endsynthese Vol. VI. P. Schebesta, *Der Urwald ruft wieder* (1936), pp. 125-130. W. Schmidt, *StZ* 134 (1938), 295-305.

pygmies, the primeval era can be reconstructed in something like the following terms: [34]

After God had created the world and humanity, he lived together with humanity on earth. He called men his children, and they called him Father. He had created mankind, not begotten it. Nowhere is there any mention of a female consort for God. God was a good Father to humanity; he had so arranged the world about them that they could spend their lives peacefully, without great effort or struggle, and particularly without need or suffering. The beasts of the forest were no more man's enemy than were the elements. And the food they needed came half-way to meet them. In a word, in the days that God lived among men, human existence was a paradise. God was not visible to men, but he lived among them and spoke with them. This paradise, if we might so refer to the world in which God had established the first humans, was the primeval forest itself. This, and everything else that he had created, he subjected to man's dominion.

He had, however, given them one commandment, and their future destiny was dependent upon keeping or transgressing it. For the transgression of his will he had threatened the most severe punishment. All creation would revolt against disloyal mankind. Animals and plants, and all the elements which had been friendly disposed towards him and ready at his command, would thereupon be his enemies. Toil and misery, sickness and death would be the result of his defection from God. But the most grievous consequences of sin would be God's departure from humanity.

Despite God's constant threat, mankind did not survive this testing; God's commandment was transgressed, and the most dire consequences of sin were immediately felt. Most fearsome of all, for mankind, was God's departure from their midst. God had disappeared; he had gone and he was no longer to be heard among them. He did not die; for otherwise his bones would have been discovered. He made his way up river, upwards.

But God did not leave mankind, his children, without protection against the hostility of their environment; he left them the tools and weapons they needed to defend themselves and to live their life. In the opinion of the pygmy authorities, God's departure from the human family was clearly the greatest of catastrophes that had ever befallen mankind. The other consequences of human sin were not so keenly felt.

These precious narratives of the primitive peoples are closest to the biblical accounts. But they obviously are not derived from it; nor could they have been taken over from the culturally superior peoples about them, since they are not to be found in these cultures; thus, they must be derivable from the nature of man as such, without postulating any dependence on one side or the other.

---

34. P. Schebesta, *Die Religion der Bambuti* (1950), p. 165ff.

CHAPTER XX

PARADISE LOST

ORDER II, GEN. 3, 22 – 4, 16

Order II can be divided into three sections: A. Cherubim and Flaming Sword (3, 22-24), B. Cain and Abel (4, 1-16), C. Early Mankind (4, 17-26). Only the total count of these sections need detain us here:

	N		I		S		
A.	29		3		19		
B.	88		18		95		
C.	116		5		19		
	233	+	26	+	133	=	392

Here too we would have to delve deep into the explanation of the individual numerical values for a satisfying commentary, but this is obviously beyond the scope of the present work. Since, however, Order I and Order II together form the first great toledot, it is the sum total of the two together that needs to be examined here. The result of this examination is such a striking series of numbers that we can hardly avoid the conclusion that the entire text has been composed, throughout, in terms of the most careful structure, right down to the least structural unit. The following are the totals we arrive at:

		N	I	S	i	s
Paradise	5 +	237	11	40		
Fall		81	38	147	11	19
Paradise Lost		233	26	133		
	5 +	551	75	320	11	19

5 + 626 + 350 = 5 + 976

INTERPRETATION OF THE TABLES:

a. DIRECT SPEECH: The direct speech sections, with the total number of 320, are simply another reference to "the 32 wonderful ways of wisdom, through which all things have been made." The 4 indirect speeches that have been incorporated raise the total to the number of a cyclical lunar year of 350 day-words.

b. NARRATIVE AND INTRODUCTION SECTIONS: There is no need to dwell at any length on the 75 words of introduction; these have already been explained in reference to the numbers that occur in the story of Abraham. At the age of 75 Abraham was called from Ur of the Chaldeans. We must rather regard the narratives and the introductions as a larger unit.

For the Paradise story we have the number: 237 + 11 = 248, the number which refers to man and commandment as such. In the Rabbinic tradition the number 248 is used as a reference to the number of bones in the human skeletal structure (Adam), since these bones form the first basis for the appearance of man in the world. To this figure is now added the number 365, the number of flesh parts in the human body, to arrive at a total of 613 parts of the human body. It goes without saying that this figure has little point of reference with a precise physiological count based on the actual study of anatomy. What is being expressed here is the essence of man. The numbers are simply raised from the physical to the psychic and spiritual plane.

The Rabbinic tradition thus prescribes that a man must perform 248 positive acts (*miswôt ta 'aseh* – Commands "Thou shalt") and avoid 365 "negative" acts (*miswôt lo ta 'aseh* – Commands "Thou shalt not"). The two numbers stand, accordingly, for command and prohibition. Moreover, the positive acts are the expression of the "male" (Adam), and the negative, passive acts are the expression of the "female" (Eve).[1]

Now it is a striking fact that the text which recounts the creation of Adam counts, without including the incorporated speech sections, a total of precisely 248 words. For the remainder of the section, however, for N and I, there are 365 + 13 words. Does this mean that the mathematics of the narrative is in error? Or are the additional 13 words there for a deliberate purpose? In my opinion, it is the latter explanation that appears closer to the truth. Let us turn to the central text in 3, 6 where we read the following of Eve, the female element: "Then the woman saw that the tree was good to eat and that it was a delight for the eyes, a tree inviting to be wise." The last word, "to be wise" (*lehaskîl*) belongs to the vocabulary of the Wisdom and Law literature, and we might thus very well be justified in excising it, with its 13 words, as a later addition.

We can thus conclude that the first toledot section follows the thematic numbers of male-female (Adam – Eve) and command-prohibition. This is already a great step forward towards interpretation. The tree of Paradise is identical with the Torah. On the basis of the individual and collective relationship to this tree-law is determined the question of human salvation or damnation.

c. GOD'S WORDS: In the total number of speech selections we discovered a reference to the lunar year. Now it would appear

1. Cf. on this subject Friedrich Weinreb, *Der göttliche Bauplan der Welt. Der Sinn der Bibel nach der ältesten jüdischen Uberlieferung*, 1966, p. 119.

that we are justified in asking how many words are attributed to God in this section. Our investigation yields the total of 235 words. Once again we are dealing with a typical value, this time a reference to the lunar and solar cycle together. Since the lunar and solar calendars exhibit considerable variation from each other, ancient scholars constantly sought some principle for reducing the two to perfect unity. They soon discovered that 19 solar years are equivalent to 235 synodic lunar months. After the completion of this length of time, the lunar and solar calendar would once again be in perfect harmony. The 19-year cycle comprises 12 normal years and 7 intercalary years, in a sequence whose ordering is not known. In determining this order, there were 110 "hollow" months of 29 days and 125 "full" months of 30 days, making a total of 6940 days.[1a] In the narrative of the fall, God is assigned precisely 110 words. Thus the division of the YHWH words, the words assigned to God, into two sub-totals of 110 + 125 is based on the text itself. This is further substantiation of the cosmic structure of the text.

A) CHERUBIM AND FLAMING SWORD (3, 22-24)

22 *And God YHWH spoke:*
See, man is become as one of us
in knowledge of good and evil!
Lest he now also stretch forth his hand
and take also of the tree of life
and eat and live for ever!
23 *And God YHWH showed him out of the garden Eden*
to cultivate the ground from which he was taken.
24 *And he drove out the man*
and placed, in the east of the garden Eden,
the cherubim and the quivering sword of flame
to guard over the way to the tree of life.

1a. *Lexikon der Alten Welt,* article: *Meton von Athen* (1965), p. 1950.

God's sentence of punishment is followed by the expulsion from Paradise, which, in turn, is based upon a final word from God YHWH. The double name YHWH-Elohim now disappears from the narrative. The very speech-form itself refers to the fact of the sin. By eating of the tree of knowledge man had become "like one of us."[2] This most likely means that man had become autonomous, without paying any heed to God's command, that he himself was determined to decide what was good and what was evil. But it was a tragically wrong decision. What he chose for himself was death. But in order to keep him from perpetuating, eternalizing, this condition of death, by eating also of the tree of life, God drove him out of the garden. In order to make it impossible for him to return, he set up cherubim at the entrance and a flaming sword.

The cherubim are elevated and mysterious creatures. They indicate the divine presence (Heb 9, 5), watch over the sanctuary (Ex 25, 18-19), and bear the throne of God. Yahweh is the God who "has his throne between the cherubim" (1 S 4, 4; 2 S 6, 2). In Gen 3, 34 they exercise their office as guardians, sealing off the entrance into Paradise.

The common conception of the cherubim in the cultures which surrounded the Biblical world can be seen in the discoveries from Byblos (King Hiram), Hamath, and Megiddo (from the time between 1200 and 800 B.C.), which represent a throne borne by cherubim.[3] In Solomon's Temple, two life-size cherubim, with wings outspread, kept watch over the ark of the covenant (Ex 26, 1; 2 Chr 3, 14); their figures were also represented on the

---

2. J. Coppens, *La connaissance du bien et du mal* (Louvain, 1948), p. 118, translates "*mimménnu*" not as "of, from us," but rather "of, from him," and refers it to Adam. Everyone who is descended "from him" must experience a like fate. The interpretation is too dependent upon other than textual considerations.

3. The Kâribi from Senjirli in North Syria are mixed creatures, bulls with human faces and eagle's wings, bearing round stone plates on their backs for supporting the throne. Illustrated in Volz, *Biblische Altertümer,* p. 13.

hangings and on the walls of the Temple (1 S 6, 29); *kərûb* is considered as equivalent to the Sumerian *kurîbi*, but there is no explanation of how the Semitic word derives from the Sumerian. On the other hand, the derivation of *kerûb* from the Akkadian *karîbu* presents no difficulties, since the *karîbu*-divinity was conceived as a gatekeeper.[4] The name *karîbu* might mean "he who blesses" or "he who prays and intercedes." This would also correspond to the function of the *karîbu*-divinity, who has access to the sanctuary. Among the mixed-figures of Babylonian art, none has yet been expressly identified as *karîbu*. An office similar to the *karîbu* is ascribed to the Egyptian sphinx. The word *karîbu* can be compared with the Indo-Germanic word *grabh* – "griffon," and the corresponding Greek root *grup*. The representation of the cherubim would thus be very ancient, dating back to the times in which Semites and Indo-Germans still shared a common territory.[5]

The enigmatic "flame of the darting sword" is probably an allusion to the avenging sword of God, which is portrayed as an autonomous independent agency or power (Is 34, 5; Jer 46, 10; Zeph 2, 12; Ez 21, 13). Thunder and lightning are signs of the divine presence (revelation on Sinai). That this lightning could take on concrete form as the expression of the most stringent prohibition is evident from an inscription of Tiglath-Pileser I (c. 1100 B.C.): "I have erected a bronze lightning, and engraved it with the booty that I took with the help of my god Ashur. Thereon I also wrote a prohibition against reoccupying and rebuilding the city. At that place I erected a house and put the bronze lightning into it."[6] Thus, whoever trespasses on that

---

4. On cherubim cf. P. Dhorme, also L.H. Vincent, "Les Chérubims," RB 35 (1926), 328-358; 481-495. On the history of religion as applied here, cf. A. S. Kapelrud, "The Gates of Hell and the Guardian Angels of Paradise," JAOS 70 (1950), 151-156. Alludes to the connection between the Cherubim in 1 Kings 6, 23 and the Sumerian "door-gods". (!)

5. J. Feldmann, *Paradies und Sündenfall*, p. 258.

6. KB I, 36, 15.

territory falls victim to the avenging sword of the gods and the king. *Kerûb* and flaming sword thus refer, in the language of Ancient Near Eastern imagery, to the most stringent prohibitions imaginable.

Whether or not this symbolic interpretation of cherubim and flaming sword – both of them merely Ancient Near Eastern images of the most strict and stringent prohibition – completely exhausts the Biblical concept is still a matter of some question. For the Old Testament, the cherubim are angelic powers, dwelling in the most immediate vicinity of God. Since human speech can express spiritual realities only in terms and images, the Bible turns to the concept of "mixed-being," familiar to the Ancient Near East; but this image thus becomes a medium for expressing the revelation of the angelic powers. In the temptation narrative, it is the satanic angelic power that we catch a glimpse of; but the gate to Paradise is guarded by God's cherub. Man's position is between the two. Human history remains open to what is above it and below it. The fact that the angel appears in the threatening position of armed guard is only a logical conclusion of God's own attitude in passing sentence and expelling man and woman from Paradise. The threatening attitude, moreover, changes with the development of God's revelation of his salvific plan. It is this same threatening angel that turns into the herald of salvation.

Thus, the first three chapters of Genesis outline the grandest perspectives of which history is capable. God, angels, devils, and man – these are the powers who make history in the proper sense of the word. If we overlook even one of these powers, we falsify the course of history. As a logical consequence of these facts, true history can be written only as a revelation; without God's revealing light, the divine and the demonic aspects of history would be hidden from the human historian.

Despite all our attempts at explanation, there are still some insoluble mysteries. "Only the New Testament is the key to this hieroglyph; only the Gospel (*Evangelium*) is the explanation of the Proto-evangelium. Only Christ has solved the difficult riddle of this sphinx, for all the saints and prophets, by fulfilling it."[7]

B) CAIN AND ABEL (4, 1-16)

The narrative of Cain and Abel still belongs to the great saga of the first man. In terms of literary history, the same principles apply here. We are not dealing with an historical account, but rather with a religious saga, which shows how the evil which entered into humanity at the first fall continued to work to the harm and calamity of all mankind. In Paradise, man had rebelled against God; the most immediate consequence of this rebellion is man's enmity towards man.

1) TEXT

1 *The man knew his wife Eva;*
and she conceived and bore Cain
and spoke:
I have made a man with YHWH!
2 *And she bore again, his brother, Abel.*
Abel was a shepherd of flocks,
a farmer was Cain.
3 *And it happened at the turn of the days,*
that Cain offered, from the fruits of the field,
sacrifice to YHWH.
4 *Abel too offered sacrifice*
of the firstlings of his flocks and their fat.
5 *Then YHWH looked upon Abel and his sacrifice,*
but upon Cain and his sacrifice he did not look.
This angered Cain so much
that his face fell.

---

7. Fr. Delitzsch, *Commentar über die Genesis* (1872), p. 151.

6 *Then YHWH spoke to Cain:*
Why are you angry,
and why has your face fallen?
7 *If you are doing good,*
is there not a lifting up?
If you are not doing good,
the sin-lurker is before the gate.
Upon you is his desire,
but you should have mastered him.
8 *And Cain spoke to his brother Abel.*
Then it happened, when they were in the field,
Cain arose against his brother Abel
and slew him.

9 *And YHWH spoke to Cain:*
Where is Abel your brother?
He spoke:
I do not know.
Am I my brother's keeper?

10 *He spoke:*
What have you done?
The voice of your brother's blood
cries out to me from the field.
11 *Then be accursed*
away from the field that opened its mouth
to receive the blood of your brother from your hand.
12 *If despite this you till the field,*
it will no longer give you its strength;
round and round will you wander upon earth.

13 *Then Cain spoke to YHWH:*
My guilt is too great to bear!
14 *Behold, you have driven me today*
away from the surface of the field.

I must hide myself from before your face,
wander round and round upon the earth.
Then it will happen that whoever finds me will
strike me dead.

15 *Then YHWH spoke to him:*
In truth, everyone who strikes Cain
shall atone sevenfold.

16 *And YHWH made a sign for Cain*
that no man who found him should strike him dead.
17 *Then Cain went away from the face of YHWH*
and dwelt in the land of "unrest," east of Eden.

2) INTERPRETATION

The introduction to the Cain-Abel narrative is loaded with plays on words. The word, after all, is primarily concerned with revealing the essence. Thus, it belongs to the essence of Hawwah – Eve, the mother of life, to produce life. The birth of the first human son is accompanied by an archaic-sounding play on words. The poet has Eve exclaim in joy: "I have gotten a man!" The word "gotten (begotten)" (*qānîtî*) is an echo of the name Cain (*qāyin*). Ancient Near East etymology is largely content with an ingenious interplay of words that sound alike, without any scientific explanation of their roots. Cain, in the Semitic languages, means simply "hammerer, smith." But there is a much deeper meaning in the present passage. The verb *qānā*, which expresses the life-creating activity of the first human mother, is unhesitatingly used also of God, the "creator (*qôneh*) of heaven and earth" (Gen. 14, 19). The birth of the first man is thus conceived of as Eve's creative activity. In the Ugarit myth, the mother of gods and men bears the honorary epithet "creatrix of the gods" (*ḳnyt'lm*). The sentence has such a proud ring about it, that the author thought it necessary to add the words "with Yahweh's help." God made use of man in order to construct woman; now the roles are exchanged: it is from woman that the first man is born.[8] Thereby, the rhythm of generation and birth is introduced on earth. It is Abel who is born as the second "man." His name already indicates his fate: *hăbel,* "breath, nothingness." [9]

When Cain is described as a farmer, and Abel as a shepherd, this already presupposes a vocation specialization which belongs to a later stage of culture.[10] The religious decision takes place at a sacrifice which is recognizable as the offering of the firstlings, the first-fruits, and as such, according to our ethnological knowledge, does belong to this early level of culture.[11] "Cain sacrificed of the fruits of the field, Abel of the first-fruits of the flocks and of their fat." Even though later conceptions of the sacrificial form are probably at work in these words, the decisive element which is pictured in the narrative is the disposition with which they each approached the sacrifice. In what manner Yahweh signified his acceptance or rejection of the sacrifice is left to our own conjecture. Was it perhaps that fire came down from heaven and consumed Abel's sacrifice (cf. Lev. 9, 24; Judg. 6, 21; 3 Kings 18, 38), or was the decision manifest only in the consequences, with God blessing the undertakings of the one brother?

The fact is that the sacrifice resulted in Cain's becoming very much embittered. "His countenance fell" (Gen. 4, 5). Does this mean that his expression was distorted by envy and bitter-

---

8. C. Hauret, "Notes d'exegèse. Genèse 4, 1: Possedi hominem per Deum," *RSR* 32 (1955), 61.

9. The name Abel has also been derived from the Sumerian *ibila,* "son." Thus, the three first humans would have been called "father" (*adamu*), "mother," (*hawwah*), and "son" (*ibila*). The Hebrew reader was certainly no longer conscious of this meaning. Cf. *VD* 4 (1924), 383.

10. W. Schmidt, *Zu den Anfängen der Herdentierzucht. Z. f. Ethnologie* 76 (1951), pp. 54-58 stresses the fact that the transition from hunting to domestication of animals took several thousands of years.

11. W. Schmidt, *StZ* 134 (1938), 303.

ness, or that he went along his way with a frown, hanging his head? At any event, Cain's attitude presents an opportunity for the author to develop a profound theology and psychology of sin.[12] "If you decide for the good,[13] your countenance will be raised up" – there is a two-fold meaning here: the good man can freely raise his head and does not need to look down upon the ground in bitterness, as Cain does; or this "raising up" can mean being heard. The petitioner lay upon his face before the king. When the king was about to grant his request, he would lift the petitioner's face from the ground. In the language of religion this means that the acceptance or non-acceptance of the sacrifice is totally and completely dependent upon the interior disposition of the man who offers it. Thus, this passage represents the primacy of conscience over external religious rites.

On the other hand, "If you decide for evil, then the (power of) sin is at the door, the lurker. Its desire is upon you and you must master it!" (Gen. 5, 7). Involuntarily we think of the *rōbēṣ,* the "lurker."

The concept of an autonomous man, relying only upon himself, is alien to Scripture. Man is always in a state of decision; either he is God's or the devil's, but never does he stand alone. The mention of the "lurker" before the door might well recall the demonic representations of the Ancient Near East; [14] but even

12. G. Closen, "Theologie der Sünde in der Genesis," *Die Sünde der Söhne Gottes,* 239ff.

13. The text uses the verb "*yätäb*" in the hiphil form, which always implies a causative element, and thus can here be translated as "make a decision for the good." G. R. Castellino, "Genesis IV, 7," *VT,* 10 (1960), 442-445. "Raise" is to be referred to "countenance." "Sin" is personified as an animal and thus construed as masculine.

14. The Akkad-Sumerian world was familiar with a demon called *rabisu-utu* (lurker, croucher). For example: "From house to house they make their way, no door can shut them out, no bolt can hold them back, through the very door, like a serpent they glide." Jastrow, *Religion der Babylonier und Assyrer,* I, p. 360. "Through the door of the house they try to make their way." That is why tutelary divinities were posted in the doorways. Cf. Closen, *Die Sünde der Söhne Gottes,* p. 248.

so the "lurker" is only a logical continuation of the serpent of Paradise, which "lurked" in ambush against the first parents and destroyed their happiness. The triad which figured in the decision in Paradise: God – man – devil, comes up again in the story of Cain. Man is called upon to master the power of sin, the demon. But as soon as he opens the door, this power asserts its supremacy, and its ultimate consequence is death.[15]

After Cain had murdered his brother, the voice of his brother's blood cried out to Yahweh. Blood is the seat of life. Life came from God and thus belongs to God alone. Whoever attacks this life, also attacks God. These concepts are also operative in the Old Testament blood sacrifices.[16] God's voice does not produce repentance in Cain; he defies God: "My guilt is too great to bear" (4, 13). The punishment to which Yahweh sentences Cain is not immediate death, but banishment into the steppe and desert country. So that no one will kill Cain, God gives him a sign.[17] This sign has been explained as a miraculous sign by which God guaranteed Cain's inviolability, or a sign in Cain himself, his troubled expression, or a tattoo mark of some kind. This last possibility appears to be the most probable, if we consider the practice of the Bedouins, among whom the law of blood vengeance still prevails.[18] The fratricide is reserved for God's judgment alone. But if another man dares to attack him,

---

15. The Pauline theology of sin develops in the same directions. For Paul sin is a "power" that has a demonic character. Man is subject to this "power." Cf. Rom. 6: 20-23.

16. In Hebrew, "blood" is a plural: "The voice of the much blood . . ." cannot be literally translated. In the prologue to John we find the same Semitic manner of speaking: "*qui non ex sanguinibus* . . . those who are born not of blood but of God."

17. O. Sauermann, "Bemerkungen zum Kainszeichen," *Antonianum* 33 (1958), 45-56.

18. A. Musil reports of the Arabians in Transjordania: When anyone kills his father or brother, he may not be put to death for it, but he shall be cast out of his family, and no stranger even from an enemy clan may take him in. Through his deed, he has forfeited companionship with the family of man. According to such ancient justice the "sign" was shown, not as a command of God, a believable miracle, but as a distinguishing

he must face a double, or even a seven-fold punishment. The fratricide is condemned to a slow and miserable death in the wilderness. That is why the country into which Cain is banished is described only figuratively by the Hebrew word Nod, "restlessness," no-man's land.

a) CAIN AND THE KENITES: among the Midianites there was a tribe called the Kenites (*Qein* and *Qayin*). According to Judges 1, 16; 4, 11, the tribe owed its origin to Hobab, Moses's brother-in-law. It always appears to enjoy friendly relations with the Israelites. Many exegetes believe that these Kenites owe their ancestry to Cain, or that Cain is a personification of the tribe of Kenites. But according to the Biblical author, the Cainites lead an existence that is alienated from God, and their life as nomads is regarded as a well deserved curse. Hobab, on the other hand, is invited by Moses to come to Canaan with him, but he prefers to live in the desert. The Kenites are small-cattle breeders (Ex. 2, 16-19). Thus it would probably be more correct to consider Abel as their ancestor. The Kenites are on terms of closest friendship with Israel, while the Cainites are rejected by Yahweh. At any rate, it is particularly surprising to note that some of these exegetes derive Israel's belief in Yahweh from the Kenites. The sign of Cain has become the sign of Yahweh! [19]

b) A SUMERIAN CAIN AND ABEL STORY: in the *Ancient Near Eastern Texts Relating to the Old Testament* (1955), S. N. Kramer presents a new Sumerian text, which he describes by the sub-title "Cain-Abel Motif." The text is preserved, only in fragments, on three tablets found in Nippur.[20]

The poem is entitled Dumuzi and Enkimdu, a discussion between the shepherd god and the farmer god. There are four principal characters: The goddess Inanna (– mistress of the sky – Astarte), the sun god Utu, the shepherd god Dumuzi, and the farmer god Enkimdu. The action begins with the sun god's ordering Inanna to marry the shepherd god Dumuzi; but she spurns him and chooses instead the farmer god. Next comes

---

mark that made known that Cain was a fratricide who should not be killed. For the knowledge of the killing of his brother set him on a course of exile so that through this indelible sign all men recognized him as a murderer. Cited by H. Junker, *Genesis,* (1949), pp. 21-22.

19. Cf. P. Heinisch, *Genesis,* p. 149. A. Keller, "Das Wort OTH als Offenbarungszeichen Gottes." (Inauguraldiss. Basel, 1946).

20. Text in paraphrase and translation interpreted by S. N. Kramer in *Journal of Cuneiform Studies* II (New Haven, 1948), pp. 60-68. *Ibid. ANET,* 1955, 41-44.

a lengthy text in which the shepherd describes the advantages he has to offer. He manages to change Inanna's mind and win her for himself. The shepherd god Dumuzi is relaxing along the river bank; there he is met by the farmer god Enkimdu; there is however, no struggle between the two; quite the opposite. The farmer gives the shepherd his land to pasture his flocks; and the shepherd invites his rival to the wedding. He comes, bringing rich presents. The poem closes upon this happy note.

There is nothing more than the farmer-shepherd "motif" in this story to remind us of the Cain-Abel narrative in the Bible. There are no other points of comparison.

C) EARLY HUMANITY

If we ask how an author of the Ancient Near East was in a position to tell the story of earliest humanity, we must realize that, in addition to the sagas of antiquity, he also had family genealogies at his disposal and was able to bridge over great intervals of time. Genesis thus presents two genealogies of Adam, one through Cain, and the other through Seth. But both end with the same figure, Lamech. Thus we must suppose that it is essentially the same genealogy, constructed in two different ways. In this saga of the first man, it is the prophetic element which is predominant. It is not so much a question of numbers and generations as it is the significant figures of Old Testament history. The Cainite genealogy (4, 17-24) presents only the external framework within which the cultural development of early humanity is described. In this connection, the name Cain has a much more positive meaning. He is actually the "smith" (*qayin*) of culture, the *homo faber*, the man who produces things.

The rhythm of this last section of the great saga of the first man is not consistent. A variety of different elements make their appearance here. The whole text belongs to the toledot additions.

1) TEXT

A. CAINITE GENEALOGY (4, 17-18)

17 Cain knew his wife;
she conceived and bore Enoch.
He was the builder of a city
and he called the name of the city
after the name of his son Enoch.
18 To Enoch was born Irad,
And Irad begot Mehujael.
Mehujael begot Methushael,
and Methushael begot Lamech.

B. LAMECH'S WIVES (4, 19-22)

19 Lamech took two wives,
the name of the one was Adah,
the name of the other Zillah.
20 Adah bore Jabal;
he is the ancestor of all
who dwell in tents with flocks.
21 His brother's name is Jubal;
he is the ancestor of all
who play upon harp and flute.
22 Zillah too bore a son,
Tubal-cain the smith,
who works with iron and bronze.
Tubal-cain's sister was named Naamah.

C. LAMECH'S OATH (4, 23-24)

23 *To his wives Lamech spoke,*
to Adah and Zillah:
Hear my word, wives of Lamech,

and listen to my saying!
I slew a man for a wound,
a young man for a bruise!
24 If Cain is avenged seven times,
then seventy and seven times Lamech!

D. THE "SUBSTITUTE" CHILD (4, 25-26)

25 And Adam knew his wife again;
she bore a son
and called his name Seth;
for, God gave me another seed
in place of Abel whom Cain slew.
26 To Seth too a son was born
and he called his name Enoch.
It was then men began to call upon the name of YHWH.

2) INTERPRETATION

a) *The Cainite Genealogy:* Together with Cain, there are 6 names: Cain, Enoch, Irad, Mehujael, Methushael, and Lamech. The seventh would be Noah; for Noah's father was called Lamech. The genealogy thus spans the interval from Paradise to the deluge. What took place in this interval? The names have been interpreted in a purely negative direction,[21] such as Mehujael, "extinguisher of God," Methushael, "man of hell," and Lamech himself can be identified as a brutal man of force. The names are already taken as an expression of the gradual decay of faith and

---

21. J. Schildenberger, *Vom Geheimnis des Gotteswortes* (1950), p. 277ff. M. Tserat, "The Canaanite *šälaḥ*," *VT* 4 (1954), 41-49. The second syllable of the name Metuschael must be associated with *še'ol*, Hell, the underworld. For further explanation of names, see B. Bonkamp, *Die Bibel im Lichte der Keilschriftforschung* (1939), p. 129 ff. For further discussion of the genealogy of Cain, see J. Gabriel, "Die Kainiten–genealogie (Gen. 4, 17-24)," *Bib* 40 (1959), 407-427.

morals. Early humanity bears the mark of Cain on its forehead, and necessarily calls down upon itself the judgment of the deluge. It is true that a negative tone does run through the entire section. But since we originally spoke of this great saga as a culture hymn, we must also examine the positive achievements side by side with the negative evidence.

The names can also be interpreted in a positive manner. The man Cain became the "smith" of culture. He built a city and called it Enoch, that is, "establishment, foundation." Man was no longer to wander aimlessly about, but rather to be permanently settled in the land. Actually, Enoch, in the legend, belongs among the greatest saints of antiquity. The other names can also be given positive meanings. Mehujael and Methushael are practically synonymous in meaning, the "man blessed of God" and the "man of God." [22] The first development of civilization exhibits not only the evidence of curse, but also the even stronger effect of blessing.

b) *Lamech's wives:* The fact that Lamech had two wives should not be a source of scandal for anyone reading the Old Testament; this was the normal practice in the patriarchal era. In this section, accordingly, the accent is not so much on the corruption of marriage, but rather on the rise of the various vocational groups. The existence of various human trade groups is explained on the basis of genealogy. Smiths, for example, could only have descended from an "original smith." We are here dealing not with history, but with symbolic interpretation. The names of the two women also point in this direction: Adah means literally "morning, dawn," while Zillah means "shade, shadow," or "twilight." [23] The Ugaritic myth also speaks of two women, "dawn and twilight" (*šahru* and *šalmu*).[24] The name Lamech has not been completely explained. The Sumero-Baby-

---

22. The derivation of the verb lies in *maḥah II,* easily, enough and *ša'al,* pray or beseech. Metuschael can also be derived from *metu-ša-'el,* man of El, that is, man of God.

23. O. Proksch, "Die Genesis," *KAT* (1913), 53.

24. W. F. Albright, *Die Religion Israels im Lichte der archäologischen Ausgrabungen* (1956), 88.

lonian god Ea, the god of wisdom and the inventor of culture, sometimes bears the epithet Lamga.[25] All this might lead us to conclude to a mythological background for this Biblical account. In the Bible, however, it is no longer a divine myth, but a simple saga. The ancestor of the nomadic Bedouins, who drive their flocks from one pasture to another, can obviously have been only Jabal, the "driver," [26] and the ancestor of the musicians could only have been Jubal, the "horn-blower," [27] and the ancestor of smiths could only have been Tubal-Cain, the "bronze-smith." The working of bronze, in the Ancient Near East, spread from the Taurus Mountains, where the land of Tubal was situated.

Since his expulsion from Paradise, man has learned much. The early culture has been produced. Side by side with the nomadic herdsmen, the established city was a reality. Artisans and artists had made their appearance. But, hand in hand with this progress, faith and morals gradually began to decay. Not without reason is Lamech's daughter called Naamah, "comely." [28] The culture hymn does not end on a happy note: Lamech's oath shows that it was a brutal era.

c) *Lamech's oath:* With the progress of civilization, human life came to be valued less and less. Whereas, in the Cain narrative, sevenfold blood vengeance was established for murder, the Lamech story raises this to "seventy-seven-fold." Not only is life to be avenged with life, but even an insignificant wound or bruise is to be avenged by murder.

This is the end of the great saga of the first man. There is no glorification, and certainly no deification of humanity. The hard reality in which the singer finds the humanity of his day, is explained in terms of man's first origins. Humanity is a rebellious

---

25. A. Clamer, "La Genèse," *ClamB I* (1953), 161.

26. Meaning of the verb *jabal,* bring, carry, travel.

27. *jôbel,* ram. With a ram's horn the Israelites were summoned to Feasts.

28. P. Flügge, "Lamechs Tochter Naema," *ZAW* 62 (1949-50), 314.

generation: God willed it otherwise. But the first man preferred to follow the serpent-demon. This was the basis for the whole subsequent history of his misfortunes. But this will be turned into a history of salvation: witness God's great promise of a serpent-vanquisher. Even though the images all belong to the realm of saga – and there is no other way to speak of these primeval eras – still, the fundamental truths of faith are expressed in them in a much more penetrating way than any abstract formulation. The saga of the first man is not a myth in the pagan sense, where even the gods themselves are swept along in an eternal cycle of death and birth. The one God stands as sovereign over world and man. He is the Creator, the Lord, and the Father of humanity, and he is also the Revealer of the mysteries of old. The saga of the first man is thus, in perfect truth, a declaration of faith.

CHAPTER XXI

THE PATRIARCHS BEFORE THE DELUGE
ORDER III, GEN. 5, 1 – 6, 9

Genealogies and Numbers

WE must begin this rather difficult section with a question. How was it possible for a scholar in ancient Israel to present the early history of humanity? The findings of archaeology and anthropology were not yet at his disposal. He did, however, have an historical sense. And this primarily on practical grounds: his business accounts had to be dated. The one secure refuge in the stream of time was the regnal dates of the individual kings. It is the royal lists which present the most ancient skeleton of the course of history. These lists claim to go back to the beginnings of humanity, where, at first, a king was ruling in a given city. Now since the Biblical genealogies also mean to span the gaping interval between the beginnings of humanity and the records of historical times, we might ask whether there is any relationship between Bible and Babel in this respect. We must first examine the Sumerian accounts of the kings and sages of the time before the deluge. A comparison with the Biblical lists could prove most enlightening.

A) THE SUMERO-BABYLONIAN ANTEDILUVIAN KINGS

Prior to the age of archaeological excavations, the only basis for our knowledge of the era before the great deluge was represented by what was generally considered the untrustworthy accounts of the Babylonian priest of Bel, Berossus, whose work *Babyloniaka* had been taken over, in part, into the church history of Eusebius of Caesarea.[1] Much to everyone's surprise, the names of the kings that were thus handed down were confirmed by the discovery of Sumerian tablets. Two such tablets are to be found in Oxford in the Weld-Blundell collection. According to their registration numbers they are referred to as W.B. 444 and W.B. 62. More recently there is another list from Uruk (Erech), W 20030,7, which was first discovered in the excavations during the winter 1959-60. Let us examine the evidence.

1) THE ANTEDILUVIAN KINGS ACCORDING TO BEROSSUS: As priest in the principal temple at Babylon Berossus had access to the temple archives. For his work *Babyloniaka,* which he completed around the year 275 B.C., he could thus draw upon ancient written sources. For the regnal dates of the antediluvian kings he uses numbers from astronomy. He counts in terms of *sars,* one *sar* being equivalent to 3600 years. The 10 kings who reigned before the great flood are assigned the following regnal dates:

1. Aloros	10 SARS	=	36000 years
2. Adaparos	3 SARS	=	10800 years
3. Amelon	13 SARS	=	46800 years
4. Ammenon	12 SARS	=	43200 years
5. Megaloros	18 SARS	=	64800 years

1. The work of Berossus is discussed by P. Schnabel, *Berossos und die babylonisch-hellenistische Literatur* (Berlin, 1923) p. 253ff. and 261ff.

6. Daonos	10 SARS	=	36000 years
7. Euedorachos	18 SARS	=	64800 years
8. Amempsinos	10 SARS	=	36000 years
9. Otiartes	8 SARS	=	28800 years
10. Xisuthros	18 SARS	=	64800 years
	120 SARS	=	432000 years

The first and most striking feature to be noted in this list is the fact that Berossus assigns 120 *sars* to the kings who reigned before the flood. In Order III, which also lists the 10 patriarchs who lived before the flood, we read: "And the days of their lives were 120 years" (Gen. 6, 3). Both Bible and Babel reckon the time in terms of the measure 120. There is great significance in that number.

The Babylonian *sar* is an astronomical measure, one *sar* being equivalent to 1 radial degree in the ecliptic. The preposterously high figures are, accordingly, nothing more than the translation of these degrees in seconds. The proper understanding of these numbers presupposes at least an elementary knowledge of astronomy.[1a] But why did Berossus decide upon precisely these numbers? The Babylonian astronomers were particularly interested in observing the course of the sun. They soon discovered that the sun does not rise in the same point of the zodiac every year. The equinox is annually displaced by 50 seconds. This law is now known as the precession of the equinoxes. After a period of 72 years the precession has advanced by one degree, one Babylonian *sar,* or 3600 seconds. What Berossus has done is to divide the celestial equator by one third, assigning 120 degrees to the 10 antediluvian kings. Now if the equinox advances by 50 seconds

1a. For a more explicit treatment of this subject, cf. P. Pavelka: *Das Geheimnis der biblischen und babylonischen Zahlen.* This important work, originally published in Czech, will soon be available in the German translation as given above.

in a single year, it will require 8640 years for the total of 432000 seconds — one third of a polar year. For the polar axis is not stable; it exhibits a rolling, somewhat circular motion, which is responsible for the precession of equinoxes. According to Berossus, one fourth of the polar year is equal to 8640 years, while a whole polar year would take 25920 years.

Berossus' numbers are, accordingly, certainly not the product of pure imagination. Since he had no reliable earthly records for determining the regnal dates of the antediluvian kings, he resorts to celestial symbolism. The significant figures for him involve the number 120, which brings us back to the total age of the Biblical patriarchs.

2) "THE KINGSHIP CAME FROM HEAVEN": The two Weld-Blundell tablets come from the era of Sumerian restoration. They might well have been written in the days of King Utu-hegal of Uruk, who liberated the land of Sumer from the yoke of the Gutaeans. In these two tablets, accordingly, the historical knowledge of around the year 2000 B.C. is summarized and catalogued. It was the great deluge which formed the most significant division point in the course of history: the kings are listed before and after the flood. We are primarily interested in the kings before the flood. This is the text:[2]

"When kingship came down from heaven, it existed first in (the city of) Eridu. In Eridu A-lulim was king; he reigned 28,800 years. Alalgar reigned 36,000 years. That makes two kings with 64,800 years of reign. From Eridu the kingship was brought to (the city of) Bad-tibira. In Bad-tibira En-men-lu-Anna reigned 43,200 years; En-men-gal-Anna reigned 28,800 years; the God Dumu-zi, the Shepherd, reigned 36,000 years. That makes three kings with 108,000 years of reign. From Bad-tibira the kingship came to Larak. In Larak En-sipa-zi-Anna reigned 28,800 years. That makes one king with 28,800 years of reign. From Larak the kingship was brought to Sippar. In Sippar En-men-dur-Anna was king and reigned 21,000 years. That makes one king with 21,000 years of reign. From Sippar the kingship

2. Text in *ANET* 265. First publication: *The Weld-Blundell Collection.* Vol. II: Historical Inscription, containing principally the Chronological Prism W-1B 444, published by S. Langdon (Oxford, 1923).

came to Shuruppak. In Shuruppak Ubar-Tutu was king and reigned 18,600 years. That makes one king with 18,600 years of reign. That makes five cities, and their eight kings reigned 241,000 years (*sic*). Then the flood swept them all off the earth."

For the sake of greater clarity, let us now examine the list independently. Once again we must interpret the high numbers as seconds which we then reproduce in their equivalent degrees as *sars*.

1. Alulim	28800 years	=	8 SARS
2. Alalgar	36000 years	=	10 SARS
3. Enmenlu-Anna	43200 years	=	12 SARS
4. Enmengal-Anna	28800 years	=	8 SARS
5. Dumuzi	36000 years	=	10 SARS
6. Ensipazi-Anna	28800 years	=	8 SARS
7. Enmendur-Anna	21000 years	=	11 SARS
8. Ubar-Tutu	18600 years		
	241200 years	=	67 SARS

This list contains, instead of 10 kings, only 8, and with entirely different regnal dates assigned. Instead of 120 *sars* we have only 67 *sars*. In the Weld-Blundell Collection referred to above (W.B. 444), 67 also occurs as the sum for the antediluvian era. This is no mere accident: 67 is the classical sum number for the Babylonian sexagesimal system, arrived at by the formula: (1 X 60) + (1 X 6) + (1 X 1) = 67. This is precisely the same number that forms the structural principle for the legislation in the Book of Deuteronomy. Moreover, the genealogy of Jesus also follows the same formula: 10 antediluvian and 67 postdiluvian (Luke 3, 23-38). Many other examples of the same symbolism could be adduced. Vera Schneider [2a] has, moreover, demonstrated that these numbers are a reference to musical relationships and thus meant to be an expression of the celestial harmony.

2a. Vera Schneider, *op. cit.*, p. 21.

If we now add the further calculation based on the precession of equinoxes, 50 seconds per year, we arrive at the following total: 241000 ÷ 50 = 4828 years, in our sense of the word, that is, 72 X 67, the product of two typical numbers. Numbers and events that could not be reckoned in terms of human records are thus measured in terms of celestial phenomena and harmony.

3) ANTEDILUVIAN KINGS AND SAGES: The newly discovered tablet from Uruk does not list any regnal dates, but it does give the names of the great sages, the Apkallu, who worked contemporaneously with the kings. This tablet stems from the Seleucid era, a time at which Sumerian science had entered upon a new period of blossom. In order to assert themselves against the Greeks, one of their scholars continued his genealogy back to the beginnings of humanity. This is the sober text: [3]

(In the time of) Ayalu, the King, U'an was Apkallu.
(In the time of) Alalgar, the King, U'anduga was Apkallu.
(In the time of) Ammelu'anna, the King, Enmeduga was Apkallu.
(In the time of) Ammegalanna, the King, Enmegalamma was Apkallu.
(In the time of) Enme'usumgalanna, the King, Enmebulugga was Apkallu.
(In the time of) Dumuzi the Shepherd, the King, Anenlilda was Apkallu.
(In the time of) Enmeduranki, the King, Utu'abzu was Apkallu.
(After the flood) under Enmekar, the King, Nungalpiriggal was Apkallu.

That makes seven kings and seven sages prior to the flood. The Apkallu are the sages known in mythology; in the most ancient times they rose out of the sea, revealing science, social systems, and art to man. Berossus also presents the names of the antediluvian sages in Grecized form.[4] As a result, there was a double genealogy for these primeval times. Not only were the

3. Explained in: *XVIII vorläufiger Bericht über die Ausgrabungen in Uruk-Warka Grabung Winter 1959-60.* Published by H. Lenzen (Berlin, 1962). The tables of the names of the kings received the signature W 20030,7. They were arranged by J. van Dijk, *Die Inschriftenfunde,* pp. 43-49.

4. The names were analyzed by a language scholar, P. Schnabel, *op. cit.* 261-264.

names of the reigning kings recorded in memory, but also the names of those sages who created the culture. At the head of these sages stands the Apkallu U'an. The name is an abbreviation for U'an-adapa, famous in myth as a hero who made his way up to An in the heavens, and was cheated out of the gift of eternal life.[5] The remaining names are all fitting ones for sages of primeval times, for example, Enmeduga, "lord of the good ME (wisdom)," Enmegalamma, "lord of the all-transcending ME,"[6] Ut'abzu, "begotten of Abzu," that is, the god of the primeval sea and primeval wisdom. The seven sages of primeval antiquity lived in the memory of posterity as the bringers of culture.

The names of the kings, in the lists, are essentially in conformity. This points to the existence of a trustworthy tradition, reaching as far back as the 3rd millennium. The regnal dates are somewhat frightening at first sight. Such numbers are simply not within the span of human life. Scholars were tempted to regard the royal lists merely as the product of some scribe's imagination. But we must also note that the five cities named there are among the most ancient in Sumer. The history of the antediluvian period is precisely located. The work must be regarded seriously. The activity of Gilgamesh, which was at first known only from the epic, appears as historical here.

This Sumerian list of the antediluvian kings might well contain some vague recollections of the era prior to the great flood. For the Sumerian historians, the flood represented an uncontestable fact. But for the time before the flood, they cannot produce any normal and usual regnal dates; thus they take refuge in symbolic numbers which betray an astonishing knowledge of astronomy.

---

5. J. van Dijk, *op. cit.* 48.
6. On Apkallu, cf. W. v. Soden, Akkadisches Handwörterbuch.

B) THE BIBLICAL ANTEDILUVIAN PATRIARCHS

When we pass from the Babylonian lists to the Bible, we are faced with the same problem. Here, too, an attempt has been made to bridge the interval between the first man and the deluge in terms of names and numbers. Closer analysis reveals the presence of three such lists.

1) THE CAINITE GENEALOGY: This genealogy was built into the great saga of the first man. We have already examined it with reference to the culture hymn. It is not a mere negative monument to the brutalization of humanity; the genealogy is an echo of the great song of humanity's first accomplishments: the building of cities, the invention of metal-working and music, the formation of humanity into vocational groups. According to the Sumerian tablets, all this was the work of the Apkallus of antiquity. There were seven of them. The Cain genealogy also counts seven members: 1. Adam, 2. Cain, 3. Enoch, 4. Irad, 5. Mehujael, 6. Methushael, 7. Lamech. The Biblical names are obviously not immediate translations of the Sumerian names; but still it is impossible to avoid the impression that there is some relation between the two. Adam and U'anadapa, the sky man, present no difficulty. The fact that the foundation of the city "Enoch" is mentioned immediately points to the five cities described in the tablets, the first of which was Eridu. Is this an echo of the name Irad? The second city was called Bad-tibira. The word *tibira* means metal-worker[7] that is, smith, *qayin*. Methushael, the "man of God," might well coincide with Anen-lil-da, in the middle of whose name we find the name of the god Enlil, which corresponds to El. The last of the wise men Utu'abzu, "begotten of Abzu," could refer to Lamga, the son of Enki, as we have explained above. If these rather vague hints can be substantiated, then the Cainite genealogy represents a reworking of the lists of antediluvian sages. In the saga of the

---

7. S. Langdon, *Weld-Blundell Collect.* Vol. II (Oxford, 1923), 8 Anm. 2.

first man, however, the barren catalogue of names has been transformed into a prophetic appeal. Despite his mighty inventions, man has kept wandering further away from God. The judgment is coming.

2) THE BEGINNINGS OF THE GENEALOGY OF SETH (Gen. 4, 25-26): "And Adam knew his wife again, and she bore a son and called his name Seth, for she said, 'God has substituted (*šāt*) another seed for Abel, whom Cain slew. To Seth also a son was born, and he called his name Enoch; it was then men began to call upon the name of Yahweh." Apart from this last sentence, the text presents no difficulty. The cult of Yahweh is not attributed to Moses' time, but dated back into antiquity. But this cannot possibly be the case. "He who calls upon the name of God" would thus have to be taken as a proper name. It would be practically identical with Mahalalel, "praises of God," which occurs in the parallel genealogy (5, 12). This broken-off genealogy shows how lists can be drawn up on the basis of variant traditions. By inserting the explanation of Seth's name, the whole narrative takes on a salvation-history overtone. The same list is taken up again and worked into a sophisticated system of numbers.

3) THE GREAT GENEALOGY OF SETH (Gen. 5, 1-32): There are ten names in the list. For each name there are three numbers: the first represents the age at which he begot his successor; the second, the number of years he lived after this; and the third, his total span of life. Apparently, this is a confused mixture of arbitrarily chosen figures. But, like the Babylonian numbers, it contains a mysterious system. The names of the ten ancient patriarchs are: "Adam, 2. Seth, 3. Enosh, 4. Kenan, 5. Mahalalel, 6. Jared, 7. Enoch, 8. Methuselah, 9. Lamech, 10. Noah.

If these names are compared with the names of the antediluvian kings, there are some surprising coincidences. Bonkamp has carried out the comparison,[8] and though professional numer-

---

8. B. Bonkamp, *Die Bibel im Lichte der Keilschriftforschung* (1939), p. 111ff.

ologists have attacked it on the grounds that it is not entirely exact, still the following observations do merit our attention. The third patriarch is called Enosh, that is, "man." The third antediluvian king is called Ame-lu-Anna. The middle word *lu* means "man." The translator has thus, occasionally, selected only the leading syllables in constructing his names. Enosh in its complete form would mean "the great man of the sky." Kenan, the "smith," is derived from Enmem-gal-Anna, "the great lord of manual work." The connection between Jared, "descent," and the shepherd Dumuzi, the vegetation god Tammuz, who descended into the underworld every year, presents no difficulty. Particularly obvious is the comparison between Enoch and Enmen-dur-Anna, "the great friend of heaven." Enoch used to walk with God and was taken up into heaven. Enmen-dur-Anna was king of Sippar (*zimbir*), the city of the sun. Enoch's life span is the solar figure, 365 years. The tenth king, according to W.B. 62, was called Ziusudda, abbreviated to Zisudda (Berossos: Sisuthros); that is, "he whose life span is long." In Akkadian, this is translated as *ut-napištim,* "long-living." The Bible has taken only the word "long"; in Ethiopian, the verb *naḥa* still has the essential meaning of "to be long." [9] Thus the name of the hero of the deluge story, Noah, (Nôªāḥ), means "the long (lived)" or the "survivor."

Obviously, Sumerologists will have to examine the names more closely; perhaps some newer tablets will be discovered. But the similarities between Bible and Babel are so clearly recognizable today, that we must assume that the author of this passage in the Bible knew and used the ancient lists. In terms of history, his knowledge does not go beyond that of the lists. He too has only fragmentary knowledge of the venerable patriarchs who lived in the days before the flood. Since he did not also take over the names of the Sumerian cities, his patriarchs cannot be identified with any locality. Nor is their lifespan to be grasped in terms of any normal reckoning of time, simply because

---

9. *ClamB* I (1953), 174.

it is unknown. That is why the Biblical author, just like the author of the lists upon which he bases his account, has taken refuge in a symbolic reckoning of time. Behind all this, we must see not a mere figment of his imagination, but a carefully preserved recollection of the early culture of Mesopotamia, before the great flood.

4) STRUCTURE OF THE TEXT: Order III, which coincides with the "Book of the Toledot of Adam," comprises the text of 5, 1 – 6, 8. The greater part of the text deals with: a. the genealogy from Adam to Noah (5, 1-32); in terms of structure, however, we must include b. the account of the giants (6, 1-4) and c. the extirpation of humanity (6, 5-8) in Order III. Dividing the text, once again, in terms of narrative (N), introduction (I), and direct speech (S), we arrive at the following outline:

	N	I	S		
A.	354	1	10	=	365
B.	49	2	13	=	64
C.	30	2	20	=	52
	433 +	5 +	43	=	481

The most surprising element in this formula is the fact that the genealogy follows the solar number 365. The incorporated S section (direct speech in 5, 29) reduces the solar year to a complete lunar year of 354 day-words. If we also examine the "open" and "closed" sections in the manuscript, the total number divides into 240 "open" + 241 "closed" sections; this is a division based on even-odd, masculine-feminine. The joining word is to be found in the introduction to the speech section, *lemor* (5, 29); this gives the division 240 + *lemor* + 240 = 480 + "speech." In addition to the solar and lunar years we thus have the further symbolism of the epochal number 480, which determines subsequent Biblical chronology.

The text of the genealogy, with its regular repetition, has a very monotonous effect. A further interesting observation is to be derived from examining the vocabulary in terms of the "basic words" and their repetition in the text. Once again, the numbers are symbolic. The author is working with a basic vocabulary of precisely 110 words. Of these, 22 are verbs and 32 are nouns. The text has been arranged and controlled down to the least word and particle. If we change or omit a single word, we destroy not only the sentence in which it stands, but also, so to speak, the harmony of the world and the word.

5) STRUCTURE OF THE NUMBERS: The list distinguishes between a. age at begetting, b. subsequent years, c. total age. In the case of Noah, the list gives only the age at begetting, a very important element for consideration. First we must examine the three lists themselves, and then attempt to interpret them with the aid of Babylonian astronomy:

	BEGOT AT AGE	SUBSEQUENT YEARS	TOTAL
1. Adam	130	800	930
2. Seth	105	807	912
3. Enosh	90	815	905
4. Kenan	70	840	910
5. Mahalalel	65	830	895
6. Jared	162	800	962
7. Enoch	65	300	365
8. Methuselah	187	782	969
9. Lamech	182	595	777
10. Noah	500	—	—
	1556	6569	7625

In terms of simple numbers, we notice that the age of generation, in the first five members, falls from 130 to 65. The unit of five is predominant. This gives the following intervals: 25:15:10:5. In the second half, the figures increase. The interval between Jared and Methuselah is 25, for Lamech, 20; both numbers multiplied together give 500, Noah's number. Adam's generation age is twice 65, the generation age of Enoch. Once again we are in the presence of solar symbolism. Enoch's life is built up on the sun. 365 is his total age; divided, this gives 300 as the years after generation and 65 as the generation age. Enoch, the sacred seventh in the series, thus represents the solar symbol as the key for deciphering the mystery hidden in the construction of the whole series of generations.[10]

Compared to the Babylonian lists, Enoch's number refers to the sun city of Sippar. Solar symbolism was also known in Egypt. From the time of the heretical Pharaoh Ikhnaton, we have representations of the solar disk, emanating its rays. At the end of these rays we find the ringed cross as the hieroglyph of life. This means that sun and life were viewed as one unity. Now, a genealogy is designed to catalogue the transmission of life. Thus, the connection with generation and solar numbers seems very significant.

a) TOTAL AGE: Pavelka's as yet unpublished book has demonstrated that all the lists – Masorah, Samaritanus, Septuagint, Flavius Josephus, and the Babylonian – can all be reduced to the same astronomical principles. The key to the whole interpretation is furnished by the discovery of the precession of equinoxes. In the Babylonian tables the measure of *sar* is interpreted as 60 minutes and 3600 seconds. But where is the key in the 9 "total ages"?

The number for Enoch, 365 "years," is "as clear as the sun." In the 6 other cases it is the number 900 that serves as the base. And this is the key to understanding the entire list. 900 is one fourth of a *sar* (4 X 900 = 3600). This is a clear point of reference to the Babylonian system of reckoning. Instead of reckoning in terms of entire *sars*, the Biblical author uses quarter-*sars*. In six cases he increases the measure, and in two cases he reduces

10. J. Schildenberger, *Vom Geheimnis des Gotteswortes* (Heidelberg, 1950), p. 267ff.

it. Omitting these additions and reductions, we arrive at the following figures for the first 4 patriarchs:

(4 X 900) + 30 + 12 + 5 + 10 = 3600 + 57 = *1 SAR* + 57.
The other 4 patriarchs apart from Enoch:
(4 X 900) + (62 + 69) – (5 + 123) = (4 X 900) + 131 – 128 = 3600 + 3 = *1 SAR* + 3.

The sum total of both groups is (2 X 3600) + 57 + 3 = 7200 + 60. The organization of the list is thus explained by the Babylonian division of 1 *sar* into 60 minutes or 3600 seconds. The number of seconds determines the hundreds, while the tens and units express the value of the minutes. Reducing the 7200 seconds to minutes, we arrive at the number 120 minutes or "years." We are thus once again confronted with the word of God which stands as introduction and leitmotiv for the whole of Order III: "No longer abide my spirit in man; for he is only flesh! the days of his life shall be a hundred and twenty years" (6, 3). Since Enoch, with the solar number 365, is carried off into heaven (5, 22), he is not included in the toledot listing. But for the others the number 120 is the key. It follows that the list and the subsequent text do actually form a definite and ordered unit.

b) AGE OF GENERATION: Here once again we can discover a similar and very simple key to the interpretation. The simpler it is, the more convincing it must necessarily appear. First of all we must take out the 6 units higher than 0, thus: 5 + 5 + 2 + 5 +7 + 2 = 26. The fundamental number underlying the whole text of the list is thus the numerical value of the name YHWH (26). The same figure is what determines the age at generation assigned to Adam (130 = 5 X 26): Eve, too, was able to give birth to the first man only "with the help of YHWH" (4, 1). In the case of Mahalalel and Enoch the number for Adam is divided in two (65 + 65 = 130). Now, we read of Enosh that at that time men began to call upon the name of YHWH (4, 26). It would thus appear justifiable for us to use, in the genealogy, not the number of Enoch (65), but rather that of

Enosh (90). This gives the following totals: 1440 + 26 (YHWH) + 90 (Enosh).

In the total ages, it is the seconds that are significant. Here perhaps the minutes might be considered as an explanation of the number 1440. The number of hours this figure represents is a significant one: $1440 \div 60 = 24$ hours $= 1$ day. The genealogical list of the ages at which the patriarchs begot their sons has been cast into the measure of a single day!

c) HORIZONTAL TOTALS: We can now raise the further question as to why it was precisely these numbers for generation, subsequent years, and total age that were chosen in preference to any others. From what has already been said it must be clear that there is some structural formula at work. This applies most obviously to the final totals, but it might well have influenced the other totals as well. One solution to the problem involves reducing the horizontal totals into their component numbers and then totaling these, thus: Enoch's number 365 is composed of $3 + 6 + 5 = 14$, etc.

In Order III, in the case of Noah, the 450 subsequent years and the total age of 950 years are not given, and thus is for a very definite purpose. The numbers are to be found only in the similar monotonous formula at the conclusion of the deluge narrative (9, 28). If we figure them into the total horizontal sums, then the sum total of all 30 figures gives the solar number 365. The numerical scheme thus produces the exact same fundamental value as the words in the genealogy. The "Book of the Toledot of Adam" is thus under the sign of the sun whose rays, in their various forms and fashions, determine the life and ways of mankind.

C) RIPE FOR DECLINE

Order III contains not only the great genealogy of the descendants of Adam, but also the judgment on the sons of God and the giants, as well as God's resolve to extirpate humanity. It is precisely these epic texts that lend the true theological meaning to the monotonous genealogy. The structure has already been discussed; we can now proceed to the text itself, and a brief explanation.

1. *Sons of God and Giants* (6, 1-4)

1 It happened,
when man began to increase upon earth,
and daughters were born to them,
2 the sons of God looked upon the daughters of men;
for they were most comely,
and they took them for wives,
whomever they wished.
3 *Then spoke YHWH:*
No longer abide my spirit in man;
for he is only flesh!
the days of his life shall be a hundred and twenty years!
4 Giants were in those days upon earth,
and then it also happened
that the sons of God went in to the daughters of men
and they bore them children.
These are the heroes of olden times,
men of name.

2. *Extirpation of Humanity* (6, 5-7)

5 And YHWH saw
that the wickedness of man upon earth had multiplied,
and all the thinking and purpose of his heart was only evil, all the days.

6 YHWH repented
that he had made man upon earth,
and he was sad in his heart.
7 *And YHWH spoke:*
I shall blot out man whom I made
from the surface of the earth,
man together with cattle,
creeping things and the birds of the heaven as well;
for I repent that I ever made them.
8 But Noah found favor in YHWH's eyes.

In terms of their literary genre, these two songs go together, because both of them refer to a sentence of annihilation upon man because of his corruption. While the second song unmistakably refers to the wickedness of the human heart as the cause for the divine judgment, the first song has taken up some mythological material, which, in the hand of the Biblical author, has been adapted to an eminently theological message.

Some authors have attempted to understand the sons of God as the posterity of the pious Seth, and the daughters of man as the descendants of the wicked Cain. It would thus be the haphazard commingling of the two that gave rise to a godless generation which deserved to be blotted out from the face of the earth. But this interpretation makes us wonder why the pious sons of Seth were also annihilated along with the godless.

Others have attempted to interpret it in terms of myth. The epics of Ugarit speak of the 70 sons of El, the sons of the god.[11] This conception is not alien to the Bible, although it is purged in monotheistic terms. The union of these sons of God and the daughters of man produced supermen, giants. The idea of giants is a widely spread belief, and yet we all know that there never were any giants.

We do the text full justice if we interpret giants as giants and

---

11. W. Herrmann, "Die Gottesöhue," *ZRelGg.* 12 (1960), 242-251, Ugaritic material collected.

saga as saga. But the saga is to serve a salvation-history interpretation. In the middle of the strophe we read: "Abide not my spirit any longer in man; for he is but flesh." [12] It is precisely in the more than human dimensions of the giants that the extravagance of human corruption is manifest.

But since the flood narrative, as we shall later see, points back to some historical event in the land between the two rivers, it is most probable that we can explain the sons of God and heroes in terms of the social conditions of this early age. The heroic epoch of ancient times lived on, in later generations, as a magnificent era of mighty deeds, but also as a brutal age. The sons of God could thus refer to city-state kings,[13] who misused their power, choosing wives from the daughters of their people according to their personal whim. Such disregard for law and justice must have called down God's vengeance upon them. This interpretation gives the proper *Sitz im Leben,* the early days of civilization in southern Mesopotamia.

---

12. N. H. Tur-Sinai, "The Riddle of Gen. 1-4," *ET* 71 (1960), 348-350, corrects the text to read: "no longer abide Noah among mankind," instead of "no longer abide my spirit."

13. M. G. Kline, "Divine Kingship and Gen. 6, 1-4," *WTJ* 24 (1962), 187-204.

SECTION THREE

ORIGIN OF PEOPLES

IN terms of world history and salvation history, Noah stands at a turning point in the story of humanity. He is the last figure in the genealogy of the antediluvian patriarchs, and the first great patriarch after the flood, after Adam the second ancestor of humanity. From him, all peoples, tribes, tongues, and nations are derived. In terms of salvation history, he opens the series of the great prophets, who set up a cry for penance in the midst of a graceless age, who announced the imminence of divine judgment and were saved from the catastrophe. Noah is the servant of God through whom life and salvation were preserved for times to come. For Biblical theology, Noah is and remains the hero of the deluge, *the* type of salvation history. The first stage of humanity ends in God's sentence of annihilation. Since the loss of Paradise, man had not been walking the path that leads to God; he had become "flesh," and thus ripe to be returned to the "dust" from which he had been taken. This would have sealed the fate of human history. But even in the midst of judgment, there is a revelation of salvation, just as the sentence that expelled our first parents from Paradise also contained the Proto-evangelium of the victory over the serpent. This sets the basic tone for the history that follows the deluge. The Bible does not subscribe to a naive faith in human progress, but neither does it exhibit a pessimism that has grown tired of life. History is the arena for God and man. From the outset it is clear that, despite all catastrophes, God will be the victor. Biblical prehistory presses on to the third great ancestor of humanity, the patriarch Abraham, the father of the faithful. The epoch from Noah to Abraham thus forms a compact interval, a span of time in which primitive humanity develops to the stage of historically recognizable peoples. There are three points to be considered: the deluge, the table of nations, and the tower of Babel. Just like the narrative of the days before the deluge, the account concludes with a genealogy, which stops with Abraham. What follows Abraham is no longer prehistory, but the early history of Israel. The task that faces us now is to examine the Biblical texts which are available to us as historical sources, in terms of their literary form and genre, in terms of their origin and transmission, and finally in terms of their historical and theological value.

CHAPTER XXII

THE BIBLICAL DELUGE NARRATIVE

A) TEXT AND NUMBER SYMBOLISM:

For determining the selection and limits of the text, our clearest signpost is the toledot inscription. In the middle of chapter 6 – and here we can see how arbitrary our modern division by chapters really is – stands the title: "These are the toledot of Noah" (6, 9). Chapter 10 begins with the title: "Toledot of the sons of Noah" (10, 1), which is introduced by the narrative of Noah's drunkenness (9, 18-28).

But this rather lengthy bloc is, in the Leningrad manuscript, divided into three Orders. Whether the division is arbitrary or imposed by some structural formula will soon enough be clear. Order IV (Gen 6, 9 – 7, 24) proceeds from the beginning to the climax of the great deluge: "The waters rose 15 cubits above the highest mountains" (7, 20) . . . "and all flesh died away" (22). Mankind had once again become clay. Only Noah remained alive, together with those who were with him in the ark. In terms of duration, the deluge reached its high-water mark 150 days after the beginning. In addition to these more general data, we also note that the precise dating for the beginning of the flood is the 17th day of the 2nd month of the 600th year of Noah's life.

Order V (8, 1-14) describes the sending out of the birds, the subsiding of the flood waters, and the complete drying of the earth. The catastrophe ended on the 27th day of the 2nd month of the 601st year of Noah's life. But how was life upon earth to survive? The answer is provided in Order VI (8, 15 – 9, 17) which proclaims the law for the postdiluvian era. Cosmos and humanity are newly received into the covenant and blessing of God.

The deluge narrative might be termed a powerful trilogy. Despite the epic restraint of the narrative, the story means to recount much more than a mere natural catastrophe. The incorporated speech sections are clearly reminiscent of a mystery play. Just as the later Greek drama attempts a meaningful and symbolic interpretation of man on earth, so the author of this narrative is clearly influenced by a theological point of view. This alone is evidence enough to support the claim that the deluge narrative is more than simply an account of a great flood catastrophe from the dim dawning of human history.

Like the Babylonian deluge accounts, which we shall also have to examine in some detail, the Biblical deluge account is not an isolated composition. In order to facilitate this comparison, we must briefly outline the peculiarities of the Biblical version. We shall not be involved here with divisions in terms of source strata in the way that most Pentateuchal criticism proceeds. In the Pentateuch Synopsis developed by Otto Eissfeldt, the deluge narrative is divided into two strains, "Priestly tradition" (P) and "Jahwist" (J). In this scheme the division often occurs in the middle of a verse. The attempt to rediscover the sources and origins of the text is certainly more than justified, but, in my opinion, this is a step that must be taken only after the present-day form of the text has first been thoroughly examined in terms of its structural principles. Thus we must call attention to a few remarks that will need fuller treatment in a more explicit commentary. But the brief description of our investigations possible within the framework of our present purposes will surely suffice to demonstrate the artistic and symbolic structural unity of the Biblical deluge narrative.

I) STRUCTURE OF THE TEXT

As has been the practice in the other textual analyses, we must first determine how many words are assigned to narrative (N), introduction (I), and direct speech (S). And once again we must have recourse to a tabular presentation. The direct speech sections are divided accordingly as they are ascribed to YHWH (YW) or to Elohim (EL).

ORDER IV (6, 9 – 7, 24)	N	I	YH	EL
Title 6, 9a	3			
Introduction 6, 9b-12	41			
Building the Ark 6, 13-21		3		133
"And Noah did . . ." 6, 22	9			
Entry into the Ark 7, 1-4		3	65	
"And Noah did . . ." 7, 5	6			
Beginning of the flood 7, 6-16	153			
Climax 7, 17-24	105			
TOTALS	317	6	65	133

ORDER V (8, 1-14)	N
Sending out the birds	192

ORDER VI (8, 15 – 9, 17)

Exit from the Ark 8, 15-17		5		30
"And Noah went out" 8, 18-19	21			
Erection of altar, 8, 20-22	19	4	37	
Blessing and Law 9, 1-7		8		82
Covenant 9, 8-11		8		44
Rainbow 9, 12-16		2		72
Sign of Covenant 9, 17		4		12
TOTALS	40	31	37	240

SUM TOTALS

Order IV	317	6	65	133	
Order V	192				
Order VI	40	31	37	240	
TOTALS	549 +	37 +	102 +	373 =	1061

EXPLANATION OF THE TABLE

A) TOTAL SUMS: If we group the 1061 words total sum as the sum of the toledot inscription plus the remaining words we reach the formula III Toledot + 1058. Now the numerical value of the name of Noah is 58 ($n + ḥ = 50 + 8$). Hence the remarkable formula: 1000 + Noah, an unforgettable aid to memory.

B) SPEECH SECTIONS: YHWH and Elohim together speak a total of 102 + 373 = 475 words. In Order VI Elohim alone has 240 words, precisely one half of the epochal number 480. Subtracting these from the total sum, we get the number 475 – 240 = 235, that is, the number that serves as guide to harmonizing the solar and lunar calendars. Of these words, in Order IV, 65 are ascribed to YHWH, that is, the number of words required to make up the symbolic value of the name ADONAY ($1 + 4 + 50 + 10 = 65$). The long speech of Elohim with the command to build the ark forms an especially artistic piece of work (6, 13-21). The ark of salvation is, so to speak, built to the measure of God himself. The text 15b-16 counts precisely the numerical value of the name of YHWH, 26 words. The preceding introductory text (13b-15a) counts 32 words, both of them together giving the above mentioned numerical value of the name of Noah ($32 + 26$), which also corresponds to the value of the saving "glory of God" (*kebôd YHWH* $= 32 + 26 = 58$). The proclamation of the flood, the promise of the covenant, and the taking of the animals into the ark (17-21) follow the numbers symbolic of Abraham's call: Abraham left Ur of the Chaldeans at the age of 75.

c) SENTENCE CONSTRUCTION: If we give our attention now to a very sober, and for that very reason all the more convincing, grammatical consideration, we find yet another key to the solution of the interior structure of the text. The poet writes in sentences of the 1st, 2nd, and 3rd person. For the Elohim speeches we can draw up the following divisions: (6, 13-21) 39 1st + ($47 + 4 + 26$) 2nd + 17 3rd = 133. The text about the ark with the command "Build yourself . . ." and its 4 words and the construction of the ark with its 26 words have been isolated from the remainder of the text. What we encounter here are clear and definitely set numerical motifs. The first person address of Elohim follows the confessional formula: "YHWH the ONE" ($26 + 13 = 39$). The second person without the Ark exhibits the number 47, which, as we shall soon see, serves as the calendar for the deluge. The Ark and the third person taken together give the same number: $4 + 26 + 17 = 47$!

There are other remarkable individual points to be observed as well. The words describing the rainbow follow the cosmic number 72. The number 47 is repeated as a reference to the chronology of the deluge. This information provides the basis for some individual points of clarification for the most difficult chapter. We have hit upon a new and unexpected source of understanding both the narrative and the speech.

II) THE DELUGE CALENDER

1) THE FUNDAMENTAL EPIC OUTLINE: The basic timetable for the deluge involves this outline: "7 more days" (7, 4), then "40 days of flooding" (7, 12, 17; 8, 6), and finally "7 days after the flood" (8, 10, 12). These are typical and very general examples of numerical symbolism. God's command and God's blessing follow the sacred number 7, while the duration of the flood corresponds to the very frequently used and at all events very general number symbolic of a generation, 40. These figures are certainly not sufficient data for reconstructing the actual temporal duration of the flooding. There is an epic dimension here. But what is the relationship between this dimension and the calendar of the deluge?

2) DELUGE CALENDAR: The flood begins on the 17th day of the 2nd month of the 600th year of Noah's life (7, 11), and rises for a period of 150 days (7, 24; 8, 3). On the 17th day of the 7th month the Ark comes to rest on the mountains of Ararat (8, 4); on the 1st day of the 10th month the peaks of the mountains were visible; on the 1st day of the 1st month of the 601st year of Noah's life the waters subsided (8, 13) and on the 27th day of the 2nd month of the 601st year the earth was once more dry (8, 14).

A) LUNAR OR SOLAR YEAR? Many scholars have argued – and in the second edition of this book I took the same position – that the calendar of the deluge is an attempt to harmonize the lunar and solar calendar. The claim was, in fact, that the author was originally dealing with a lunar year of 354/55 days, which he equated to a solar year of 365 days by the addition of 10 days.

Accordingly, the period from the 17th day of the 2nd month, 600 to the 17th day of the 2nd month, 601, is a lunar year; and continued to the 27th day of the 2nd month, 601, it becomes a solar year. But a more accurate calculation shows that this hypothesis is inadequate.

The author places particular emphasis on the number 150, which he uses twice in the account: 150 days for the flood's rising (7, 24) and after 150 days the highwater mark (8, 3). The second reference to the "end of 150 days" is precisely fixed by a calendar reference: (17th day, 6th month). Thus from the 17th day, 2nd month, to the 17th day, 7th month, 150 days must have passed. If we suppose this calculation to be based on the lunar calendar with alternating months of 29 and 30 days, we reach the number 147 days. Now in the actual lunar calendar which we can verify for Babylonian usage the schematic sequence of 29-30 days was not at all a fixed rule. It was quite possible for there to be as many as 3 months in a row with 30 days each.[1] But even this does not give the proper total. To reach the sum required, we should have to postulate a calendar which contained nothing but months of 30 days each. This leads us to the hypothesis that the deluge calendar must be based on a solar year, or more precisely a jubilee solar year, traces of which we have also discovered in the creation narrative. There is thus nothing new about the solution.

B) THE QUARTERS OF THE JUBILEE CALENDER. The jubilee calendar reckoned primarily in months of 30 days each; the peculiarity of this calendar, however, is the fact that it intercalates a "day of remembrance" or a "memorial day" in each of the four quarters so that the four quarters each number 91 days and the whole year thus counts 364 days. The year invariably begins on a Wednesday, since it was on this the fourth day that the great luminaries of the heavens were first created as "signs for days and seasons

1. R. A. Parker and W. H. Dubberstein, *Babylonian Chronology*, Brown University Studies XIX (1956), 25ff.

and feasts." The rhythm of the sabbath days was thus never disturbed.

Now the great flood began on the 17th day of the 2nd month; this is the day that serves as point of departure for the 150 days. The text itself stresses this fact: "On that very same day" (7, 13). Counting from that date, and allowing 30 days to the month, we arrive at the 16th day of the 7th month as the 150th day; on the following day, the 17th day of the 7th month, the ark came to rest upon the Mount Ararat. This interval of time cuts across three distinct quarters of the jubilee calendar; this means that three intercalary days are still to be reckoned. This might be the meaning of a sentence in the text that has been the subject of a variety of unsatisfactory interpretations: "And YHWH closed his space (*ba ʿadô*)." The 150 days are clearly expressed, but really it is the 153 that are understood. According to the jubilee calendar, the 16th day of the 7th month was a Friday, the day of preparation. The 17th day was thus a Sabbath, the day on which the ark "rested."

These calendar data are also clearly stamped onto the structure of the text. The narrative of the beginning of the flood (7, 6-16b) counts 150 words, and these are raised to 153 words by the addition of the text quoted above, "and YHWH closed his space."

The fact that the author means to lay special stress on the quarters of the jubilee calendar also follows from the rest of the dates he mentions. On the 1st day of the 10th month, 600, begins the 4th quarter, and on the 1st day of the 1st month, 601, begins the 1st quarter of the new year. Each of the two dates, one as the beginning of the year and the other as the beginning of a quarter within the year, falls on a Wednesday.

c) 2,17,600 AS THE BEGINNING OF THE FLOOD. The ancient epic outline exhibits the numbers 40 and 7, together, 47. This is the very number that has been taken as the point of departure for the calendar reckoning. For, presupposing that it is a jubilee year, there are precisely 30 + 17 = 47 days from 1, 1 to 2, 17. If we now look ahead from this date and ask how many days of the year 600 (of Noah's life) are assigned to the flood, we come across the dating 1, 1 at the beginning of the 601st year. Including this first day of the new year in the total sum, the interval from 2, 17 to 1, 1 comprises exactly 318 days, the familiar numerical value of the moonlight year. We might say that the author of the calendar has subtracted one full moonlight year from the Jubilee year, in order to arrive at the date for the beginning of the deluge. In this connection 17 is also a very obvious lunar number: it is composed of 14 days of moonlight and 3 days of dark moon.

Passing now from the calendar to the text again, it is once again obvious that the text has been worked out on the basis of the calendar. In answering the question of how many days of the year are assigned to the flood we arrive at the value 318. But this calculation includes the dating formula 1, 1, 601. If we leave out this new year's day, we arrive at 317 days for the duration of the deluge. Now this is a familiar number from the above treatment, in Order IV. The speech sections in Order IV exhibit this total: 65 + 133 = 198. If we now include the 47 days which we have subtracted from the total year, that is, if we begin to count from 1, 1, 600, the 198th day coincides with the 150th day of the flood. But this can happen only in the jubilee calendar. The system is, in itself, absolutely clear and simple. Provided only that we have made one very essential discovery: the author is determined to emphasize the jubilee calender in practically every single line. This preoccupation is even more evident from a consideration of the sums of the individual years.

D) SUMS OF THE YEARS. Why is the end of the flood assigned as the date 2, 27, 601? In order to establish a comparison with the solar year? No. It is, rather, simply one more attempt to stress the rhythm of the jubilee calendar. If we add the days together: 317 old year + 56 new year (N.B. up to 2, 26, inclusive) = 373, that is, the sum of the Elohim speeches in all three Orders. Now we also have to include the intercalary day in this first quarter of 601, and together with it the date of 2, 27, that is, two intercalary days in a row, so that from 2, 17, 600 to 2, 27, 601 we must count a total of 375 days. But what is the meaning of this final total? The key to the solution is hidden in the text itself: "The flood covered the highest mountains, fifteen cubits deep." Applied to the total number, this gives the following figure: 360 + 15, that is, a cyclical lunar year of 360 days and 15 intercalary days. But where are these additional days to be found? In the quarterly intercalary days of the year 600 and the first quartal day of the year 601, to which must be added the 10 days from the 17th to the 27th of the 2nd month, 601.

The prolongation of the flood into the year 601 has, in my opinion, one obvious purpose: it is meant to further stress the name of the hero of the flood story. For the new year contains the intercalary day plus 57 (including 2, 27) for a total of 58, the numerical value of the name of Noah.

E) THE MEANING OF THE CALENDAR. We have already pointed out the fact that reference to the construction of the ark (6, 15b-16) contains 26 words, a reference to the sacred name of YHWH. The ark is thus bound up with the symbolism of the divine name. The same name is also the structural principle beneath the jubilee calendar. The purpose here is to emphasize the inviolable and inalienable holiness of the Sabbath. By the very fact that the matrix of the Jubilee Year has been imposed upon the epic outline, the Ancient Near Eastern deluge narrative has taken on a true theological depth. The deluge is not simply something that took place in the dim dawn of history; it is present and at work today. In this deluge only the just are saved, those who take refuge in the ark, that is, in YHWH. Or to put it more simply, only the just man who keeps the Sabbath can hope for salvation.

YHWH and Sabbath are thus the true ark into which our narrative, in its every sentence and outline, warns mankind to seek refuge. It is in this connection that we must briefly allude to the Rabbinical principle of synchronization: "There is, in the Bible, no earlier and no later." It is precisely in terms of this very sober and sterile sounding calendar outline that the diachronistic and historical perspective is, as it were, elevated to the sphere of the synchronistic and the individuality of one historical fact is raised to the level of integral awareness of a constantly new present reality.[2]

In this we have uncovered something of far-reaching importance not only for the proper understanding of the deluge narrative, but for our interpretation of all prehistory as a whole. The scholar who approaches these narratives simply in terms of historical sources and strata, approaches the sacred text with a sharp but very false perspective. What has gone before in the text is certainly most helpful, since it is the only avenue to proper appreciation of what is new in the text's point of view and message, taken as a whole. But the earlier state of the text is and remains largely something unknown, while the total point of view leads us deep into the mysteries of Biblical theology. The primary accent here is not upon the historical event – historicity is presupposed as self-evident – but the primary accent is on the kerygma, the constantly renewed appeal to the present generation.

III) THE YEAR OF THE FLOOD

The sum of the generation years from Adam to Noah is 1556 years. Now Noah begot his son at the age of 500 years, while the flood began in the 600th year. This would make the year of the deluge the 1656th year. What is behind this number?

As in the interpretation of the genealogies of the Adamites, we must once again turn to the painstaking investigations of P. Pavelka, which are as yet unpublished. The key to the proper understanding is once again supplied by the calculation of the equinox. We must repeat the observation that according to the

---

2. Cf. W. Schlepper, Rezension zu Fr. Weinreb: "Der göttliche Bauplan der Welt," and "Die Rolle Esther," *Theologie und Philosophie* 45 (1970), 595-600.

Babylonian calculation, the equinox advances by 50 seconds every year. In 72 years this precession would total 1 full degree. Applying these data to the date of the flood, we have the following figures: $1656 \div 72 = 23$; that is, from Adam to the year of the flood the precession of equinoxes has advanced to the 23rd degree.

This might, in fact, well prove to be a most opportune key to solving the more general problem of all Biblical chronology. The chronology has been constructed upon an outline which has been known from later history as the Pythagorean Tetraktys, but can be clearly identified with ancient Babylonian origins. If we write the digits from 1 to 10 in a pyramid arrangement as follows:

1
2 – 3
4 – *5* – 6
7 – 8 – 9 – *10*

the three apex numerals and the middle numeral together add up to the sum of 23; the sum of the other numbers (the hexagon that remains) is 32, and the sum of the total is 55. The perfection of this number 55 has been extensively discussed as early as Philo.[3] If the 23rd degree has been achieved in the time of the deluge, where are we to find the remaining 32 degrees? The solution is quite simple. We need only examine the numbers that appear in the Biblical text. The narrative after the deluge begins with the quite unmistakable notice: "In the 2nd year after the flood" (Gen 11, 10). Following a brief schematic outline of the remaining text, which is dominated by symbolic numbers, we obtain the following results:

---

3. Philo von Alexandria, *Die Werke im deutschen Ubersetzung*, Vol. I (2nd ed.) Berlin, 1962: Leben Mosis, Book II (III), par. 79ff.

After the flood, Gen 11, 30	II
Generations from Arpachshad to Terah, Gen 10- 11	290
Generation of Abraham, Gen 17	100
Generation of Isaac, Gen 25, 20	40
Jacob into Egypt, Gen 47, 18	130
Israel in Egypt, Gen 15, 13	400
Exodus to the Building of the Temple, 1 Kg 6, 1	480
	II + 1440

The time from the flood up to the building of the Temple thus comprises four solar periods (4 X 360 = 1440) or, in terms of the precession of equinoxes, 20 degrees (20 X 72 = 1440).

If we now take up the summary figure of 480, from the Exodus to the building of the Temple and continue the calculations down to the destruction of the Solomonic Temple (and these general numbers are all given in more specific form in the Book of Judges), we find, for the Era of the Judges, 18 figures (cf. Judges 10, 8), and for the Kings of Judah, 21, for a combined total of 39. The figures are as follows:

Judges	I + 392
Kings	469
	I + 861

Combining these two totals we arrive at the following calculation:

1. First calculation	II + 1440 =	1442
2. Second calculation	I + 861 =	862
Total		2304 = 32 X 72

The final total for the time after the flood thus yields the postulated value of 32 degrees in the precession of the equinox. The only conclusion from this evidence is that the numbers of Genesis, and the deluge narrative in particular, presuppose the destruction of the Solomonic Temple. The time from Adam to the destruction of the Temple is composed on the system of the "Pythagorean Tetraktys," which is to be regarded as the sum of all perfection and thereby expressing the perfect compact cycle of historical epic.

This knowledge is of the greatest importance for the interpretation of the Biblical text. There can be no doubt as to the fact that ancient traditional material was used. There are Babylonian deluge narratives still extant for the flood story. But this numerical formula cannot be seen simply as an outline imposed by later redaction. The number system thoroughly permeates the very structure of the text, whether it is a question of the Jahwistic or Elohistic strata, or even the Priestly tradition. Thus we are justified in concluding that the so-called final editors were not only editors, but actually authors engaged in the more primary work of forming and molding the text. The historical point of origin, that is, the *Sitz im Leben* and thus the era and milieu in which the present-day text was actually formed, is thus to be sought in the era after the destruction of the Solomonic Temple. We are, moreover, in Babylonia, the land of precise celestial observation. The Prophet Ezekiel had sketched the new outline for the Temple. His era and his circle of followers might well be responsible also for the new holy year of jubilee which is so clearly stamped upon the Biblical text.

The above discussion has already touched upon the most essential features of the interpretation of the deluge narrative. Epic tradition and kerygmatic re-presentation (adaptation to the contemporary situation) are inextricably bound up together. Since we cannot reproduce the entire text, we shall be content with Order IV, which contains the narrative of the deluge itself, and thus the two narrative sections in which the numerical structure is especially clear and evident. The entry into the ark (7, 6-16) follows the number 153, which is the number of water and fish (cf. John 21, 11). Mathematically, it is the sum of arithmetic series 1-17; and, in point of fact, this section numbers precisely 17 verbs. In the account of the flood itself (7, 17-24), with its 105 words, we are once more confronted with the total of the basic vocabulary of the creation narrative. Mathematically, 105 is the sum of the arithmetic series 1-14.

ENTRY INTO THE ARK (7, 6-16):

6 *And Noah was a son of 600 years*
then came the deluge over the land;
7 *and Noah went into the ark away from the flood waters,*
and his sons, his wife and the wives of his sons with him.
8 *Of the clean animals and of the animals that are not clean,*
of the birds and everything that creeps on the earth,
9 *there came two and two into the ark to Noah,*
male and female
just as Elohim had commanded Noah.
10 *After 7 days it happened*
there came the deluge over the land.
11 *In the year 600 of the life of Noah,*
in the 11th month, on the 17th day of the month,
on precisely this day
broke open all the springs of the great primordial deep
and the floodgates of the heaven were opened.
12 *and rain was for 40 days and 40 nights upon earth,*
13 *On precisely this day went Noah,*
Shem, Ham, and Japheth, the sons of Noah,
Noah's wife and the three wives of his sons with him,
into the ark.
14 *They and all living things according to their kind*
and all the cattle according to its kind,

and all the beasts that creep upon the earth according
to their kind,
and all the flying creatures according to their kind,
all the birds, and all winged creatures,
15 *and they came to Noah into the ark*
two and two from all flesh
in which there is the breath of life,
16 *and those who came came from all flesh*
male and female,
just as Elohim had commanded him.
And Yahweh shut up after him (153 *words*).

THE DELUGE (7, 17-24):

17 *And the flood was* 40 *days upon the earth,*
and the waters swelled and raised the ark
and they were high above the earth.
18 *And the waters swelled exceedingly strong upon the earth,*
and the ark floated along on the surface of the waters.
19 *And the waters rose higher, high over all the earth,*
and they covered all the highest mountains
that are under the sky,
20 15 *cubits above them rose the waters,*
and they covered the mountains.
21 *Then there died all flesh, everything that moves*
upon earth,
all birds, cattle and wild beasts,
all that crawls upon the earth, and all men,
22 *everything that lives through the breath of air in its nose,*
everything that lives on dry land – they all died.
23 *Thus did he blot out all creatures upon the surface*
of the earth,
men and cattle, creeping animals and birds of the heaven,
they were all blotted out from the earth,
and Noah alone was left

and those with him in the ark.
24 But the waters continued to rise on earth 150 days (105 words).

B) INTERPRETATION OF THE DELUGE NARRATIVE:

The most important information for understanding the deluge narrative has already been supplied by the sober appraisal of the numbers. The calendar datings have transformed the epic event into a new and contantly repeated present. The deluge is not something that took place only once: the deluge is an abiding reality. Only the *saddîq*, the just man, will be saved, the man who takes refuge in the ark of faith in YHWH. It is this very point of view which already suggests the symbolism of seeing synagogue and Church after it as a further embodiment of the saving ark. The epic text itself, the foundation for the whole process, can, moreover, still be verified in the culture history of ancient Mesopotamia.

The deluge narrative exhibits an unexpected internal harmony and compactness, not only in terms of the numerical symbolism, but in its content as well. The hero of the flood is Noah alone, the just man. The sons and wives are mentioned because they are included in the fate of Noah. But Noah is not a hero in the epic sense, a man who has accomplished mighty deeds. His one and all-embracing accomplishment is the fact of his faithful obedience to the word of YHWH. The real actor in this drama is God himself.

The deluge has a theological motivation. There are two references to the fact that God repents of having made man. Man has strayed from the original plan of creation; his heart has been wholly corrupted. At the beginning of Order IV the text introduces a further motive, that the world was filled with violence. Evidence of this fact is the inclusion of the mythical tradition of the giants and the sons of God.

In this violent world, filled with wickedness, Noah alone finds favor before the Lord. God has determined to annihilate the world by flood; but he also determined to preserve Noah from destruction. He commands him to build a great "chest" or "coffer"; this is the real meaning of the Hebrew word *tēbâ,* which is generally translated as ark. The precise building directions, the dimensions, and the furnishings, all recall the ancient ship-builder's art. Since the most ancient times, the Babylonians made use of asphalt, which was abundant in their territory (oil wells), to make their ships water-tight.

After completing the building, Noah went into the ark. With him he took seven of every kind of animal, not every imaginable animal, but only domestic animals (*bēhēmâ*). He had already taken care of food and provisions. For his contemporaries all this gave the impression of preparing for a great sea voyage. Seven days after the completion of the building, the flood broke loose. Two causes are assigned: 40 days of rain from the flood-gates of heaven, and a violent storm from the sea. The rising waters raised the ark, but every other living thing perished in the catastrophe.

But God thought of Noah. He made the wind blow, and shut up the gates of heaven, so that the waters receded and the peaks of the mountains began to appear and the ark landed on one of them. Then Noah three times sends out a bird. This is a clear reminiscence of the ancient sea voyage. The seafarers took birds with them which they frequently sent out to determine the direction of the land. If the bird sensed the nearness of land, he would fly in that direction without returning.[4] First, Noah sent out the raven, then, twice, the dove. The text for this third sending has obviously been tampered with in its present condition. The dove with the olive branch in his beak makes a strong

---

4. M. V. David, "L'Episode des Oiseaux dans le Récit du Deluge," *VT* 7 (1957), 189-190. The use of birds in sea voyages. H. Heras, "The Crow of Noe," *CBQ,* 10 (1949), 131-139. Presents old Indian accounts of sea trade with Mesopotamia.

impression; but the older form of the text probably had the dove not return at all. From the behavior of the birds, Noah realized that land was in sight. Finally, the ark landed on a mountain peak. Noah got out, immediately built an altar, and offered sacrifice for his salvation. The Lord smelled the fragrant odor. The song begins with God's divine sentence of judgment; but it closes with a new proclamation of salvation: "A flood will nevermore be!" As guarantee for this promise, the rainbow stands in the heaven. A new time of salvation is beginning, the era of God's covenant with new humanity.

In the form described, the song presents an internal compactness. The flood narrative turns into a prophetic sermon on judgment and salvation. The flood is not a mere natural catastrophe; it is God's activity for judgment and salvation. If we prescind from this prophetic garb, we are faced with the simple nucleus of a flood narrative, which, in its basic elements, is no different from the Babylonian flood narrative. But it is here that we can recognize the Biblical poet-theologian at work. He has given this ancient song a salvation-history overtone. The flood tradition itself must, accordingly, be older than Israel.

C) THE TIME AFTER THE FLOOD

ORDER VI (GEN 8, 22 – 9, 17)

The structure of this Order has already been discussed. It contains 6 speeches of Elohim with 240 words and one speech of YHWH with 37 words. In these speech sections the order of human life is established for mankind after the flood. What is required is the securing of the cosmic order, the securing of human life, and also the securing of the new order of salvation, in the sign of the covenant. Curse and blessing are pronounced, and hereafter salvation begins to focus upon the posterity of Shem.

1) THE COSMIC ORDER (8, 21-22)

After leaving the ark, Noah built an altar. The text describes, not an apparition from God, but only a divine word which takes up the deluge as the foundation of a new cosmic order:

6, 21c Never again will I annihilate
the earth on account of man;
for the impulse of the heart of man
is wicked from the time of his youth.
Never again will I strike
all life, as I have just done.
22 For all times of the world
shall nevermore cease:
sowing and harvest, frost and heat,
summer and winter, day and night.

The first person is used 3 times; if we isolate the corresponding sentences, we have 17 words, the symbolic number of the whole flood narrative. In terms of structure, accordingly, the flood is clearly echoed in this divine speech: there will be no further flood, despite the constant wickedness of the human heart. In the oracle of the seasons, there might be an echo of some ancient popular proverb.

2) THE LAW OF BLOOD VENGEANCE

In order to secure human life, Yahweh reserves blood for himself. Man is free to eat the flesh of animals as his food, but blood is sacred to Yahweh. The blood sentence is pronounced upon the man who sheds human blood. This is to serve as a restraint against the brutalization encountered in the time before the flood, as it was expressed in the sword-song of Lamech, for whom human life had no value. For peoples and times in which no clear civil order has yet been established, the law of blood vengeance is the final guarantee for the security of human life (9, 6-7).

3) THE COVENANT AND THE SIGN

For this new world order, the rainbow is chosen by God as the sign of the covenant. When God struck a covenant with Abraham, he determined upon circumcision as its sign. This was not the first invention of circumcision; the already prevalent practice took on a new significance. The same thing might be said of the sabbath, which figures as the sign of the Mosaic covenant. Similarly, the rainbow existed in the heavens long before Yahweh concluded his covenant with Noah; as a natural phenomenon it was always there. But now it takes on a salvation-history significance; it becomes the sign of a new humanity, the seal of a new covenant. The Noah-covenant is, for its state of development, just as precisely structured as the New Testament. The covenant with Noah does not represent some sort of a trade agreement, in which the advantages of both parties are arbitrated; quite the contrary. It is wholly and simply the unilateral ordinance of God. This fact is expressed, in terms of simple grammar, in the verbs employed: "God gives the covenant (9, 12), establishes the covenant (9, 9, 11)." "*Hāḳīmôtî* – I establish" is the causative form, that is, God is the cause behind the covenant (6, 18). The Noah covenant is completely God's establishment, ordering, *testamentum*. And since it involves the concept of a free decision on the part of a merciful God, it is, wholly and absolutely, a covenant of grace.[5]

For this kind of new beginning, the rainbow, which appears in heaven after rain or thunder storms, is a significant sign: Gen. 9, 13: "I set my bow in the cloud, and it shall be a sign of the covenant between me and the earth." – As distinguished from the rainbow, the Old Testament repeatedly refers to a different bow of God (1 Kings 2, 4; 3, 12; Hab. 3, 9; Ps. 7, 13); God's arrows are also mentioned (Deut. 32, 23, 43; Hab. 9, 14;

---

5. On the theology of the Noah covenant see the very stimulating presentation in *Theologie des AT in heilsgeschichtlicher Entwicklung* by W. Möller (1934), 105-128.

Ps. 7, 14; 18, 15; 38, 3; 114, 6; Job 6, 4). The bow generally refers to the weapon of war, and in the passages listed above God is spoken of as a warrior, bending his bow and shooting his arrows against his enemies. This, obviously, is a figure of speech. On the other hand, the bow which God sets up in the clouds is something visible. The bow is something that Yahweh always uses; in fact God is begged to shoot his arrows, that is, to annihilate his opponents. But in the covenant with Noah, God has put aside his bow, never to take it up again. The bow (as weapon) is the symbol of God's wrath; the rainbow, however, is the symbol of divine love and predilection.

CHAPTER XXIII

EXTRA-BIBLICAL FLOOD NARRATIVES

A) EXTENT OF THE FLOOD

AS far as the geographical extent of the flood is concerned, it must be pointed out that in the flood narrative, just as in the creation narrative, the Ancient Near Eastern picture of the world is presupposed. The earth is thought of as a round disk anchored in the primeval ocean. The flood is caused by the inroads of the upper water masses of the ocean of the heavens, since God opens the "flood-gates" (Gen. 6, 11), and by the rising of the water from the ocean underneath (6, 11). The earth is flooded with water from above and below, just as it had been in the time before the ocean above and below was separated. It is against this same background that we must understand the statements regarding the geographical universality of the flood. God threatens to blot out "all" flesh under the heaven (6, 17); the water covers "all" the highest mountains under the whole heaven (7, 19). This word "all" is formulated from the standpoint of the Ancient Near Eastern narrator, as far as his point of view extended, and in this sense it was also understood literally by the ancient scribes and authors.

With the gradual expansion of the geographical picture of

the world, and particularly with the palaeontological investigation of the earth's crust, a growing tide of reflection has been mounting against the geographical universality of the flood. For some time it was believed that the discovery of the fossil remains of living creatures, fish and shellfish, on the highest peaks of the mountains necessarily substantiated the historicity of the flood catastrophe. Today, there is hardly any serious scholar who attempts to correlate these geological deposits in the earth's strata with the Biblical flood narrative. Our natural science has thus surpassed the Ancient Near Eastern picture of the world, as recorded in the Bible, and clearly indicated its historical limitations.

If the flood was geographically limited, we might begin to suspect that it was also bounded ethnologically, and thus that not all men on earth perished in the flood, but only that segment of humanity which had settled in a geographically compact area, had succeeded in developing a high degree of culture, and had then fallen into a state of moral decay and were ripe for destruction. Thus it would be primarily the Cainites and the Sethites who were struck; the Bible makes no mention of what happened to the other children of our first parents. Since the fact of human universality, in the flood narrative, is not necessarily bound up with any truths of faith, or teaching of the Church,[1] every possibility is open to the freedom of argument and opinion, and only the relative merit of the various arguments advanced can decide for or against them.

The results of ethnological investigation force us to date the flood at a very early age, since it belongs to the earliest traditions of the most ancient peoples. Flood narratives are to be found in Syria, Asia Minor, Iran, India, Siberia, South Asia, among the Greeks, Germans, and Slavs, in Australia and America. They

---

1. Cyprian's dictum, "outside the church no salvation," which is modeled on the ark, is based on the ancient picture of the world, and cannot be appealed to as a geographical testimony. The anthropological universality of the deluge is maintained by D. Poulet, *Tous les hommes sont-ils fils de Noe?* (Ottawa, 1941).

have not yet been demonstrated among the Arabs, Chinese, Japanese, and many African peoples. Riem counts 68 related flood sagas.[2]

In terms of ethical content, the Iranian flood narrative is closest to the Biblical. Ahuramazda foretells the coming of the flood to Jima, who is to be saved. The flood is a divine judgment upon sinful humanity. The flood comes not by a rainstorm, but by a massive blizzard whose snows melt and overrun the country. Jima saves himself by building a lofty stronghold.

The Indian saga shows marked individualities: Manu, the first man, caught a fish in his hand which promised him: "Raise me, and I will save you!" When the fish had grown up, it told Manu that in a certain year a great flood was coming; thus, he should build himself a ship. Manu obeyed and bound his ship to the horn of the fish, who pulled it towards a northern mountain. There the ship landed. The flood, however, had blotted out all other creatures. Manu longed for a family. One day as he was offering sacrifice, a woman appeared, whom he took for his wife and begot the present generation.[3]

In the Greek saga, it is Deucalion and Pyrrha who produce the next generation, after the flood, in a miraculous manner; they throw stones backwards over their heads, and the stones turn into humans.[4]

How are we to explain this wide spread of the flood saga? Must we postulate the existence of a nature myth, which develops, independently, in different areas, to a poetic formulation? Obviously, natural catastrophes may have been the occasion for

---

2. J. Riem, *Die Sündflut, eine ethnographisch-naturwissenschaftliche Untersuchung*. A. R. Herrmann, "Die Sintflut im Volkerleben," *Benedictine Monthly* (Beuron, 3/4, 1951), 153ff.

3. Text in *ATAO*, 3rd edition, 132. W. Koppers, *Der Urmensch und sein Weltbild*: "Die Urflutmythe bei den Bhil" (1949), 130.

4. A. G. Galanopulos, "Die deukalionische Flut aus geologischer Sicht," *Altertum* 9 (1963), 3-7. The volcanic eruptions of the former island of Strongyle gave rise to a spring-tide in the Mediterranean, which found its echo in the saga. Dated around 1529.

such poems. Boklen [5] sees Noah as a moon hero, the ark being the moon, the three stories the three phases of the moon, as well as the three sons of Noah, and the rainbow at the end of the flood narrative being the sickle of the new moon. Obviously there is no merit in such imaginative explanations.

A more reliable foundation, however, is offered by the excavations carried on in Mesopotamia. Archaeology has not yet succeeded in isolating traces of the great flood at various places; but the results of the excavations in the ancient Sumerian metropolis of Ur are well deserving of consideration. The first newspaper accounts of the discovery of the deluge site were not, of course, authentic. If, however, we take up the official excavation account of L. Woolley, we must pause for thought. Ur had been known primarily for the royal graves with their mass burials. In the deepest levels, which lie far beneath the era of the royal graves, the excavation, in many areas, came upon strata of alluvial sand, as much as 2.5 to 3.7 m. thick. In order to have deposited a layer of sand almost 4 meters thick, there must have been a flood half again, or even twice, that high. The southern part of Babylonia is an absolute flat land. A flood which attained a height of 8 meters in the area of Ur would have put almost the entire country south of the chain of hills from Hit to Kurnab under water, and completely covered any cities built on that plain. In the flood narrative, we read that the flood covered even the heights of the mountains. The Iraqi, even today, refer to these small hills in the plain country, hills which could not be reached by the irrigation system, as "mountains," although they stand only a few meters higher than the surrounding country. The ark's landing on Mount Ararat would thus be a legendary addition.

The course of the flood could be reconstructed as follows. A strong southern wind, even today, can raise the water level

---

5. Böklen, "Die Sündflutsage," *Archives of Religion Research* 6 (1903), 1-61; 97-150.

6. L. Woolley, *Ur Excavations.* Vol. IV: *The Early Periods* (Philadelphia, 1955).

of the Persian Gulf by at least a meter, and block the normal outlet of the river water. Rainfall alone, no matter how strong, could hardly have produced an inundation of the proportions described above. "The flood came from the sea," as the song expressly states. The rain only helped to make the catastrophe complete. Strong rainfall in the Persian Mountains can produce landslides along the banks of the Tigris, so that wide stretches of land are inundated. If the Euphrates and Tigris both rise at the same time, there is catastrophe and flood even today. The last time this happened with really serious consequences was in the year 1929. If there is a series of long, cold winters, with short, cool summers, so that the masses of snow and ice are forced to collect in the Armenian Mountains, then the arrival of a particularly hot summer necessarily results in a catastrophic flood. Such an inter-glacial occurrence has been computed for the time around 4500 B.C.[7] Woolley, the excavator of Ur, arranges all these factors into place within the course of the early development of civilization, insofar as it can be determined by excavation, and comes to the prudent conclusion that, in the alluvial sand strata discovered in Ur, we are actually dealing with the sediment deposited by the great deluge. Shortly after this stratum of destruction, civilized remains make their appearance again; they show some relation to the artifacts of the earlier age, but are much sparser and much poorer. This means that the earlier city culture of southern Mesopotamia was annihilated by a catastrophic flood.

It is no wonder that the great flood figures as a decisive point of division in the Sumero-Babylonian reckoning of time. Conditions before the flood were known only on the basis of vague memories and recollections. But the great event itself was passed on, in poetry and song, from generation to generation, in the famous saga of the flood.

---

7. *Ibid.*, Wooley's claims were at first accepted rather skeptically, since, in nearby Kish, excavation yielded strata of debris that clearly dated into the 3rd millennium. Further excavations, however, confirmed the traces of a much older inundation.

B) THE BABYLONIAN DELUGE SAGA

Prior to the discovery of the cuneiform literature, the Babylonian deluge narrative was known only fragmentarily, from the history of Eusebius of Caesarea, *Praeparatio evangelica* (IX, 12, 414-15). The fragments date from the work of the Babylonian priest of Bel, Berossus, who wanted to pass on both the *enûma eliš* as well as the Gilgamesh epic to the Greek world.

The first cuneiform source for the Babylonian deluge was discovered in 1872. George Smith, one of the assistants to the British Museum, discovered a fragment of a clay tablet which amazed him by referring to the landing of a ship on a mountain. In the following lines he read how a dove was sent out and returned again, how a swallow was let loose and also came back, and how finally a raven was let loose and did not return. This was enough to clearly fix the interpretation of the text. Smith searched tirelessly for further fragments, and was able to assemble a large collection of fragments of two other copies of the same narrative. He was thus able to establish the fact that the description belonged to the 11th tablet of a larger work, written on 12 tablets, which today, in its totality, is known as the Gilgamesh epic.[8] The epic is divided into two principal parts: the heroic activities of Gilgamesh and the deluge narrative. The unifying leit-motif is the thought of death and immortality.

---

8. The first lengthy edition of the Gilgamesh Epic, with text transcription and German translation, was published in *Keilinschriftliche Bibliothek IV* (1900): "Assyrisch - babylonische Mythen und Epen." Further texts in A. Ungnad and H. Gressmann, *Das Gilgamesch Epos* (1919). E. Ebeling in *AOT,* 2nd edition (1926), 198. A. Schott, *Das Gilgamesch Epos* (1958). A. Heidel, *The Gilgamesch Epic and Old Test ment Parallels* (1946). F. M. Th. Böhl, *Le problème de la vie éternelle dans le cycle épique sumérien et dans l'épopée accadienne de Gilgameš* (1948). *ANET* (1955), 42ff.

1) GILGAMESH AND HIS HEROIC DEEDS

Gilgamesh, the strong and powerful king of Uruk, the builder of the city walls, three-fourths god and one fourth man, piled so much hard forced labor upon his subjects that, from their oppression, they turned to the gods for help. They importune the mother goddess to create a friend and rival for Gilgamesh, equal to him in birth. She immediately sets to work, washes her hands, pinches off a piece of clay, and shapes Enkidu, a being of powerful physical strength and extraordinary sensuality; he is covered with hair like an animal and, at first, also makes his home with the beasts of the field, eating grass, although he has all the other properties of man.

Upon Gilgamesh's orders, a hunter brings a prostitute to Enkidu, who succeeds in bringing the wild man back to Uruk. The two heroes take each other's measure in a wrestling bout, in which Enkidu is overcome. The two then conclude a firm friendship.

They go out into the world together, upon great heroic adventures. One day, however, Enkidu falls prey to a sickness which causes his death on the 12th day. Gilgamesh is deeply shaken, and at first thinks it is only sleep. But when his friend's eye no longer opens and his heart beats no more, he covers him, the way a bride is veiled, and abandons himself to his grief. Six days and six nights he cries for Enkidu; then he buries him.

Suddenly he is assailed by fear of his own death. He will some day also die, just like Enkidu. In order to achieve immortality, he makes his way, amid many adventures, into the underworld, to his ancestor Uta-Napishtim, whom he begs for counsel and advice. This narrative serves as introduction to the second part of the epic. It is here that Uta-Napishtim advises him how he is to be saved from the great flood and thus attain immortality.

2) UTA-NAPISHTIM AND THE GREAT FOOD

Uta-Napishtim says: "I will reveal to you, Gilgamesh, hidden tidings; a mystery of the gods I will entrust to you!" Through the wall of a reed hut, he listens to the dreamlike warning: "Man of Shurippak, destroy the house, build a ship, let go your riches, seek life, bring the seed of life of every kind into the ship."

As his reason for building the ship he is to say that the earth god Enlil has conceived hatred against him, and thus he must betake himself into the territory of the water god Ea. The poem next describes the building of the ship, into which Uta-Napishtim brings his treasures and then assigns its steering to an experienced helmsman. The storm breaks loose, thunder and lightning, like a mighty battle:

The gods were frightened by the deluge,
And, shrinking back, they ascended to the heaven of Anu.
The gods cowered like dogs
Crouched against the outer wall.
Ishtar cried out like a woman in travail . . . .
"The olden days are alas turned to clay."
The gods, all humbled, sit and weep.

Finally, the ship lands on Mount Nisir. On the 7th day, Uta-Napishtim sends out a dove, which returns, since it can find no place to rest. Then he sent out a swallow, with no better success. Finally a raven, who flew out, saw that the waters had dried, and did not return. Uta-Napishtim came out of the ship and offered sacrifice to the gods:

The gods smelled the savor
The gods smelled the sweet savor,
The gods crowded like flies about the sacrificer.

In gratitude for the sacrifice, Uta-Napishtim and his wife are accepted into the ranks of the gods.

Thereupon Enlil went aboard the ship.
Holding me by the hand, he took me aboard.
He took my wife aboard and made her kneel by my side.
Standing between us, he touched our foreheads to bless us:
"Hitherto Uta-Napishtim has been but human.
Henceforth Uta-Napishtim and his wife shall be
like unto us gods.
Uta-Napishtim shall reside far away,
At the mouth of the rivers."
And they took me, and they made me to dwell
at the mouth of the rivers.[9]

The best known form of the Gilgamesh epic comes from the library of Ashurbanipal (668-626). But it has many older predecessors. About 1250 B.C. there was already a Hittite translation of this heroic epic. There are also many other Sumerian, Old Babylonian, and Assyrian versions. The flood myth, in all these texts, is not recounted for its own sake; it is largely built into some concrete need of human life. Thus, an incantation text, to be used for pregnant women in order to assure a happy delivery, also contains the deluge myth; despite all the storm and thunder which were let loose, the elements did not succeed in annihilating the human race. In like manner, may the birth of N.N. be a happy one.[10]

The hero of the flood story has different names. In the Sumerian account he is called Zui(d)sudda, that is, the "long-lived, the distant," at the mouth of the rivers. Since it was by his particular cleverness that he managed to save himself from the general destruction, he receives the Akkadian name Atar-hasis, that is, "the arch-wise, he who is clever beyond all measure." When the Bible uses the name Noah for him, we have the same phenomenon as in the translation of the genealogy. Sumerian names are translated and popularly interpreted in Hebrew, insofar as this is possible. Lamech says this upon Noah's birth: "Out of

---

9. Text in B. Bonkamp, *Die Bibel im Lichte der Keilschriftforschung* (1939), pp. 130-170.

10. Further texts in *AOT*, 2nd edition (1926), 203.

the ground which the Lord has cursed this one shall bring us relief from our work and from the toil of our hands" (5, 29). Noah is thus the "comforter, appeaser," in the midst of the accursed earth: a redeemer figure.

The concluding judgment on Bible and Babel we leave to A. Jeremias,[11] who clearly stresses the individual and proper value of the Biblical narrative as opposed to the Babylonian flood tradition, without, however, sharing his astro-mythological viewpoints:

"The Biblical tradition, in both recensions, displays a relationship with the Babylonian tradition, and a considerably closer relationship than in the case of the creation narrative. The material of the narrative had made its way from people to people; still, we must warn against the concept of a direct literary dependence.

"At all events, the important element, in terms of religion, is not to be found in what Bible and Babel have in common, but rather in the elements that distinguish them. The account that Berossus presents to the Greeks is significantly more refined than the account preserved in the cuneiform texts. We must not exclude the possibility that this priest of Marduk in Babel was influenced by Jewish thinking.

"In place of the mythological world of gods which, in the Babylonian account, are constantly lying and scheming against each other and ruling the world of men according to their changing moods, appearing in childlike anxiety before the flood and then greedy in their demands at the sacrifice, we find, in the Bible, a wrathful God who judges the world and has mercy on the just.

"The Biblical deluge narrative still has the power to awaken the conscience of the world. And the Biblical story-teller wrote it down with this pedagogical and moral purpose in view. There is no evidence of any such motivation in any of the extra-Biblical deluge narratives."

---

11. A. Jeremias, *ATAO* 4th edition (1930), 160.

CHAPTER XXIV

THE RISE OF THE NATIONS

ORDER VII, GEN. 9, 18 – 10, 32

Quite disparate blocs of material have been combined to form a structural unit in Order VII. The principal bloc comprises the lists of peoples who are derived from Noah and his sons. This is preceded by the account of Noah's drunkenness (9, 18-29); the emphasis here is not upon Noah's agriculture, but rather Noah the great ancestor whose curse and blessing continues to have its effects for generations of future peoples. In the genealogical tables we find not merely "sons," but rather peoples, cities, and tribes. And yet right in the very middle of these genealogies and tables of nations, we find the sober outlines of the catalogue interrupted by the narrative of the powerful and violent Nimrod (10, 8-12). If we examine the word count in terms of these blocs of text, we reach the following conclusions:

	N		I		S		
1. Curse and Blessing (9, 18-29)	95	+	2	+	24	=	121
2. Table, first part (10, 1-7)	58					=	58
3. Nimrod (10, 8-12)	46	+	3	+	5	=	54

4. Table, second part (10, 13-32)	175	= 175
		374 + 5 + 29 = 408

Without going into individual details, we are immediately struck by the fact that, without the 54 words about Nimrod, the whole of Order VII is clearly bound up with the moon: 408 – 54 = 354. The Adamite genealogy in chapter 5 was related to the solar number 365. The Paradise narrative was controlled by the number of the morning star. The great luminaries of the heaven cast their light not only upon day and night; they also have a formal and structural influence on the literary text.

A) NOAH'S CURSE AND BLESSING

After the flood, Noah, in keeping with the earthly makeup of humanity, turns again to the earth: "Noah was the first tiller of the soil. He planted a vineyard . . ." (Gen. 9, 20). The work of the days before the flood is taken up again. Agriculture and viniculture clearly imply the existence of a sedentary establishment; Noah, however, following the example of the semi-nomads, lives in a tent. It might be that the Bible text shows evidence of historical abbreviation here. The Bible does not attempt to describe the cultural milieu, but only to record the religious evolution. The religious level of this human family after the flood is revealed by the conduct of Ham, when he saw his father, overcome by the strength of the wine, lying naked in his tent. He made fun of his father in the presence of his brothers Shem and Japheth. When Noah awoke and learned of the behavior of his youngest son, he was seized not only with anger, but also with the spirit of prophecy, so that he spoke words of blessing and curse, which were to have their effect upon the generations to come.

The curse of Ham is, if we examine it closely, based on how painfully shameful and humiliating the ancient Israelite mentality regarded nakedness, not only in a woman (Is. 47, 3;

Ex. 16, 37; Hos. 2, 11; Nah. 3, 5), but also in a man (2 Sam. 6, 20; 10, 4; Hab. 3, 15). This lack of reverence is an offense against his father. Ham is degraded to the position of servant and even slave.

The effects of this curse could clearly be seen, in ancient Israel, in the lot of Canaan, who was considered the son of Ham. It is worth noting that in the text the words of the curse are addressed not directly to Ham, but to his son Canaan (Cf. Gen. 9, 22: The sin of Ham; 9, 25: Cursed be Canaan!). Parents are struck most deeply in their children. The religious-moral degeneracy of the Canaanite population, which had reached its nadir in the practice of sacred prostitution, is a spiritual offspring of the frivolous behavior of Ham. The narrative of the curse of Canaan was, at the same time, a religious exhortation to avoid the company of the Canaanite population. There is no community between Israel and Canaan.[1]

While the curse dissolves community with God, the blessing establishes this community all the more strongly.[2] Yahweh binds himself so strongly to Shem, that he is called the "God of Shem." The name Yahweh, the name of the later God of the covenant, is deliberately used here. The Noah covenant is here focused more directly upon the Semitic people. The text yields no further information, apart from the fact that Japheth is also included in this religious community: he is permitted to live in the tents of Shem, whereas all religious communion with Canaan is forbidden (Ex. 23, 31-33; Deut. 1-4). Japheth's blessing reveals a Hebrew play on words: "God enlarge (*yapt*) Japheth, and let him dwell in the tents of Shem, and let Canaan be his slave" (Gen. 9, 27).

---

1. H. Heras suggests that, even in the Indian literature, there is a reminiscence of the curse of Canaan. *CBQ* 19 (1950), 64-67.

2. In our civilization, words have turned into empty sound: on the power of words see P. Heinisch, *Das "Wort" im AT und im Alten Orient* (1922). L. Róst, "Noah der Weinbauer," *Bemerkungen zu Gen. 9, 18 in Fs für A. Alt,* (1953), 163-78, interprets the curse in terms of the political situation in Solomon's time.

The text is most easily explained if Noah, Shem, Japheth, and Ham are taken as historical personalities, who were the object of blessings or curses. Opposed to this is the typical interpretation, which regards these four names only as the personification of the political conditions verified in later history. With respect to Canaan, the answer is obvious. Canaan is the ethnic groups which Israel encountered in taking possession of Palestine. Israel is identified with Shem. With respect to Japheth, however, there are several interpretations. Some think of the Phoenicians, who, in the time of David, were close allies of Israel. Others see Japheth as the Philistines, who, however, according to the Table of Nations, belonged to the posterity of Ham; others propose the Hittites, or they regard the Japheth oracle as an expression of the sentiments which the Jews, at the time of Alexander the Great, harbored towards the Greeks.[3] These attempts at identification serve only to show how uncertain the interpretation is in individual details. The religious line of development, however, is clearly visible. Salvation history is no longer on the universal plane; it is now focused on the Semitic people.[4]

B) THE TABLE OF NATIONS (GEN. 10, 1-32)

Pentateuchal criticism has distinguished two sources which are easily recognizable in terms of content and language. The original, deeply-moving account of Nimrod and the building of the tower is from the pen of the Yahwist. The editor in the time of the Babylonian exile, or shortly afterwards, worked the Yahwist's narrative into his outline. He took over the Yahwist's Folk

3. For a more explicit presentation of the individual opinions, see the commentaries mentioned at the head of this chapter. See also P. Heinisch, *Genesis* (1930): "Noes Fluch und Segen," 184ff.

4. Proof of the close relationship between Semites and Hamites is presented in the new linguistic investigations of O. Rössler, "Verbalbau und Verbalflexion in den semito-hamitischen," *ZDMG* 100 (1950), 461-514.

Table of Nations, which is characterized by the formula "X begot Y (*yālād*)," whereas his own catalogue uses the formula "These are the sons of N.N." There is no mistaking the difference between the two catalogues; but perhaps it is possible to contest the interpretation. Who made use of whom? According to the classical critical position, it was naturally the more recent P (Priestly) who used the older J (Yahwist). But is this necessarily the case? It is certainly possible for P to be the more ancient document, and for J to have enlisted it in the service of his own act of faith.

At any rate, we are dealing with a catalogue of peoples. The science of such genealogies was already developed to the point of virtuosity by the Sumerians, then taken over by the Babylonians and even further developed. Students of the Ancient Near East are not surprised to discover tables of nations available for school use, already towards the end of the 2nd millennium. The geographical and ethnic horizons which form the background of the present table fit much better into the era prior to 1000, when Canaan still belonged to the Egyptian sphere of influence, than in the time after the Babylonian exile. Catalogues naturally invite additions and supplements. After the political appearance of the Cimmerians, Scythians, Medes and Lydians, these peoples were also fitted into the outline. But the original Table of Nations is redolent of the era of the migrations of the sea peoples.

In the treatment of the Table of Nations, we find the same structure with which we are already familiar from the preceding chapters. Historically, geographically, and ethnologically, our modern-day knowledge has outstripped the times in which the Table of Nations was first composed; not only our cosmological picture of the world, but also our historical knowledge has grown much deeper and much more detailed. We can follow the path of humanity, from the dawn of prehistory, through the discovery of cave dwellings, to the formation of the first village, the evolution of the earliest civilizations, much better than the editor of the Table of Nations was in a position to attempt.

The Table of Nations does not recognize the real value of this "human progress." It represents an attempt to encompass the whole of humanity within a unified framework, and to do this in a manner which surpasses the egocentric philosophy of the other ancient histories of early humanity. It is not the tiny polis which occupies the focus of our editor; his horizon includes the entire world known to the scientific investigation of his day.

Many scholars are of the opinion that this attempt must have been based upon an ancient map, similar to the map of Herodotus.[5] But the Biblical editor goes beyond mere geography and ethnology. He has turned this ancient map into a document that has relevance in the theology of history.[6] For him, the individual accounts of the nations and their interdependence are only a medium of expression to develop an idea which is central to the theology of history: humanity, in the sight of God, is one big family. At the beginning of the splitting up of the various peoples stands Noah, who still knew the God of primeval times, under whose protection the peoples spread across the whole earth. If the nations have fallen away from the god of antiquity, they have not thereby fallen out of God's salvific activity. God's will, which is the source and principle of human history, still determines the fates of the nations, who are to be brought back to a new unity. For the whole Table of Nations is only an overture to the story of Abraham, through whom the blessing was to be poured out upon all peoples.

The first reading of this Table of Nations is confusing. It appears to be a mixture and a composite. Shem, Ham, and Japheth are clearly conceived of as persons, and so is Nimrod, who conquered a kingdom and achieves pre-eminence as a hunter. But Misrayim, Cush, and Ophir are countries, Elishah is an island, Tarshish, Sidon, and Arvad are cities, Gomer and Madai are peoples.

Strangely enough, nations and peoples are represented as

---

5. Herodotus' "Table of Nations" in Guthe, *Bibelatlas,* No. 6. With maps.
2. Junker, "Genesis," *EB I,* 49.

"begotten" and as "sons" or as "begetting": Seba and Havilah are the sons of Cush, a people; Egypt, a country, "begets" the Ludim; Canaan "begets" the city of Sidon. . . . The expression "sons" and "beget" are not to be understood literally. And yet it is precisely these words which contain the whole basic idea of a family of nations. The table presents a universal spirit. All peoples are placed on the same level. Israel is not in the primary focus. She does not come first, but is included among the posterity of Heber. Other ancient nations were not so objective in their philosophies; they looked upon their neighbors as "barbarians" and treated them with contempt.[7]

The principle of division: According to what points of view did the author of our table arrange his material? Certainly not according to language. Canaan is counted together with Cush, even though it has a Semitic language. Nor was it in terms of ethnic blood relationship, for the Hittites actually belong to the Indo-Germans (Japhethites) and still they are numbered among the sons of Canaan. The riddle of the Table of Nations is easiest understood if it is attacked in terms of the world political situation which is mirrored in the catalogue.

1) THE SONS OF JAPHETH

Our scholarship in this respect would be considerably advanced if we could interpret the name of Japheth. The Biblical author, at all events, understood it in terms of the curse spoken by Noah, which develops the Semitic interpretation "may God enlarge Japheth," that is, "give him wide territory." But since we are here dealing with non-Semitic peoples, the original ancestor of these peoples might, at all events, have borne a non-Semitic name. There is a striking similarity with the Greek Iapetos, the son of Uranos (heaven) and Gaia (earth). He belonged to the Titans, whom Zeus cast down from Olympus

7. P. Heinisch, *Genesis*: *Zur Beurteilung der Völkertafel*, p. 194ff.

into Tartarus. His son was called Prometheus, who taught mankind how to build fire, and thus introduced the beginnings of civilization. But apart from this similarity of name, there are certainly no grounds for comparison between the Greek myth and this unmythical Biblical account.[8] We are once again referred back to the testimony of the list itself, in which we can distinguish two levels. The more ancient level bears traits of the migration of the sea peoples, while the more recent stratum shows evidence of being composed in the Scythian era.

a) *The more ancient stratum:* Among the sons of Japheth belong: JAVAN with Elishah, Tarshish, Kittim, and Dodanim; TUBAL, MESHECH, and TIRASH.

The interpretation of the list has generally been attempted in terms of simply identifying JAVAN with the Ionians along the west coast of Asia Minor. But more precise philological and historical investigation has pointed in a different direction.[9] The most ancient mention of the Ionians (*Ymnym*) occurs already in the texts of Ugarit (14th century). Since Ugarit's knowledge of the west and northwest was not very extensive, we cannot proceed, in our attempt to localize these Yamanim, much beyond Cyprus and Cilicia, that is, not far beyond their immediate neighborhood. The victory inscriptions of Sargon II (722-705) point in the same direction, speaking of Cyprus and "Ionia" as synonymous. In the annals he speaks of Yadna, the man from Cyprus; in the corresponding passage in the official royal inscription, however, he speaks of Yamani, the "Ionian."[10] In the cylinder inscription[11] he claims that he fished this Yamani out of the sea, like a fish, and made peace in Kue (Cilicia) and Surri (Tyre.).

---

8. *EncMikr* III, 746.

9. W. Brandenstein, *Bemerkungen zur Völkertafel in der Genesis*. Fs. A. Debrunner (1954), 66ff. Based on the following.

10. *ANET* 286: in terms of linguistic history, *m* can be replaced by *v* and conversely. Thus, *yavan-yaman*. The disappearance of the digamma *v* (w) produces the form Ionia.

11. *ANET* 285a.

He refers to three coast countries, whom he overcame with one campaign. The grouping in the account of Esarhaddon (681-669) is significant: [12] "All the kings of the middle of the sea, from Yadnana (Cyprus), Yamani, to Tarsis, cast themselves at my feet." Once again the land of Yavan lies in the neighborhood of Cyprus. Finally, Nebuchadnezzar (605-562) understands Yaman as "Cilicia." [13] The same practice can be verified for the Persian era. Thus we can conclude with certainty that the "Ionians" of the Table of Nations are to be sought, not on the western coast of Asia Minor, but rather in the Taurus district. The name Ionian, accordingly, did not migrate from west to east, but from east to west. The form Ia-vones is not Greek, but Asia Minor, more precisely, Hittite hieroglyphic, where it ends in *-awana.* The decisive element in this argument is the fact that this suffix was used primarily to designate cult communities, and only within a narrowly circumscribed area. The Hittite sources, once again, point to the district of the Taurus and Antitaurus.

The coast of Asia Minor had already been settled by the Greeks in the 2nd half of the 2nd millennium. As an example we might mention the rich and famous island of Rhodes; the Mycenaean Achaeans made their way to Rhodes around the 14th century B. C. The Rodanim, that is, the inhabitants of the island of Rhodes, are considered the "sons" of the Yavan (Javan) who live on the mainland. The other three sons are to be sought in the same general area. Authors have been inclined to identify Tarshish with Tartessos in Spain; but the geographical horizons of those times were not so broad as this; Tarshish is simply Tarsus in Cilicia, the town in which the Apostle Paul was born. Tarsus [14] was joined to the sea by a short and navigable river, and thus became a famous seaport and commercial city. Timber

12. *ANET* 290a.

13. E. Weidner, Fs. für Dussaud (1939), 932.

14. Tarsus was destroyed by an attack from the sea, 1225. This date marks the disappearance of the Mycenaean pottery, pottery from Cyprus making its appearance more and more strongly in its stead. Excavation

from Taurus, metals, silver and lead sulphite, as well as precious gems, were all shipped to this port from time immemorial (cf. Ez. 27, 12; Jer. 10, 9). The ships of Tarshish, already in the days of Solomon, were considered the most seaworthy; it was possible to make trips as far as Ophir in them (1 Kings 22, 49).

Javan's 3rd son is called Elisha. The identification of this name with the island of Cyprus can be considered as definite. Elisha - Alashia is apparently the name of the ancient city near Enkomi, which has recently been excavated. The name of the city gradually came to be used for the whole island. According to a vocabulary discovered in Nuzi, Alas means simply "copper." Cyprus was considered as simply the island of copper. Since the middle of the 2nd millennium, great quantities of copper were mined here.

Javan's 4th son, Kittim, leads us back to the mainland. He is not to be identified with the city of Kition on Cyprus; Brandenstein[15] has established the fact that *kittim* is identical with *ḥittim*, that is, the Hittites. After the great Hittite empire collapsed in the storm of the sea peoples' inroads around 1200, individual Hittite principalities still held out in the southeast. Thus, Tiglath-Pileser I (c. 1100) refers to the land of Carchemish as the "land of the Chatti." The fact that the Hittites are referred to as the sons of Javan might point to a political dependence. This would also give us a clearer understanding of the "Ionians" in the table. They would comprise the two islands of Rhodes and Cyprus, including the commercial city of Tarsus on the mainland, together with the neighboring Hittite principalities.

The names of the next three sons of Japheth, Tubal, Meshech, and Tiras, point, geographically, to eastern Asia Minor, and, historically, to the era of the sea peoples' migrations. Shortly

---

accounts in "Excavations at Gözlü Kule, Tarsus III," *The Iron Age,* published by H. Goldmann (Princeton, 1963), p. 93.

15. Brandenstein, *op. cit.,* 73ff.

after the fall of the great Hittite empire, Indo-Germanic tribes make their appearance in the Assyrian sources. Tiglath-Pileser I (1112-1074) recounts that 50 years before his time some 20,000 Mushki (Meshech) invaded the territory of the Upper Tigris. In the time that follows they were a constant threat to Assyria. Tiglath-Pileser was forced to undertake a campaign against them. He made his way through Armenia up to the Black Sea. In this campaign he also came to grips with the Tabal (Tubal), a tribe related to the Mushki, which eventually established itself on the Antitaurus.[16] The name Mushki, Moschoi in Greek, is an obvious reference to the migrations of the sea peoples. It means simply "young manhood."[17] In the ancient tribal territories, probably on the southern steppe of Russia, there was not enough land to support the population; thus the younger element of the population, as the *ver sacrum,* "sacred spring-time," was forced to migrate to a new location. For the later psalmist, the lands of Meshech and Tubal are places of the most extreme exile, equivalent to the end of the world (Ps. 120, 5). The list of sea peoples, finally, included also the Tiras (*turša,* Tyrsenians, Etruscans), which Merneptah numbers among the conquered peoples in his inscription. They were widely feared as pirates; their homeland is also to be sought in Asia Minor. Ancient saga[18] recounts that, on the occasion of a famine, the younger element of the population split in two; one half migrated over the Aegean towards Italy, while the other remained in Lydia in Asia Minor. Since this migration did not take place until 800 B.C., the united nation must have played a significant role in Asia Minor in the centuries prior to that time.[19]

b) *The younger element:* Whereas the sons of Japheth described above clearly belong to the time of the sea peoples,

---

16. Moortgat, *GVA*, 386, 398.

17. *Muški* is made up of the root *moz,* "young, young man," and the plural suffix - k'. Brandenstein, *op. cit.,* 82.

18. Herodot, I, 94.

19. Brandenstein, *op. cit.,* 82.

his other 6 sons belong to a much later era, even though they are placed first in the list. Their names are: *Gomer*, together with his sons Ashkenaz, Riphath, and Togarmah; *Magog* and *Madai*.

Towards the turn of the 8th century, new Indo-Germanic peoples were making their way across the Caucasus southwards. Their goal was the countries of the Fertile Crescent. The first wave was made up of the Cimmerians (Gomer); their name is still to be recognized in the Peninsula of Crimea, their original home. They annihilated the kingdom of the Mushki, with their legendary king Midas.[20] The Magog belong to the same migration. Attempts have been made to derive the name from *mat-gog*, "land of Gog," but this is not satisfactory. Brandenstein[21] seems to have pointed out the proper direction here. Herodotus[22] reports that the Scythians derive their origin from the earth-mother. Now, Ma-guga[23] actually means "having the earth-mother Ma as ancestral Lady." Such name formations, in this era of history, were of frequent occurrence.[24] For Ezekiel (38 and 39), in his apocalyptic writing, Magog, together with its leader Gog (Attila), is a type for the wild and godless people of the end-time, who will rise up against Sion, from the ends of the earth, but will eventually be defeated. The Magog are thus related to the Cimmerians and the Scythians who follow them. One of Gomer's sons is called Ashkenaz. He has been identified with the Scythians who followed on the heels of the Cimmerians and established themselves in the district around

---

20. Not a proper name, but a royal title, like Mithras "sun." The old Hittite kings liked to be addressed as "my sun." Brandenstein, *op. cit.*, 61.

21. *Ibid.* 65.

22. Herodot, IV, 5ff.

23. Hittite *huhhas* means "grandfather, ancestor"; in Lycian *kuga;* hence the king's name, Gyges, Gog in the Bible, which like Attila, means "little father."

24. Cf. the hieroglyph-Hittite *karua-huhas,* "grandfather stag."

Lake Urmia. From this position they harassed the Assyrian kingdom for a long time, until Esarhaddon concluded an alliance with them, which he sealed by sending his daughter to join the harem of the Scythian king. The Scythians kept faith, and, at the destruction of Nineveh, fought on the side of the Assyrians.

There is much to substantiate the opinion that the Ashkenaz are identical with the Ashkuz of the Assyrian sources. Their home would thus be in Ararat-Armenia.[25] Finally, Riphat and Togarmah point to the same general area. The Togarmah might well be identified with the Tilgarimmu of the Assyrian sources, north of Carchemish.

At the same time, in the Cimmerian era, the Medes (Madai) were harassing the Assyrian empire. One fortress after another fell into their hands, until they eventually managed to conquer the "great city," Nineveh, together with the Neo-Babylonians, and annihilated the Assyrian empire. Their rise is treated more explicitly in connection with the history of Israel.[26]

The editor of the Table of Nations has added a much greater northern belt to the relatively small area of the "Ionians." The "sons of Japheth" include the peoples who dwell along the outermost margin of the earth, to the north. The ancient catalogue listed only 8 peoples, while the more recent list enlarges the number to 14. It might seem more appropriate to follow this northern belt of the sons of Japheth by the immediate mention of the "Semitic" peoples in the middle. But the Table of Nations first pushes far to the south, and mentions the peoples who dwell in the middle only at the very end.

---

25. *EncMikr,* 763. J. Wiesner, "Kimmerier und Skythen" im Lichte neuer Indogermanenforschung, FF 19 (1943), 214-217. The Cimmerians are pre-Scythian Iranians, who had completed the transition to cavalry warfare and thereby gained the upper hand over their enemies. W. Brandenstein, "Die Abstammungssagen der Skythen," *WZKM* 52 (1953-55), 182-211.

26. Cf. Vol. IV, 310f.

2) THE SONS OF HAM

The derivation of the name Ham is lost in vague conjectures.[27] The Semitic ear might well have thought, consciously or unconsciously, of "hot, sun, south" (*ḥam*). Actually, the name is used to include the peoples of the then known southern world. But it is not the ethnological point of view that is predominant here; there seems, rather, to be an attempt to catalogue the sphere of influence of the Egyptian kingdom. It is no surprise that the land of Canaan, predominantly Semitic in population, is counted among the sons of Ham. The four sons *Cush, Misrayim,* (Egypt), *Put,* and *Canaan,* stand for the four principal divisions of the Pharaonic kingdom. The list begins in the extreme south with Cush, then follows the Nile Valley, in Egypt proper (Misrayim), and finally mentions the two outlying provinces, Libya in the west and Canaan in the east.

As we discussed more fully in the section on the geography of Egypt,[28] the land of Cush embraced the country between the first and fourth cataract, from the modern dam at Aswan southwards to Wadi Halfa. The "royal son of Cush" ruled here as a representative of the Pharaoh. In the course of time, the word Cush probably took on a broader meaning and came to refer to the southern regions whose boundaries were lost in the uncharted wilderness. Since Egypt already engaged in commerce on the Red Sea at a very early era and sent her ships into the distant countries of Ophir and Punt,[29] the tribes and cities of the Arabian Peninsula also came under Egyptian influence. This might be why they are here introduced as "sons of Cush."

---

27. *EncMikr* III, 163f.

28. See above, p. 10f.

29. V. Bissing, "Pyene (Punt) und die Seefahrten der Ägypter," *WOr* 3 (1948), 146-157, (Punt - Erythrea). H. Quiring, "Die Lage des Gold und Antimonlandes Punt und die erste Umfahrung Afrikas, *FF* 21/23 (1947), 161-163. (Punt - eastern coast of Africa from the Gulf of Aden southwards. The first circumnavigation of Africa from East to West took place, if not already in the 20th, at least in the 16th century B.C.)

The individual names can be identified only in the broadest terms. *Seba* refers to the southern coast of the Red Sea, where the Latin geographer Strabo was familiar with a port named Sabai or Sabat (the present Massawa in Eritrea). *Havilah* means, approximately, "sand country." This name appears in various territories. In this connection, it is probably a reference to the tribes in the Arabian Desert. *Sabtah* is probably to be identified with the capital of present-day Hadramaut. Somewhere in this same general area *Raamah* and *Sabteca* are to be sought. From Raamah in turn, the two sons *Sheba* and *Dedan* are descended. These two are more easily identified. Sheba (Vulg. Saba) is the Arabian kingdom, famous in antiquity, with its capital city of Marib, which has been recently excavated.[30] The Sabaeans were famous for their caravan trade. The visit of the Queen of Sheba was primarily commercial and political in purpose. Since the zenith of the kingdom of Sheba occurs only in the 8th century, we might well suppose that the Sabaeans were settled further to the north. But an equally probable solution is the supposition that the commercial traders maintained their outposts along the caravan route. *Dedan* is likewise an Arabian oasis in northern Heja (modern *ed-dağan*). Cush and his "sons," the Arab tribes along the coast of the Red Sea, mark the southern horizon of the Table of Nations.[31]

Next comes the Egyptian heartland, *Misrayim*, with his seven "sons." First we shall examine the names that are easiest to understand. Ancient Egypt was a double kingdom. In the word *Pathrusim* we find evidence of the ancient name[32] for Upper Egypt: "Land of the lotus plant" (Egyptian: *p'-t'-rś*, Assyrian *paturisi*). In *Naphtuhim*[33] we find the name for Lower Egypt: either "land of the north" (Egyptian *p-t-mahi*) or "land of the

30. W. Phillips. *Kataba und Saba. Entdeckung der verschollenen Königreiche an den biblischen Gewürzstrassen Arabiens* (1955).

31. For the identification of the individual name, see Simons, *GTT* 60, 207, 218, 219, 223, 232.

32. Erman, *ZAW* (1890), 118.

33. A. Clamer, *ClamB* I, 214.

delta district" (*na-patûh*). Since the island of Crete was considered as an extension of Egyptian power, it is no wonder that the people of Crete (*Caphtorim*) are counted among the children of Egypt. The next four names remain a puzzle. The *Ludim* cannot, in any event, refer to the Lydians of Asia Minor, since they are mentioned among the Semites. It is possible that an ancient name for Palestine is to be recognized here,[34] more precisely, a name for the coastal land of Palestine, which does not appear in the Canaan list.

The *Ananim* might well be identified as the ʿAmu, the desert dwellers of the Sinai Peninsula, against whom the Pharaohs frequently made war.[35] The *Lehabim* are explained by some as the Libyans, while others explain them as some other desert tribe; the *Casluhim* are identified as Cyrenaica or the eastern delta. The phrase "whence came the Philistines" no doubt refers to the land of Caphtor, already mentioned as the home of the Philistines, and not to the Casluhim.

Next comes the third son of Ham, whose name is *Put*. Most exegetes, somewhat too hurriedly, identify this with the incense country of Punt. But it is hardly probable that this distant country supplied mercenaries for the wars of the Pharaohs (cf. Jer. 46, 9; Ez. 27, 10, 38, 5). The Vulgate and Septuagint (LXX Jer. 26, 9 – Mt. 46), already translated Put as Libya. The prophets speak of Cush and Put in one and the same breath. Thus, it could hardly refer to the incense country *pwn-t*.

Ham's fourth son is *Canaan*. Here the editor of the list has more to say; he is discussing his own country. He counts 11 sons of Canaan, 7 of them cities and 4 of them tribes. *Sidon*, the powerful commercial city, is considered as Canaan's first-born. Then follow the cities on the Syrian coast: *Arka, Sin, Arvad,*

34. *EncMikr* IV, 439: Since the Middle Kingdom, the Palestinian coastland had been referred to as Retenu. By dropping the local ending *-enu*, we have the stem *Ret;* since the Egyptians substitute an *r* for the Semetic *l*, we would thus arrive at the name of the city Lut or Lod.

35. S. Yeivin, "Topographical and Ethnic Notes," ʿAtiqot 2 (1959), 155-164.

Simir, in the interior, *Hamat,* the much attacked fortress on the Orontes, and *Jebus* (Jerusalem). Then follow, under their collective national names, the *Hethites,* that is, the states in north Syria descended from the Hittites, the *Amorites,* that is, the city of Amurru in middle Syria, the *Hivites* in middle Palestine, and the *Girgashites,* which cannot be further identified.[36] The catalogue is striking both in what it says and in what it does not say. There is no mention, for example, of the cities of Ugarit and Tyre. The former had been completely destroyed by the invasion of the sea peoples, whereas the latter had not yet won its position of precedence over Sidon. Jerusalem is still referred to under the name of *Jebus,* which was certainly not the case after the city had been conquered by David. All this points to a date somewhere between 1200 and 1000 B.C. for the origin of the catalogue. The antiquity of the list is also evidenced by its mention of the cities of Sodom and Gomorrha (verse 19) as still existing. The list is not interested in sketching the boundaries of Canaan, but rather in establishing the fact that the south country too, the home country of Abraham, was a Canaanite territory. A fixed point is established in Gerar,[37] and a line described as running westward to Gaza and eastward to the 5 cities along the Dead Sea, a district in which a great part of the patriarchal history took place.

It follows that the sphere of influence of the Egyptian kingdom is comprised under the sons of Ham. In the later songs, the "land of Ham" no longer refers to Egypt proper (Pss. 78, 51; 105, 23, 37, 106, 22). It has undergone a change of meaning, which mirrors the rise and fall of the Egyptian kingdom.

3) THE SONS OF SHEM

The Semitic genealogy is different from the other two, already in terms of its formal outline. Immediately after Arpachshad,

---

36. Simons, *GTT* 239, 94. The question is whether, behind the name Girgas, we are perhaps to see a city name, such as Karkar on the Orontes.

37. On the location of Gerar see Vol. IV, 30f.

the son of Shem, his 17 descendants are already mentioned.

Shem's youngest son is called *Aram*. Here, an editor of the Davidic era would have had abundant opportunity to elaborate a long series of related names. The Aramaeans had taken definitive possession of their country around 1000 B.C. But the list mentions nothing of the Aramaic principalities of Syria, under the leadership of Aram-Damascus; only four unimportant desert tribes, *Uz, Hul, Gether,* and *Mash,* are numbered as sons of Aram. Insofar as these names can be identified at all – Hul and Gether are completely unknown, Mash might refer to Mount Masius near Nisibis, and Uz might be a north Syrian Bedouin tribe – the evidence all leads back to the territory from which the Aramaean migration originated.[38] The genealogy of Aram is thus very archaic.

The two oldest sons of Shem are *Elam* and *Ashur*. It might seem surprising to note that Elam, which is certainly not Semitic, is here counted among the Semites. But since it is not biological or racial elements, but rather political determinations which form the basis of the division, we must attempt to reconstruct the historical possibilities of bringing all four sons, Elam, Ashur, Arpachshad, and Aram, under one title. This should not prove too difficult. The name Shem stands for the empires founded in Mesopotamia. Then why is not Babel, the capital of the four ends of the earth, explicitly named as a son of Shem? This omission enables us to reconstruct the historical order of development evident in the catalogue; Babel is hidden behind the name *Arpachshad*. Earlier scholarship had no clue to this fact, but now it has been discovered[39] that the name Arpachshad is Indo-Iranian in origin. It is composed of two elements *arpa* "middle," and *-kshad,* "ruling, having dominion." Together with the mountain peoples, an Indo-Arian ruling class had penetrated into the Fertile Crescent. With the Hyksos, it made its way into

38. Simons, *GTT* 19.

39. W. Brandenstein, *Bemerkungen zur Völkertafel der Genesis*. Fs. A. Debrunner (1954), 59ff.

Egypt, and then, in Upper Mesopotamia, established the remnant state of Mitanni; in Babylonia itself, the Kassites (Kassu) maintained political power for many centuries. The Ancient Near East was thus ruled by an Indo-Arian ruling class, who fought from war chariots. It is precisely this foreign nobility that can be designated as Arpachshad. Around 1200, the sea peoples, in the west, and the Assyrians, in Mesopotamia, change the face of the earth. That is why, side by side with Arpachshad, on equal terms, we have the brothers Elam and Ashur. The greatest Assyrian ruler of the 13th century was Tukulti-Ninurta I (1243-1207). He annihilated the kingdom of Mitanni and brought the Kassite supremacy in Babylonia to an end. Now the time was ripe for *Elam* to rise in the east: around 1200 begins the classical era of the Elamite kingdom.[40] Around this time, Aram was, as the catalogue explains, only an insignificant Bedouin tribe. The fact that the tribe of Arpachshad is subdivided, in the catalogue, into "division" (*peleg*) and "diminution" (*yoktan*) already points to the subsequent fall of the Babylonion-Kassite empire. In the middle stands *Eber* (*Haber*). As we have already explained, the Biblical Eber is identical with the cuneiform Habiru, which, according to the evidence of the Amarna texts, had, at this same era, achieved the possession of the land of Canaan. The fact that Abraham, and, in his turn, Israel, are not directly descended from Aram, but rather from Arpachshad, thus corresponds to the historical facts. The patriarchs came from Upper Mesopotamia, the land of Mitanni (Arpachshad). The terse and sober words of this genealogy contain a brief but pregnant insight into the history of the Ancient Near East.

The genealogy of Shem, just like that of Japheth, was enlarged in terms of a new historical situation. Since it was the sons of Eber who were the more closely related to the Hebrew editor, he filled in the catalogue with 13 names (only 12 in LXX) of Bedouin tribes, whose territory reaches from Transjordan down into south Arabia. The identification of the individual

40. Moortgat, *GVA* 390.

names remains obscure. Particularly significant is the position of *Lud,* as a son on equal terms with Elam, Ashur, Arpachshad, and Aram. Either we must postulate the existence of a kingdom of Lud in Upper Mesopotamia, for which we have no other evidence,[41] or we must identify Lud as the normal term for the Asia Minor kingdom of Lydia. But how did this kingdom come to be reckoned among the sons of Shem? In an effort to contain the inroads of the Persians, the Babylonian kings, around 550 B.C., contracted a defensive and offensive alliance with Lydia.[42] Thus, Lud (Lydia) made its way into the Semitic family of peoples. Textual criticism reveals that the Table of Nations owes its final form to the era of the Babylonian exile, precisely the time at which Lud was a brother to Babel.

In outline form, we thus have the following general picture:

JAPHETH

Gomer, together with 1. *Ashkenaz* (*'aškenaz*) 2. *Riphath* (*rîphat*) 3. *Togarmah* (*togarmah*)

Magog, Madai, Javan, Tubal, Meshech, Tiras, together with Elishah, Tarshish, Kittim, Dodanim (Rodanim)

HAM

Cush together with 1. Seba (*seba'*) 2. Havilah (*ḥawîlah*) 3. Sabtah (*sabtah*) 4. Raamah (*ra'mah*) 5. Sabteca (*sabteka*) 6. Sheba (*šeba'*) 7. Dedan (*dedan*)

Misrayim (Egypt): 1. Ludim (*ludîm*) 2. Ananim (*'ananîm*) 3. Lehabim (*lehabîm*) 4. Naphtuhim (*naphtuḥîm*) 5. Pathrusim (*patrusîm*) 6. Casluhim (*kasluhîm*) 7. Caphtorim (*kaphtorîm*) [8. *Philistines* (*pelištîm*)]

Put: no sons

Canaan, together with the cities: 1. Sidon 2. Arka - Arkites

41. Simons, *GTT* 150-151.

42. More explicit treatment on the political conditions of that time in Vol. V, 9f.

(*'arka*) 3. *yebusî* (Jebusites) 4. Arvad (Arvadites) 5. Ṣimir (Zemarites) 6. Hamat(h) (Hamathites) 7. Karkar (Girgashites) and together with the districts: 8. Heth (*ḥet*) 9. *'emôrî* (Amorites) 10. Sianu (Sinites) 11. *ḥiwwî* (Hivites).

SHEM

Elam, Ashur, Arpachshad, together with: 1. Shelah (*šelaḥ*) 2. Eber (*ḥeber*) 3./4. Peleg (*peleg*) and Joktan (*yokṭan*) Joktan begot: 1. *Almodad* (*'almodad*) 2. *Sheleph* (*šelep*) 3. *Hazarmaveth* (*ḥaṣarwawet*) 4. *Jerah* (*yaraḥ*) 5. *Hadoram* (*hadoram*) 6. *Uzal* (*'uzal*) 7. *Diklah* (*diklah*) 8. *Obal* (*'obal*) 9. *Abimael* (*'abima'el*) 10. *Sheba* (*šeba'*) 11. *Ophir* (*'opîr*) 12. *Havilah* (*hawîlah*) 13. *Jobab* (*yobab*)

Lud, Aram, together with 1. Uz (*ḥûṣ*) 2. Hul (*ḥûl*) 3. Gether (*geter*) 4. Mash (*maš*)

If we now take the lists as a total, and isolate the primogenitures, we have the following results:

Japheth:	VII + 7 = 14
Ham	IV + 26 = 30
Shem	V + 21 = 26
	16 + 54 = 70

The table thus numbers precisely as many peoples as there were souls in Jacob's company when he emigrated from Egypt (Gen 46, 27). The sacred number 7 is once more the basis. Also, the seal of the name YHWH (26) appears twice in the table.

The compass of the known world is not a limited or narrow one, in ancient conception. It embraces the districts which modern history refers to as the lands of the Ancient Near East. Nor is the editor so narrow-minded as to insist on putting his own country in the middle. There is a world-wide and universal atmosphere in this account. As soon as the geographical horizon enlarges, the newly discovered peoples are fitted into the overall human genealogy as brothers and sons. There is nothing strange about the fact that the African and Asiatic peoples are not included, since at that time they represented an unexplored and little known land.

In this universality of attitude, the Table of Nations is a document unique in the literature of the Ancient Near East. Its value rises and falls with the faith in one God. Humanity forms a unity, brothers and sons, since the one God is their Father. The fact that, from this multitude of nations, only 70 peoples are numbered is evidence of a deliberate plan in the table. Just like the story of salvation, the Table of Nations is oriented towards the holy sabbath. The world of nations is created by God and for God.

But in the very middle of this Table of Nations, an almost erratic bloc, we find the account of the mighty Nimrod, the founder of a world kingdom. It is followed by the narrative of the tower of Babel, in which the author makes the point that the unification of mankind against God remains an impossible undertaking. The Table of Nations leads to the historical moment at which this unity collapses.

C) NIMROD, THE MIGHTY HERO

(Gen. 10, 8-12)

The monotonous lists make it very clear that all humanity represents one single family. The inserts, which introduce an element of life into this monotony, give the catalogue a dynamic and salvation history character. The section on Nimrod has been called an erratic bloc in the midst of a balanced context. It does introduce an element of motion into the history. *"Cush became the father of Nimrod; he was the first on earth to be a mighty man. He was a mighty hunter before the Lord; therefore it is said, 'Like Nimrod a mighty hunter before the Lord.' The be-*

ginning of his kingdom was Babel, Erech, and Akkad, all of them in the land of Shinar. From that land he went into Assyria, and built Nineveh, Rehoboth-Ir, Calah, and Resen between Nineveh and Calah; that is the great city" (Gen. 10, 8-12).

The peoples of the Ancient Near East are particularly fond of preserving the names of ancient heroes. The name Nimrod is attached to a ruin mound Birs Nimrud, under which the ancient Calah lies buried. At this strategically important point, in the triangle formed by the Euphrates and the upper Zab, Shalmaneser I (1276-1246) founded the new Assyrian capital Calah. His son Tukulti-Ninurta I (1246-1209), a very talented but immoderate prince, led the Assyrian kingdom to its first great golden age. Even the Greeks knew him under the name Ninos.[43] After successful campaigns against the Hittites and the mountain tribes of the Zagros mountain range, he turned his whole force against Babylon. The war ended with the defeat of the Kassite king Kashitiliash IV (1239-1231). Even the statue of Marduk was carried away to Ashur. For our knowledge of the accomplishments of Tukulti-Ninurta we are not dependent only on his military journals and inscriptions; a court poet composed an epic in his honor with some thousand verses. The epic gives an extremely broad account of the war against Babylon, often in a very bombastic style. After his victorious wars, Tukulti-Ninurta dedicated himself to an extensive building program. In the city of Ashur he built three temple towers; Nineveh was enlarged and beautified. The palaces were adorned with glazed bricks. His great passion, however, was big game hunting.[44] He succeeded in killing four aurochs in Mitanni, ten elephants in the neighborhood of Haran, and 120 lions; all this on foot; from his war chariot he killed 800.[45]

Exegetes have good reason to conclude that in the Biblical

---

43. W. v. Soden, "Der Nahe Osten im Altertum," *PropWG* II, 62.
44. *Ibid.*, 66.
45. E. Dhorme, "Les religions de Babylonie et d'Assyrie," *MANA* (1949), 104.

Nimrod we have an echo of the fame of the Assyrian king Tukulti-Ninurta. How, then, can he be called a son of Cush? The Assyrian king certainly had nothing in common with the Egyptian Cush. One possible grounds for the insertion is to be found in the fact that the words *kûš* and *kaššu* have somewhat the same sound.[46] These last are simply the Kassites already well known to history. When the author writes "and Cush became the father of Nimrod," this means, translated into our way of thinking, "from the kingdom of *kaššu,* the Kassites, proceeded the kingdom of Nimrod." This corresponds perfectly with the facts of ancient history described above. Reference to the Sumerian kingdom of Uruk (Erech), the kingdom of Sargon in Akkad, as well as the kingdom of the Amurru and the Kassites at Babel is frequently recalled; but now they are all dissolved by the kingdom of Nimrod. He transfers the center of power from the Babylonian south to the Assyrian north, where he builds new cities. Nineveh and Calah are sufficiently known; the position of Rehoboth-Ir and Resen remains an unsolved puzzle. This account is also composed on the basis of the sacred number 7; exactly 7 cities are mentioned.[47]

Behind the figure of the Assyrian king Tukulti-Ninurta, we also see the figure of the god Ninurta. The king seems to be the incorporation of the characteristics of this god. His name was originally read, erroneously, as Ninib.[48] Ninurta is the son of Enlil, the god of thunder, war, and, primarily, world dominion.[49] He has taken on many characteristics of Nergal. This fact is best appreciated by examining a Sumerian hymn to Nergal,

---

46. Others explain Cush as the name of the Babylonian city Kish, from which the Amurru established their kingdom and founded Babylon. Fr. Nötscher, *EB I,* 50.

47. The word *klnh* was formerly read as a city name Kalneh. But since such a city is completely unknown in Babylonia, it was read *kullānâ,* "all of them." *ClamB* I, 212.

48. Witzel, *Der Drachentöter Ninib* (1920).

49. On Ninurta, in greater detail, cf. E. Dhorme, *Les Religions de Babylonie et d'Assyrie,* pp. 102-109.

which, in the opinion of its translator,[50] can also be interpreted as applying to Ninurta: "Lord, bearing dread in heaven and on earth . . . begotten by your father for kingly dominion. . . . Hero, on the day on which your father begot you, your father Enlil made a present to you of the "mountain of the earth,"[51] together with all its people; he set the decision of human destiny firmly into your hand: "hero, Nergal, their king you are!" Ninurta is *the* "hero of Enlil" par excellence. The Bible gives this name an orthodox ring, by interpreting it as "heroic hunter, mighty hunter before the Lord." The Sumero-Babylonian god Ninurta and the bearer of his name, the king Tukulti-Ninurta, may have been so well known in the era of the ascendancy of Assyrian world rule, that they turned into a proverb still used in later years. The Bible has blotted out the mythological background, but the appearance of Nimrod reawakens the idea of world empire in the Table of Nations. The Hebrew reader might have heard a connotation of "rebel, revolutionary" in the name Nimrod. Thus, the erratic bloc of the Nimrod account prepares the way for the narrative of the tower of Babel. In terms of their contemporary history, these verses, like the older section of the Table of Nations, point to the time of the migration of the sea peoples.

---

50. J. J. A. van Dijk, *Sumerische Götterlieder,* Part II, 12. Text, p. 9ff.
51. Allusion to the world mountain of mythology: cf. Tower of Babel account.

CHAPTER XXV

THE FULLNESS OF PREHISTORY

ORDER VIII (GEN. 11, 1-32)

The last Order of ancient history once again focuses upon the nations of the world. Something gigantic is in progress: the attempt to combine all humanity into one single kingdom. The Babylonian tower (Tower of Babel, 11, 1-9) rises high in the midst of the nations of the world. But this gigantic work of human endeavor collapses. A new beginning must be sought. The toledot of Shem (11, 10-26) carry the genealogical line further, as far as Terah, father of Abraham. The toledot of Terah (11, 26-32) is already a prelude to the patriarchal narratives which follow. The principal characters of the new drama of history are introduced: Abram, Sarah, and Lot. Terah's death in Haran forms the conclusion of prehistory. In the manuscript, accordingly, these three divisions are carefully marked. The text presents the following picture:

	N		I		S		
Building of the Tower	65	+	7	+	49	=	121
Toledot of Shem	182						182
Toledot of Terah	89						89
	336	+	7	+	49	=	392

It is immediately obvious that the speech sections follow the jubilee number 49. Equally obvious are the 65 narrative words in the story of the tower building; these follow the numerical value of the name Adonai. The toledot of Shem form half a jubilee year (2 X 182 = 364): moreover, the first 5 generations number 110 words, while 7 and 8 have 72 words: these too are familiar numbers.

The total sum of 392 is best analyzed as the total sum of 360 + 32, that is, a cyclic solar year plus the number of wisdom. But is there some clear indication in the text itself that these 32 words are to be so isolated? There is. In the toledot of Terah we find two notices of death: "Terah begot . . . Nahor; and Nahor died . . ." (27-28) with 22 words. Also: "And all the days of Terah were . . ." (vs. 32) with 10 words. This is the classic composition of the number of wisdom: 32 = 10 primordial words and 22 letters/elements. Order VIII is thus under the influence of the solar numbers.

A) TOWER OF BABEL

As contrasted with the monotonous catalogue of the table, we are here faced with a dramatically constructed ancient song, which is framed in arsis and thesis. In the arsis we find this theme: The whole world was one tongue and one language; the thesis on the other hand, must confess that the whole world was a babel of languages and peoples. In between, we have two scenes of unparalleled drama. The first is played on earth, the second in heaven.

11 1 All the world was once one language
and one in its words.
2 Then it happened as they migrated eastwards,
in the Land of Shinar a valley they found
and settled there.
3 Each to the other now spoke:

"Come, let us make us bricks
and burn them hard!"
4 *The brick served for their stone*
asphalt was their mortar.
They said: "Come!
5 *Let us build city and tower,*
and its head in the heaven!
6 *We will establish for us a name;*
in all the world shall we otherwise scatter!"
7 *Then Yahweh looked down*
on the city and the tower,
that the men had built.
8 *And Yahweh spoke: "One people are they,*
and one language all of them!
9 *Nothing now seems impossible to them*
that they plan to accomplish.
10 *Let us go down and confuse*
their language there below,
11 *that none hear and understand*
the tongue of the other!"
12 *Thus the Lord scattered them*
in all the world's direction.
The tower building they had to leave.
13 *Thus their name is also Babel;*
for there did the Lord confuse
all the world's tongue.
14 *From there did the Lord scatter them*
in all the world's direction.

The narrative of the tower building is set in a cosmic framework: "All the world was one language..." (Gen. 11, 1). "The Lord confused the language of all the earth; and from there the Lord scattered them abroad over the face of all the earth" (11, 9). Humanity's natural tendency to work at cross purposes is to be channeled into one mighty unified effort; the martial air of unity has already sounded in the rhythm of the advancing world. Humanity wants to be a unity, and, as an expression of this unity, they mean to build a world capital with a mighty tower. The unifying motif in the tower building narrative is thus the concept of a world kingdom. In the literature of the Ancient Near East there is no parallel. Perhaps we are to understand this as an abbreviated statement of history, a short and dramatic representation of the long historical process by which the pagan world empire evolved, forgetting the true God of antiquity and, in its unbounded development of power, attempting presumptuous undertakings against the will of God, a narrative and world power that are both concentrated in the world capital of Babel.[1]

That the Tower of Babel is not simply a religious monument, but actually the exponent of political power is easily understood on the basis of an outline view of the history of the Babylonian tower. The most ancient story of the tower is not yet known. Since the ascendancy of the first dynasty of Babel, which, since Hammurabi's time, had claimed sovereignty over the then-known world, the tower must have played a great role; but our oldest historical records speak only much later of a reconstruction, collapse, and destruction of the Tower. The fate of the Tower mirrors the rhythm of the world empires of the Ancient Near East.

In the Table of Nations, the figure of the mighty Nimrod has been inserted. As explained above, this is probably a reminiscence of the Assyrian king Tukulti-Ninurta. It was precisely this Nimrod who destroyed Babel and carried off the statue of Marduk to Ashur. It is thus quite possible that the Biblical account of the Tower building relates to this episode. The text, in Pentateuchal criticism, is attributed to the Yahwist, whose activity is dated in the Davidic-Solomonic era, a time at which Israel had no eye-witness familiarity with the Tower of Babel. Since it is also possible to establish literary correspondences

---

1. H. Junker, "Genesis," *EB I* (1955), 54. *Ibid.*, "Die Zerstreuung der Völker nach der biblischen Urgeschichte," *TTZ* 70 (1961), 182-185.

with the *Enûma eliš* epic,[2] the Biblical account is most likely a commentary on the Babylonian epic of the Tower building, which was known throughout the whole of the Ancient Near East. But since the Tower of Babel was the symbol of world sovereignty, its later history must be briefly sketched.

In his war against Babel, the Assyrian king Sennacherib had both the city and tower of Babel destroyed (689 B.C.), but his son Esarhaddon began its reconstruction in the year 681, a task which his son Ashurbanipal completed in the year 668. In the civil war (652-648) between Ashurbanipal and Šamaš-šum-ukin, who, as king of Babel, wanted to be independent of his brother, the tower is once again destroyed. The neo-Babylonian kings Nabopolassar and Nebuchadnezzar II, immediately upon their accession to power, undertook a completely new structure, which spread the fame of Babel throughout the whole of the then-known world.

During the Persian era, the Tower still stood in all its magnificence. Cyrus adopted a conciliatory politics in religion. Upon his triumphal entry into Babel, he did not have the temples destroyed, but rather "himself grasped the hand of Marduk," as a sign of sovereignty. It was not until the time of Xerxes, about 478 B.C., who had the statue of Bel-Marduk destroyed, in order to quell revolutionary activities, that the tower was once again attacked. At any event, the tower was a complete ruin when Alexander the Great, in the year 331, began the reconstruction of Babylon as the capital city of his world empire. He had great mounds of plaster and brick carried away, in order to lay a new foundation for the tower, which was to rise in all its former splendor. His sudden death prevented the execution of this gigantic plan. His successors moved to other capitals, and abandoned the tower to its fate.

The Tower today is less than a ruin; it is a vast depression, in the middle of which, even today, there is a mighty mound

---

2. E. A. Speiser, "World Plays on the Creation Epic's Version of the Founding of Babylon," *Orientalia* 25 (Rome, 1956), 317-323.

of clay, whose covering of well baked bricks is still used by the Arabs as a quarry. This accounts for the rather insignificant remains of the ground plan which has been unearthed by excavation. The inscription of the Greeks (Herodotus) and the cuneiform texts which have been discovered enable us to somewhat reconstruct the style and magnitude of the tower in the Golden Age of the neo-Babylonian kingdom.[3]

The ground plan of the Tower is, according to the excavations, a square of about 91 m. The massive inner structure measures 61 m. square. The outer layer of burned brick thus presented a wall strength of 15 m. From the southeast side, a great approach way, 9.35 m. in width, led up to the tower; to the right and to the left there were imposing entrances. The Tower itself was a step pyramid, with seven storeys, diminishing towards the top.

The first storey had a height of 33 m. At this height the terrace diminished from 91 to 78 m. and rose in a second storey of 18 m. In a series of gradually diminishing squares (60, 51, 42, 24 m.) the 3rd, 4th, 5th, and 6th storeys all arose to the same height, 6 m. The 7th storey, with the temple sanctuary, rose 15 m. It was decked with blue glazed bricks, and vied with the color of the sky. The "roof" of the Tower was, perhaps, adorned with splendid, cast-metal horns, like the temple in Susa, whose horns were broken up by Ashurbanipal.

A description of the dimensions in terms of feet or meters makes it easier to grasp the overall plan and effect of the structure, but it makes it all but impossible to appreciate the underlying symbolism. But when we examine into the ancient Babylonian units of measure, we are no longer dealing with mere surmise. In the cuneiform tablet of Anubêlshunu, from the year 229 B.C., the 83rd year of King Seleucus (Seleucid Era), there is a precise reference to the dimensions of the tower: side, front, and height. This table does indeed date from an era in which the tower itself

---

3. The descriptions of the tower, together with the dimensions assigned is from E. Unger, *Babylon, die heilige Stadt. Nach der Beschreibung der Babylonier*, Berlin (1970, 2nd. ed.), Cuneiform Tablet on p. 248.

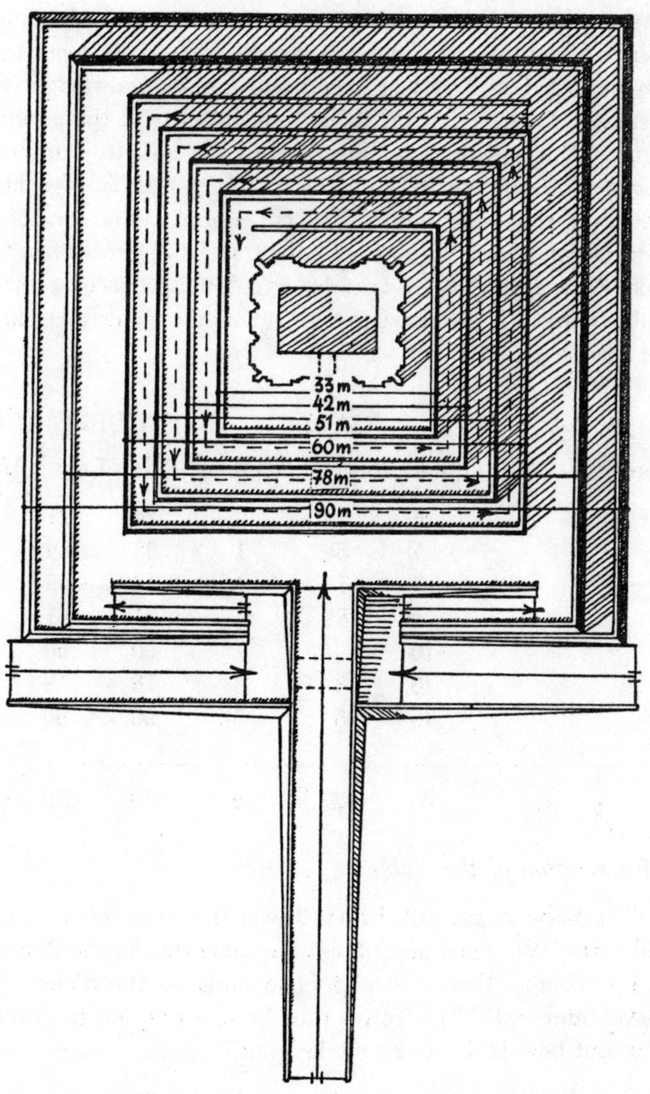

Ill. 3: Ground Plan of the Tower of Babel

had long been destroyed. But the writer bases his data on an ancient model from the city of Borsippa. Even these sober figures were regarded as a sort of sacral and initiate knowledge of the mysteries. That is why the tablet concludes with these ominous words: "The initiate is to show this to the initiate. But the un-initiate shall not see it!" What is the secret knowledge hidden beneath these dimensions? The cuneiform tablet measures in terms of *gar,* a measure which can be translated into various types of cubit measure: 1 GAR = 12 lesser cubits = 8 paced cubits = 6 double cubits. The following table gives the dimensions in *gars* and double cubits.

	GARS			DOUBLE CUBITS		
Storey	Side	Front	Height	Side	Front	Height
VII	4	3½	2½	24	21	15
VI	5½	5½	1	33	33	6
V	7	7	1	42	42	6
IV	8½	8½	1	51	51	6
III	10	10	1	60	60	6
II	13	13	3	78	78	18
I	15	15	5½	90	90	33
	63	62½	15	378	375	90

Interpretation of the Table:

The Babylonians called their Tower the "foundation of heaven and earth." We must accordingly presume that in the dimensions of the Temple there are also some hints of the dimensions of heaven and earth. The Tower thus becomes an image of the cosmos. But how is this to be worked out?

1. Solar Year: The first origins of the sexagesimal system are hidden in the shadows of prehistory. At all events, the system was known to the Sumerians. Both space and time were measured according to this system. If we look at our clock today we realize our debt to these ancient cultures; we still reckon time in terms of the ancient Babylonian and Sumerian measures. An average man walking was presumed to be able to cover 360 double cubits (DC) in 4 minutes, and 90 DC in a single minute. This is the key to understanding the dimensions of the first storey of the Tower: 4 X 90 = 360, the square of the side. This is clearly a reference to the solar year. The particularly effective result of this system is the fact that the structure can translate time in measurable degrees of length and breadth. The following table will make these relationships clearer: double cubits (DC) are shown as equivalent to cables or watches. The distance that can be covered in terms of minutes is as follows:

	1 minute	90 DC		
	4 minutes	360 DC	6 cables	
	1 hour	90 cables		
	4 hours	360 cables		1 watch
1 day	24 hours	2160 cables		6 watches
6 days	144 hours	12960 cables ..		36 watches

7th day as day of rest. . . .

2. *Dimensions of the earth*: If we assume 6 days of walking and the 7th day as a day of rest, and if we also keep in mind the ancient wisdom oracle: "If a man keeps walking straight ahead, he is back to where he started in one year," we get the figure 364 – 52 sabbaths = 312 days of walking, the precise number of Storey II of the Tower of Babel (4 X 78 = 312). Translating these temporal measures into a measure of distance, we get the following results:

1 week = 6 days = 12,960 cables
52 weeks = 312 days = 673,960 cables

Now since, upon the termination of this amount of walking, a complete circle of 360 degrees has been accomplished, we can take the final sum as the circumference of a circle and then calculate its radius. Since, moreover, the Babylonians were familiar with the function of Pi, we have

$$\text{circumference} = 2\pi r \qquad r = \frac{c}{2\pi} = \frac{673.960}{2x3.1444} = 107{,}160 \text{ cables.}$$

Turning now to the stone stele of Gudeas for a key to the value of the individual dimensions, we find that one cable is equivalent to 59.54 meters. This gives us a radius of 6380 kilometers. This figure is, in actual fact, the radius of the earth, the modern calculation being generally given as 6378 kilometers. This makes it very clear that the ancients actually regarded the Tower of Babel as the center or focus of the "globe" and thus the very foundation of the world.

3. *Celestial Polar Year:* In discussing the Biblical chronologies, we have already touched upon the phenomenon known as the precession of equinoxes. The Babylonians calculated the precession as 50 seconds per year, and thus one degree in 72 years. This makes it easy enough to calculate the amount of time it would require to complete the circle of 360 degrees; 360 X 72 = 25,920, that is, the figure we call the celestial polar year. Furthermore, this makes it easy to understand how the Babylonians regarded their tower as the foundation of the heaven.

This brief explanation should be sufficient. It is enough to show that the Tower was not a primitive or unsophisticated structure. It presupposes a high degree of astronomical expertise, precise celestial observation, and considerable mathematical concentration. One might truly admit that here mankind had achieved a climax of abstract cosmic knowledge. If, now, we can discover the very same basic conception at work in the Bible, that can only mean that the Biblical writers have incorporated the secular wisdom of their day into the sacred text. They meant to show that it was not the Tower of Babel, but rather the word of YHWH, that is the one true foundation of the cosmos. The text itself is thus structured on a cosmic measure.

Since we have already considered the deluge calendar in considerable detail, we need now refer only to the fact that the front of the Tower of Babel is given as 375 cubits. The flood, from 2,17,600 to 2,27,601 lasts for 375 days. In the deluge narrative we read that the waters covered the highest peaks by 15 cubits. Now, the highest and 7th storey of the Tower has a height of precisely 15 cubits. Is there some connection here?

In considering the total chronology of the Bible, we discovered that from Adam to the destruction of the Solomonic Temple, the precession of equinoxes had advanced 55 degrees. The number 55 is therefore a structural number. What are we to say to the fact that, on a cuneiform tablet,[3a] we read that the Temple of Marduk, the principal god in Babylon, had precisely 55 cells. It is in terms of observations such as these that the relationship between the Bible and the sphere of Babylonian influence is more and more strongly demonstrated.

The text of the Tower of Babel narrative numbers, in the Hebrew text, 121 words. To divide this total into 1 + 120 might at first seem quite arbitrary. But in the Greek Septuagint there is an equally obvious additional unit (181 = 1 + 180) in the word count. The figures in both these texts are so surprisingly similar in structure that one must necessarily postulate some knowledge of the dimensions of the Tower of Babel. We have already mentioned that the cuneiform tablet gives the dimensions only in *gars*, which we have translated into equivalent values for double cubits (DC). There is also, however, an equivalent in lesser (*suklu-*) cubits (12 *suklu*-cubits) or paced cubits (8 paced cubits). The height of the Tower would thus give the following equivalents: 15 *gars* = 180 lesser or *suklu*-cubits and 120 paced cubits. The Hebrew and the Greek text are expressing the same value in terms of different cubit equivalents!

3a. *Loc. cit.*, p. 244.

The Tower bore the name "*E-temen-an-ki,* that is, temple of the foundation of heaven and earth." It belonged to the great temple structures, which bore the name "*E-sag-ila* - temple which raises its head." In the tower sanctuary, there was no cult image. This room was regarded as the *Šaḫaru,* that is, the most intimate nuptial chamber of the god. It contained only a nuptial bed for the divinity. The Tower was, essentially, an "epiphany-temple," the place of the theophany. This probably also explains the position of the Tower in the direction of the favorable winds. His worshippers thought of Marduk as coming in the wind, to take possession of his nuptial chamber, and by performing the nuptial rites with a "divine bride," endowing all creatures with life and fertility. He would come down from the Tower, and take his place in the temple at the foot of the Tower, and there appear to mankind in the cult statue. The Tower probably played a significant role at the New Year's Feast, and the ceremony of the "sacred wedding" (*hieros gamos*).

The Tower of Babel, in its original construction, dates back to the origins of the Sumerian architecture. The step-temple goes back to the terrace-form foundation for the hut-dwellings, in the flood districts.[4] Every Sumerian city state had its step-tower and temple. The best preserved today is to be found in Ur. But in the Bible, it is the Babylonian tower which turns into a point of departure for a theology of world empire.

In order to give a clearer picture of the significance of the Babylonian tower, we present an excerpt from the building records of Nabopolassar and Nebuchadnezzar.

On a clay cylinder, discovered in the year 1910 in the depression of the tower, Nabopolassar (626-605) says this: "When, upon the command of Nabu and Marduk (I had struck down the enemies), Marduk the Lord ordered me to work on the foundation of Etemenanki, the step-tower of Babel, which, even before my time, had begun to collapse and fall into ruin, to

---

4. Cf. Galling in *Reallexikon für Antike und Christentum.* (*RAC*): Babel.

build up the ground walls on the solid earth and to make its head vie with the heaven. The pick, the spade, the brick-mold of ivory I supplied. Countless people, the work-levy of my country, I enlisted in the project. I had tiles made, and had bricks prepared . . . I had a flood of asphalt and bitumen brought in. . . Wise building masters I engaged. . . I laid its foundation; gold, silver, and stones from the mountain and the sea I worked into its foundation. . . Fine oil, and fragrant herbs I poured under the tiles. An image of my majesty, bearing a basket of tiles, I prepared and laid into the foundation. Before Marduk my Lord I bowed my neck. My garments, the magnificent garment of my majesty, I girt up about me and I bore clay tiles upon my head. . . Marduk, my Lord, look down graciously upon my work. . . Just as the tiles of Etemenanki are set firm for ever, establish firmly the foundations of my throne for days far off."

Nabopolassar was unable to finish the building that he began when "Marduk gave him land and people to rule over, and ordered him to plunder the lands of his enemies." His son Nebuchadnezzar II (605-562) brought it to a conclusion. Among his achievements he recounts the following: "I set my hand to the work of raising Etemenanki, making its head to vie with the heaven. The men who dwell in the far distance, whom Marduk, my Lord, has entrusted to me, all the lands, the totality of all the peoples, from the upper to the lower sea, distant lands, the kings of distant mountains and out-lying islands. . . I forced them all to bear the yoke of Marduk. . . I lay the tile basket upon them. . . I had Etemenanki, the step-tower of Babel, made brilliant with asphalt and bright blue gilded tiles. . . To cover its rooms I used mighty cedars. . . ." [5]

Even though these texts date from the late Babylonian era, they give us some appreciation of the structure of the first Tower. The Tower is the symbol of world dominion and the seat of

5. The texts are taken from Fr. Wetzel and F. H. Weissbach, "Die Hauptheiligtum in Babylon, Esagila und Etemenanki," *WVDOG* 59 (1938). An outline survey of the literary sources and text excerpts in A. Jeremias, *ATAO,* 3rd edition, 1916, "Urkunden zum Turmbau von Babel," 170-175.

Ill. 4: View of the Tower of Babel from the Southeast

the gods. The construction of the world empire is a gigantic undertaking, which could not be accomplished without doing violence to human rights. It has a certain note of opposition to God about it. That is why Yahweh comes down to look at the city and the Tower (Gen. 11, 5). There is a certain irony in this statement. The gigantic human accomplishments are so great that Yahweh has to come down in order to see them. In order to put an end to this arrogant enterprise of united humanity, and their attempts to scale the heavens, he confuses their languages, so that men no longer understand each other and the completion of their great plans is impossible. Psalm 54/55, 10 helps us to understand the real meaning of this confusion of language: "Destroy their plans, O Lord, confuse their tongues; for I see violence and strife in the city." This prayer for help is certainly not a reference to the formation of new languages. Language is an expression of human thought. The growing divergence in patterns of thinking is the deeper grounds behind this inability to understand each other. The Tower narrative is not merely a document which explains the evolution of the various human languages; this may have occurred at a much earlier age; already in most ancient times, in the territory of the Babylonian plain, various peoples and tongues have mixed together. The new element of the Biblical narrative is to be found in the interpretation that this loss of the one and universally understandable human language is the expression of a divine judgment which was called down upon humanity by its own titanic undertakings against the will of God. This basic truth is concentrated on the word Babel, a name which in the popular Hebrew etymology is easily connected with the verb "*bālāl* (older form *balbila*), multiply, confuse," a stem which, in the Akkadian language, means gate of God, *bab-ilu.*[6] The manifold variety of peoples, as presented in the Table of Nations, portrayed the creative activity of God; the confusion in the

---

6. The plural form "*bab-ilani*" - gate of the gods, developed into the Greek form Babylon.

world of nations can now be expressed and understood only in terms of a divine judgment.

B) CONCLUSION AND TRANSITION

When we give Order VIII the title "Fullness of Prehistory," the word fullness implies that something is coming to an end. In the toledot of Shem the transmission of life is recorded as far as Terah (11, 10-26). Then the list starts all over again with the inscription: "Toledot of Terah" (11, 27). Now it would be the place of Abram, son of Terah, to continue the genealogy, but his wife Sarah is reported as being barren. Thus, from the human point of view, the road has simply come to a dead end. If life is to pass on from here, it can only be the result of God's special intervention. That is why this brief mention (11, 30) is already an introduction to Abram's supreme test of faith in his God. The significance of the numbers in this genealogy has already been discussed in the preliminary sketch of the problems of Biblical chronology. We proceed now to a brief comment upon the structure.

The Semite genealogy (Gen. 11, 10-26) is a continuation of the genealogy of Seth. Here, however, it is only the age of generation and the subsequent years that are given, the total number of years not being mentioned. The genealogy contains 182 words, half a solar year. The sequence of generation overlaps with the first half of the Table of Nations (10, 21ff).

	Begot at Age	Subsequent Years
1. Shem	100	500
2. Arpachshad	35	403
3. Shelah	30	403
4. Eber	34	430
5. Peleg	30	209
6. Reu	32	207

7. Serug	30	200
8. Nahor	29	119
9. Terah	70	135

The numbers of the Semite catalogue are thus a continuation of the Adamite catalogue. The key to understanding these new lists is the generation age of Adam. Adam's generation number is 130, which, divided into 100 and 30, gives the numbers of Shem, Shelah, Peleg, and Serug. Terah's number 70 is derived from 100 less 30; Arpachshad's 35 is half of this. The numbers of Eber, Arpachshad, Reu, and Nahor form an ascending series, in terms of the numbers 1, 2, 3. The intervals from Arpachshad to Eber, from Eber to Reu, and from Reu to Nahor, progress in a series of 1, 2, and 3. The total of the generations is 3 times the generation age of Adam: 100 plus 30 equals 130; 30 plus 30 plus 70 equals 130; 35 plus 34 plus 32 plus 29 equals 130. Translated, this means that the new humanity, after the flood, is the continuation of humanity as first founded in Adam. From Adam alone is the current of life derived.

RETROSPECT ON PREHISTORY

The story of the Tower of Babel is the final chapter in prehistory. It would be wise to take a brief retrospect over the important Biblical-theological events that take form and figure in this period.

Prehistory sketches the way of God with humanity. From humanity's point of view, it is characterized by an avalanche of growing sinfulness: the sin of the first man; Cain; Lamech; marriage prior to the flood; the Tower of Babel. These are the stages of the path that led man farther and farther away from God. It is thus a constantly widening gulf between man and God which is narrated in this series of events.

Then God reacts to this outbreak of human sinfulness, in a series of strict divine judgments. The punishment of the first man was severe; even more severe was that of Cain, who was forced to make his way forever from the face of God; then came the deluge, and finally the confusion of tongues and the eventual dissolution of the unity of mankind. Prehistory ends with a serious question: What will be God's future relationship with his rebellious, but now prostrate humanity? Is this catastrophe the final one?

Side by side with the divine sentence, there is always an element of God's grace, shining through his renewed mercies: the Proto-evangelium in Paradise, the line of Patriarchs faithful to God, the new covenant with Noah, the blessing on Shem. If the sin was great, the grace was more powerful (Rom. 5, 20). All this is, of course, not formulated in terms of theological concepts. Concepts such as *salvation, grace, forgiveness,* are sought for here in vain; it is only the facts which are related, turning into reality in the words of divine patience.

The story of the Tower closes with an unrelieved judgment upon humanity. And thus the whole of prehistory seems to break off on a shrill note of dissonance. Is God's relationship to humanity now definitely broken? This is the question that no careful reader of chapter 11 can keep from asking.

In fact, we might go so far as to say that the Biblical author has arranged the content of his prehistory in precisely such a way as to give rise to this question, and pose it in all its unrelieved severity. It is only against this background that we are properly prepared to accept the incomprehensibly good news that follows the unconsoling story of the Tower of Babel, namely the choice, blessing, and promise of Abraham.

We are standing at a point where prehistory and salvation-history overlap, and thus at the most important passage of Old Testament history. Prehistory recounts the constant breakdown of the relationship between humanity and God, and concludes with God's judgment upon the nations. The question of God's salvation for the nations remains open.

All of a sudden, this universal frame of reference fades into the background; the whole ecumenical world drops away, and all our interest is concentrated on one individual man. Earlier chapters told of general humanity: creation of man, woman, humanity, nations – all universal themes; chapter 12, 1, is the first hint of the particularism of election, the beginning of the "great scandal." From among the fullness of the nations, God chooses one man for himself, takes him away from his tribal bonds, and makes him the beginning of a new people, the recipient of the great promise of salvation. This blessing promised to Abraham is destined to extend far beyond Israel; in fact, it has a universal significance for every generation on earth.

Prehistory thus pushes on with an inner necessity towards the election of Abraham: it is clearly recognizable as a universal preconstruction for the salvation history which now begins in its full scope.[7]

The peculiar accomplishment of the Biblical prehistory just presented in this text might very well lie in the fact that here for the first time proper attention has been accorded the structural principles of the sacred text. Even in terms of its content, we are necessarily forced to conclude that prehistory forms one unit in the progress of salvation history. Can this final fact be demonstrated on the basis of structure? I think it can. The speech sections must serve as our point of departure here.

A) HOW MANY SPEAKERS? In considering the structure of Genesis, we came upon the 11 toledot, each of them to be interpreted as either a repetition or a resumé. The same principle was evident in the creation narrative, with its 10 words of creation and the 1 word of law. Now, in the whole of prehistory, there are also exactly 11 speakers: 1. YHWH-Elohim, 2. YHWH, 3. Elohim, 4. Adam, 5. Eve, 6. dragon, 7. Cain, 8. Lamech, 9. Noah, 10. Nimrod, 11. Babel. If, once again, in terms of the earlier discussion of the 10 + 1, we look for one of the 11 to be singled out from the other 10, we immediately hit upon the speaker YHWH-Elohim,

7. The thoughts expressed in this retrospect are taken largely from G. von Rad, "Das erste Buch Mose," *ATD* (1949), 127-29.

who stands out as a clear example of resumé. Thus we once again have the structural principle of 10 + 1.

b) HOW MANY SPEECHES? These 11 speakers are made to share a total of 55 speeches. Now we have already discovered that this number is the real key to the mystery of Biblical chronology. The date for the deluge forms, as it were, the caesura, while the destruction of the Solomonic Temple is the endpoint. The two periods yielded the relationship of 23 + 32 = 55. We also observed that the Temple of Marduk has precisely 55 cells. The number is clearly meant to express all-perfection (*panteleia*) and be symbolic of a compact and self-contained unity. This is only a further confirmation of the unity of the Biblical prehistory.

The distribution of the speeches among the individual speakers also betrays a conscious and deliberate structural principle. The confessional number 39 dictates that God be assigned a total of 39 speeches: 13 YHWH-Elohim + 9 YHWH + 17 Elohim (13 + 26 = *YHWH 'ehed*, "Yahweh the One"): of the other speakers, Adam and Eve and Noah have 3 each, Cain and Babel have 2 each, and the dragon, Lamech, and Nimrod 1 each. It would take us too far afield to consider the individual totals here. We must be content with the final totals.

c) THE SEALED BOOK: If we combine the word count of the 8 orders of prehistory with the prefatory beginning of the creation narrative, in terms of the component elements we have described earlier, we obtain the following results:

$$\underbrace{2523\ \mathrm{N} + 157\ \mathrm{I}}_{2680} + \underbrace{1082\ \mathrm{S} + 11\ \mathrm{i} + 19\ \mathrm{s}}_{1112} = 3792$$

The total number for the speech sections – the 11 words of introduction (i) in the quoted speeches, in the temptation story, are also direct speech – is the sum of 1112 words, which obviously suggests the resolution into 1000 + 112. The peculiarity of the prehistory lies in the use of the double divine name. Now the numerical value of this doubled name YHWH-Elohim is 26 + 86 = 112. The entire unit is thus sealed by the formula: Large Aleph + YHWH-Elohim.

The narrative sections (N) include the 6 toledot inscriptions with a total of 25 words. If we isolate these as titles, and there would appear to be good justification for this, we arrive at the following structural formula: XXV + 2600 + 55. Once again we have the seal of the Name of YHWH (26) raised to a higher level (X 100) and the number of all-perfection, 55.

We are, accordingly, quite justified in claiming that any interpretation of prehistory as told in the Bible must necessarily rest on a preliminary examination of the structural principles of the text itself. Only then does the Pentateuchal critic dare to attempt the second step, the concentration on the actual data from the past. Our investigations have shown that the author or authors of this prehistory were not only redactors or editors of an ancient body of traditional material, but actually true and proper authors in their own right. One might, in fact, go so far as to maintain that this new discovery of the fact that the high numbers we find everywhere in the dates and ages of prehistory are based upon an ancient astronomical heritage, handed down from one generation to the next, could well prove to lead the way towards some new and essential understanding of the text and message of Scripture, especially today, in the age of space flight.

INDEX

PHOENICIAN COSMOGONIES 265

ORIGIN OF MAN 271

ORIGIN OF PEOPLES 371ff

RISE OF THE NATIONS 407ff

GEOGRAPHY OF THE OLD TESTAMENT

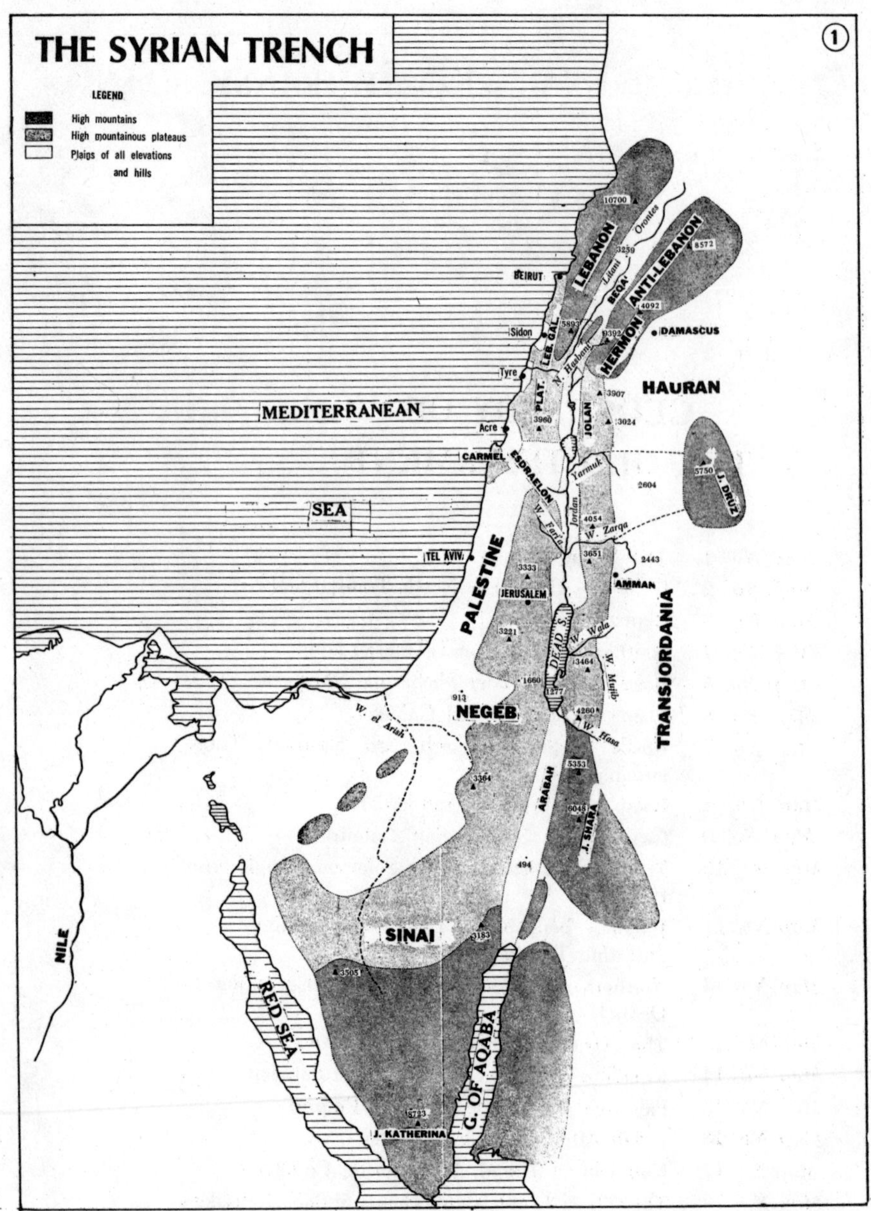
THE SYRIAN TRENCH
1
LEGEND
High mountains
High mountainous plateaus
Plains of all elevations and hills
LEBANON
ANTI-LEBANON
Orontes
Litani
BEQA'
10700
3250
8572
BEIRUT
4092
5893
Sidon
LEB. GAL.
N. Hasbani
9392
HERMON
DAMASCUS
Tyre
PLAT.
3907
HAURAN
MEDITERRANEAN
3960
JOLAN
3024
Acre
CARMEL
ESDRAELON
Yarmuk
5750
J. DRUZ
2604
SEA
Jordan
W. Far'a
4054
W. Zarqa
PALESTINE
TEL AVIV
3651
2443
3333
AMMAN
JERUSALEM
TRANSJORDANIA
DEAD S.
W. Wala
3221
3464
W. Mujib
1660
1277
913
NEGEB
4260
W. Hasa
W. el Arish
5353
ARABAH
3364
6048
J. SHARA
494
SINAI
3183
3505
NILE
RED SEA
G. OF AQABA
5723
J. KATHERINA

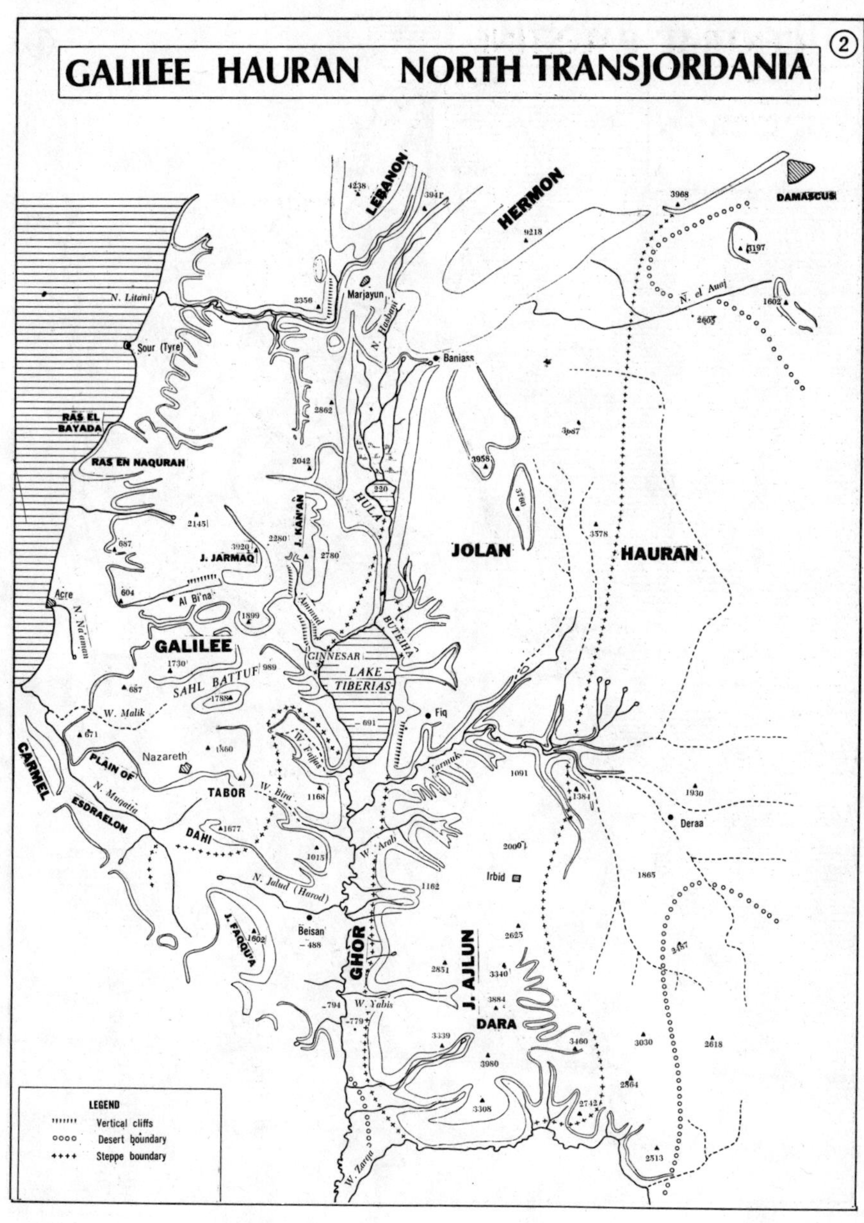
GALILEE HAURAN NORTH TRANSJORDANIA
2
LEBANON
HERMON
DAMASCUS
N. Litani
Marjayun
N. Hasbani
Sour (Tyre)
Baniass
RAS EL BAYADA
RAS EN NAQURAH
HULA
J. KAN'AN
JOLAN
HAURAN
J. JARMAQ
Acre
Al Bi'na
N. Na'aman
GALILEE
GINNESAR
LAKE TIBERIAS
BUTEIHA
SAHL BATTUF
W. Malik
Fiq
Yarmuk
CARMEL
PLAIN OF
ESDRAELON
Nazareth
TABOR
N. Muqatta
W. Fajjas
W. Bira
DAHI
W. Arab
Deraa
Irbid
N. Jalud (Harod)
Beisan
J. FAQQU'A
GHOR
J. AJLUN
W. Yabis
DARA
W. Zarqa
N. el Awaj
LEGEND
Vertical cliffs
Desert boundary
Steppe boundary

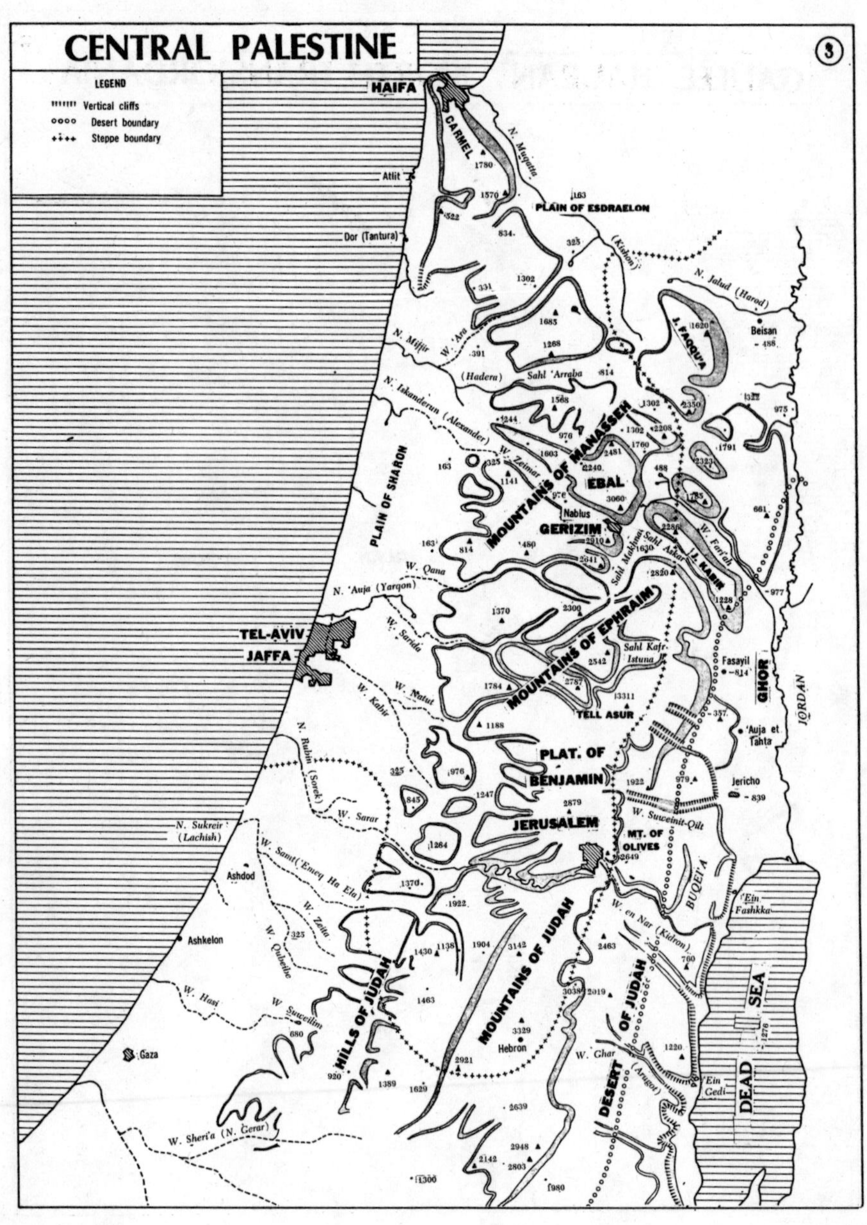
CENTRAL PALESTINE
3
LEGEND
Vertical cliffs
Desert boundary
Steppe boundary
HAIFA
CARMEL
Atlit
Dor (Tantura)
PLAIN OF ESDRAELON
N. Muqatta
(Kishon)
N. Jalud (Harod)
J. FAQQU'A
Beisan
N. Mifjir
W. 'Ara
(Hadera)
Sahl 'Arraba
N. Iskanderun (Alexander)
W. Zeimar
PLAIN OF SHARON
MOUNTAINS OF MANASSEH
EBAL
Nablus
GERIZIM
Sahl Makhneh
Sahl Askar
J. KABIR
W. Far'ah
W. Qana
N. 'Auja (Yarqon)
MOUNTAINS OF EPHRAIM
TEL-AVIV
JAFFA
W. Sarida
Sahl Kafr Istuna
Fasayil
GHOR
JORDAN
W. Natuf
W. Kabir
TELL ASUR
'Auja et Tahta
N. Rubin (Sorek)
PLAT. OF BENJAMIN
Jericho
W. Sarar
JERUSALEM
W. Suweinit-Qilt
N. Sukreir (Lachish)
MT. OF OLIVES
W. Samt (Emeq Ha Ela)
Ashdod
BUQEI'A
'Ein Fashkka
W. Zeita
W. en Nar (Kidron)
Ashkelon
W. Qubeibe
HILLS OF JUDAH
MOUNTAINS OF JUDAH
DESERT OF JUDAH
W. Hasi
W. Suweilim
Hebron
W. Ghar
(Arugot)
'Ein Gedi
DEAD SEA
Gaza
W. Sheri'a (N. Gerar)

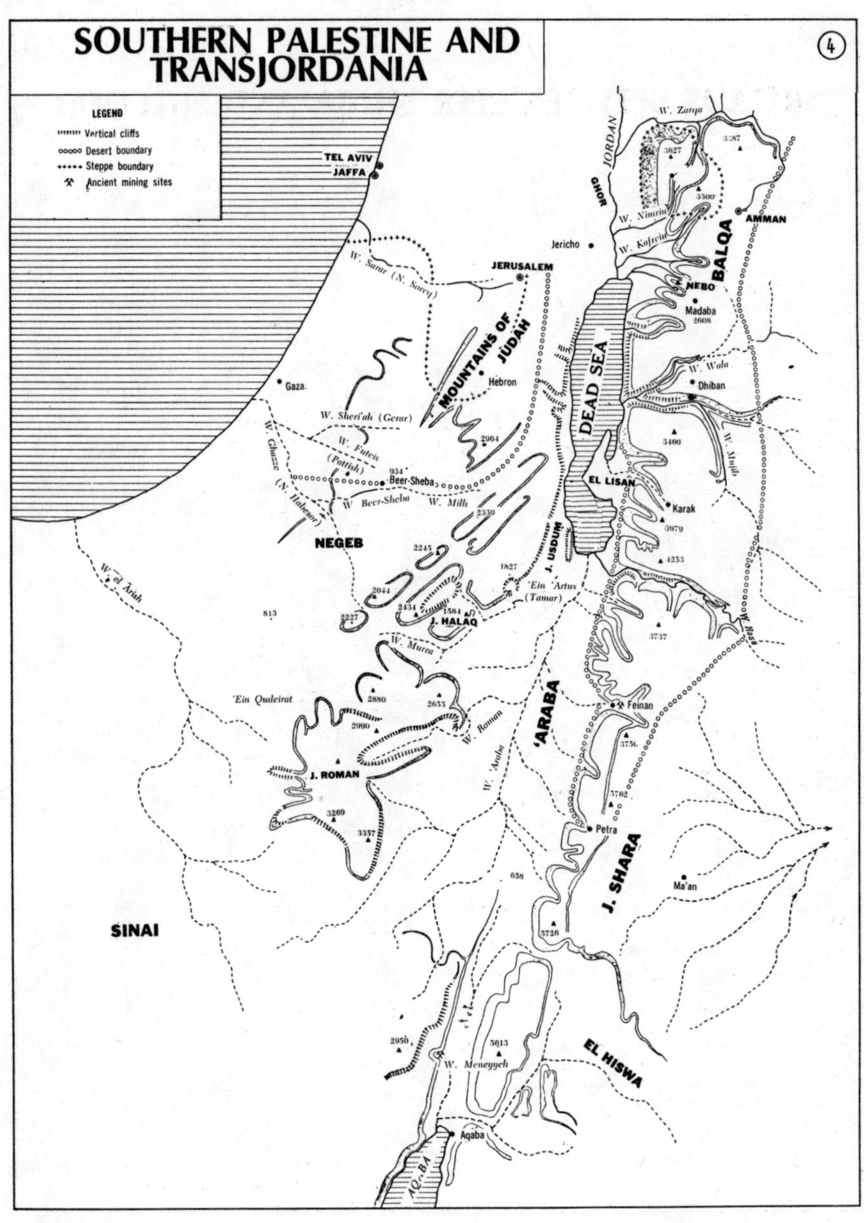
SOUTHERN PALESTINE AND TRANSJORDANIA
4
LEGEND
Vertical cliffs
Desert boundary
Steppe boundary
Ancient mining sites
TEL AVIV
JAFFA
JERUSALEM
Jericho
JORDAN
GHOR
W. Zarqa
W. Nimrin
W. Kafrein
AMMAN
BALQA
NEBO
Madaba
W. Sarar (N. Soreq)
MOUNTAINS OF JUDAH
Hebron
Gaza
DEAD SEA
W. Wala
Dhiban
W. Mujib
W. Sheri'ah (Gerar)
W. Futeis (Pattish)
W. Ghazze (N. Habesor)
Beer-Sheba
W. Beer-Sheba
W. Milh
EL LISAN
Karak
J. USDUM
NEGEB
W. el 'Arish
'Ein 'Artus (Tamar)
J. HALAQ
W. Murra
W. Hasa
'Ein Qudeirat
'ARABA
Feinan
W. Roman
W. 'Araba
J. ROMAN
Petra
J. SHARA
Ma'an
SINAI
EL HISWA
W. Meneyyeh
Aqaba
AQ. BA

5

ROADS BETWEEN BEER SHEBA AND SHECHEM

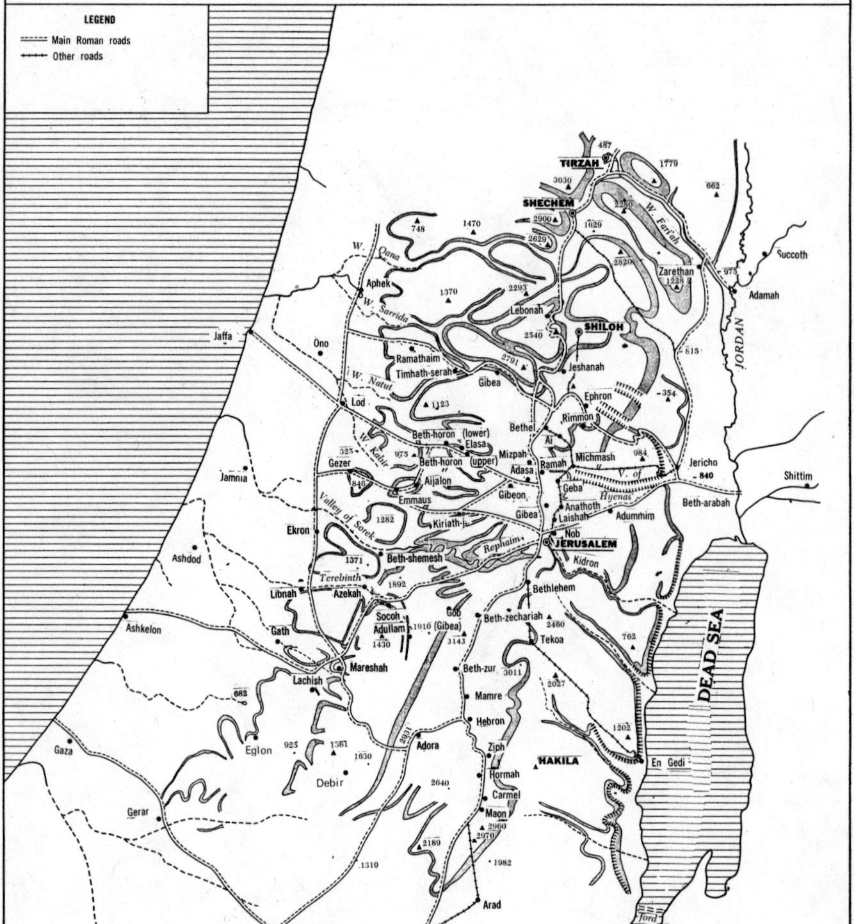

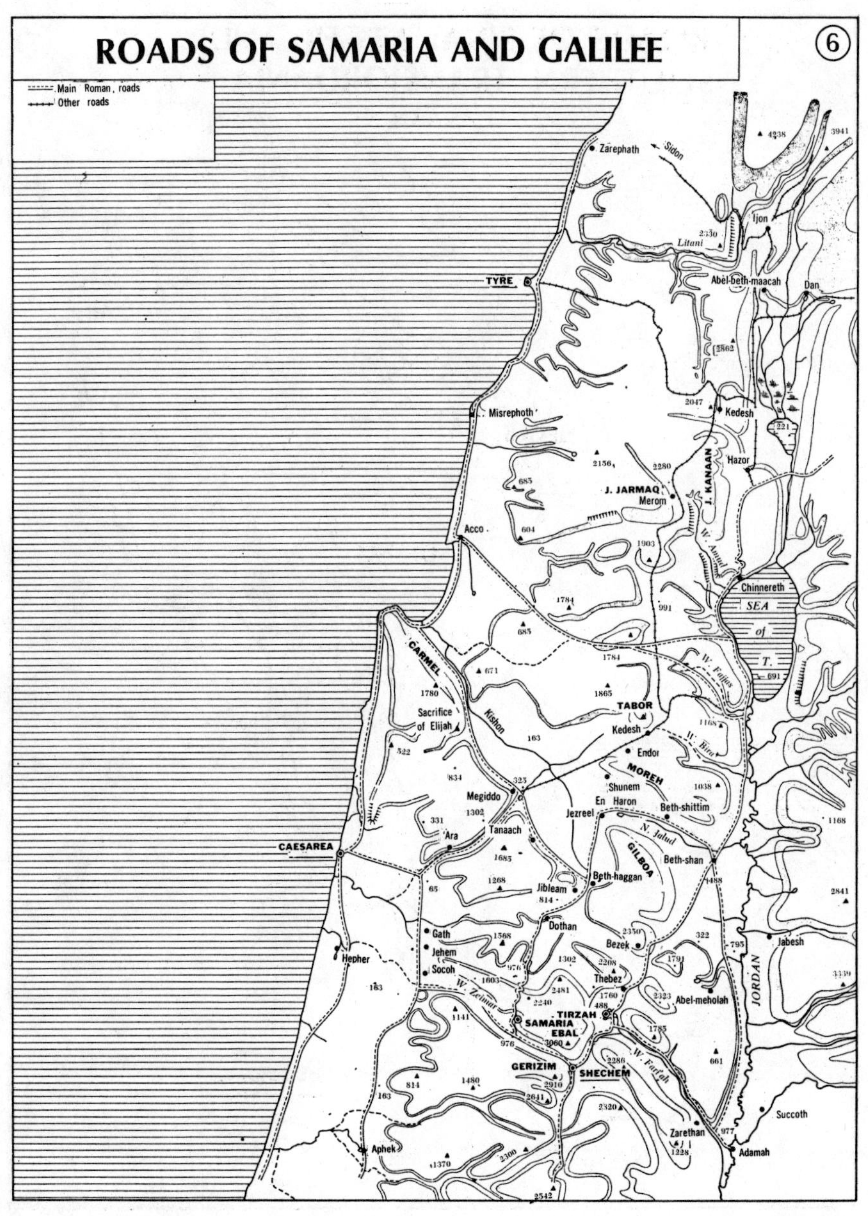
ROADS OF SAMARIA AND GALILEE
6
Main Roman roads
Other roads
Zarephath
Sidon
4238
3941
Ijon
Litani
2330
TYRE
Abel-beth-maacah
Dan
2862
Misrephoth
2047
Kedesh
221
2156
2280
Hazor
683
J. JARMAQ
Merom
J. KANAAN
Acco
604
1903
W. Ammud
Chinnereth
SEA
of
T.
691
1784
991
685
CARMEL
671
1784
1865
W. Fajjas
1780
TABOR
Sacrifice of Elijah
Kishon
163
Kedesh
1168
522
Endor
W. Bira
834
MOREH
325
Shunem
1038
Megiddo
1302
Jezreel
En Haron
Beth-shittim
1168
331
Tanaach
N. Jalud
Ara
CAESAREA
1683
GILBOA
Beth-shan
1268
Jibleam
Beth-haggan
65
814
1488
2841
Dothan
Gath
1368
2350
Bezek
322
795
Jabesh
Jehem
1302
2208
1791
Hepher
Socoh
976
Thebez
JORDAN
1603
2481
163
W. Zeimar
1760
2323
Abel-meholah
1141
2240
488
TIRZAH
SAMARIA
EBAL
1785
976
3060
2286
661
GERIZIM
SHECHEM
W. Far'ah
814
1480
2910
2641
163
2320
Succoth
Zarethan
977
Aphek
1370
2300
1228
Adamah
2542

ROADS OF SINAI, NEGEB, AND SOUTHERN TRANSJORDANIA

7

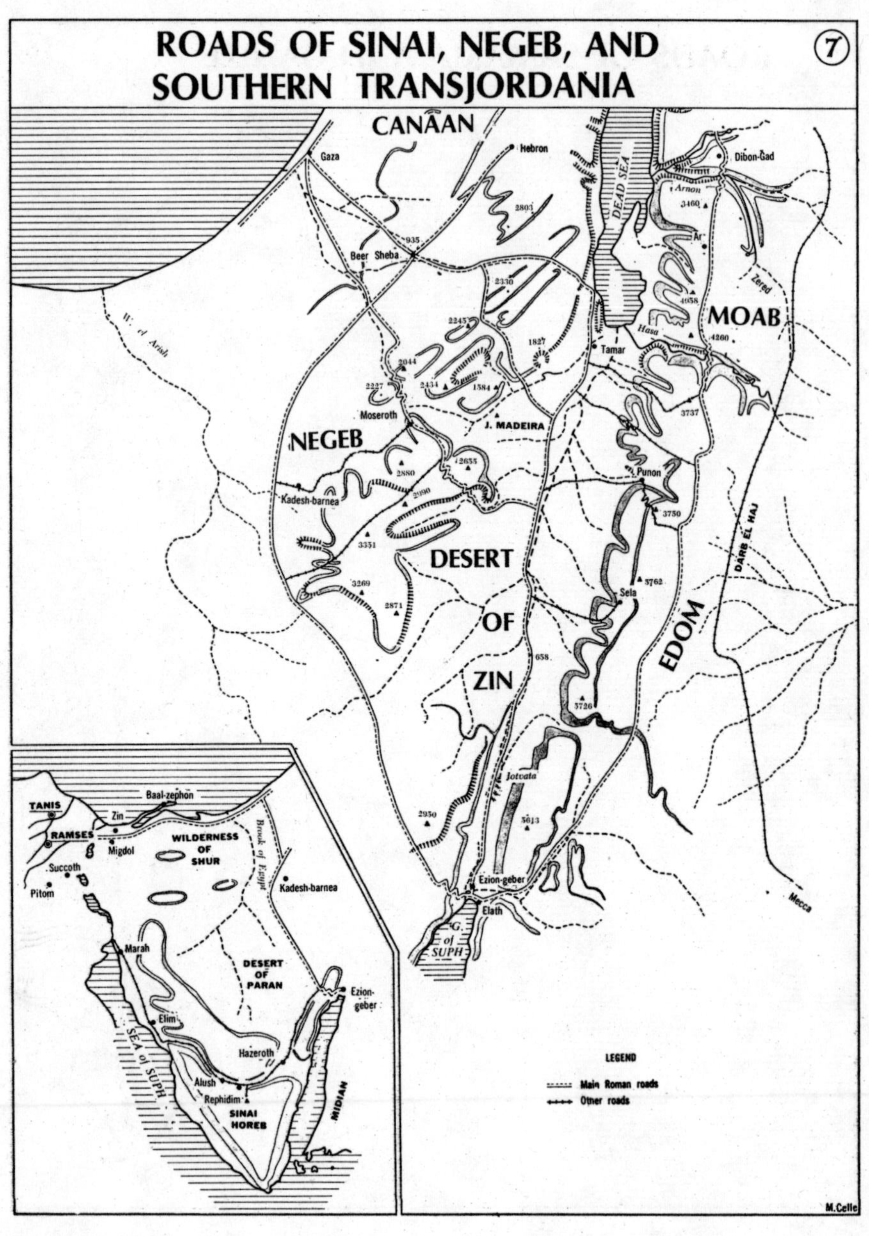

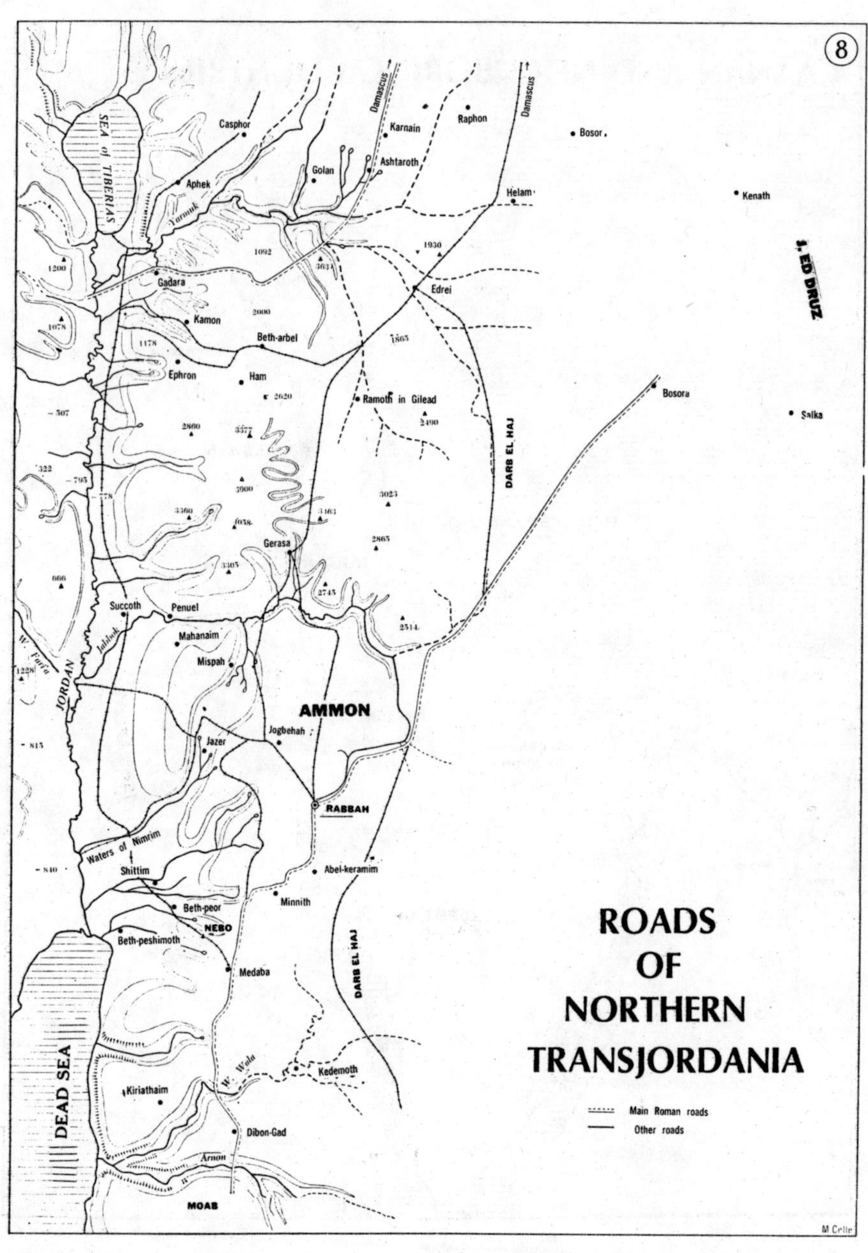
8
ROADS
OF
NORTHERN
TRANSJORDANIA
Main Roman roads
Other roads
SEA of TIBERIAS
Damascus
Damascus
Casphor
Karnain
Raphon
Bosor
Golan
Ashtaroth
Aphek
Yarmuk
Helam
Kenath
J. ED DRUZ
Gadara
Edrei
Kamon
Beth-arbel
Ephron
Ham
Ramoth in Gilead
Bosora
Salka
DARB EL HAJ
Gerasa
Succoth
Penuel
Jabbok
Mahanaim
Mispah
W. Farfa
JORDAN
AMMON
Jogbehah
Jazer
RABBAH
Waters of Nimrim
Shittim
Abel-keramim
Minnith
Beth-peor
NEBO
Beth-peshimoth
Medaba
DARB EL HAJ
DEAD SEA
W. Wala
Kedemoth
Kiriathaim
Dibon-Gad
Arnon
MOAB
M Celle

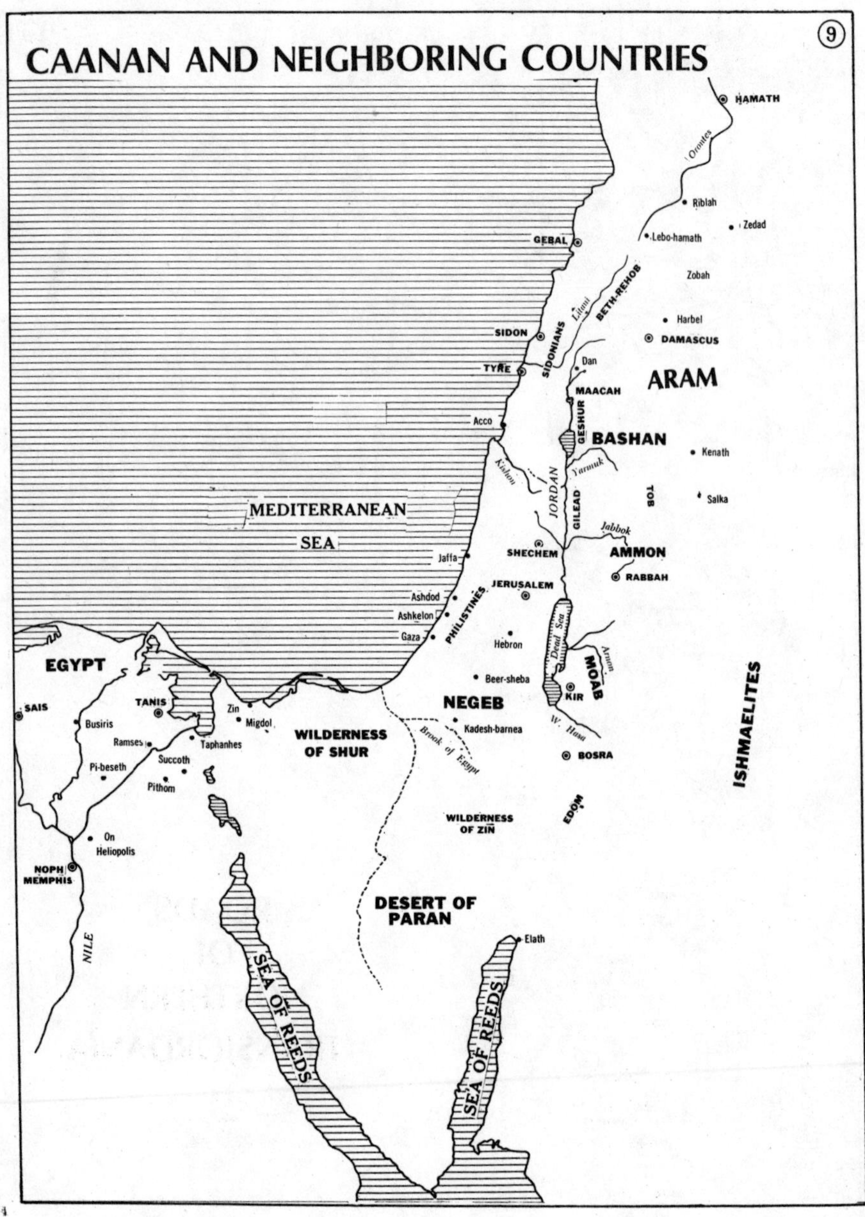
9
CAANAN AND NEIGHBORING COUNTRIES
HAMATH
Orontes
Riblah
Zedad
Lebo-hamath
GEBAL
Zobah
BETH-REHOB
Litani
Harbel
SIDON
SIDONIANS
DAMASCUS
Dan
TYRE
ARAM
MAACAH
Acco
GESHUR
BASHAN
Kenath
Kishon
Yarmuk
JORDAN
TOB
Salka
GILEAD
MEDITERRANEAN
SEA
Jabbok
Jaffa
SHECHEM
AMMON
RABBAH
JERUSALEM
PHILISTINES
Ashdod
Ashkelon
Gaza
Hebron
Dead Sea
Arnon
EGYPT
Beer-sheba
MOAB
KIR
ISHMAELITES
SAIS
TANIS
NEGEB
Zin
Migdol
Busiris
Kadesh-barnea
W. Hasa
WILDERNESS
OF SHUR
Brook of Egypt
Ramses
Taphanhes
BOSRA
Succoth
Pi-beseth
Pithom
EDOM
WILDERNESS
OF ZIN
On
Heliopolis
NOPH
MEMPHIS
DESERT OF
PARAN
Elath
NILE
SEA OF REEDS
SEA OF REEDS

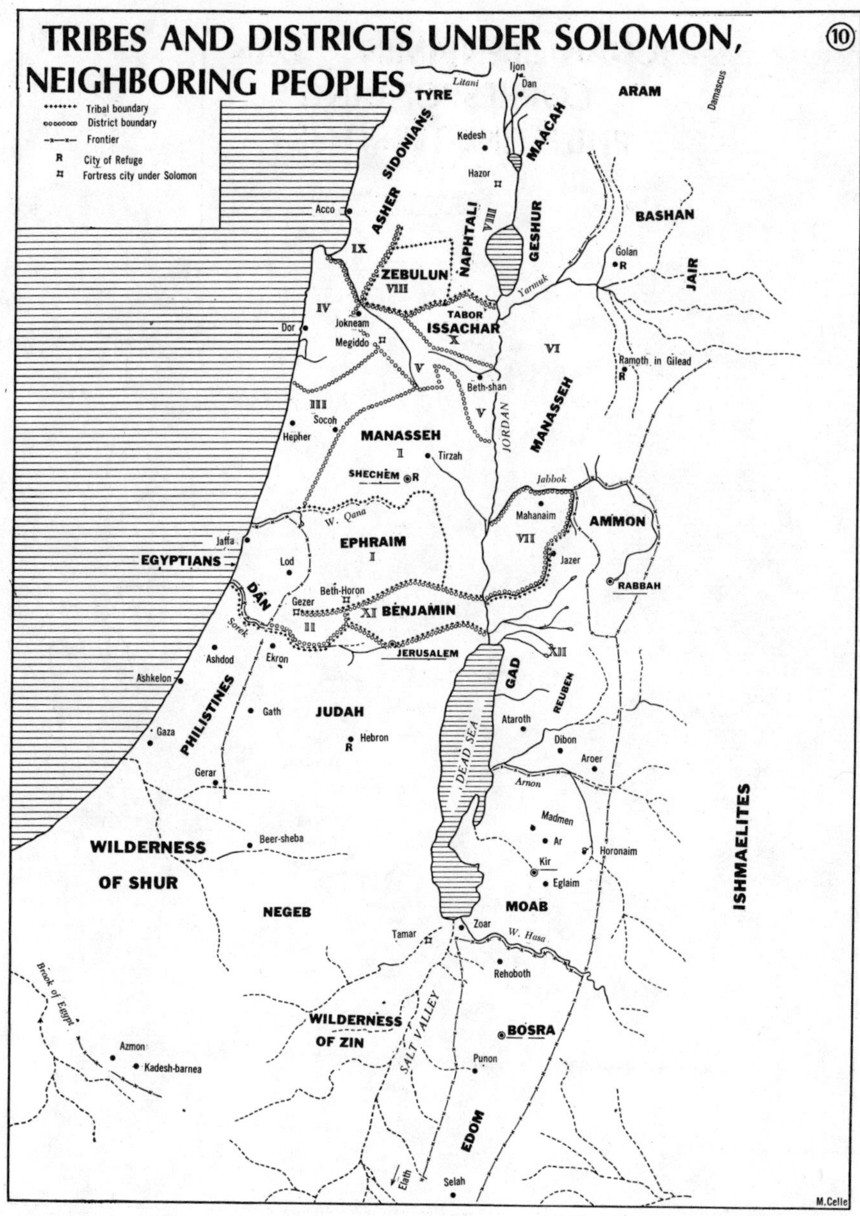

TRIBES AND DISTRICTS UNDER SOLOMON, NEIGHBORING PEOPLES
10
Tribal boundary
District boundary
Frontier
R City of Refuge
Fortress city under Solomon
Litani
Ijon
Dan
TYRE
ARAM
Damascus
SIDONIANS
MAACAH
Kedesh
Hazor
Acco
ASHER
NAPHTALI
VIII
GESHUR
BASHAN
IX
Golan
JAIR
ZEBULUN
VIII
Yarmuk
IV
TABOR
Dor
Jokneam
ISSACHAR
Megiddo
X
VI
V
Ramoth in Gilead
Beth-shan
III
Socoh
V
Hepher
MANASSEH
JORDAN
MANASSEH
II
Tirzah
SHECHEM
Jabbok
W. Qana
Mahanaim
AMMON
Jaffa
EPHRAIM
VII
EGYPTIANS
Lod
I
Jazer
RABBAH
DAN
Beth-Horon
Gezer
XI
BENJAMIN
II
Sorek
Ashdod
Ekron
JERUSALEM
XII
GAD
Ashkelon
PHILISTINES
REUBEN
Gath
JUDAH
Ataroth
DEAD SEA
Gaza
Hebron
Dibon
Aroer
Gerar
Arnon
ISHMAELITES
Madmen
Ar
WILDERNESS
Beer-sheba
Horonaim
Kir
OF SHUR
Eglaim
NEGEB
MOAB
Zoar
Tamar
W. Hasa
Rehoboth
Brook of Egypt
WILDERNESS
OF ZIN
BOSRA
SALT VALLEY
Azmon
Punon
Kadesh-barnea
EDOM
Elath
Selah
M.Celle

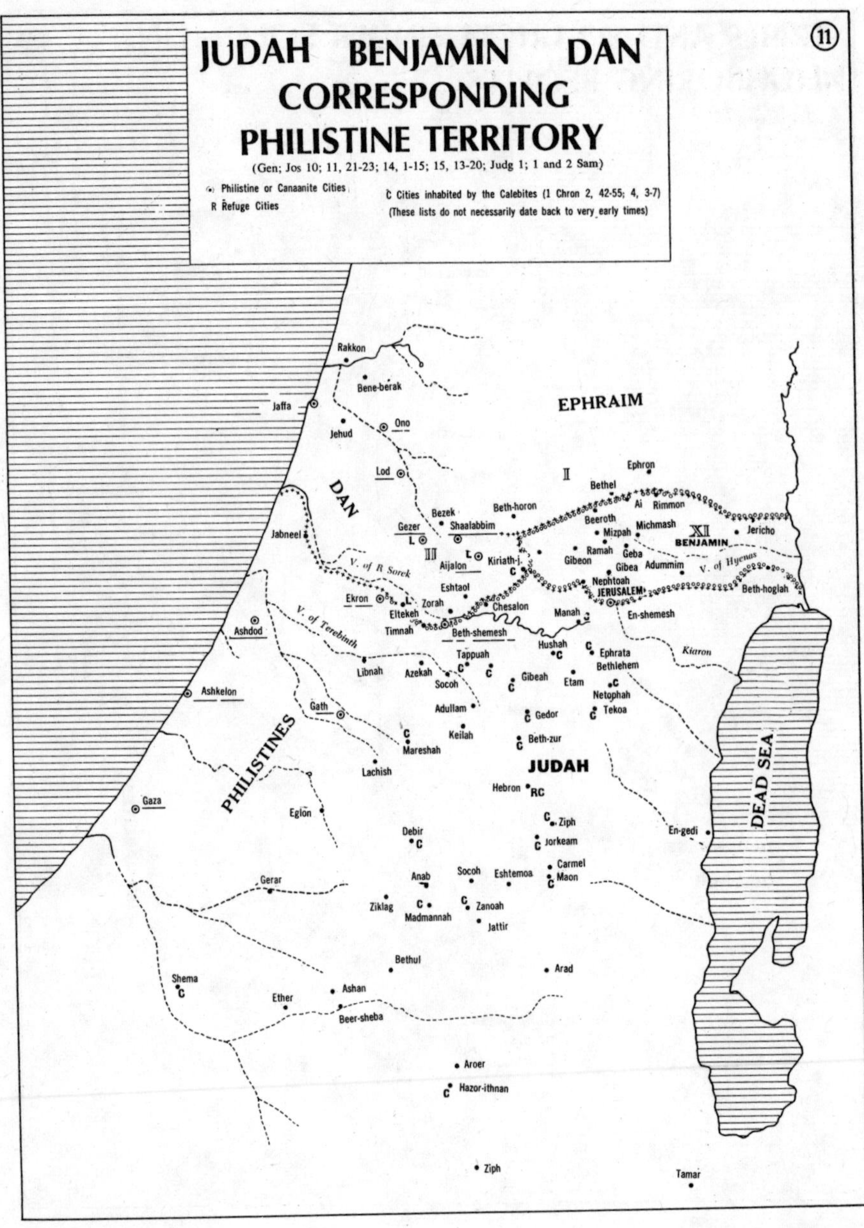
11
JUDAH BENJAMIN DAN
CORRESPONDING
PHILISTINE TERRITORY
(Gen; Jos 10; 11, 21-23; 14, 1-15; 15, 13-20; Judg 1; 1 and 2 Sam)
Philistine or Canaanite Cities
R Refuge Cities
C Cities inhabited by the Calebites (1 Chron 2, 42-55; 4, 3-7)
(These lists do not necessarily date back to very early times)
Rakkon
Bene-berak
EPHRAIM
Jaffa
Ono
Jehud
Lod
Ephron
I
Bethel
DAN
Ai
Rimmon
Beth-horon
Bezek
Beeroth
Gezer
Shaalabbim
Mizpah
Michmash
XI
Jericho
Jabneel
L
III
BENJAMIN
Ramah
Geba
L
Aijalon
Kiriath-j.
Gibeon
C
Gibea
Adummim
V. of Hyenas
V. of R Sorek
Eshtaol
Nephtoah
JERUSALEM
Beth-hoglah
Ekron
Zorah
Chesalon
Eltekeh
Manah
En-shemesh
V. of Terebinth
Ashdod
Timnah
Beth-shemesh
Hushah
C
Ephrata
Kiaron
Tappuah
Bethlehem
Libnah
Azekah
Gibeah
Etam
Socoh
Netophah
Ashkelon
Adullam
Gath
Gedor
Tekoa
Keilah
PHILISTINES
Mareshah
Beth-zur
DEAD SEA
JUDAH
Lachish
Hebron
RC
Gaza
Eglon
Ziph
En-gedi
Debir
Jorkeam
Carmel
Socoh
Eshtemoa
Anab
Maon
Gerar
Ziklag
Zanoah
Madmannah
Jattir
Bethul
Arad
Shema
Ashan
Ether
Beer-sheba
Aroer
Hazor-ithnan
Ziph
Tamar

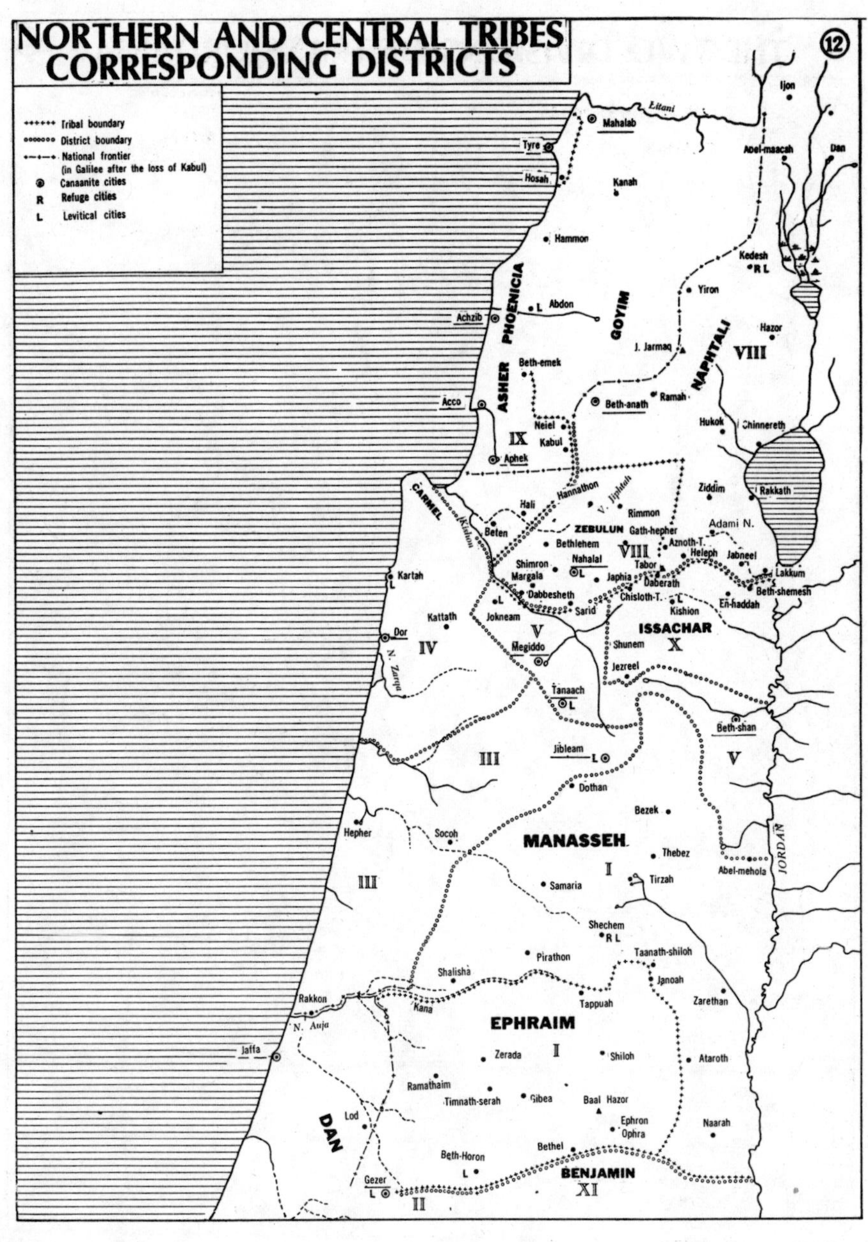
NORTHERN AND CENTRAL TRIBES
CORRESPONDING DISTRICTS
12
Tribal boundary
District boundary
National frontier
(in Galilee after the loss of Kabul)
Canaanite cities
R Refuge cities
L Levitical cities
Litani
Mahalab
Tyre
Hosah
Kanah
Ijon
Abel-maacah
Dan
Hammon
Kedesh
R L
Yiron
PHOENICIA
GOYIM
Abdon
Achzib
Hazor
J. Jarmaq
NAPHTALI
VIII
ASHER
Beth-emek
Acco
Beth-anath
Ramah
Neiel
Hukok
Chinnereth
IX
Kabul
Aphek
CARMEL
Hannathon
Hali
Ziddim
Rakkath
Rimmon
Beten
ZEBULUN
Gath-hepher
Adami N.
Bethlehem
Aznoth-T.
Heleph
Jabneel
Shimron
Nahalal
Tabor
Lakkum
Kartah
Margala
Japhia
Daberath
Dabbesheth
Beth-shemesh
Chisloth-T.
Kishion
En-haddah
Kattath
Jokneam
Sarid
ISSACHAR
Dor
V
X
IV
Megiddo
Shunem
N. Zarqa
Jezreel
Tanaach
Beth-shan
III
Jibleam
V
Dotham
Bezek
Hepher
Socoh
MANASSEH
Thebez
III
I
Tirzah
Abel-mehola
JORDAN
Samaria
Shechem
R L
Pirathon
Taanath-shiloh
Shalisha
Janoah
Rakkon
Tappuah
Zarethan
Kana
N. Auja
EPHRAIM
Jaffa
Zerada
I
Shiloh
Ataroth
Ramathaim
Timnath-serah
Gibea
Baal Hazor
DAN
Lod
Ephron
Ophra
Naarah
Bethel
Beth-Horon
BENJAMIN
Gezer
XI
II

THE TWO DIVISIONS OF TRANSJORDANIA ⑬

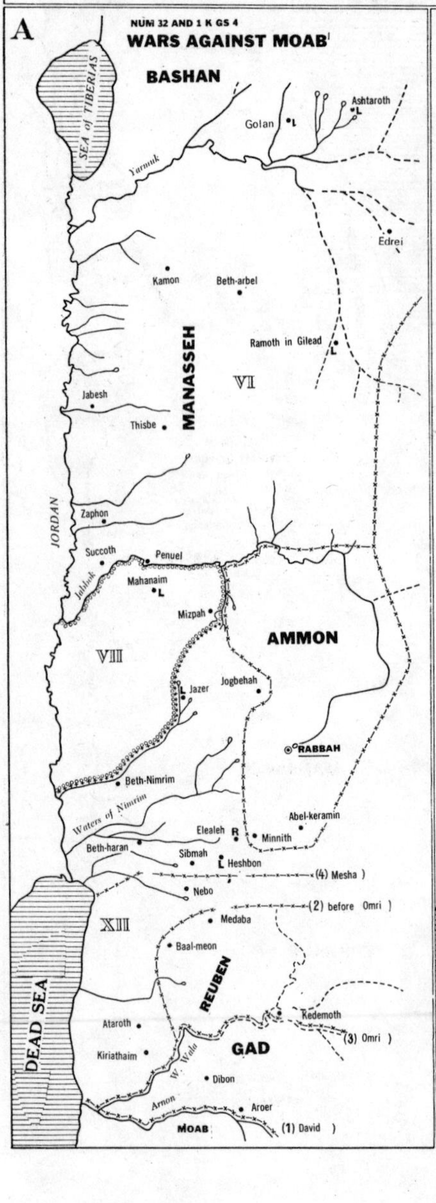

A

NUM 32 AND 1 K GS 4

WARS AGAINST MOAB

SEA of TIBERIAS
BASHAN
Golan
Ashtaroth
Yarmuk
Edrei
Kamon
Beth-arbel
Ramoth in Gilead
MANASSEH
VI
Jabesh
Thisbe
JORDAN
Zaphon
Succoth
Penuel
Jabbok
Mahanaim
Mizpah
AMMON
VII
Jazer
Jogbehah
RABBAH
Beth-Nimrim
Waters of Nimrim
Elealeh
Minnith
Abel-keramin
Beth-haran
Sibmah
Heshbon
(4) Mesha)
Nebo
(2) before Omri)
XII
Medaba
Baal-meon
REUBEN
DEAD SEA
Kedemoth
Ataroth
(3) Omri)
Kiriathaim
GAD
W. Wala
Dibon
Arnon
Aroer
MOAB
(1) David)

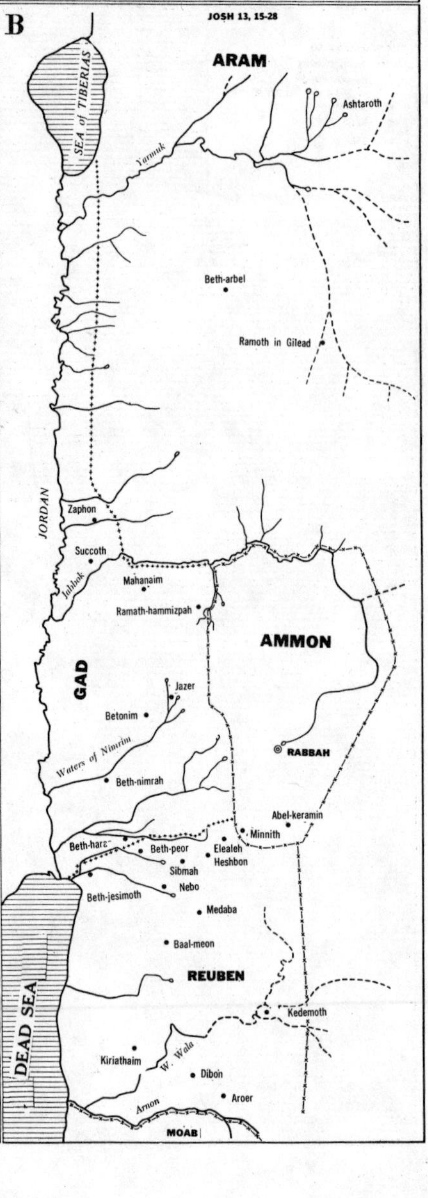

B

JOSH 13, 15-28

SEA of TIBERIAS
ARAM
Ashtaroth
Yarmuk
Beth-arbel
Ramoth in Gilead
JORDAN
Zaphon
Succoth
Jabbok
Mahanaim
Ramath-hammizpah
AMMON
GAD
Jazer
Betonim
Waters of Nimrim
RABBAH
Beth-nimrah
Abel-keramin
Minnith
Beth-haran
Beth-peor
Elealeh
Heshbon
Sibmah
Nebo
Beth-jesimoth
Medaba
Baal-meon
REUBEN
DEAD SEA
Kedemoth
Kiriathaim
W. Wala
Dibon
Aroer
Arnon
MOAB

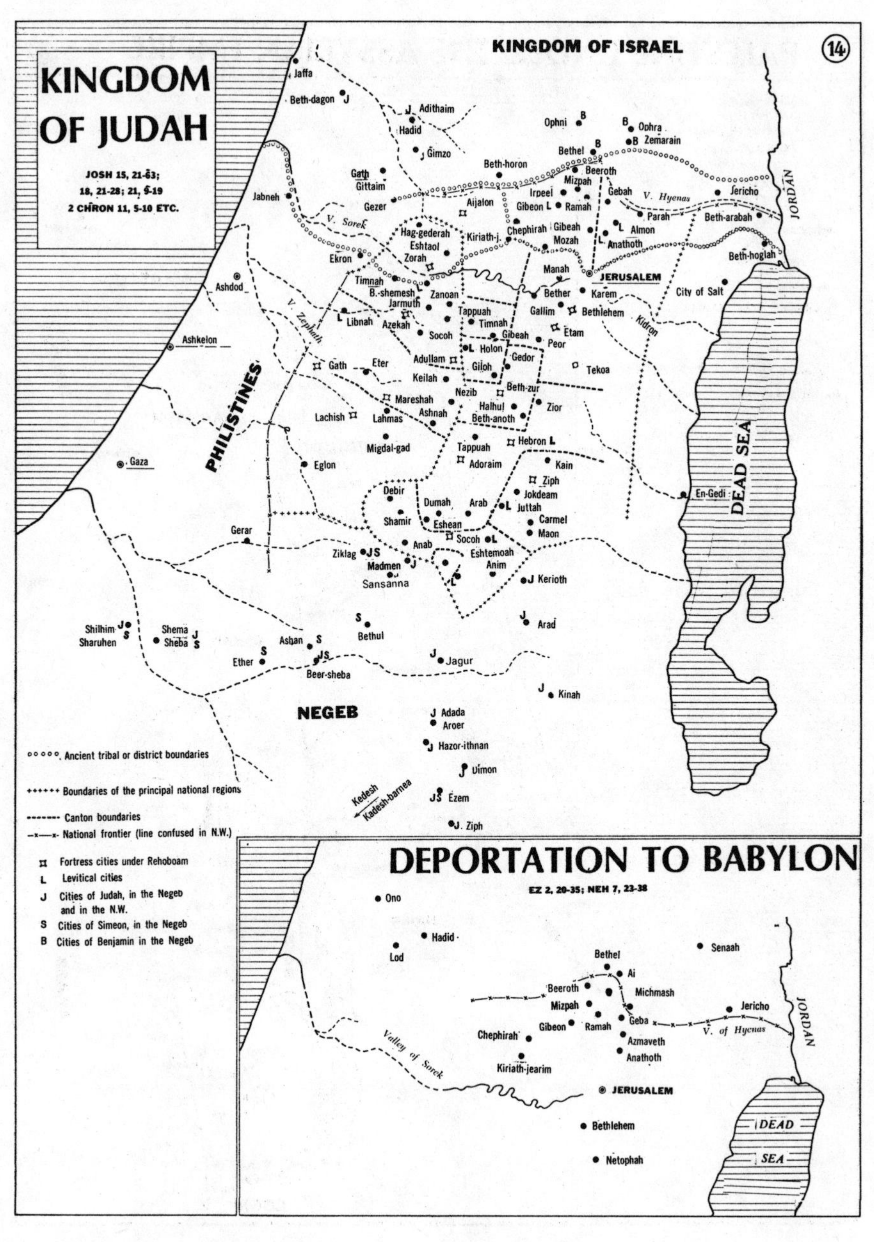
KINGDOM OF JUDAH
JOSH 15, 21-63; 18, 21-28; 21, 9-19
2 CHRON 11, 5-10 ETC.
KINGDOM OF ISRAEL
14
Jaffa
Beth-dagon
Adithaim
Hadid
Gimzo
Ophni
Ophra
Zemarain
Bethel
Beth-horon
Beeroth
Mizpah
Gebah
Jericho
Irpeel
Ramah
Gibeon
V. Hyenas
Parah
Beth-arabah
Almon
Anathoth
Beth-hoglah
Gath
Gittaim
Gezer
Jabneh
Aijalon
V. Sorek
Hag-gederah
Eshtaol
Zorah
Ekron
Kiriath-j.
Chephirah
Gibeah
Mozah
Manah
JERUSALEM
Ashdod
Timnah
B.-shemesh
Zanoan
Jarmuth
Bether
Karem
City of Salt
JORDAN
Libnah
Azekah
Tappuah
Timnah
Gallim
Bethlehem
Kidron
V. Zephath
Ashkelon
Socoh
Gibeah
Etam
Peor
Holon
Gedor
Adullam
Giloh
Tekoa
PHILISTINES
Gath
Eter
Keilah
Beth-zur
Mareshah
Nezib
Halhul
Beth-anoth
Zior
Lachish
Lahmas
Ashnah
DEAD SEA
Migdal-gad
Tappuah
Hebron
Adoraim
Kain
Gaza
Eglon
Ziph
Debir
Jokdeam
Dumah
Arab
Juttah
En-Gedi
Shamir
Eshean
Carmel
Gerar
Maon
Socoh
Anab
Eshtemoah
Ziklag
Madmen
Anim
Sansanna
Kerioth
Arad
Bethul
Shilhim
Sharuhen
Shema
Sheba
Ashan
Ether
Beer-sheba
Jagur
Kinah
NEGEB
Adada
Aroer
Hazor-ithnan
Dimon
Ezem
Ziph
Kedesh
Kadesh-barnea
Ancient tribal or district boundaries
Boundaries of the principal national regions
Canton boundaries
National frontier (line confused in N.W.)
Fortress cities under Rehoboam
L Levitical cities
J Cities of Judah, in the Negeb and in the N.W.
S Cities of Simeon, in the Negeb
B Cities of Benjamin in the Negeb
DEPORTATION TO BABYLON
EZ 2, 20-35; NEH 7, 23-38
Ono
Hadid
Lod
Senaah
Bethel
Ai
Beeroth
Michmash
Mizpah
Jericho
Geba
Gibeon
Ramah
Chephirah
V. of Hyenas
JORDAN
Azmaveth
Anathoth
Valley of Sorek
Kiriath-jearim
JERUSALEM
Bethlehem
DEAD SEA
Netophah

PALESTINE UNDER THE ASSYRIAN EMPIRE ⑮

Biblical sources
Texts from Tiglath-pileser III and Sennacherib and province lists
(Assrian names given in their Biblical equivalents)

SIDON:	Phoenician confederacy, with **TYRE** remaining independent
MEGIDDO:	the former V, VIII, and X. districts of Solomon
DOR:	III and IV
SAMARIA:	I
KARNAIM:	Ancient **BASHAN**
GILEAD:	VI and VII
MOAB:	Extended at the expense of XII
PHILISTINES:	only 4 cities, extends to Japho and its vicinity
JUDAH:	Retains its northern frontier; difficult to establish contact with Philistines

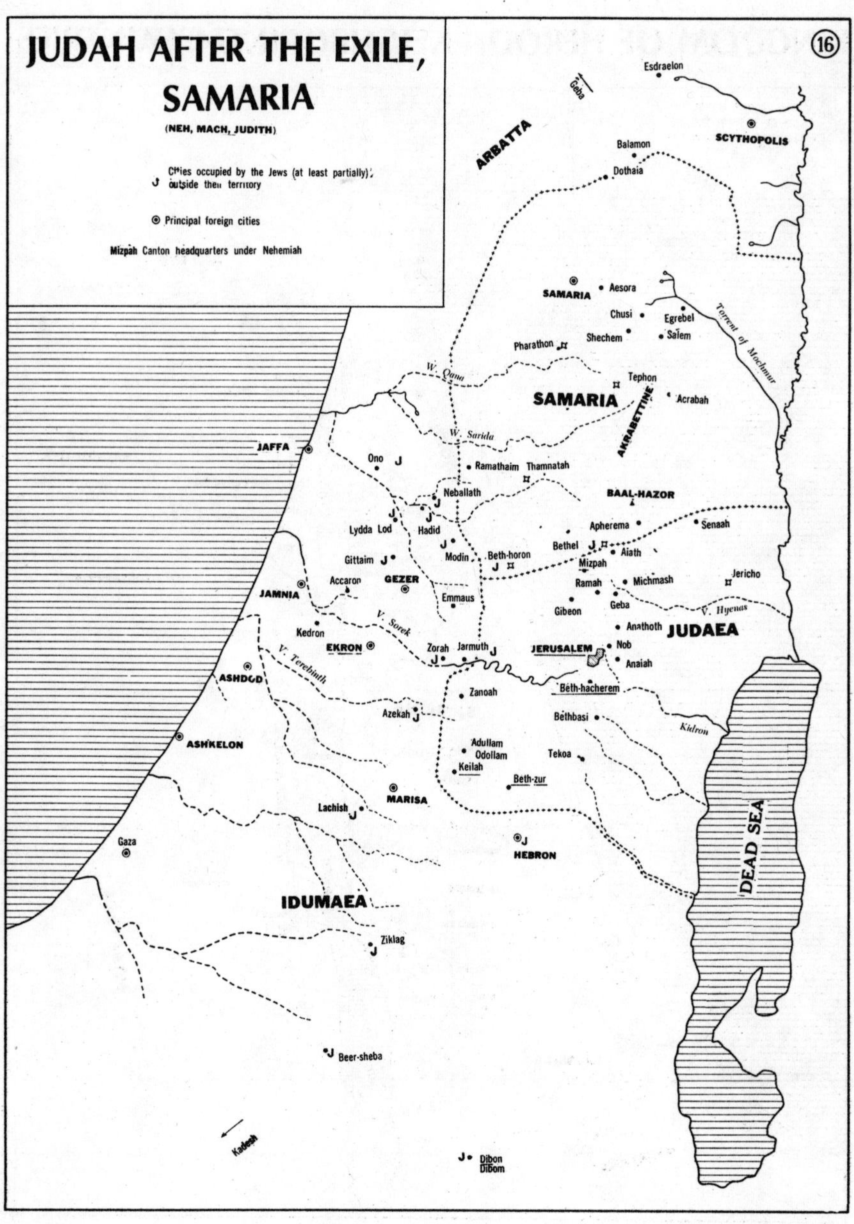
JUDAH AFTER THE EXILE, SAMARIA
(NEH, MACH, JUDITH)
Cities occupied by the Jews (at least partially) outside their territory
Principal foreign cities
Mizpah Canton headquarters under Nehemiah
16
Esdraelon
Geba
ARBATTA
SCYTHOPOLIS
Balamon
Dothaia
SAMARIA
Aesora
Chusi
Egrebel
Shechem
Salem
Torrent of Mochmur
Pharathon
W. Qana
Tephon
SAMARIA
Acrabah
AKRABETTINE
W. Sarida
JAFFA
Ono
Ramathaim
Thamnatah
Neballath
BAAL-HAZOR
Lydda Lod
Hadid
Apherema
Senaah
Gittaim
Modin
Beth-horon
Bethel
Aiath
Mizpah
Jericho
Accaron
GEZER
Ramah
Michmash
JAMNIA
Emmaus
Gibeon
Geba
V. Hyenas
Kedron
V. Sorek
Anathoth
JUDAEA
EKRON
Zorah
Jarmuth
JERUSALEM
Nob
Anaiah
ASHDOD
V. Terebinth
Beth-hacherem
Zanoah
Azekah
Bethbasi
Kidron
ASHKELON
Adullam
Odollam
Keilah
Tekoa
Beth-zur
MARISA
Lachish
DEAD SEA
Gaza
HEBRON
IDUMAEA
Ziklag
Beer-sheba
Kadesh
Dibon
Dibom

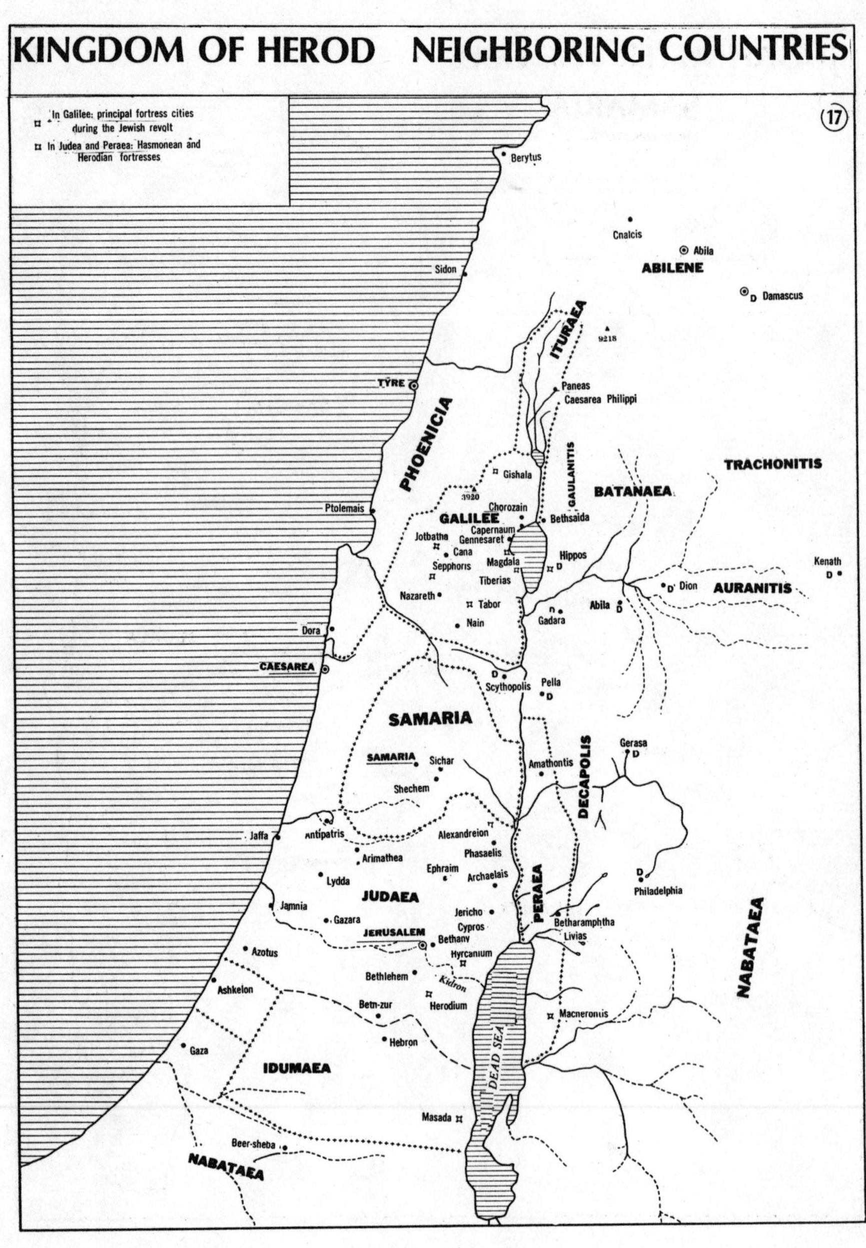
KINGDOM OF HEROD NEIGHBORING COUNTRIES
17
In Galilee: principal fortress cities during the Jewish revolt
In Judea and Peraea: Hasmonean and Herodian fortresses
Berytus
Cnalcis
Abila
ABILENE
D Damascus
Sidon
ITURAEA
9218
TYRE
Paneas
Caesarea Philippi
PHOENICIA
Gishala
GAULANITIS
TRACHONITIS
BATANAEA
3920
Ptolemais
Chorozain
GALILEE
Bethsaida
Capernaum
Jotbatha
Gennesaret
Cana
Hippos
Kenath
Sepphoris
Magdala
D
Tiberias
D
D Dion
AURANITIS
Nazareth
Tabor
Abila
D
Gadara
Nain
Dora
CAESAREA
D
Scythopolis
Pella
D
SAMARIA
Gerasa
D
DECAPOLIS
SAMARIA
Sichar
Amathontis
Shechem
Jaffa
Antipatris
Alexandreion
Arimathea
Phasaelis
Lydda
Ephraim
Archaelais
D
Philadelphia
JUDAEA
PERAEA
Jamnia
Jericho
Betharamphtha
Gazara
Cypros
JERUSALEM
Bethany
Livias
NABATAEA
Azotus
Hyrcanium
Bethlehem
Kidron
Ashkelon
Herodium
Betn-zur
Macneronis
Hebron
DEAD SEA
Gaza
IDUMAEA
Masada
Beer-sheba
NABATAEA

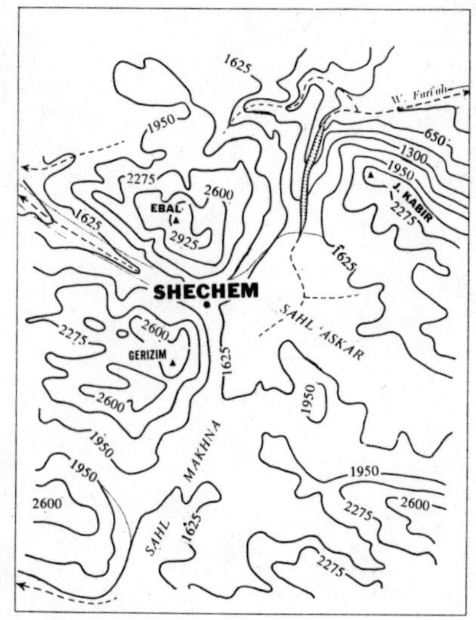

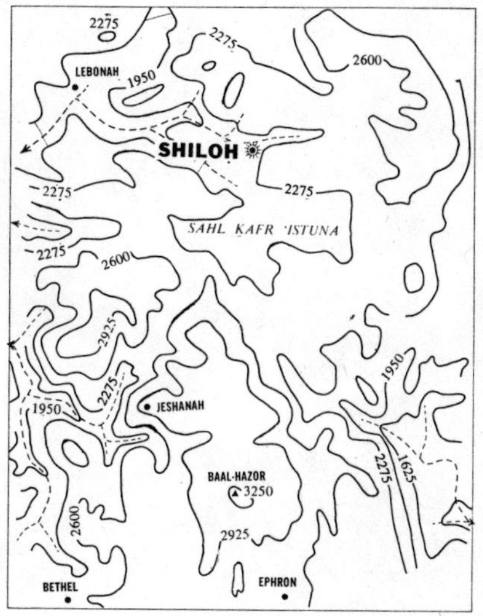

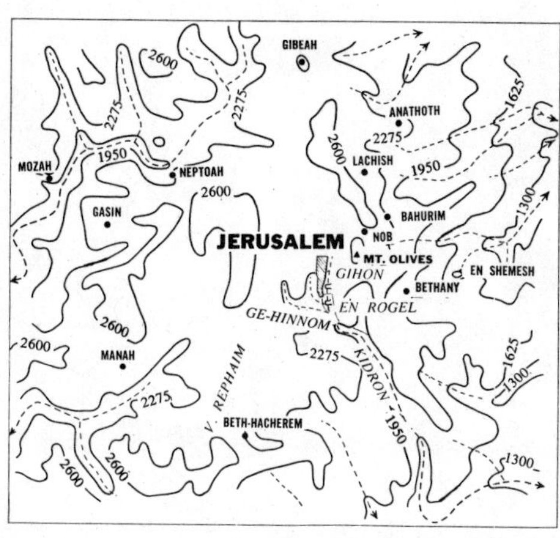

THE THREE CAPITALS

SHECHEM: Good soil, easy communications to North, East, and West; no natural defenses.

SHILOH: Good soil, difficult communications in all directions; natural defenses.

JERUSALEM: Mediocre soil, easy communications to North and South, difficult in other directions; natural defenses.

Geological Morphology

Hard Limestone: vicinity of **SHILOH** and West of **JERUSALEM**

Soft Limestone: East of **JERUSALEM**

Soft Limestone with overlying nummulite: West of **SHECHEM**

Plains or alluvial valleys.